Criticism of Earth

Historical Materialism Book Series

The Historical Materialism Book Series is a major publishing initiative of the radical left. The capitalist crisis of the twenty-first century has been met by a resurgence of interest in critical Marxist theory. At the same time, the publishing institutions committed to Marxism have contracted markedly since the high point of the 1970s. The Historical Materialism Book Series is dedicated to addressing this situation by making available important works of Marxist theory. The aim of the series is to publish important theoretical contributions as the basis for vigorous intellectual debate and exchange on the left.

The peer-reviewed series publishes original monographs, translated texts, and reprints of classics across the bounds of academic disciplinary agendas and across the divisions of the left. The series is particularly concerned with encouraging the internationalization of Marxist debate and aims to translate significant studies from beyond the English-speaking world.

For a full list of titles in the Historical Materialism Book Series
available in paperback from Haymarket Books, visit:
www.haymarketbooks.org / category / hm-series

Criticism of Earth

On Marx, Engels, and Theology

Roland Boer

Haymarket Books
Chicago, IL

First published in 2012 by Brill Academic Publishers, The Netherlands
© 2012 Koninklijke Brill NV, Leiden, The Netherlands

Published in paperback in 2013 by
Haymarket Books
P.O. Box 180165
Chicago, IL 60618
773-583-7884
www.haymarketbooks.org

ISBN: 978-1-60846-274-2

Trade distribution:
In the US, Consortium Book Sales, www.cbsd.com
In Canada, Publishers Group Canada, www.pgcbooks.ca
In the UK, Turnaround Publisher Services, www.turnaround-uk.com
All other countries, Ingram Publisher Services International, ips_intlsales@
ingramcontent.com

Cover design by Ragina Johnson.

This book was published with the generous support of
Lannan Foundation and the Wallace Global Fund.

Library of Congress Cataloging-in-Publication data is available.

Entered into digital printing August 2018.

Contents

Preface

I have put off writing this book for too long, daunted by the endless volumes of Marx and Engels's writings. At long last, I opened the first volume of their *Collected Works*. Over the next eight months, I read the whole lot, instead of the select pieces I had read until then, finishing the last volume on the evening before boarding a freighter-ship bound for New Zealand in June 2008. Vast, tiring and exhilarating, it was one of the greatest reading experiences I have ever had.

From the nooks and crannies of their youth, with bad poetry, love-letters, angry and worried parents, the story unwound in volume after volume. Marx soon showed up as an obsessive and brilliant writer who cared nothing for his health, even when there was a long history of unstable health on his side of the family. Engels, by contrast, obviously knew how to enjoy himself and unwind: good beer, fine wine, exquisite tobacco and women, mixed in with long-distance hiking and a love for swimming. We follow them through the obstacle-course of early political journalism in the face of censorship, arrests and exile in Paris, Brussels and then London. I found myself enticed by Engels's background, one that was so similar to my own, as well as his remarkable ability with languages (I have come across French, English, Spanish, Italian, Portuguese, Danish, Dutch, Frisian, Russian, Bulgarian, Romanian, Devanagari or Sanskrit, as well as classical Hebrew and Greek). While Engels passed through his hawkish phase and wrote some amazing pieces on battles, campaigns, and the histories of matters such as infantry, rifles and castles, Marx buried himself in piles of economic data and wrote endless notebooks working out his breakthrough-theories. As Marx peaked and burned himself out with the monumental first volume of *Capital*, Engels kept the whole show together, maintaining his partnership in the firm in Manchester, sending Marx endless pound-notes in the post, until at last he could retire and set up both Marx and himself in relative comfort. The formality of intellectual work and the immediacy of journalism finally make way for the intensely personal correspondence. Here, Marx's obsession with his declining health – especially the interminable reports on those famous carbuncles – shows up starkly (if before he disregarded his health, now it is at the centre of his attention), as does Engels's patience and irrepressibly jovial take on life. And this is how the story closes, with Engels dutifully ensuring Marx's legacy through a mountain of editorial work on Marx's unfinished manuscripts (not always understanding them) and yet utterly enthused by the strides taken by the working-class and socialist movement.

When I began writing, I became conscious of the fact that Marx and Engels too were primarily writers. I started to gain respect for Engels as a writer. At times, he may have been too categorical and doctrinaire, not quite shining as bright as Marx, but, at other times, his texts sparkle with insight and observation. Unlike Marx's intense and obsessive prose, Engels could have a lightness of touch and way of turning a phrase that draws one in. I have read his accounts of the walk from Paris to Berne in Switzerland many times, the travel-notes on Sweden and Denmark, his glorious description of the cotton-bale that passes through so many handlers and merchants (swindlers) before reaching Germany, or his letters full of comments on smoking, drinking and women, or indeed his continuous doodles, portraits and battle-scenes. Only Engels could write, '...now I can shit in peace and then write to you in peace.... Damn, there's somebody sitting in the lavatory and I am bursting'.[1] No wonder he lived to a good age. His motto, written in young Jenny's notebook, would have helped: 'Your favourite virtue – jollity; Motto – take it easy'.[2]

Often, Engels had to remind Marx to get some fresh air and exercise instead of sitting on a broken chair at a worn desk in order to write. For Marx was driven by a demanding muse, one that allowed him three or four hours' sleep a night, rushed breaks for meals and those endless cups of coffee and reams of tobacco. There are plenty of notes in the letters about working all night, or for thirty hours straight until his eyes were too sore to go further, or Jenny taking over letter-writing since he had dropped from sheer exhaustion. No wonder he became so ill – liver, carbuncles, sores, abscesses, rheumatism, lungs (the letters are full of them) – and no wonder he recovered when on the sea at Margate where he ate well, went for long walks (up to 27 kilometres to

---

1. Engels 1839ff, p. 411; Engels 1839gg, p. 354.
2. Engels 1868k, p. 541.

Canterbury), swam every day and slept. He was already sick from overwork in his 30s, was alternating between periods of enforced rest and frenetic writing in his 40s, was spent after *Capital* appeared at the age of 49, and he could not write anything substantial after that. He was lucky to get to 65.

The image Marx's father, Heinrich, had of his son in Berlin pretty much sums up the way Marx wrote: 'God's grief!!! Disorderliness, musty excursions into all departments of knowledge, musty brooding under a gloomy oil-lamp; running wild in a scholar's dressing-gown and with unkempt hair instead of running wild over a glass of beer'.[3] Or, in Marx's own words:

> The writer does not look at all on his work as a *means*. It is an *end in itself*; it is so little a means for him himself and for others that, if need be, he sacrifices *his* existence to *its* existence. He is, in another way, like the preacher of religion who adopts the principle: 'Obey God rather than man'.[4]

The result was that Marx's texts are often rushed, dense, endless and written in that atrocious hand. Yet he could also rise from that tangle and produce extraordinarily brilliant stretches of text, such as the *Eighteenth Brumaire* and *The Civil War in France*, but it came less naturally to him. I find myself caught in between, preferring Engels as a writer over against Marx, but then taken up with Marx's sheer originality. And I must confess that I too often succumb to that demanding muse.

In citing the many works of Marx and Engels used in my research, I have opted to list both German and English where the work was first published in German. However, by the 1850s, both Marx and Engels wrote a good deal that was first published in English and then translated into German (and often other languages). In these cases, I cite only the English version. When a work was first published in a language other than German or English, I provide both references. The references mention the date the work was first written (when not published until much later) or first published (when it appeared in the lifetimes of Marx and Engels). Anyone who works with the various 'collected works' of Marx and Engels soon realises that the overlap between them is not very neat. The standard collection in the *Werke* (*MEW*) is highly selective, not merely in terms of the earliest writings, but also the multitude

---

3. Marx (Heinrich) 1837, p. 688.
4. Marx 1842i, p. 175.

of journalistic pieces. Initially, some of the early material appeared in two extra volumes not listed in the official 39 – the two *Ergänzungsbande*, one for Marx and one for Engels. In later editions, they became Volumes 40 and 41, and then another couple of volumes were added, especially with the text of the *Grundrisse*. The comprehensive *Gesamtausgabe* (*MEGA*), projected to be a mammoth 114 volumes, is barely halfway through to completion. For these reasons, my references move between the three collections, at times finding that a work is published in one and not found in another.

This volume is the fourth in the series called *The Criticism of Heaven and Earth*. It was written during a hermit-like period while those close to me were busy in their own lives. But those who read my blog – *Stalin's Moustache* – will have seen quotations, comment and reflections as I wrote this book. I would like to thank Peter Thomas and Sebastian Budgen for their enthusiasm for the project, Sara Farris for our ongoing discussions over Marx, Calvin and Weber, Jan Rehmann and David Roberts for insightful comments on an earlier version of the manuscript, as well as Marti Huetink at Brill for his keenness to get the whole lot into print. There is also an increasing number of readers who send me comments, observations and requests after having come across *Criticism of Heaven*, the first book in the series. Among others, they include trade-unionists from Norway, theologians from Taiwan, activists from Australia, and an increasing number of translators. I can honestly say that all this has come as a complete surprise, so I thank them sincerely. Above all, Christina has found herself listening to all manner of quotes, comments, questions and ideas. For her patience (not a gift for her) I am deeply thankful.

The Hill
December 2008

Introduction

This is a work of intimate commentary. Before an image comes to mind of all those voluptuous volumes by Marx and Engels sharing my bed or snuggling up sensuously on a couch, let me explain what I mean. By intimate, I mean the patient and careful reading of texts, especially of the primary sources. It entails that one does not rush over texts, paying attention to the various twists, contradictions, problems and insights of a text. No small feat, I must admit, since Marx and Engels wrote an astounding amount. But I can say that I have come to know their works rather well. Actually, the source of this approach is none other than the age-old practice of biblical commentary. Too often left in the hands of that insular group of biblical critics, it really is an approach suited to all manner of texts.

I need to be more specific: this is a theological commentary. By that, I mean not the recourse to some transcendent authority in order to assess Marx and Engels. Not at all. Instead, I read their texts with an ear tuned to the various theological allusions, references, undercurrents, protests and arguments that turn up all too often. That process includes arguing with them when I feel that they have come up short. It is common enough to deal with the question of 'religion' in Marx and Engels.[1] But I want to be far

---

1. After the drought of the 1980s and 1990s, the Marxism-and-religion question is beginning to generate renewed interest. It does not take too much effort to realise that

more specific than that, for what they engage with overwhelmingly is not so much 'religion' but theology and often the Bible itself.[2] I should not have to make this point, but it is still needed: in a Europe still saturated with its Christian heritage, 'religion' really means Christian theology. Even today, we find 'religion' used as a stand-in for theology. Whenever I hear the term, I find myself wanting greater specificity, a grounded sense – historically, socially and culturally – of what religion we are talking about. The same applies to Marx and Engels.

I should no longer be surprised by the way Marxists keep engaging with theology – ostensibly a discipline that concerns itself with what does not exist and has no independent history. When I first began this project (this is the fourth volume), I kept coming across more material than I first imagined there would be. One by one, the major Marxists turned out to have produced extensive studies of theology. Adorno, Bloch, Benjamin, Luxemburg, Kautsky, Goldmann, Althusser, Gramsci, Lefebvre, Thompson, Žižek, Badiou, Eagleton... the list goes on. So it was time to turn to the daunting task of becoming intimate with Marx and Engels.

Standing before the vast pile of their interactions with theology, I have wished on more than one occasion for a smoke to help me ponder how on earth to deal with it all. I might have taken what has become with many retellings the standard approach, ordering my whole discussion in terms of the well-worn development-of-thought model with its various 'conversions' to Hegel or Feuerbach or communism.[3] In following this path, I would have picked out the threads that eventually led into the 'mature' historical materialism of a few years down the track. The problem is that one's thoughts never seem to develop in a neat temporal sequence and they certainly do not appear in the order in which they are published (or not). More importantly, it makes no sense of the continued interest in theology by Marx and Engels in

this resurgence is directly related to global politics. See, for example, Bhattacharyya 2006, Molyneux 2008, and Löwy 1996. The brilliant study by Kouvelakis (Kouvelakis 2003) tends to take Marx at his word when he states that he has moved beyond theology, which Kouvelakis takes as a marker of the Prussian 'Christian state' from which Marx went into exile.

2. Their very occasional comments on Islam, Buddhism and so on are therefore outside my scope.

3. In what seems to be an effort to outdo the conventional search for Marx's 'conversion' to communism (as Avineri 1968, pp. 33–4, and Hunt 1974, pp. 74–5, do), Breckman 1999, pp. 258–97, is after multiple conversions over a very few years.

their later years – for example, Marx's fascination with fetishism or Engels's unflagging concern with Christianity and its origins.

So, I prefer to organise my discussion in terms of some key-themes that wind through their work, some with a longer shelf-life than others. These include: the continual myriad allusions to the Bible and theology that run into the hundreds if not thousands; the ever-present Bruno Bauer and his alternative path to radical politics; the need for producing a narrative of world-history and its crucial lever in response to Max Stirner; the breakthrough of Feuerbach's inversion; the question of the theological or secular state; the long-running concern with fetishism; the hint of ambivalence in theology in Marx and its full-scale articulation in Engels; the extensive engagement with the Bible and theology in Engels's writings, which would become his famous argument for the revolutionary origins of Christianity. Each of the topics forms a chapter by itself, so let me say a little more about them.[4]

Synopsis

In the first chapter, I set out to trace the various types of biblical and theological references and allusions in the texts of both Marx and Engels. I begin with these allusions since they provide a synoptic view of many of the issues in this study, especially those of ambivalence over theology, the context in which Marx and Engels operated, and the overlap between theology and economics. Anyone who reads their works soon picks up this pattern of allusions, but, to my knowledge, the mammoth task of tracking all of them and identifying their different functions has not yet been undertaken. In the chapter itself, I have chosen the best examples of each type. Initially, I began compiling

---

4. An adequate introductory survey on Marxism and religion may be found in McLellan 1987, although he is dismissive of Engels. At times, I engage with the double volume by Arendt van Leeuwen (Van Leeuwen 2002a and 2002b). Despite languishing out of print for almost four decades, this deep theological engagement with Marx is well worth a read, even if van Leeuwen is a bit too sincere, has a tendency to find 'confessions' and go off on all manner of tangents, theological and otherwise. Van Leeuwen is the only one I know who suggests that Marx had a religious commitment, so much so that he was fully ready for confirmation in light of his *Gymnasium* examination-paper on the Gospel of John. Needless to say, I am not so reverent. All the same, I agree with van Leeuwen's premise that Marx could never quite escape the criticism of heaven in his work. Despite my criticisms, van Leeuwen is a better read than the blustery and eclectic discussion of Milbank 1990, pp. 177–205, who plunders Marx for his own development of 'radical orthodoxy'.

an appendix of the remainder of these allusions but soon realised that they would form a massive volume on their own, so I resigned myself to referring to them in the footnotes. These allusions and references are quite revealing. While we would expect those that attack the ruling classes, whether the vestiges of the old nobility in Germany or the relatively new bourgeoisie in England, or indeed the side-swipes at the clergy as part of that corrupt ruling class, the others are less known. They include the attempts to outsmart the censor, the huge number of theological allusions in economic texts such as *Capital*, the thick use of such allusions against other opponents, usually within the communist movement, and – of most interest to me – those that are appropriated positively. In this case, Marx and Engels refer to a biblical text or theological motif and take its meaning on for themselves. In the midst of these appropriations, we come across the occasional reference that recognises the political ambivalence of the Bible or theology. These allusions cluster in some works more than others, but they appear throughout their writings.

After this synoptic sweep, I focus on specific pieces and arguments. So, in Chapter Two, I comment in detail on a neglected early essay by Marx. It comes from 1842 and has a title one can only wish to emulate – 'The Leading Article in No. 179 of the *Kölnische Zeitung*'. It is written in response to the editor of a rival newspaper by a certain Hermes, who was not only the editor of that paper but also a conservative Roman Catholic and government-agent. Here, Marx responds to a broadside against the young Hegelians and the relatively new critical approach to the Bible and theology. So Marx touches on the relations between theology on the one side and scientific research and history on the other. We also find the vexed issue of church and state turning up, especially in the context of the 'Christian state' of Prussia. Finally, we come across one of the first mentions of fetishism. Here it is a response to Hermes's schema of history that moves from sensuous animal-worship through fetishism to the highest form of Christianity – which just happened to exist in Germany at the time. Marx is scathing in his reply, pointing up contradictions, trading in *ad hominems* and generally sharpening his polemical skills. Apart from showing us a Marx who tackles theology at some length, this essay introduces some themes that would stay with him, especially those of church and state, and fetishism.

There follow three chapters that deal with what is mainly Marx's struggle with the theological Hegelians, Bruno Bauer, Max Stirner and Ludwig

Feuerbach. Bauer was Marx's one-time teacher, friend and mentor who taught him a course on the book of Isaiah at the Friedrich Wilhelm University in Berlin in 1839. Soon enough, Bauer becomes a target for Marx's polemic in *The Holy Family* and *The German Ideology*, as well as *On the Jewish Question*. The problem with Bauer is that he developed a reasonably radical political position – his later works dealt extensively with politics – through his work as a biblical critic. Marx sought to close this path off entirely, although he does admit in a telling phrase that Bauer follows the 'detour of theology'. For all the polemic, Bauer and Marx kept in touch, the former visiting Marx in London many years later. By contrast, Engels developed a rather different approach to Bauer, using his New Testament criticism to argue for the revolutionary origins of Christianity, as we shall see in Chapter Ten.

Max Stirner was a different proposition. In by far the longest part of *The German Ideology* – it runs to hundreds of pages and is all too often ignored – Marx and Engels undertake a detailed demolition of Stirner. Or, rather, they tackle his effort to identify a lever of history – the ego – and then rewrite history itself. Stirner felt that he was dispensing with theology entirely, but Marx and Engels point out that his alternative is still deeply historical. This is especially so with Stirner's identification of a very human Jesus Christ as the model of the lever he seeks. Jesus is actually a signal that the individual human being with no social ties may rise up to be the key to history. In reply, Marx and Engels gradually develop their own position. Its content may be a radical break, with its collective focus on division of labour, class-struggle and mode of production, and the lever of history – contradiction – is a world away from Stirner's ego. Yet, this alternative theory of history is formally related to theology. I realise this is a contentious issue, especially in light of the persistent criticism that Marxism is really secularised theology. The final section of the chapter on Stirner deals at length with this question, especially to make the point that I am not trying to uncover some embarrassing theological skeleton beneath the floorboards. Rather, I seek a productive way of dealing with their very complex relation with theology.

The interaction with Feuerbach – the topic of Chapter Five – is vastly different, for Marx and Engels were very taken with what I call the Feuerbachian inversion: God may appear to be an omniscient and omnipotent being to whom limited human beings are subject, but we actually create this God by projecting and hypostasising the best of ourselves. This argument becomes the theological springboard for the most famous of Marx's arguments concerning religion – that it is the 'opium of the people' and the 'heart of a heartless world'. As far as Marx was concerned, this was the vital breakthrough, so much so that the criticism of theology was complete, at least in Germany. He would, of course, extend the argument to point out that religion is not the projection of the best in human beings but the sign of alienated social and economic conditions – they should be the focus of criticism from now on. The catch is that Feuerbach also pointed this out, for Christianity diminished human beings in relation to the God to whom they attributed all their best attributes. However, the solutions differed: Feuerbach wanted to recover these projected items for human beings and thereby show the truth of Christianity; Marx wanted to deal with the alienating conditions that produced a religion such as Christianity and then leave Christianity by the roadside. I close with a surprising turn in Marx's argument: the invocation of Luther as a revolutionary forebear, albeit one who falls short.

The following three chapters explore the ramifications of the Feuerbachian inversion along a number of different paths. Initially (in Chapter Six) it takes me to Hegel, especially the *Contribution to the Critique of Hegel's Philosophy of Law*. In contrast to the many readings of this text, which take it as a move from theology to politics and law, I move in reverse, reading it as an engagement with theology. Here, Marx deploys the inversion again and again to show that Hegel is a formal theologian. His arguments concerning the state need to be inverted or stood on their feet, as one of Marx's favourite expressions would have it. Marx tries to rule theology completely out of court by arguing that it is otherworldly, heavenly and simply not real. Needless to say, I give close attention to the turns of this argument. From there, I pick up and assess various statements by Marx (and, at one point, Engels) on the secular state. I am particularly interested in the fact that they take up contradictory positions. On the one hand, otherworldly theology has no business dealing with the state; on the other, the secular state actually emerges out of the contradictions of the Christian state.

The seventh chapter, 'Idols, Fetishes and Graven Images', picks up one of the most interesting motifs in Marx, namely fetishism. In this case, I trace the way he first comes across the idea in the early ethno-anthropological work of Charles de Brosses, how he uses it in a religious sense in his early polemic, and then its various permutations in relation to economics, especially in terms of money, labour, commodities and capital itself. All the while, the basic assumption remains the same: fetishism involves the transfer of human social characteristics to the products of labour while we human beings seem to become objects. The connection with Feuerbach should be obvious, although here Feuerbach's inversion mutates in contact with the history of religions. I stress two features of this multiple use of fetishism: for Marx, it is illusory and the subjects of attack are the other political economists with whom he engages. However, what draws me into the whole question of fetishism is the way Marx never lost sight of the religious sense of the term, as *The Ethnological Notebooks* show, as well as the striking connection with the biblical critique of idolatry – an assumption common to de Brosses and, I suggest, Marx himself.

'Of Flowers and Chains', the eighth chapter, picks up one last item from the engagement with Feuerbach, namely the ambivalence of theology. This is really a search for hints and unwitting clues in Marx's texts. Every now and then, Marx recognises this ambivalence, especially in his point that religious suffering is both the expression of real suffering and the protest against it. But it also turns up in the multivalent metaphor of opium, which was both a medicine Marx regularly used along with most of the population and a drug that was progressively vilified in the nineteenth century. This chapter is also an opportunity to comment in detail on Marx's very early essay, 'The Union of Believers'. It is the only direct attempt at biblical exegesis by Marx and a little precocious. Yet what interests me about it is the fact that Marx cannot avoid struggling with contradictions when faced with a biblical text. On top of all this, Marx skilfully uses the Bible in some of his polemical works in a way that illustrates the ambivalence I pursue in this chapter. While this awareness of political ambivalence is muted in Marx and usually inadvertent, it is one that Engels would take up with gusto.

The last two chapters are given over entirely to Engels. I actually have a soft spot for Engels, partly because he grew up in a very similar environment to mine – a staunchly Calvinist household. That background left its mark on him, not least the habit of quoting a biblical text at will when it suited his purpose. But it also meant that he kept up an interest in matters theological and biblical, returning to them on a regular basis, even if it was from a very different perspective. In contrast to Marx, who would occasionally touch on theology in the context of other topics, Engels wrote a good number of pieces that are exclusively concerned with theology. So, in this chapter, I dig deep into his writings about Elberfeld, his hometown, and then Bremen where he spent a couple of years. I also track the central issue of biblical contradictions in his correspondence with his good friends and ministers of the church, Friedrich and Wilhelm Graeber. And I see what he is up to in his three pieces on Schelling, whose lectures he attended in Berlin when on military service. All of this is actually quite personal, for we encounter a young man coming face to face with the radical biblical criticism of the time, his rapid shifts, and his senses of loss and liberation. It is personal for me too, since it does show that the path from Calvinism to Marxism is not such a strange one.

While Chapter Nine shows that Engels was no stranger to the intricacies of biblical criticism and theology, the tenth chapter picks up a theme of Chapter Eight – the political ambivalence of theology. It will lead us to Engels's extraordinary piece, *On the History of Early Christianity*, which was written not long before his death. It really is his final coming to terms with his background, especially with his arguments for the revolutionary origins of Christianity, the appeal to the lower classes and the myriad parallels with the communist movement in his own day. In order to get to that point I follow two lines. One is his persistent interest in the book of Revelation, moving all the way from his uses of its apocalyptic language, in jest, satirically or to express his own jubilation, to treating it as a purely historical work that provides a window into early Christianity. The other line is his clear awareness of the political ambivalence of Christianity. It can be the most oppressive religion and needs to be debunked, criticised and held to account. But then it can also give voice to revolutionary impulses. Both lines would lead him to Thomas Müntzer and early Christianity.[5]

Some of the texts with which I deal are all too familiar. These are the usual suspects one finds in any line-up when 'Marxism and religion' is the topic. But there are others that sit on the periphery, at times troubling the fairly uniform picture and nature of the debates. I include both types of text in this book, not merely because they provide a fuller sense of the theological concerns of Marx and Engels, but also because these less travelled routes often have a surprising turn or two, especially when juxtaposed with the well-known texts.

---

5. One topic with which I do not deal is the question of the Asiatic mode of production, mainly because it is part of another project called *The Sacred Economy*.

Above all, I offer a critical commentary, exploring, expositing, questioning and, where appropriate, extending the issues raised.

The terrain of struggle: theology and the Bible

> There are two kinds of facts, which are undeniable. In the first place religion, and next to it, politics are the subjects, which form the main interest of Germany today. We must take these, in whatever form they exist, as our point of departure.[6]

So wrote Marx in 1844. In order to set the context for the following chapters, I draw a sketch of the entwinement of religious and political issues in the formative period for Marx and Engels – the 1820s and 1830s in Germany.[7] Although it is going too far to argue that the idea of separating religion and politics was simply not possible in those years, it is true that there was a massive effort to make sure they stayed an inseparable married couple, however much they might have squabbled.[8] As I pointed out earlier, at stake were not merely religion but theology, which I take as a distinctly Christian activity with its own history, language and modes of argument. As for politics, that took the specific form of the drive for a 'Christian state' under the pious Friedrich Wilhelm III and his equally reactionary son, Friedrich Wilhelm IV. Let me say a little about them before returning to theology.

When the new Prussian king, Friedrich Wilhelm IV, took power in 1840 he succeeded a father who had begun a process of ensuring the restoration of authority in the monarchy. Frightened by those dreadful Frenchmen and their revolutionary fervour across the border, one after the other, the two Friedrichs busily set about shoring up their domain against the hordes of

---

6. Marx 1844k, p. 143; Marx 1844l, p. 344.
7. A few basic points are in order: 'Germany' in the eighteenth and nineteenth centuries refers to a loose conglomerate of independent states, namely Prussia, Westphalia, the Rhineland and East Prussia. Westphalia and the Rhineland had been under French rule for almost two decades, had absorbed French culture and politics (including the abolition of feudal social relations) and often looked to Paris rather than Berlin. However, in 1815 they were annexed to Prussia.
8. See Breckman 1999 for a good treatment of this period, although he tends to deal with it in terms of the history of ideas, especially by means of the key-motif of 'Christian personalism'. Kouvelakis 2003, pp. 243–6, has an insightful treatment of the tensions between an archaic bedrock and the reforming push by a small group of liberals in the Rhineland.

barbarians keen to lop off their heads. In 1822, the devoutly Calvinist Friedrich Wilhelm III had brought together the Calvinist and Lutheran churches to form the Prussian Union [*Preussische Landeskirche*]. He enforced a single liturgy for the church, ensured a strict hierarchy and in all modesty promptly placed himself at the head of the church. One would have had to be a complete hermit not to notice the impression that theology and politics were united in a broad reactionary front, all of it concentrated in one person who was both political leader and Christ's representative on earth.[9] To use terms of which Americans are fond, he was commander-in-chief and theologian-in-chief – all rolled up into one humble person. Despite a few vague hints at reform to keep the liberals hopeful, his son was even more reactionary, seeking to wind back the clock even further. The 'Christian state' would be restored no matter what stood in its way. One by one, the reforms that had been imposed on his father in a moment of republican ferment after the unrest of 1805–15 (which in its turn followed in the wake of the French Revolution) were rolled back. In effect, what Friedrich Wilhelm numbers III and IV were trying to do was hold back the push for political power from a newly wealthy bourgeoisie. At all costs, that anti-church, anti-aristocratic and democratic impulse had to be resisted in Germany.

For intellectuals, this reactionary tendency had a real effect on livelihoods and opportunities. The monarch had a direct hand in university-appointments, ensuring conservative appointments to positions in philosophy, law and, above all, theology. Feuerbach ran foul of the system and ended up running the porcelain-workshop of his wife's family (Bertha Löw) in the small Bavarian town of Bruckberg. Bruno Bauer was removed from Berlin and then Bonn and ended up living on a farm. David Strauss was dropped at Tübingen and struggled to be appointed. Marx did not even bother with a university-career. One of the most notable moments was the direct invitation from Friedrich Wilhelm IV to a retired and increasingly reactionary Schelling in 1841 to take up Hegel's chair of philosophy in Berlin in order to 'slay the dragon-seed of Hegelian pantheism'. The young Hegelians were certainly not in favour.

---

9. It is this concentration that leads Breckman to speak of a type of personalism in German thought and practice, a personalism that became the focus of struggle.

So far the story is reasonably well known, at least for anyone with a passing knowledge of German politics in the early-nineteenth century.[10] However, for my purposes, the theological questions are even more interesting. In contrast to the radical anticlericalism of the Enlightenment *philosophes* in France or the deism of English intellectual culture, Germany fought its cultural battles on a different ground, namely that of theology.[11] Or, rather, theology was crucial to all three, but in very different ways. While the French radicals either rejected it and its institutions or developed a rather Christian form of communism, and while the radicals in England tended to slide from religious dissent to deism (with a good dose of anti-establishment polemic against the Church of England),[12] in a Germany still saturated with the pietistic revival of the 1810s and 1820s as well as the well-known German backwardness in economics and politics, German intellectuals could hardly avoid fighting their battles with and through theology. More specifically: they waged furious controversies over the Bible, especially the New Testament and its Gospels. In short, the stories about Jesus in the Gospels were political gunpowder, precisely because political and ecclesiastical power hinged on this figure. To offer an immanent analysis of these texts, one that made no reference to God as cause or agent, was a fundamental challenge to the structures of power which relied on transcendent justification. So the Bible was the terrain of battle for the knot of political struggles in nineteenth-century Germany – over the state, politics, freedom of the press, secularism, immanence and transcendence, reason and religion.

It should come as no surprise, then, that both Marx's and especially Engels's earliest writings should have so much theological and biblical commentary in them. I must admit that even I am surprised at how much there is, much more than the occasional collections on 'Marx and Religion' would lead us to

---

10. For more detail, readers may consult any number of histories of the period, although Kroll 1990, Berdahl 1988 and Blasius 2000 are worth a look.

11. Or, as Engels puts it, 'the battle for dominion over German public opinion in politics and religion' is in fact a battle 'over Germany itself' (Engels 1841a, p. 181; Engels 1841b, p. 256). Marx often becomes exasperated at the backward religiosity and piety of bourgeois German economists and political theorists, especially as compared to those in England and France (Marx 1845a, pp. 266, 284–5).

12. See Thompson 1966.

believe.[13] But the question is: why theology, of all things? Let me suggest four factors, one from France and the other three relating to Germany itself.

The type of socialism that did emerge from France was of a distinctly Christian type. Or, rather, arguing that the original form of Christianity was communist – as found in the legendary accounts of Acts 2:44–5 and 4:32–5 that the early communities had 'all things in common' – it sought to transform Christianity's teachings into codes of ethics without all the supernatural trappings. So we find Saint-Simon's critique of capitalism tied in with an argument that both the Protestant Reformation and medieval Catholicism had distorted the nature of early Christianity, which was really a religion of brotherly love and not a dualistic one that elevated heaven and debased earth. The communities that formed after his death established themselves as a 'church' replete with a priesthood that proclaimed Saint-Simon himself as the messiah. Despite the inevitable fractions in the movement, the defections to Fourier who had until then managed to attract only a small band of followers for his phalansteries, and even the much ridiculed venture to the Middle East to find a female messiah, this type of early socialism washed over the border to affect some German radicals. It was the moral vision and sense of progress in human society towards brotherly love that inspired characters such as Heinrich Heine, August von Cieskowski and an early collaborator with Marx and Engels, Moses Hess.[14] It also influenced some of the early leaders of the German communist movement, such as Wilhelm Weitling, Hermann Kriege, Karl Grün and Gottfried Kinkel, against whom Marx and Engels worked overtime to denounce and excise from the communist movement.[15] Marx could be scathing about this French socialism, which 'sentimentally bewails the sufferings of mankind, or in Christian spirit prophesies the millennium and universal brotherly love, or in humanistic style drivels on about mind, education and freedom'.[16] And, of course, Engels's popular work, *Socialism: Utopian and*

---

13. Marx and Engels 1976a; Marx 2002. Less useful is Padover (ed.) 1974.
14. See especially Breckman 1999, pp. 131–76.
15. Marx and Engels 1845–6a, pp. 484–530; Marx and Engels 1845–6b, pp. 473–520; Marx and Engels 1852a; Marx and Engels 1852b; see also Marx and Engels 1850c, pp. 528–32; Marx and Engels 1850d, pp. 459–63.
16. Marx 1852c, p. 142; Marx 1852d, p. 153. Despite his criticisms of Proudhon's economics, Marx did appreciate his resolute atheism: 'Nevertheless his [Proudhon's] attacks on religion, the church, etc., were of great merit locally at a time when the French socialists thought it desirable to show by their religiosity how superior they

Scientific, argued that this type of socialism was fine for the early, crude stage of socialism, but it really was not going to help mature socialism all that much.[17] Indeed, the old League of the Just, which Marx and Engels joined before changing its name to the Communist League, had a distinctly French socialist and Christian slogan, 'all men are brothers'. One example of this struggle will suffice here. In the attack on Kriege, who was based in the United States, Marx and Engels go to great lengths to debunk his emphasis on Christian love, the holy spirit of community, cup of community and other biblical platitudes: 'Kriege is therefore here preaching *in the name of communism* the old fantasy of religion and German philosophy which is the *direct antithesis of communism. Faith*, more specifically, faith in the "holy spirit of community" is the last thing required for the achievement of communism'.[18]

As for Germany, it is often pointed out (following Marx and Engels, and even Hegel) that Germany was economically and politically backward, with industry barely established and the state engaged in a last gasp of absolutism. For this reason, it did not feel the full effect of the radical anticlericalism of France or the extremes of deism in England. Yet this is far from the full picture, for there are three other historical reasons, one much deeper and longer, and the other two more immediate. In one sense, the controversies of the 1830s and 1840s provided yet another turn in the rumbling history of the Reformation. From Luther's defiance (and assistance by the Duke of Saxony) in the sixteenth century to the Thirty Years' War (1618–48) between Protestants and Roman Catholics that raged over the German states, Italy and the Low Countries, Protestants in the North and Roman Catholics in the South had dug themselves in to become deeply conservative. The Roman Catholics looked to the Pope, while the Protestants (a mix of Lutherans and some Calvinists in the far North) drew upon conservative streams of pietism, marrying an inner walk with God to a tenacious hold on the Bible as the 'word of God'. Despite all the best efforts of the state to keep both Protestants and Roman Catholics in a civil if often fractious relationship, the mutual antagonism ran deep. Thus, during his early experiences with journalism, Marx found that

---

were to the bourgeois Voltairianism of the eighteenth century and the German godlessness of the nineteenth' (Marx 1865a, p. 32; Marx 1865b, p. 31).

17. Engels 1880a, especially pp. 285–97; Engels 1880b, especially pp. 189–201; see also Engels 1892a, pp. 283–300; Engels 1885a, pp. 316–20; Engels 1885b, pp. 210–14.

18. Marx and Engels 1846a, p. 45; Marx and Engels 1846b, p. 12.

one of the major dividing lines between the various newspapers was in terms of the Protestant/Catholic divide.[19] There was one point on which these various conservative newspapers could agree: the young Hegelians were a threat. These impertinent young radicals challenged the very foundations of Christianity; they were really atheists (Bauer ended up becoming one) hell-bent on destroying everything that the Protestants and Roman Catholics held sacred.[20] And they said so as often as they could in the various church-sponsored newspapers, as well as in the ear of the new king.

A more recent factor was the pietistic revival in the 1810s and 1820s. It was a confluence of the longer history of German pietism and revivalist waves that rose across Europe in response to Enlightenment rationalism, 'Godless' revolutionary republicanism and the social dislocation produced by the inroads of industrial capitalism. The emphasis was on recovering one's walk with God, the inner life of faith, the priesthood of all believers and the all-important rôle of God's word, the Bible. The big difference from earlier moments of pietistic fervour in the eighteenth century was that the nobility and intellectuals took it up with not a little enthusiasm. This combination of the aristocracy and bourgeois intellectuals meant that it was not merely a revival from above, but that it also took a distinctly conservative turn. Misgivings in the Prussian state – for pietism could easily reject the state in favour of one's direct relation with God and others – soon gave way when it dovetailed nicely with obedience to God's regent on earth and the purity of the Reformation itself. Crown Prince Friedrich Wilhelm declared himself in favour (why would he not?) and theology-faculties became watchdogs for orthodoxy. Among these was Ernst Hengstenberg in Berlin, against whom Bruno Bauer directed his attack in *Herr Dr Hengstenberg* of 1839 – one of his less-than-astute political acts, for it led to his removal from Berlin.

---

19. This deep tension shows up in various observations and passing comments concerning German politics and society in Marx's endless journalistic pieces. For example, see Marx 1858e, p. 57; Marx 1858h, pp. 96, 99; Marx 1858b, p. 127.

20. In his broad survey, 'Progress of Social Reform on the Continent', Engels presents the young Hegelians as a loose group that relied on shock and surprise rather than any organised and broad-based movement as such. Even though they claimed to be Christians and Protestants and did their work on the Bible, they did not realise that they were actually atheists until Engels pointed it out to them, or so he claims (in his *Schelling and Revelation*). See Engels 1843e, pp. 404–5.

A more immediate event still was a particular book by David Friedrich Strauss called *Das Leben Jesu*. Not so much a book, it was a bomb. It was lobbed out of the midst of that radical group known as the young Hegelians who met in the small Hippel Café in Berlin from 1837.[21] One feature of the writings (and limited teaching) of this energetic group cannot be emphasised enough: a good number of them were biblical scholars or at least theologians, and their chosen ground of battle was nothing other than the Bible. The decades of the 1830s and 1840s trembled and indeed rumbled with the seismic shift taking place. Bruno Bauer threw out his deep challenges to the Bible, in studies on both the Hebrew Bible and the Gospels in the New Testament.[22] Ludwig Feuerbach's *Das Wesen des Christentums* of 1841 caused a furore and sold out a number of print-runs in a short time. Above all, it was David Strauss's book that set the hares running.

After deliberately taking time off from his first teaching position at the theological faculty in Tübingen (where he taught for only three semesters from the summer of 1832 to autumn 1833 in logic, metaphysics, the history of philosophy, and ethics) in order to focus on his writing, Strauss published in 1835 his *Das Leben Jesu, kritisch bearbeitet* in two volumes. It really is the kind of work that most writers would dream of producing – a controversial, landmark text that makes its mark way beyond the narrow confines of intellectual work.[23] I must admit, however, that I could have done without the stress. Although the liberals held Strauss up as something of a champion, he was surprised

---

21. For some strange reason, we seem to be living once again the time of the young Hegelians. As Alberto Toscano put it to me (private communication), we, in our own time, have not yet reached 1840. That may explain why interest in these rabble-rousers and party-animals has revived somewhat. Three decades and more ago it seemed impossible to discuss Marx without considering the young Hegelians (for example, Berlin 1978, pp. 47–60; McLellan 1969; Hook 1994 and the unreliable Kolakowski 1981, pp. 81–95), but the interest waned. Breckman's study of 1999 is the first of a small revival, but see also Moggach 2006 and the anthology edited by Stepelevich 1997. One rule of the game that has not changed is trying to determine who influenced Marx and when they did so. That game is not for me.

22. Bauer 1838, 1839, 1840, 1841, 1842a, 1842b, 1843a, 1850–1, 1852.

23. In the shadow of such a great book, Strauss was never quite able to repeat the performance. Apart from the four editions of the *Leben Jesu* itself (Strauss 1835, 1836, 1839, 1840a), he kept producing support-works, responses to critics and further explorations (Strauss 1840b, 1864, 1865, 1873, 1980, 1983, 1997, 2000), apart from his penchant for biographies during a twenty-year hiatus from theology (Strauss 1851, 1858–60, 1924, 1978, 1991), along with the odd satirical and very polemical political work (Strauss 1992).

to find himself vilified and roundly attacked by both young Hegelians such as Bruno Bauer (for 'misreading' Hegel)[24] and a range of conservative forces in theology-faculties, the churches and government, so much so that he lost any chance of further offers of positions in either church or university.[25] The theology-faculty at Tübingen sacked him as soon as the book came out. The closest he came to any university-position at all was in Zurich the year after. Some of the liberal burghers invited Strauss to take up a chair in dogmatics and church-history. Twice, their proposal was overcome by conservatives, but in January 1839, with a majority in the city-government, they were successful. However, his arrival was anticipated with fear and trembling and in the face of huge protests, and the government gave him a lifelong pension in compensation.

So what was it about the *Leben Jesu* that so offended people? Strauss argued that the key to the Gospels and their depiction of Jesus lay in myth. He played off a double sense of myth: it did mean that we can never recover a distinct picture of the historical Jesus (fiction), but he also argued that myth should be read in a positive light, as a poetic expression of deeper truths that cannot be expressed in any other form. Focusing on the miraculous dimension of the Gospel narratives, from virgin-birth through the various miracles performed by Jesus to the ultimate miracle of the death and resurrection, Strauss argued that both a supernaturalist and interventionist understanding were hopelessly wrong and that the rationalist effort to explain the miracles in naturalistic terms (for example, Jesus did not walk on the water but walked on a sand-spit so that he seemed to do so) simply missed the point. If the former accepted the record at face-value, the latter argued that the New-Testament writers misrepresented or misinterpreted what had actually happened. For Strauss, however, what the New-Testament writers did was draw deeply upon the mythical Jewish-messianic traditions which they knew all too well and used these to portray Jesus as the Messiah. Indeed, myth is the natural way in which life and indeed religion was understood by pre-scientific peoples (Lévi-Strauss was by no means the first to develop this idea).[26] Strauss's

---

24. See his response in Strauss 1980, 1983.
25. In 1830–1 he had briefly been a pastor's assistant for a local parish in Kleiningersheim near Ludwigsburg, his hometown, after studying theology at Tübingen.
26. The key-figures on whom Strauss relied in his treatment of myth are the classicist Christian G. Heyne (1729–1812), and the biblical scholars Johann Gottfried

challenge was to apply such a mode of mythic interpretation to the New Testament in as rigorous a fashion as possible.

The result: after a lengthy introduction that establishes the need for mythical interpretation, with a characteristically German propensity for trawling through all of the previous studies on both the Gospels and myth, Strauss painstakingly works through each episode in the Gospels. In each case, he presents the supernaturalist position, negates it with the naturalist one and then offers a mythical interpretation in order to resolve the contradiction: in light of the lack of corroborating evidence, the contradictions with known physical laws, the presence of poetic language and the heavy use of prophecies from the Hebrew Bible (in both the narratives and in Jesus's mouth), what we have is mythic construction of the first order. The Hegelian echo in his plan was not a mistake.

He then takes the final Hegelian step in the third part of the book (the first two parts move through the Gospels) to offer his own positive proposal. In short, he wants to 're-establish dogmatically that which has been destroyed critically'.[27] His proposal is what he calls a speculative Christology, produced with a helping hand from Hegel. God is nothing other than the infinite spirit that moves out of itself to produce 'the Finite, Nature, and the human mind' from which it eternally returns to itself in unity.[28] Neither the finite spirit of man nor the infinite spirit of God have any reality without being in contact with one another. So, the 'infinite spirit is real only when it discloses itself in finite spirits; as the finite spirit is true only when it merges itself in the infinite'.[29] The result is none other than Jesus Christ, for the following reason: 'If God and man are in themselves *one*, and if religion is the human side of this unity: then must this unity be made evident to man in religion, and become in him consciousness and reality'.[30] The catch is that this union and this appearance are not restricted to one person, as the church would have it. By contrast, this dialectical unity of infinite and finite can take place in every person, or preferably in the whole of humanity.

Eichhorn (1752–1827), Johann Philipp Gabler (1753–1826), Georg Lorenz Bauer (1755–1806), Wilhelm Martin Leberecht de Wette (1780–1839) and Ferdinand Christian Baur (1792–1860).

27. Strauss 1902, p. 757.
28. Strauss 1902, p. 777.
29. Ibid.
30. Ibid.

> This is the key to the whole of Christology, that, as subject of the predicate which the church assigns to Christ, we place, instead of an individual, an idea; but an idea which has an existence in reality, not in the mind only, like that of Kant. In an individual, a God-man, the properties and functions which the church ascribes to Christ contradict themselves; in the idea of the race, they perfectly agree. Humanity is the union of the two natures.[31]

The question remains as to why this book, a lengthy and detailed work in New-Testament criticism (where it has a lasting influence) should have had such a wide political impact. And why was it the text around which much of the ferment of the time took place, a ferment in which Marx and Engels were also caught? There have been far more critical works that have hardly had the same impact. Here I draw on Marilyn Massey's *Christ Unmasked*,[32] where she argues that it was understood, championed and opposed as a text that espoused 'radical democratic politics'.[33] Not only did its undermining of any verifiable historical record of Jesus of Nazareth challenge the basis of both Protestant and Roman-Catholic assumptions about the Bible and Christianity, it also shook up the theological justifications for the hold of the old aristocracy on power and of the Prussian king himself. Even more, in developing a Christology in which the divine and human rested not with one man but with all humanity, Strauss was giving voice to a theological agenda with radical-democratic tendencies. Rather than God's chosen ruler being, like Christ, a chosen individual, all may potentially rule. In short, Strauss attempted a reinterpretation of Christianity that questioned its cosy relationship with the power of the state. In making a shift from the heroic individual to the general community, 'the potentiality seeming to belong only to one exalted human belonged, rather, to humanity itself'.[34] Massey's conclusion is that by 'unmasking' Christ not as the God-man of Christian doctrine but as the democratic Christ, as the one who shows that the human species itself is the embodiment of God-man, Strauss pointed to a model of popular sovereignty instead of the monarchy.

---

31. Strauss 1902, p. 780.
32. Massey 1983.
33. Massey 1983, p. 12.
34. Massey 1983, p. 79.

There are a number of ways of reading such a situation. A conventional one is to suggest that Strauss used the dominant language of his time – theology and biblical studies – to make political points. Should he have lived in a different time, such as ours or perhaps in ancient Greece, his language may well have been economic or political. Theology thereby becomes a code for something else – in this case, the politics of German self-determination. Another approach is to argue that Strauss's purely theological work had unforeseen and unexpected political consequences. Strauss's own surprise and dismay at the massive reaction suggest that any political consequences were by-products.

A third possibility – the one that Massey pursues – is that Strauss clearly articulated despite himself the key-tensions of the time. She points to the differences between the first and third editions. In the first (the one I have outlined all too briefly above) Strauss pursued his radical critique of existing scholarship and understandings of Jesus, concluding with a democratic rein-terpretation of Christology. By contrast, in the third edition he made many concessions to his critics and elevated the individual figure of Christ. In this 1838 edition, Strauss 'offered the palliative of an aristocratic Christ, a genius Jesus, who was the epitome of the perfection of the inner life'.[35] He gave up a massive amount of ground, allowing for the unique unity of divine and human in Jesus's religious consciousness and even granting a category of miracles based on the unusual powers of nature. Partly an effort to secure a teaching-post, Strauss soon regretted his back-peddling and in the fourth edition of 1840 he returned to his former hard-hitting arguments. For Massey, this tension within Strauss himself gave clear expression to the struggles within Germany between the liberal, democratic movements and the forces of reaction which waged a consistent campaign against Strauss and the liberals.

I would add a couple of points. First, the analysis developed by Strauss was indebted to and characteristic of the new model of biblical criticism developing in Germany at the time. It was an immanent analysis of the text, eschewing the transcendent reference to God. In order to distinguish itself from traditional theological exegesis, 'scientific' biblical criticism did not avail itself of God as historical cause, reason for the actions of people, or as a factor in the formation of the Bible. Instead, they sought for cause and effect in the

---

35. Massey 1983, p. 149.

same places as other historians and literary critics – in politics, economics, culture, individual psychology and so on. The text was no longer a witness to God but to history, both of the texts themselves and the history behind those texts. That is to say, the assumed signifying link between the character known as 'God' in the text and a being to whom the text referred was broken for the purpose of biblical analysis (what people did in their lives outside biblical criticism is another matter). This may seem commonplace in biblical criticism today, but it was widely perceived in the mid-nineteenth century as a threat to one's faith, the church and the state. The first two are obvious, but the state? A major reason for the challenge posed by David Strauss, Bruno Bauer and a host of lesser biblical critics was that a criticism which removed God from the picture and focused on immanent analysis challenged the claims that the state and the monarchy were appointed and sanctioned by God. If the Bible, which was the basis of the church and the state, could be understood perfectly well without any transcendent reference-point, then so, by implication, could the state. As we will see in the chapter on Engels's engagement with biblical criticism, these assumptions of immanent biblical criticism may be seen as one of the influences on the immanent approach of historical materialism.

Secondly, and following on from the previous point, it is no surprise such an articulation took place in the realm of biblical criticism and theology. As I pointed out earlier, all of these furious debates were not purely the fussy and pompous struggles of academics, the hot air of intellectuals vainly feeling that they were important for shaking up a few of their colleagues in the faculties of theology at Berlin, Bonn or Tübingen. These debates hit at the crux of the idea and practice of the 'Christian state' at the time. They also fed off the long history of bitter struggles between Roman Catholics and Protestants, with their resultant conservatism, and the immediate situation of a reactionary king, Friedrich Wilhelm IV, who sought to recover the lost glory of Christendom. Apart from having a say in university-appointments, he also oversaw the tightening of censorship-regulations. Besides liberal and republican movements, one of the main targets of this censorship were the young Hegelian radicals. Wilhelm IV had, in fact, called for an answer from young Hegelians in response to Strauss's claim that he had made use of Hegel. Bauer was nominated to take up the attack, but the King was not altogether pleased with the result. The conservative papers had a field day, feeling that their assaults on the young Hegelians were fully justified in light of the Crown's support. In this context, the young Hegelians were both cornered and became the champions of the liberal and republican cause.

Conclusion

These titanic struggles had an immediate effect on both Marx and Engels, which often felt to their participants like the Reformation all over again with its battles over the Bible, theology and the state.[36] They left their mark not merely in the pressing need to respond to this theological context, but also in specific references to biblical matters. For example, in the midst of reading and absorbing all these new works in biblical studies, we find Engels writing to his friend Wilhelm Graeber:

> Now, manikin, now you're going to hear something: I am now an enthusiastic Straussian. Just you come here, I have now got arms, shield and helmet; now I am secure, just you come here and I'll give you such a drubbing, despite all your theologia, that you won't know where to run. Yes, Guillermo, *jacta est alea* [the die is cast] I am now a Straussian; I, a poor, miserable poet, have crept under the wing of the genius David Friedrich Strauss.[37]

His enthusiasm is hard to miss. For Engels, at least when he was nineteen, Strauss's mythicism is like the 'dawn-reddened, snow-capped peaks' that signal a whole new world.[38] In many ways, a book like *Das Leben Jesu* was the decompression-chamber for Engels from his Calvinist upbringing. He may have moved past Strauss, but he certainly made good use of the insights from critical study of the Bible (see Chapters Nine and Ten).

---

36. As we will see, Marx saw Luther as a hero and nearly always cites him approvingly. Engels was less enthused, although he still felt Protestantism was superior to Roman Catholicism. Gustav Mayer argued back in 1920 that the debates in the 1820s and 1830s were the most intense since the Reformation (Mayer 1920, p. 416).

37. Engels 1839x, p. 471; Engels 1839y, p. 419. To Friedrich Graeber he also writes: 'Your orthodox psychology must necessarily rank me among the most wicked, obdurate sinners, especially as I am now wholly and utterly lost. For I have taken the oath to the flag of David Friedrich Strauss and am a first-class mythic; I tell you, Strauss is a grand fellow and a genius, and with powers of discernment such as nobody else has' (Engels 1839bb, pp. 479–80; Engels 1839cc, p. 429).

38. Engels 1839dd, p. 486; Engels 1839ee, p. 435.

While Marx, and later Engels, lost their enthusiasm for the young Hegelians,[39] they never ceased to be interested in the battles over the Bible. In a letter to Engels in 1864, written while Marx was travelling after the death of his mother, he points out that, although Ernst Renan's popular *The Life of Jesus* (which introduced critical biblical scholarship to France) has its problems, it is a step beyond the German studies on which it is based. 'Here in Holland', he writes, 'the German critical theological school is so much *à l'ordre du jour* that clerics openly proclaim their allegiance to it from the pulpit'.[40] Some two decades earlier, at the height of the furore, Marx thought about engaging in some theological criticism. His close association with Bauer led him to plan a review of a book by K. Fischer called *Die Idee der Gottheit*,[41] a critique of Hegel's *Philosophy of Religion* and to edit a journal together with Bauer called *Archiv des Atheismus*. None of these works came to fruition, or if they did they have not survived. Further, in a letter to Ruge (10 February 1842) he offers to write a review for the *Deutsche Jahrbücher* of a book, *Die menschliche Freiheit in ihrem Verhältniss zur Sünde und zur göttlichen Gnade*, written by the Hegelian biblical critic and theologian Wilhelm Vatke.[42] He writes, 'my critical zeal

---

39. While on military service in Berlin in 1841, Engels soon joined the amorphous group at the Hippel Café and became an active member. While he was busy defending their positions in attacks on Schelling or in his marvellous poem 'The Insolently Threatened Yet Miraculously Rescued Bible', Marx was already becoming disenchanted with the Berlin section of the group. He derides their 'mania for genius and boasting', frivolity, 'insipid aping of the French clubs', rowdiness, blackguardism, 'vague reasoning, magniloquent phrases and self-satisfied self-adoration' (Marx 1842a, p. 287; Marx 1842b, pp. 371–2; Marx 1842ff, p. 394; Marx 1842gg, p. 412; see also Marx 1842dd, p. 390; Marx 1842ee, p. 406).

40. Marx 1864b, p. 507; Marx 1864c, p. 386. See also Marx's comment to Engels in 1864 concerning a book from Holland by Professor Dozy of Leyden (the leading orientalist in Holland) in which Dozy argues from what would now be called a classic biblical-minimalist position – the characters of Abraham, Isaac and Jacob are fictional characters, the Israelites were idolaters, and Ezra made up Genesis-Joshua in order to generate reform. Marx comments that it is causing quite a stir, and: 'Outside Germany at any rate (Renan, Colenso, Dozy, etc.) there is a remarkable anti-religious movement' (Marx 1864d, p. 541; Marx 1864e, pp. 414–15). In a letter of the same year to his uncle, Lion Philips, he points out that Spinoza had already argued that the Pentateuch was concocted after the Babylonian exile (Marx 1864f, p. 542; Marx 1864g, p. 665).

41. Fischer 1839.

42. Marx 1842v; Marx 1842w. Vatke (1806–82) was one of the significant contributors to the developing theories about sources in the Hebrew Bible (Old Testament). See also Marx's sarcastic comments in the letter to Ruge on 27 April 1842: 'We were very much amused with what you wrote in your letters about Vatke's lack of a "full heart". This super-clever, diplomatic Vatke, who would so much like to be the greatest critic and the greatest believer who always knows everything better than anyone else, this

is at your disposal'.[43] More substantially, there is the lost manuscript called
A Treatise on Christian Art that he also mentions to Ruge. It seems that at the
time Marx wrote to Ruge (5 March 1842) the manuscript was one step away
from a fair copy – he mentions that he would need to write one up and make
a few corrections before it would be ready for the *Anekdota* which Ruge
planned to publish in Switzerland.[44]

This, then, is the context in which Marx and Engels began their critical
explorations. Due to the proverbial tardiness of German economics and politics, as well as the Lutheran doctrine of *sola scriptura* and the long history of
struggles between Protestants and Roman Catholics,[45] the debates over reason, secularism and politics took place on the territory of theology and the
Bible. Implicit in this historical situatedness is an assumption concerning theology that runs throughout this book: theology is a very particular beast that
occasionally makes false claims to absoluteness and universality. That theology has a beginning and a history is all too often forgotten. So the reason Marx
and Engels must engage with and try to extract themselves from theology is
because it was one of the dominant modes of thought and practice at that time
in Germany. Let me close with a dialectical point: the radicalism of German
biblical and theological scholarship, engendered from the deep conservatism
of their context, gave that scholarship a radical edge it was not to lose for
some time. Indeed, German biblical and theological scholarship was able to
surge to the lead in biblical scholarship for about a century, until a good number of the leading figures moved to the USA before World-War II.

Vatke has for one party no heart, and for the other no head. *Hic jacet* Vatke – a notable
example of what the passion for cards and religious music leads to' (Marx 1842bb,
p. 388; Marx 1842cc, p. 403).
    43. Marx 1842v, p. 381; Marx 1842w, p. 395.
    44. Marx 1842x; Marx 1842y. Only one volume of *Anekdota zur neuesten deutschen
Philosophie und Publistik* ever appeared, in 1843, so the treatise never made it in.
    45. Engels is somewhat correct when he points out that German Protestantism was
the basis of this critical scholarship, although he turns it into a good old Protestant
diatribe against the Roman Catholics (Engels 1873e, p. 608; Engels 1873f, p. 594).

Chapter One
The Subterranean Bible

> Moses said: Thou shalt not muzzle the ox when
> he treadeth out the corn. But the Christian lords
> of Germany say on the contrary: 'Serfs should
> have a big wooden board fastened round their
> neck, so that they can't use their hands to put
> flour into their mouths'.[1]

I begin with a synoptic effort, casting my eye over
the whole range of both Marx's and Engels's allusions
to the Bible and theology. Rather than begin with the
sustained treatments of theology in their works (they
will turn up in the chapters that follow), I open with
the allusions for a number of reasons. At the simplest level, these references show how extensively
Marx and Engels knew the Bible and theology; they
use these resources as a ready reserve of raw materials on which they call again and again for all manner
of purposes. Further, this synoptic view introduces
a number of key-themes that appear in their more
direct engagements with theology – themes such as
anticlericalism, the connections between economics
and theology, the context in which Marx and Engels
worked, and the ambivalence of their interactions
with theology.

---

1. Marx 1861–3f, p. 400.

It would be tempting to sideline these biblical and theological allusions as mere examples, as illustrations peripheral to the main argument. The catch is that they are so *persistent*. I have noticed these for many years – a brief reference to the Bible or theology or church-history. But when I began gathering material for this chapter by collecting the various references in a pile, all too soon the pile became a massive mountain. So in an effort to discern the various types, I tried to imagine myself sitting in a vast shed, sorting an immense mound of bolts, nuts, washers and what have you into their respective tins. In what follows I outline the major types of allusions, offer a few select examples and then relegate the remainder to the notes.

These biblical and theological allusions cover the full range of Marx and Engels's writings, from the earliest letters and articles through to the last. The references cluster more tightly in some areas than others, such as Marx's journalistic essays in the *Rheinische Zeitung*, or Engels's letters to his friends, joint works such as *The Holy Family* and *The German Ideology*, or Engels's occasional essays on biblical and theological topics. The early texts by both Marx and Engels were written under the vigilant gaze of the censor. So we find them working hard to outwit the censor, either by writing under pseudonyms (Engels), or provoking and attacking the censor directly, or neutralising him through ingenious arguments. Next, we find that many of the allusions are polemical uses of the Bible and theology to attack the assumed privilege of the ruling classes. In their earlier texts, such a class was still made up of the remnants of the old feudal aristocracy, although now in the form of landed nobility. These texts refer mostly to the German situation where the bourgeoisie was still largely excluded from power and pursued a vigorous liberal agenda attacking the old ruling class. Closely connected with these polemical allusions are the delightful anticlerical pieces, where the clergy as part of a corrupt ruling class come in for a beating. On this matter, Marx and Engels are part of a long German tradition that goes back at least to Luther. However, as Marx's economic studies gained momentum, the focus shifts to the new ruling class of the bourgeoisie. By this time, Marx's family was based in England where industrialisation was far more advanced and where the bourgeoisie had a distinct political party – the Whigs – that first undermined and then joined forces with the Tories. The polemical attention shifts and the Bible and theology become useful tools indeed for attacking the systemic exploitation by the new capitalists, especially factory and mill-owners. From this point

I move to consider the increasing number of economic allusions, especially when Marx's economic studies gained momentum.

The final cluster shifts emphasis. I track the ways Marx and Engels make use of the Bible as a polemical resource against opponents, within and outside the communist movement. This use is often a positive one; that is, the Bible is appropriated by Marx and Engels and used to criticise someone else. It is a short step to the next category, namely, the act of lining oneself up with the Bible and using it favourably for oneself. All of which leads me to the final group where the ambivalence of the Bible comes to the fore.

Outwitting the censor

Much of Marx's early journalistic material, especially for the *Rheinische Zeitung*, was written in the shadow of vigorous censorship from the Prussian government. In the context of the 'Christian state', this censorship had a distinctly religious edge. Some of these articles are still a pleasure to read. Witty, cutting and polemical, they delight in showing up the inconsistencies and weaknesses of any rival. But they are also, as Kouvelakis points out, manifestations of a political style that tried to find room to move in the small space opened up by the pause in state-censorship.[2] Mixing up mockery and serious argument with a good deal of humour, these pieces fed a public starved of open debate, as evidenced by the rapid increase in circulation of the *Rheinische Zeitung*. Marx does not mind using whatever comes to hand, whether *ad hominem* attacks on the intellectual weakness of an author,[3] mockery, satire, an over-abundance of puns[4] (he does have a tendency at times to run on like the proverbial spermatic spluttering pen), close reading whereby he pulls to pieces the arguments of the latest target sentence-by-sentence and phrase-by-phrase, the merciless exposure of contradictions, inconsistencies and sloppy thinking. Some of Marx's phrases are delightful, such as 'buffoon by

---

2. Kouvelakis 2003, pp. 256–7. Indeed, for Kouvelakis, the repression that followed in 1843 closed down this space and brought on the political crisis that pushed Marx to take the crucial steps to a revolutionary position (Kouvelakis 2003, pp. 276–8).

3. See the descriptions of Dr O.F. Gruppe as a dilettante and 'comical character' in Marx 1842t; Marx 1842u. Gruppe wrote a short critique, *Bruno Bauer und die akademische Lehrfreiheit* (Gruppe 2010), of Bruno Bauer's *Kritik der evangelischen Geschichter der Synoptiker* (Bauer 1841).

4. Marx 1842h, pp. 184–5; Marx 1842i, pp. 172–3.

profession'[5] or 'that egregious literary laxative';[6] so also with sentences such as this: 'The style of the whole is pretentious, puerile, piffling and of a complacent stupidity unequalled in the annals of world history'.[7]

When I first sank into these texts, I had the impression of a long period of writing (they run to 268 pages of *MECW*). Looking again at the dates I realised it was barely over a year: his first piece was written between 15 January and 10 February 1842,[8] and the last, a note concerning his resignation as editor, appeared on 18 March 1843. And what a tumultuous, productive and provocative year it was, ending with the closing-down of the *Rheinische Zeitung* by order of the King of Prussia himself, Friedrich Wilhelm IV. By April, Marx had married Jenny von Westphalen; by November, they found other ways to outsmart the censor, such as leaving Prussia for Paris, and then Brussels and London.

Marx uses all manner of tactics to slip by the censor, whether it is biting criticism of the state's censorship where he delights in showing up its contradictions,[9] or responses to efforts at censoring the *Rheinische Zeitung* by the Rhine authorities,[10] or yet another polemical piece directed at his favourite target, the right-wing *Kölnische Zeitung*,[11] or short, sharp articles defending Bruno Bauer[12] and the like-minded Friedrich von Sallet, the army-lieutenant, poet and critic of Christianity,[13] or even the occasional lost pieces such as the one attacking the Archbishop which he fears (as he writes to Ruge) may not be approved by the censor.[14] Throughout these various tactics, theology and the Bible are not far from the scene.

---

5. Marx 1842t, p. 211; Marx 1842u, pp. 245–6.
6. Engels 1851k, p. 417; Engels 1851l, p. 305.
7. Marx 1851f, p. 360; Marx 1851g, p. 263.
8. Intended for Arnold Ruge's *Deutsche Jahrbücher* (see Marx 1842v; Marx 1842w), the first piece, 'Comments on the Latest Prussian Censorship Instruction', never appeared there due to the heavy hand of the censor. It did eventually see the light of published day in *Anekdota zur neuesten deutschen Philosophie und Publicistik* in Switzerland in 1843.
9. Marx 1843a, pp. 116–21; Marx 1843b, pp. 103–9.
10. Marx 1842p; Marx 1842q.
11. Marx 1842h; Marx 1842i; Marx 1843e; Marx 1843f.
12. Marx 1842t; Marx 1842u.
13. Marx 1843o; Marx 1843p. A couple of articles deal with other matters, such as the law punishing the use of fallen wood by impoverished peasants (Marx 1842n; Marx 1842o), or taking up the cause of the Moselle vine-growing peasants who faced tough economic conditions (Marx 1843g; Marx 1843h).
14. On 9 July 1842, Marx wrote to Ruge: 'What do you advise if the article on the Archbishop is not stamped for publication by the high police censorship? It must

Among many, I give three examples, two of them merciless uncoverings of contradictions in the Prussian censorship-laws concerning religion and the other a reply to a series of questions from the censor himself, namely the stern Oberpräsident of the Rhine Province, von Schaper. So, in the article concerning the revision of the Prussian censorship-laws in 1842 (ironically, the article itself could not be published due to censorship and appeared later in Switzerland), Marx points up one contradiction after another.[15] The list grows and grows: the original law of 1819 fell into the trap of protecting all religions and thereby ended up being irreligious, for each religion lays claim to the truth at the expense of the others. The particularity of each cancels out any notion of religion in general. Or the new law of 1842 forbids both frivolous and hostile attacks against Christianity itself or religion in general. Marx points out that it thereby restricts the nature of attack to either frivolous (light-hearted and particular) or hostile (serious and general) forms; no other forms are permissible. Then again, in repeating the ban on confusing faith and politics from the earlier decree, the new legislation actually bans its own underlying agenda, which is none other than the desire to establish a Christian state. Even with this point he is not finished, for he goes on to ask how a state can be Christian when it has Lutheran and Roman-Catholic elements within it. Which creed is to be the official faith of this Christian state? On it goes, until he identifies the final contradiction, where the charge is nothing less than hubris, arrogating God's own rôle:

> Thus the instruction wants to protect religion, but it violates the most general principle of all religions, the sanctity and inviolability of the subjective frame of mind. It makes the censor instead of God the judge of the heart. Thus it prohibits offensive utterances and defamatory judgments on individuals, but it exposes you every day to the defamatory and offensive judgment of the censor.[16]

The second example involves Marx's effort to overturn the argument that the actual existence of the laws against freedom of the press is enough of a refutation of freedom of the press. Based as it is on a conservative argument

---

appear in print because of 1) our Provincial Assembly, 2) the government, 3) the Christian state. Should I, perhaps, send it to Hoffmann and Campe? It does not seem to me suitable for the *Anekdota*' (Marx 1842dd, p. 391; Marx 1842ee, p. 407).

15. Marx 1843a, especially pp. 116–21; Marx 1843b, especially pp. 103–9.

16. Marx 1843a, p. 121; Marx 1843b, p. 109.

that assumes and respects the wisdom of one's forebears (i.e. the ruling class), Marx cites some other examples of such residual convictions and legal sanctions:

> People were once ordered to believe that the earth did not go round the sun. Was Galileo refuted by this? Similarly, in *our Germany* legal sanction was given to the conviction of the empire, which the individual princes shared, that serfdom was a quality inherent in certain human beings, that truth could be made most evident by surgical operation, we mean torture, and the flames of hell could already be demonstrated to heretics by means of flames on earth.[17]

I hardly need to explicate the reference to Galileo's 'heresy' or indeed to the Inquisition, but with a couple of examples from the history of Christianity what might have looked (at least to those stuffed up with inherited wealth and titles) perfectly reasonable becomes quite ridiculous. Galileo too was censored, as were the heretics at the stake – hardly an argument for the wisdom of censorship.

Finally, there is Marx's reply to the charges of the censor, von Schaper, a reply in which Marx draws heavily on the Bible.[18] In response to the charge of being 'impudent and harsh' against the government, Marx offers a skilful mix of obsequiousness and defiance that effectively removed the possibility of immediate prosecution. He makes a whole series of points – that the paper was already subject to strict censorship, that a 'noble purpose' lies behind the paper's criticisms, that it wishes to enhance Prussia's progress and so on. But I am interested in his answer to the charge of being 'irreligious'. His reply is threefold. First, drawing on an argument he would use more than once, he points out that Germany is divided between Protestants and Roman Catholics, so it is hardly appropriate to take one side in an unresolved debate.[19] Second, he invokes the censorship-legislation itself, especially on the point

---

17. Marx 1842l, pp. 138–9; Marx 1842m, p. 127.
18. Marx 1842p; Marx 1842q. It is actually written in the name of Engelbert Renard, the publisher of the paper, but Marx is the author.
19. See also his comments on the religious party-polemics between the Roman-Catholic (*Rhein- und Mosel-Zeitung* and *Kölnische Zeitung*) and Protestant (*Leipziger Allgemeine Zeitung*) papers (Marx 1843e; Marx 1843f). Once again, Marx asserts that the *Rheinische Zeitung* does not engage in such one-sided polemic. Alternatively, 'North-German' and 'South-German' culture stands in for Protestant and Roman-Catholic (Marx 1843l, p. 364; Marx 1843m, pp. 352–3).

that religious concerns should not be transferred to the realm of politics.[20] On this score, the *Rheinische Zeitung* actually carries out a necessary duty, for it criticises those who would confuse religion and politics. Finally, Marx goes as far as to promise not to raise theological or ecclesiological matters, with the qualification: 'so long as other newspapers or political conditions themselves do not necessitate reference to them'.[21] In other words, if they are going to do it, we will do it. In the end, he asserts that the *Rheinische Zeitung* will remain a vigorous and free newspaper, even threatening to take up legal action if needed. Now, all this is good liberal defence, stressing the separation of church and state, the need to attack those who would confuse religion and politics, and proclaiming freedom of the press. There is, however, one point that it far more intriguing. In a passage deleted in pencil, Marx wrote: 'If Luther is not blamed for having attacked, in defiance of emperor and realm, the sole mode of existence of Christianity at that time, the Catholic Church, in a form that was even unbridled and exceeded all bounds, should it be forbidden in a Protestant state to advocate a view opposed to current dogma, not by isolated frivolous invectives, but by the consistent exposition of serious and primarily German science?'[22] It is not clear who deleted this stronger statement, whether the publisher Renard before he sent the letter or Marx himself. But it shifts the defence to another level. Quite simply, Marx invokes Luther himself and the challenge of the Reformation to argue that defiant criticism is at the heart of the German theological tradition. It is, of course, a clever move, for it invokes a hero of the German Protestant state. More than that, however, Marx also claims to stand in Luther's own footprints.[23] I will have more to say

---

20. Marx cites Article II of the 1819 censorship-decree on a number of occasions. It stated that censorship is 'to oppose fanatical transference of religious articles of faith into politics and the *confusion of ideas* resulting therefrom'. Marx quotes it directly and then later asserts that the *Rheinsiche Zeitung* had heeded it to the extent of criticising others who did not (Marx 1843a, p. 117; Marx 1843b, p. 105, and Marx 1843l, p. 364; Marx 1843m, p. 352).

21. Marx 1842p, p. 285; Marx 1842q, p. 396.

22. Marx 1842p, p. 284, n. a; Marx 1842q, p. 395, n. 1.

23. See also his delight in heretics who sought to bypass religious censorship by disguising their works under innocent titles: 'In Rome, the publication of the Koran is prohibited. But a cunning Italian found a way out of the situation. He published a *refutation* of the Koran, i.e., a book, the title page of which bore the heading "Refutation of the Koran", but after the title page it contained a simple reprint of the Koran. Have not all heretics employed such a ruse?' (Marx 1843e, p. 323; Marx 1843f, p. 341).

later about Marx's soft spot for Luther and sense that he followed the path first blazed by this Augustinian monk.

Censorship, then, was the constant backdrop to Marx's writing even from the earliest days. And his dealing with religious censorship was the continuation of a long history that preceded him.[24] It would not leave him alone until he and his family finally arrived in London. As for this short stint with the *Rheinische Zeitung*, eventually he tired of the constant twisting, paying lip-service and trying to outsmart the censor. Indeed, later, after he had resigned as editor, Marx admitted to Ruge, 'As far as the *Rheinische Zeitung* is concerned I would not remain *under any conditions*; it is impossible for me to write under Prussian censorship or to live in the Prussian atmosphere'.[25] It was not merely the constant dealings with the censor, but also the desire of the paper's liberal backers to tone down the polemic that frustrated him.

Against the ruling class

What often got Marx into trouble was his constant polemic against the churches, Christianity and theology. Given Friedrich Wilhelm IV's desire to re-establish Christendom in the 'Christian state' of Prussia, any political criticism was bound to attack the Christian churches, and vice versa. Marx (and Engels in his own essays) was merciless in his attacks on the old aristocratic ruling class, the clergy and the new bourgeois rulers.

As for the German landed nobility, meeting every now and then in the Assembly of the Estates in the different provinces, they could certainly find plenty of justification in the Bible for their privilege and support of the king. It may be Romans 13:1 ('Let every person be subject to the governing authorities') or the divine sanction promising to King David to establish the 'throne of his kingdom forever' (2 Samuel 7:8–17), or the long and cosy relationship between the churches and the state-powers of Europe. Marx's response is both mischievous and more serious. In using the same biblical text, the same theology and the same church-history as they used to justify their position, he shows how these materials are shaky foundations indeed. They often speak with two or more voices, and he has little trouble in turning biblical texts and

---

24. Ibid.
25. Marx 1843q, p. 400; Marx 1843r, p. 418.

theological examples against the privilege of the ruling class. Every now and then, the Bible, theology and church become in Marx's hands ambiguous and ambivalent resources that provide plenty of polemical weapons.

Marx attacks this old nobility in a couple of overlapping ways, first by breaking open the seamless connection between theology and the ruling class and then by attacking the ruling classes directly. On this matter we find delightfully ironic comments and asides that tend to belittle those in authority. Out of an insurmountable pile I choose the following. These include the lightly ironic comment on the development of windmills – 'In Germany the nobles at first maintained that the wind was their property; but then the bishops challenged them, claiming it as ecclesiastical property'.[26] – as well as the comment to Ruge concerning the pietistic relatives of Jenny, for 'whom "the Lord in heaven" and the "lord in Berlin" are equally objects of religious cult'.[27] Or in response to the claim to divine inspiration by the Rhine Assembly, or at least its speaker: 'If a private person boasts of divine inspiration, there is only one speaker in our society who can refute him officially, viz. the *psychiatrist*'.[28] One of my favourites from this massive collection is the following. On 26 July 1844, the Prussian king survived an assassination-attempt. Soon afterwards he wrote a cabinet-order, which was duly published as an open letter. Marx pulls it to pieces sentence-by-sentence and word-by-word with great relish. So, when Friedrich Wilhelm IV writes 'when the hand of the Almighty cast the deadly bullet away from My breast to the ground', Marx observes: 'It does not seem altogether appropriate to cause the *"bullet"* to be warded off directly by the hand of God, since in this way even a slight degree of consistent thought will arrive at the false conclusion that God at the same time both guided the hand of the criminal and diverted the bullet away from the king; for how can one presume a one-sided action on the part of God?'[29] Not a bad theological point, for God makes the sun to shine and the rain to fall on both the righteous and unrighteous,[30] but it is a point that could easily land one in prison at the time. While Marx is dissecting the epistolary style of his beloved sovereign, I cannot help giving one more example. In response to the Prussian

---

26. Marx 1861–3f, p. 399.
27. Marx 1843q, p. 399; Marx 1843r, p. 417.
28. Marx 1842l, p. 156; Marx 1842m, p. 144.
29. Marx 1844i, p. 209; Marx 1844j, p. 440.
30. Matthew 5:45.

king's comment that he goes 'while looking upward to the divine Saviour', Marx observes dryly: 'That His Majesty "*goes* while *looking upwards to God*" "to complete what has been begun, to carry out what has been prepared", does not seem to offer a good prospect for either the completion or the carrying out. In order to complete what has been begun and to carry out what has been prepared one must keep one's eyes firmly fixed on what has been begun and prepared and not look away from these objects to gaze into the blue sky'.[31] I can well imagine the laughter of the eager readers of Marx's pieces and the white rage of the king and his sycophants.

In the process, the Bible and theology become weapons against ruling-class privilege.[32] In the backward German situation, the ruling class was made up largely of the older nobility, so they are criticised extensively. For instance, against the law which censors anonymous writers, Marx points out: 'Moreover, when Adam gave names to all the animals in paradise, he forgot to give names to the German newspaper correspondents, and they will remain nameless in *saecula saeculorum*'.[33] More substantially, in his first piece for the *Rheinische Zeitung*[34] he keeps returning to make theological jabs at his opponent (apparently a speaker in the Rhine provincial assembly). To begin with, this speaker argues that freedom of the press in other countries gives free licence to all manner of boorish political debate. Apart from England and the Netherlands, Switzerland is snobbishly dismissed (at the hands of the speaker) for its party-quarrels in the newspapers. What can you expect, he points out, when they use animal parts – such as the 'claw-men' and 'horn-men' – as names for their parties? Marx swoops:

> But there is a press which he will hardly want to subject to censorship: we refer to the *holy press*, the *Bible*. Does this not divide all mankind into the two great parties of *sheep* and *goats*? Does not God Himself describe his attitude

---

31. Marx 1844i, pp. 209–10; Marx 1844j, p. 441.
32. That the Bible is such a ready tool for political satire and polemic should come as no surprise, since it contains a good deal of such polemic and has been used for this purpose for centuries. See especially the useful study by Weisman 1998.
33. Marx 1842l, p. 178; Marx 1842m, p. 166.
34. With the long-winded title, 'Proceedings of the Sixth Rhine Province Assembly: Debates on Freedom of the Press and Publication of the Proceedings of the Assembly of the Estates', it actually appeared in a series of instalments between 5–19 May 1842 (Marx 1842l; Marx 1842m).

to the houses of Judah and Israel in the following terms: I shall be to the
house of Judah as a *moth* and the house of Israel as a *maggot*?[35]

The references are to the apocalyptic parable in Matthew 25:31–33 and Hosea
5:12. Add to this the earlier allusion, 'By their fruits ye shall know them',[36]
and we start to see that Marx uses the Bible against this noble speaker of the
Assembly precisely because it is a sacred text, one that was used to shore up
the tradition of privilege, wealth and power. This close connection between
the assumptions of the aristocratic rump of the ruling class and Christianity
often draws from Marx not merely irony but white fury. These purveyors of
inherited superiority may keep their 'emotional affection' and 'fantastically
extravagant unction'[37] in check, hiding behind the nonchalant and sober exterior of privilege. But, every now and then, the religious side comes forth, and
Marx cannot stand it. He fires off one insult after another: it is mystical, arbitrary, base, fantastical, imaginary, other-worldly, and a sham, for it functions
as a 'holy cloak' for secular, political aims. It is no wonder that the communists tended to be atheists.

By contrast in England – 'that land of Mammon'[38] – in which Marx and the
family made their home and where he undertook his economic studies, the
ruling class was the result of a fractious alliance between the old aristocracy
and the newly powerful bourgeoisie keen to flex its muscles. When directed
against the bourgeoisie, the polemic becomes directly economic. One of the
best examples comes from the auspicious opening address to the inaugural
meeting of the International Working Men's Association. Proclaiming the
success of the Ten Hours' Bill as a high-point of working-class action, Marx
draws on the Bible: 'Through their most notorious organs of science, such
as Dr. Ure, Professor Senior, and other sages of that stamp, the middle-class
had predicted, and to their heart's content proved, that any legal restriction
of the hours of labour must sound the death knell of British industry, which,
vampire-like, could but live by sucking blood, and children's blood, too. In
olden times, child murder was a mysterious rite of the religion of Moloch, but
it was practiced on some very solemn occasions only, once a year perhaps,

---

35. Marx 1842l, p. 144; Marx 1842m, p. 133.
36. Ibid. Here the biblical reference is to Matthew 7:20.
37. Marx 1842l, p. 152; Marx 1842m, p. 140.
38. Marx 1877g, p. 283; Marx 1877h, p. 302.

and then Moloch had no exclusive bias for the children of the poor'.[39] Moloch (or Molech or Milcom) is one of the ancient Near-Eastern gods who appear in the mythical and legendary accounts of the Old Testament.[40] 'To burn one's son or daughter as an offering to Molech' (or as the older King James version has it, 'to pass through the fire to Molech') became proverbial as the lowest act one could commit. For Marx, however, the dreadfully barbaric Ammonites – the main worshippers of Moloch – appear in a much better light than the factory-owners. The former might have demanded a few children once a year on a solemn occasion, but the factory-operators demand poor children every hour of the day.[41]

---

39. Marx 1864a, pp. 10–11. See also Marx 1840–1a, p. 104; Marx 1840–1b, p. 90; Marx and Engels 1845a, p. 21; Marx and Engels 1845b, p. 21; Marx 1845a, p. 266; Marx 1882a, p. 234; Marx 1882b, p. 54; Marx 1855a, p. 95; Marx 1855b, pp. 132–3; Marx 1859a, p. 294; Marx and Engels 1848f, p. 264; Marx and Engels 1848g, p. 251; Engels 1846a, p. 474; Engels 1846b, p. 405; Engels 1893e, p. 234; Engels 1893f, p. 171; Eichhoff 1868, p. 330.
40. On Moloch, see Leviticus 18:21; 20:2–5; 1 Kings 11:7; 2 Kings 23:10; Jeremiah 32:35; Amos 5:26; Acts 7:43. Also, for Milcom, see 1 Kings 11:5, 33; 2 Kings 23:13. The variation between Moloch, Molech and Milcom comes from the different arrangement of the vowels (Hebrew vowels appeared much later than the consonants). So with the root *mlch* one may obtain a number of different words depending of which vowels you slip in between the consonants. The accounts are largely mythical and legendary and provide little actual historical data.
41. I had originally set out to provide a full appendix of all the theological allusions and references in the work of Marx and Engels, but that would have become a massive work on its own. So I have reconciled myself to listing further examples in each category. It approaches a complete inventory. Marx 1842l, pp. 146, 168–9; Marx 1842m, pp. 134, 156–7; Marx 1844c, p. 178; Marx 1844d, p. 381; Marx 1844e, pp. 191, 198; Marx 1844f, pp. 394, 401–2; Marx 1842n, pp. 230–1, 258; Marx 1842o, pp. 205, 232; Marx 1843i, p. 369; Marx 1843j, p. 359; Marx 1842z, p. 384; Marx 1842aa, p. 399; Marx 1842dd, p. 390; Marx 1842ee, p. 406; Marx 1848a, p. 154; Marx 1848b, p. 102; Marx 1858e, pp. 56–7; Marx 1859b, p. 272; Marx 1859c, pp. 439–40; Marx 1859d, pp. 444–5; Marx 1860c, p. 161; Marx 1860d, p. 518; Marx 1860a, p. 330; Marx 1862g, p. 131; Marx 1862h, p. 434; Marx 1862i, p. 240; Marx 1862j, p. 545; Marx 1861i, p. 286; Marx 1861j, p. 165; Marx 1857f, p. 5; Marx 1856b, p. 106; Marx 1856c, p. 156; Marx 1857b, p. 219; Marx 1857c, p. 216; Marx 1857e, p. 296; Marx 1871a, pp. 317, 325, 353; Marx 1871b, pp. 325, 333, 360; Marx 1858i, p. 482; Marx 1871e, p. 501; Marx 1871f, p. 559; Marx 1858d, p. 518; Marx 1877e, p. 275; Marx 1877f, p. 294; (also Marx 1868j, p. 148; Marx 1868k, p. 574; Engels 1865a, p. 58; Engels 1865b, p. 58; Engels 1868c, p. 509; Engels 1868d, p. 531; Engels 1849j, p. 252; Engels 1862b, p. 428; Engels 1862c, p. 299; Marx (Jenny senior) 1876a, p. 442; Marx (Jenny senior) 1876b, p. 520); Marx 1872b, p. 255; Marx 1872c, p. 160; Marx 1870a; Marx 1870b; Marx 1861–3f, p. 400; Engels 1840c, p. 97; Engels 1840d, p. 129; Engels 1844f, pp. 491, 493, 503–4; Engels 1844g, pp. 571–3, 582–3; Engels 1844a, pp. 525–6; Engels 1843e, p. 393; Engels 1853e, pp. 307, 310; Engels 1853f, pp. 579, 581; Engels 1872–3a, p. 322; Engels 1872–3b, p. 218; Engels 1882o, p. 349; Engels 1882p, p. 381; Engels 1885g, p. 304; Engels 1885h, p. 331; Engels 1885i, p. 361; Engels 1885j, p. 397; Engels 1851i, p. 392; Engels 1851j, p. 287; Engels 1845–6, pp. 20, 24–5, 30–1; Engels 1847k, p. 94; Engels 1847l, p. 60; Engels 1847i, pp. 235–49; Engels 1847j, pp. 207–22; Engels 1847h,

Clergy as part of a corrupt ruling class

A good dose of anticlericalism never goes astray and Marx and Engels do not disappoint. By and large, the clergy fell into two groups: either they hung onto the vestiges of feudalism and saw themselves as part of the ruling classes, supporting king and nobility, or they had become part of the newer class-configurations where they found themselves among the petty bureaucrats and state-employees such as schoolmasters and lawyers. All too often, we find them in precisely such a grouping when Marx and Engels roll out a list of reactionary opponents and impediments to communist agitation, especially when it took the form of the International. So Marx writes, 'In the eyes of these honest advocates of religion, order, the family and property the crime

---

pp. 283, 287; Engels 1847a, pp. 362–3; Engels 1847b, p. 386; Engels 1847c; Engels 1847d; Marx 1847c, p. 405; Marx 1847d, p. 422; Marx 1848bb, p. 455; Marx 1848cc, p. 447; Marx and Engels 1848v, p. 487; Marx and Engels 1848w, p. 465; Engels 1848c, pp. 527–8; Engels 1848d, pp. 501–2; Marx and Engels 1848hh, p. 451; Marx and Engels 1848mm, p. 66; Marx and Engels 1848nn, p. 57; Marx and Engels 1848h, p. 68; Marx and Engels 1848i, p. 59; Marx and Engels 1848oo, p. 103; Marx and Engels 1848pp, p. 93; Marx and Engels 1848l, p. 108; Marx and Engels 1848m, p. 97; Marx and Engels 1848r, p. 112; Marx and Engels 1848s, p. 101; Marx and Engels 1848d, pp. 280–2; Marx and Engels 1848e, pp. 265–7; Marx and Engels 1848kk, pp. 310–11; Marx and Engels 1848ll, pp. 296–7; Marx and Engels 1848ff, p. 324; Marx and Engels 1848gg, p. 308; Marx and Engels 1848n, pp. 377, 380; Marx and Engels 1848o, pp. 359, 362; Marx and Engels 1848a; Marx 1848y, pp. 464–5; Marx 1848z, p. 421; Marx 1848w; Marx 1848x; Marx 1848u; Marx 1848v; Marx 1848s, p. 489; Marx 1848t, p. 444; Marx 1848e; Marx 1848f; Marx 1848m, p. 38; Marx 1848n, p. 32; Marx 1848c; Marx 1848d; Marx 1848o, p. 75; Marx 1848p, p. 56; Marx 1848dd, p. 81; Marx 1848ee, p. 62; Engels 1848a, pp. 67, 73; Engels 1848b, pp. 47, 53; Marx and Engels 1848ii, pp. 90, 92; Marx and Engels 1848jj, pp. 71, 73; Marx and Engels 1848z, p. 94; Marx and Engels 1848aa, p. 75; Marx 1848a, pp. 159–61, 170, 174, 178; Marx 1848b, pp. 106–7, 115, 119–20, 124; Marx 1848q, p. 197; Marx 1848r, p. 138; Marx 1849g, p. 258; Marx 1849h, p. 187; Marx 1849c, pp. 273–4; 1849d, pp. 201–2; Marx and Engels 1849c, p. 310; Marx and Engels 1849d, p. 227; Marx and Engels 1849a, p. 23; Marx and Engels 1849b, p. 333; Marx 1849e, pp. 66–9; Marx 1849f, pp. 347–50; Engels 1849g, p. 94; Engels 1850e, pp. 14–15; Marx 1850a, pp. 55, 60, 77, 83, 118, 124–5, 131, 141; Marx 1850b, pp. 19, 24, 40–1, 47, 81, 87–8, 94, 104; Marx and Engels 1850a, pp. 257–8; Marx and Engels 1850b, pp. 213–14; Engels 1850c, pp. 292–5; Engels 1850d, pp. 235–8; Marx and Engels 1850g, p. 332; Marx and Engels 1850h, p. 287; Engels 1850i, pp. 363–4; Engels 1851–2, p. 5; Marx 1852c, pp. 105–6, 125, 132, 141, 158, 169–70, 196–7; Marx 1852d, pp. 116–18, 137, 143, 152, 170, 181–2, 206–7; Marx 1853o, pp. 408, 412, 421, 457; Marx 1853p, pp. 419, 423, 432, 469; Marx 1853h, p. 185; Marx 1853n, p. 464; Marx 1854j, p. 155; Marx 1854a, p. 197; Marx 1855p, p. 577; Marx 1855q, p. 607; Marx and Engels 1855a, p. 616; Marx and Engels 1855b, p. 19; Marx 1855v; Marx 1855w; Marx 1855z, p. 57; Marx 1855aa, p. 98; Marx 1855r, p. 239; Marx 1855s, p. 265; Marx 1855h, p. 244; Marx 1855i, p. 269; Marx 1875c, pp. 52–3; Marx 1875d, pp. 569–70; Marx 1878b, p. 247; Marx (Jenny senior) 1844, p. 580; Marx (Jenny junior) 1870a, p. 423; Marx (Jenny junior) 1870b, p. 586; Marx (Jenny junior) 1871a, p. 631.

of *falsification* is not even a peccadillo'.[42] At times Marx felt as though they were lining-up all too gleefully to attack him and his family: 'During the past few days I have been pressed very hard by the baker, cheesemonger, assessed taxes, God and the Devil'.[43]

It is no wonder that we come across regular pieces of pure anticlericalism. Given his background, Engels could produce some delightful observations: 'In the countryside and in the towns of England nothing is more hateful and more contemptible to the people than a Church of England parson'.[44] The parsons were a bad lot, seeking favours from the decrepit aristocracy and, more often, the newly wealthy owners of factories, mills and mines. They tended to care little for their flocks and a great deal for their own comfort. The situation in England was exacerbated by the fact that dissenting ministers were often far closer to the people.

One more example: in their extended discussion of the priest Rudolph in Eugene Sue's novel *Fleur du Marie*, Marx and Engels write:

> He [Rudolph] wants to teach him to *pray*. He wants to convert the Herculean robber into a *monk* whose only work is prayer. Compared with this Christian cruelty, how humane is the ordinary penal theory that just chops a man's head off when it wants to destroy him.[45]

Knowing the church and its apparatchiks all too well I can only nod my assent to such comments. With some two millennia of honing its skills, the church is able to pinpoint one's most vulnerable spot, hold onto it and then stretch it to breaking-point on the rack.[46] This Christian cruelty renders all external

---

42. Marx 1871c, p. 291; Marx 1871d, p. 301.
43. Marx 1868f, p. 62; Marx 1868g, p. 114.
44. Engels 1844f, pp. 502–3; Engels 1844g, pp. 581–3. See also: 'At present, however, the mere cry: "He's a parson!" is often enough to drive one of the clergy from the platform of a public meeting' (Engels 1846a, p. 421; Engels 1846b, p. 353). Here is Marx: 'They know now, from the official declaration of Mr. Bruce, the liberal Home Minister, in the House of Commons – firstly, that without going through the premonitory process of reading the Riot Act, any country magistrate, some fox-hunter or parson, has the right to order the troops to fire on what he may please to consider a riotous mob; and, secondly, that the soldier may give fire on his own hook, on the plea of self-defence' (Marx 1869e, p. 81).
45. Marx and Engels 1845a, p. 179; Marx and Engels 1845b, p. 190.
46. As Marx points out, 'General exploitation of communal human nature, just as every imperfection in man, is a bond with heaven – giving the priest access to his heart' (Marx 1844g, p. 307; Marx 1844h, p. 547).

forms of torture crude and ineffective (although it has never hesitated to use these too).

All the same, we need to reiterate the old point that it is one thing to attack a corrupt and venal clergy for its support of the ruling classes, for its condoning of exploitation and repression, and for its sheer reactionary nature. But it is another thing to recognise that many groups and individuals belong to what may be called the religious Left, especially the various Christian communists, socialists and anarchists. I am saying nothing new by pointing out that the churches are by no means monolithic and that they are multifarious institutions, often struggling within themselves over these matters.[47]

---

47. See further Boer 2007b and Löwy 1988, 1996. Here are the remaining references for the clergy as part of the corrupt ruling classes: Marx 1842l, pp. 174–6; Marx 1842m, pp. 162–4; Marx 1842r, p. 294; Marx 1842s, p. 274; Marx 1844g, p. 241; Marx 1844h, p. 477; Marx 1858h, p. 99; Marx 1861e, p. 130; Marx 1861f, p. 433; Marx 1871a, p. 332; Marx 1871b, p. 339; Marx 1857d, pp. 353, 356; Marx 1871e, pp. 485, 502; Marx 1871f, pp. 541, 560; Marx 1866i, p. 338; Marx 1866j, p. 268; Marx 1872d, pp. 223, 225; Marx 1872e, pp. 133, 135; Marx 1861–3a, pp. 205, 290; Marx 1861–3h, pp. 195, 285; Marx 1861–3g, p. 154; Marx 1861–3b, pp. 30, 33, 184, 194–7; Marx 1861–3c, pp. 145, 148, 271–4; Marx 1875e, pp. 84–5; Marx 1875f, pp. 8–9; Marx 1894a, pp. 595, 607; Marx 1894b, pp. 614, 626. Marx and Engels 1845a, pp. 168–76; Marx and Engels 1845b, pp. 178–87; Engels 1844f, pp. 501–4, 512; Engels 1844g, pp. 580–3, 591; Engels 1846a; Engels 1846b, pp. 492–3; Engels 1845c; Engels 1856c, p. 49; Engels 1856d, p. 56; Engels 1871e, p. 58; Engels 1872c, p. 64; Engels 1872d, p. 475; Engels 1868g, p. 137; Engels 1868h, p. 184; Engels 1869b, p. 246; Engels 1869c, pp. 286–7; Engels 1872–3a, p. 318; Engels 1872–3b, p. 214; Engels 1871f, p. 145; Engels 1871g, p. 220; Engels 1884g, p. 216; Engels 1884h, p. 233; Engels 1895a, pp. 446–7; Engels 1895b, p. 412; Engels 1840m; Engels 1840n; Engels 1839p, p. 449; Engels 1839q, p. 396; Engels 1840e, pp. 73–4; Engels 1840f, pp. 87–8; Engels 1865a, p. 47; Engels 1865b, p. 47; Marx 1847h, p. 179; Marx 1847i, p. 145; Engels 1847g, pp. 217–19; Marx 1847a, pp. 222–34; Marx 1847b, pp. 193–203; Marx and Engels 1848v, pp. 481, 494–5, 508; Marx and Engels 1848w, pp. 461, 472–3, 483–4; Engels 1848c, pp. 524–5; Engels 1848d, pp. 498–9; Marx 1848k, p. 537; Marx 1848l, p. 511; Marx and Engels 1848bb, p. 546; Marx and Engels 1848cc, p. 520; Marx and Engels 1848b, pp. 80–5; Marx and Engels 1848c, pp. 71–6; Marx and Engels 1848dd; Marx and Engels 1848ee; Marx and Engels 1848t, p. 385; Marx and Engels 1848u, p. 366; Marx and Engels 1848a; Engels 1848i, pp. 109–10; Engels 1848g, p. 85; Engels 1848h, p. 66; Marx 1849k, p. 385; Marx 1849l, p. 293; Engels 1849c, p. 137; Engels 1849d, p. 374; Engels 1850a, p. 155; Engels 1850b, p. 116; Engels 1850h, p. 272; Marx 1851a, p. 570; Engels 1851–2, pp. 23–4, 28, 35; Marx 1852c, pp. 110–14, 126–8, 135, 138–42, 150, 171, 181–3, 192–4; Marx 1852d, pp. 121–5, 137–9, 147, 149–56, 162, 183, 194–5, 202–4; Marx 1852e, p. 331; Marx 1852a, p. 334; Marx 1852b, pp. 342–4; Marx 1852f, p. 350; Marx 1853b, p. 517; Marx 1853m; Marx 1855jj; Marx 1855kk; Marx 1855e, p. 599; Marx 1855ff, pp. 51–2; Marx 1855gg, pp. 93–4; Marx 1855l, p. 64; Marx 1855m, p. 105; Marx 1855a, p. 95; Marx 1855b, pp. 132–3; Engels 1882g; Engels 1882h; Marx 1863a, p. 468; Marx 1863b, p. 342; Marx (Jenny senior) 1866a, pp. 571–2; Marx (Jenny senior) 1866b, p. 587; Marx (Jenny senior) 1867a; Marx (Jenny senior) 1867b; Marx (Jenny junior) 1870a, p. 440; Marx (Jenny junior) 1870b, p. 600; Marx (Eleanor) 1876a, p. 444; Marx (Eleanor) 1876b, p. 522.

Economic allusions

So much for the attacks levelled at various layers of the ruling class. There are, however, other uses of the Bible and theology that make the whole situation far more complex. A sizeable group falls into the category of economic allusions. The first volume of *Capital* is peppered with these types of allusions, although we find them less frequently in the other two volumes.

As tends to happen with one who writes so much and at such a pace, some favoured motifs and turns of phrase keep recurring in Marx's texts. These include images such as the inversion which stands an idea on its feet, or Marx's love of flowers being plucked and chains being broken. He also had his favourite biblical texts:

> Thus political economy – despite its worldly and voluptuous appearance – is a true moral science, the most moral of all the sciences. Self-renunciation, the renunciation of life and of all human needs, is its principal thesis. The less you eat, drink and buy books; the less you go to the theatre, the dance hall, the public house; the less you think, love, theorise, sing, paint, fence, etc., the more you *save* – the *greater* becomes your treasure which neither moths nor rust will devour [*den weder Motten noch Raub fressen*] – your capital.[48]

Such a glorious passage gains an added dimension in light of the fact that Marx was notoriously hopeless with money, spending when he had a little without thought for tomorrow, more often in debt than not, so much so that he and Jenny had to fight off creditors again and again. Most of the time they simply could not afford to sing, dance and go to the theatre, so I suspect that passages such as these express a utopian wish for something beyond their reach.

The biblical reference is to a saying placed in Jesus's mouth by both the Gospels of Matthew and Luke: 'Do not lay up for yourselves treasures on earth, where moth and rust consume and where thieves break in and steal, but lay

---

48. Marx 1844g, p. 309; Marx 1844h, p. 546. See also: 'He [Bruno Bauer] could just as well...call *theology* heavenly *political economy*...since it is the theory of the production, distribution, exchange and consumption of "*spiritual wealth*" and of the treasures of heaven' (Marx and Engels 1845a, p. 110; Marx and Engels 1845b, pp. 116–17). 'Our readers will then find out how the "treasures" are obtained that neither "moths nor rust" doth corrupt and they will learn in which way the economic background of the "loyal way of thinking" is acquired' (Marx 1848y, pp. 464–5; Marx 1848z, p. 421). See also Marx 1842h, p. 199; Marx 1842i, p. 186; Marx 1859a, pp. 362–3, 457.

up for yourselves treasure in heaven, where neither moth nor rust consumes and where thieves do not break in and steal. For where your treasure is, there will your heart be also'.[49] Marx has captured the sense of this saying rather well. It appears in the context of a collection of sayings concerning prayer, fasting and the need not to worry. The saying that follows[50] draws as a consequence the point that one should not worry about food or clothes or where one is to live, for the birds of the air and lilies of the field care not for these things but receive them all from God. One's heart is all too often where one's treasure is. But, then, Marx gives it one of his characteristic twists, for it is not the treasure in heaven of which he speaks but treasure on earth. Yet this is no ordinary treasure, a hoard of material possessions that could rot, burn, turn to mould or be eaten by vermin. It is that 'eternal' treasure known as capital.

More substantial is the use of what I call the Feuerbachian inversion. I will have much to say on this inversion in the chapters on Feuerbach and fetishism, but what is striking about it is the way a theological argument makes the transition to economics within Marx's own text. Feuerbach argued that the understanding of religion was topsy-turvy: it is not that God or the gods exist prior to human beings who are their creation and who therefore remain subject to God. Rather, human beings create the gods. They extrapolate their best and project them into the beyond, so much so that God appears as a distinct and superior being. Once created, this being becomes far superior to human beings, who worship it, attribute creative powers to it and seek its favour. Marx took this argument and gradually turned it into a materialist argument, modifying it, using it over and again in many places. But what I search for is the transition from theology to economics. Marx does not disappoint:

> If man attributes an independent existence, clothed in a *religious form*, to his relationship to his own nature, to external nature and to other men so that he is dominated by these notions, then he requires *priests* and *their* labour. With the disappearance of the religious form of consciousness and of these relationships, the labour of the priests will likewise cease to enter into the social process of production. The labour of priests will end with the existence of the *priests* themselves and, in the same way, the labour which the capitalist

49. Matthew 6:19–21; see also Luke 12:33–4.
50. Matthew 6:25–34. Luke 12:22–34 rolls both sayings into one.

performs *qua* capitalist, or causes to be performed by someone else, will end
together with the existence of the capitalists.[51]

The parallel is explicit: priests and their labour are analogous to capitalists
and their labour. In the same way that the labour of the priests slips away
when priests themselves drop out of the picture, so also will the labour of
capitalists disappear. Is this not tautological? It is until we bring in a missing feature of the parallel: the reason for that labour. Marx lays out what the
priests' labour involves, namely, religion – or, in his circumlocution, the independent existence of one's relationship to one's own nature, external nature
and other people, which is clothed in religious form; or, more concisely, the
religious form of consciousness. The priest's labour, then, consists in dealing
with this religious system that human beings conjure out of themselves. This
is where we need to fill in the missing item, which is nothing other than capitalism. This too is a system produced out of the relationship between human
beings and themselves, nature and other people. And, like religion, it is a
system that dominates one's everyday life. Let me return to the circumlocution. Marx could have simply stated that priests and religion are analogous to
capitalism and capitalists. Why use the circumlocution? It makes explicit the
Feuerbachian move in which religion is a product and projection of human
bodies and minds. But then so is capitalism as an abstract category. Now, we
might expect that such an argument comes out of Marx's early texts – say,
the *Economic and Philosophic Manuscripts of 1844*. Not so, for it comes from the
endless manuscript of 1861–3. Running into thousands of pages, it is where
Marx did most of the groundwork for *Capital* itself. What it does is enable
Marx to shift the Feuerbachian inversion from its initial theological context to
economics. In case we might suspect that Marx later discarded the plank that
allowed him to walk from theology to economics, then the following example
from the first volume of *Capital* should put that suspicion to rest: 'Thus the
linen acquires a value form different from its physical form. The fact that it is
value, is made manifest by its equality with the coat, just as the sheep's nature
of a Christian is shown in his resemblance to the Lamb of God'.[52]

---

51. Marx 1861–3d, p. 496; Marx 1861–3e, pp. 486–7.
52. Marx 1867a, p. 62; Marx 1867b, p. 66. The allusion is to John 1:29. See also: 'In
order, therefore, that a commodity may in practice act effectively as exchange-value, it
must quit its bodily shape, must transform itself from mere imaginary into real gold,
although to the commodity such transubstantiation may be more difficult than to the

On a different note, ever since I first read *Capital* more than twenty years ago, I have always been intrigued by the use of the family-bible in the list of everyday exchangeable items. Along with the famous piece of linen and the coat, they form part of Marx's effort to provide concrete examples for his theory. But I suspect they were also the sorts of things Marx would cart off to the pawnbroker at regular intervals when they were short of food or rent was due. Here is the first appearance of the Bible:

> Let us now accompany the owner of some commodity – say, our old friend the weaver of linen – to the scene of action, the market. His 20 yards of linen has a definite price, £2. He exchanges it for the £2, and then, like a man of the good old stamp that he is, he parts with the £2 for a family Bible of the same price. The linen, which in his eyes is a mere commodity, a depository of value, he alienates in exchange for gold, which is the linen's value-form, and this form he again parts with for another commodity, the Bible, which is destined to enter his house as an object of utility and of edification to its inmates.[53]

Once the Bible enters the equation, it stays there for the next dozen or so pages as Marx works towards his crucial formula, namely, C-M-C. We may write this appearance off as a convenient and everyday example and leave it at that, but I would suggest that it is a signal of the pervasive presence of the Bible and its texts throughout *Capital* and indeed Marx's writings as a whole.[54]

Hegelian "concept," the transition from "necessity" to "freedom," or to a lobster the casting of his shell, or to Saint Jerome the putting off of the old Adam' (Marx 1867a, pp. 112–13; Marx 1867b, pp. 117–18). Or from the third volume, 'The monetary system is essentially a Catholic institution, the credit system essentially Protestant. "The Scotch hate gold." In the form of paper the monetary existence of commodities is only a social one. It is *Faith* that brings salvation. Faith in money-value as the immanent spirit of commodities, faith in the mode of production and its predestined order, faith in the individual agents of production as mere personifications of self-expanding capital. But the credit system does not emancipate itself from the basis of the monetary system any more than Protestantism has emancipated itself from the foundations of Catholicism.' (Marx 1894a, p. 587; Marx 1894b, p. 606). As a further example, there is this use of the inversion from the endless manuscript of 1861–3: 'It is clear, therefore, that the worker cannot *enrich* himself through this exchange, since in exchange for the available value magnitude of his labour capacity he surrenders its *creative power* like Esau his birth-right for a mess of pottage' (Marx 1861–3a, p. 160; Marx 1861–3h, p. 152).
   53. Marx 1867a, pp. 114–15; Marx 1867b, pp. 119–20.
   54. Here are the remaining economic allusions: Marx 1844g, pp. 271, 307; Marx 1844h, pp. 511, 547; Marx 1860e, p. 342; Marx 1853dd, p. 381; Marx 1865a, p. 27; Marx 1865b, p. 26; Marx 1869a, p. 53; Marx 1869c, pp. 57–8; Marx 1869d, pp. 359–60;

Against other opponents

We have already seen Marx and Engels use the Bible and theology as a resource against the press, various elements of the ruling class and the church. Yet they do not restrict their polemical use of theology to these groups. Others also turn up, such as philosophers like Comte and Proudhon, or opponents within the communist movement, or members of the young Hegelians such as Bruno Bauer. However, the reason I have gathered them here is that they begin to reveal a tendency in relation to the Bible and theology. Indeed, as we will see in the next section, this bottomless resource is every now and then appropriated in a positive way. I do not mean that they buy into the Bible and its associated religious assumptions. Rather, they link their arms with whatever allusion comes from the Bible, placing themselves on its side.

For example, opponents within the communist movement often end up being compared unfavourably with one or other character or motif from the Bible. So the much-vaunted prophetic gifts of Herr Vogt – to whom Marx devoted a large polemical volume – end up being no better than the speaking ass in the story of Balaam in Numbers 22:21–33.[55] While Hermann Kriege is the 'apostle of love [*Liebesapostel*]',[56] Gottfried Kinkel, leader among the German refugees in London, is described as 'Jesus Christ-Kinkel', or the 'theologising belletristic Kinkel' who had the habit of adopting a pose that

---

Marx 1865c, p. 105; Marx 1858g, pp. 512–13; (also Marx 1894a, pp. 392–4; Marx 1894b, pp. 407–9; Marx 1851j, pp. 423–4; Marx 1851k, p. 313; Marx 1857–8b, pp. 218–19); Marx 1861–3a, pp. 306–10; Marx 1861–3h, pp. 302–5; Marx 1861–3b, p. 184; Marx 1861–3c, p. 148; Marx 1877g, p. 283; Marx 1877h, p. 302; Marx 1861–3f, p. 397; Marx 1861–3g, pp. 406–7; Marx 1867a, p. 97; Marx 1867b, p. 101; Marx 1885a, p. 390; Marx 1885b, p. 390; Marx 1894a, pp. 244, 328; Marx 1894b, pp. 256, 342; Engels 1844j, p. 439; Engels 1844k, p. 520; Engels 1844b, pp. 451, 457–61; Engels 1844c, pp. 532, 538–43; Engels 1862a, p. 374; Engels 1872–3a, pp. 323, 331, 341, 353; Engels 1872–3b, pp. 219, 227, 236–7, 249; Engels 1851a, p. 280; Engels 1851b, p. 180; Engels 1851e; Engels 1851f; Engels 1869d, p. 382; Engels 1869e, p. 400; Marx 1857–8a, pp. 18, 25, 43, 154, 162–4, 192, 233, 251, 257, 401, 408, 464, 529; Marx 1857–8c, pp. 20, 23, 40, 148, 156–8, 185–6, 228, 245, 250, 385, 392, 446, 512; Marx 1857–8b, pp. 149, 177, 215–16, 218; Marx 1859a, p. 278, 294, 299, 303, 359, 363–4, 374, 387, 389, 446, 448–9, 457, 475, 481; Marx 1867a, pp. 142–3, 146, 149, 162, 165–6, 186, 189, 202–3, 242, 250, 257, 260, 266, 270–1, 300, 314, 366, 375, 377–8, 412, 440, 471–2, 488, 580, 589–91, 605–6, 611–13, 616, 638, 640–1, 663–4, 668, 683, 704, 711–12, 733, 738–45; Marx 1867b, pp. 146–7, 149, 152, 166, 169–70, 189, 194, 206–7, 248, 257, 264, 267, 274, 279–80, 313, 328, 382, 393, 395, 431, 461, 492–3, 510, 607, 619–21, 636–7, 644–6, 649, 673, 675–6, 700–1, 705, 721, 741, 748–50, 772–3, 777–85.

55. Marx 1860c, p. 72; Marx 1860d, p. 432.
56. Marx and Engels 1846a, p. 50; Marx and Engels 1846b, p. 17.

was 'a synthesis of the "dying gladiator" and "Christ crucified"'.[57] A more positive use of the Bible emerges in a comment against Freiligrath: 'Does the brute believe that I couldn't, if so minded, immerse him up to the eyebrows in the lake of brimstone [*Schwefelpfuhl*]?'[58] The allusion is to Revelation 20:10, but here Freiligrath becomes the Beast of Revelation and Marx joins forces with the returning Christ. In my last example, Marx takes on the rôle of King David in relation to Uriah the Hittite: 'I thought it necessary to write to you about it 1. because you knew Heise well enough, 2. because he wrote to me, humbly asking to be recommended to you and I didn't want to give him a letter of Uriah'.[59] The allusion is to 2 Samuel 11:14–15, although Marx appropriates a rather ambiguous figure, for David was known as much for his devious dealings and brutal self-advancement as for his legendary status as the great king of ancient Israel.

Part of the reason for such polemic was that Marx everywhere encountered the Christian background of the communist movement. The League of the Just, the organisation Marx and Engels first joined, stated that it was 'based on the ideals of love of one's neighbour, equality and justice' – a rather biblical motto. Formed in 1836, the League of the Just was heavily influenced by the currents of French socialism with its distinct Christian flavour. Marx and Engels joined it in 1847 and were influential in changing its name to the 'Communist League'. But this did not stop those who had espoused Christian-communist ideals from continuing their work. It also meant that Marx and Engels waged a constant battle to rid the movement of this religious element. For example, Wilhelm Weitling, who had done an extraordinary amount of groundwork in establishing the League and who appears as a signatory to early circulars from the International, became a constant target. As one example: 'Then Weitling took the floor and proceeded to prove that Jesus Christ

---

57. In sequence, Marx 1851d, p. 323; Marx 1851e, p. 226; Marx 1851h; Marx 1851i; Marx 1861k, p. 311; Marx 1861l, p. 189. See also Marx 1851l, pp. 428–9; Marx 1851m, pp. 574–5; Marx 1851p, p. 483; Marx 1851q, p. 363; Marx 1851r, p. 501; Marx 1851s, p. 590; Marx 1852g, p. 42; Marx 1852h, p. 494.

58. Marx 1860f, p. 36; Marx 1860g, p. 32.

59. Marx 1854o, p. 442; Marx 1854p, p. 350. Not one to miss the opportunity of using a good allusion more than once, Marx refers to Uriah once again in regard to C. Schramm and a letter he was carrying from Marx establishing the latter's bona fides (Marx 1851n, p. 467; Marx 1851o, p. 351).

was the first communist and his successor none other than the well-known Wilhelm Weitling'.[60]

Apart from the opposition-press and sundry philosophers,[61] the great target is the young Hegelians, especially Bruno Bauer. Both *The Holy Family* and *The German Ideology* have multiple biblical and theological references on page after page. At this point both Marx and Engels are keen to show how theological Bauer really is, especially with his theory of self-consciousness, so they draw upon one theological motif after another, each time stitching Bauer ever more closely in with the Bible. I will have more to say on Bauer in a later chapter, so I restrict myself to one example:

> Critical Criticism, however superior to the mass it deems itself, nevertheless has boundless pity for the mass. And Criticism so loved the mass that it sent its only begotten son, that all who believe in him may not be lost, but may have Critical life. Criticism was made mass and dwells amongst us and we behold its glory, the glory of the only begotten son of the father.[62]

I have touched on a couple of themes that will become familiar as the book proceeds, especially the struggles over the theological nature of the early communist movement, the titanic effort against Bruno Bauer and a use of the Bible that will become more complex as I move on. I have had to restrict the number of examples given, but, by this stage, it should be clear that this allusive use of the Bible and theology was no means a peripheral practice.[63]

---

60. Marx 1853z, p. 296; Marx 1853aa, p. 229.

61. For further references, see note 63.

62. Marx and Engels 1845a, p. 9; Marx and Engels 1845b, p. 9. The allusion is to the well-known texts of John 3:16 and John 1:14.

63. Here are the remaining theological allusions and references against other opponents: Marx 1843e, pp. 325–6; Marx 1843f, pp. 343–4; Marx 1843i, p. 368; Marx 1843j, p. 358; Marx 1843o, p. 372; Marx 1843p, p. 362; Marx 1858a, p. 78 (also Engels 1859c, p. 327); Marx 1860c, pp. 228, 243; Marx 1860d, pp. 583, 600; Engels 1859d, p. 370; Engels 1859e, p. 568; Engels 1851l, p. 428; Marx 1851m, p. 574; Marx 1852i, p. 73; Marx 1852j, p. 43; Engels 1851g; Engels 1851h; Marx 1852k, p. 269; Marx 1852l, p. 568; Marx 1853dd, p. 349; Marx 1859k, p. 535; Marx 1859l, p. 513; Marx 1861i, p. 286; Marx 1861j, p. 165; Marx 1856a, p. 115; Marx 1866e, p. 274; Marx 1866f, p. 215; Marx 1877a, p. 190; Marx 1877b, p. 243; Marx 1877c, p. 247; Marx 1877d, p. 54; Engels 1851m, p. 488; Engels 1851n, p. 368; Engels 1873b, p. 439; Engels 1873c, p. 319; Engels 1871i, p. 282; Engels 1871j, p. 361; Marx and Engels 1845a, pp. 7, 134–5, 140, 157; Marx and Engels 1845b, pp. 7, 142–3, 148–9, 166; Marx 1844c, p. 177; Marx 1844d, p. 380; Marx 1842bb, p. 388; Marx 1842cc, p. 403; Marx 1871e, p. 498; Marx 1871f, p. 555; Marx 1859i, p. 483; Marx 1859j, pp. 474–5; Engels 1873–82a, pp. 345–55; Engels 1873–82b, pp. 337–47; Eichhoff 1868, p. 347; Engels 1846g, p. 61; Engels 1846h, p. 40; Engels 1851c, p. 290; Engels 1851d, p. 190;

Appropriation and ambivalence

In the previous section, I mentioned a tendency of Marx and indeed Engels to appropriate the Bible and the occasional theological idea for themselves. Now it becomes interesting, for that appropriation is but a first step to an awareness of the political ambivalence of the Bible and theology. In this section, then, I collect those allusions that mark a more positive appropriation of the Bible before turning to the texts that unwittingly recognise the presence of some ambivalence.

As far as appropriating the Bible is concerned, one of the best examples is Marx's comment: 'Our Association is a thorn in their flesh'.[64] However, most of these allusions are far more personal, especially in reference to Marx's multitude of ailments. It may be a personal note to Engels, in reference to a rotten tooth: 'By following Christ's precept "if thy tooth offend thee, pluck it out", I have at last found relief'.[65] Or it may be those persistent carbuncles: 'The wound hasn't stopped discharging yet, but all along the route I should find some good Samaritanesses to apply the plaster for me'.[66] This allusion is to Luke 10:33–4, but he also calls on Job: 'As you see, I am as tormented as Job, though not as god-fearing'.[67] Indeed, this last reference to Job's suffering is a common way that Marx appropriates the Bible, often from the Psalms. So

---

Marx and Engels 1846a; Marx and Engels 1846b; Engels 1847i, pp. 257, 262, 270; Engels 1847j, pp. 230, 235, 244; Engels 1847e, p. 301; Engels 1847f, p. 319; Marx 1847f, pp. 321, 325–6; Marx 1847g, pp. 340, 344–5; Marx 1847j, p. 403; Marx 1847k, p. 420; Marx and Engels 1848v, p. 511; Marx and Engels 1848w, p. 487; Schaper, Bauer and Moll 1847, pp. 605–9; *A Circular of the First Congress of the Communist League to the League Members, June 9, 1847* 1847, p. 593; Marx 1849a; Marx 1849b; Marx and Engels 1850g, pp. 302–3, 305–6; Marx and Engels 1850h, pp. 256–7, 260; Marx and Engels 1850c, pp. 528–32; Marx and Engels 1850d, pp. 459–63; Marx and Engels 1852a, pp. 229–37, 241–56, 259, 262–4, 278, 282–4, 297, 299, 304, 312–16; Marx and Engels 1852b, pp. 235–43, 247–63, 266–7, 270–2, 285, 290–2, 304, 306–7, 311, 320–4; Marx 1854g, p. 487; Marx 1854h, p. 497; Marx 1875a, pp. 93; Marx 1875b, p. 27; Marx 1878a, pp. 235–9; Marx 1881a, p. 551; Marx 1881b, p. 375; Engels 1877–8a, pp. 29, 93, 104, 286; Engels 1887–8b, pp. 28, 93, 104, 280; Engels 1891a, p. 116; Engels 1891b, p. 117. There are hundreds more in *The Holy Family*, *The German Ideology* and Engels's early texts (see Chapter Nine).

64. Marx 1868f, p. 63; Marx 1868g, p. 114. The allusion is to 2 Corinthians 12:7.

65. Marx 1857j, p. 122; Marx 1857k, p. 125. The text is Mark 9:47 where the offending item happens to be an eye.

66. Marx 1863c, p. 495; Marx 1863d, p. 376. Again on the carbuncles: 'This is a disease of truly Christian perfidiousness...In the meantime, I can neither walk, stand, nor sit, and find even lying down damned difficult. So you see, *mon cher*, how nature in her wisdom is persecuting me. Would she not be better advised to inflict these trials of patience upon a good Christian?' (Marx 1864b, p. 507; 1864c, p. 386).

67. Marx 1861g, p. 247; Marx 1861h, p. 144.

in reference to their perpetual money-problems, he writes that he pants 'for money as doth the hart for cooling streams'.[68] And Marx, writing to Hermann Becker, describes the family as 'we here by the rivers of Babylon',[69] an allusion to Israel weeping in exile in the well-known Psalm 137:1.

But now we find the shift to a distinct sense that the Bible is far more politically ambivalent than may at first appear to be the case. An excellent example comes from the early article in which Marx attacks the positions taken in the Rhine Province Assembly.[70] In a characteristic pattern, he cites a series of statements and lampoons them one after another with his own comments. The most intriguing is the story of the Fall from Genesis 2–3. The Assembly speaker quotes the words of the serpent to the woman in Genesis 3:4–5: 'You will not die. For God knows that when you eat of it your eyes will be opened, and you will be like God, knowing good and evil'.[71] Marx retorts that 'the devil *did not lie to us then*, for God himself says, "Behold the man is become as one of us, to know good and evil" '.[72] This text is from Genesis 3:22, immediately preceding the wish expressed by the 'gods' that the man should not eat from the tree of life and live forever. Now, there are a host of delectable problems with this text, not the least of which is the presence of two trees (one of good and evil and the other of life), the intriguing plural 'us [*mimmennu*]' and the fact that the devil appears nowhere in this text. However, note especially the way Marx lines up the critics of the government (himself included) with Eve and Adam. Thus, '*we* negotiate today as *then*' for the fruits of the tree of knowledge, and the devil does not lie to 'us'. Over against him stand the speaker and the assembly, who take the side of God (or the gods) and warn against taking what is forbidden (freedom of the press, democracy and so on). What Marx has done here, somewhat unwittingly, is tap into a long tradition in which the serpent is the hero of the story and God the oppressor. The serpent, after all, is the only one who speaks the truth. The fact that the woman heeds the serpent's advice was read by some, such as certain gnostic groups

---

68. Marx 1848ff, p. 179; Marx 1848gg, p. 129. The allusion is to Psalm 42:1.
69. Marx 1851b, p. 273; Marx 1851c, p. 544.
70. Marx 1842l; Marx 1842m.
71. Revised Standard Version translation. The plural *Elohim* is ambiguous here: one of the names for God in the Hebrew Bible, it also means 'gods' in some contexts and may well refer to the man and woman becoming like 'gods'.
72. Marx 1842l, p. 168; Marx 1842m, p. 156.

and the Ophites, as a rebellion against an oppressive deity. In this light, other references in the Bible to serpents took on a new look: stories such as the one about Moses's staff turning into a serpent,[73] and the bronze-serpent set up by Moses in the desert for healing,[74] or texts such as John 3:14 in the New Testament: 'And just as Moses lifted up the serpent in the wilderness, so must the Son of Man be lifted up'.[75] Marx's satirical response, then, has touched on a revolutionary reading of the Bible.

Marx does not restrict himself to the Bible. If history provides an example, then he will use it. So, in response to the claim that governments or kings rule by divine sanction and inspiration, Marx retorts: '*English history*, however, has sufficiently well demonstrated how the assertion of divine inspiration from above gives rise to the counter-assertion of divine inspiration from below; Charles I went to the scaffold as a result of divine inspiration from below'.[76] A passing dismissal, perhaps, but it once again touches on the political ambivalence of Christianity. Oliver Cromwell and the Puritans overthrew the monarchy by drawing upon the same sacred theological tradition as that by which the British monarchy justified itself.

One thing is certain: this revolutionary touch is by no means a common theme in Marx's work (Engels is a different story). Yet there is some grudging awareness of a radical edge, one that shows up as well when Marx claims a biblical or theological moment for the poor, workers or the communists. For example, in his long treatment of the new law criminalising the gathering of fallen wood by the poor, Marx writes: 'Therefore, the wood thief, like a second St. Christopher, bore the state itself on his back in the form of the stolen wood'.[77] In the fable of St Christopher, our saint agrees to carry a child across a river only to find that the child becomes unbearably heavy in the midst of the river. When he looks back to see why this has happened, he sees that Christ is on his shoulders – so also does the poor peasant need to carry the state. In the process, St Christopher becomes one with these desperate peasants. Yet, despite Marx's ability to claim such symbols for the poor, or even to note the

---

73. Exodus 4:2–5; 6:8–12.
74. Numbers 21:4–9.
75. See further Boer 2007a, pp. 41–3; Bloch 1972, pp. 183–9; Bloch 1970, pp. 166–71.
76. Marx 1842l, p. 156; Marx 1842m, p. 144.
77. Marx 1842n, p. 253; Marx 1842o, p. 227.

appeal of religion to the poor,[78] he usually does not see that the resistance of the poor is often couched in biblical language.

Conclusion

For some time now, I have asserted that Marx and Engels knew their Bible rather well. But I did so on the basis of impressions gained from scattered reading. Now, at least, that assertion has the basis of more sustained reading. If this chapter does nothing else, it shows how extensive and complex those references and allusions really are. Even more, at the moments when Marx and Engels drew on theology, we find a number of crucial ideas that will recur in the following chapters. It may be the attacks on young Hegelians such as Bruno Bauer, or a critique of the hold that the ruling class has on the state, the appropriation from theology of a crucial move such as Feuerbach's inversion, or indeed the inadvertent awareness that theology is politically ambivalent.

---

78. As he does when visiting Ryde, where he puzzles over how the poor fishermen should be so religious (Marx 1874a; Marx 1874b). The remaining theological allusions and references that are appropriated and ambivalent are: Marx 1837c; Marx 1837d; Marx 1836a, p. 526; Marx 1836b, p. 536; Marx 1836–7a, p. 528; Marx 1836–7b, p. 545; Marx 1837q, pp. 543–5; Marx 1837r, pp. 588–90; Marx 1837a, p. 563; Marx 1837b, p. 640; Marx 1837i; Marx 1837j; Marx 1837s; Marx 1837t; Marx 1837m, p. 566; Marx 1837n, p. 497; Marx 1837k; Marx 1837l; Marx 1837e, pp. 575–6, 578–80; Marx 1837f, pp. 643–4, 646–8; Marx 1837g, p. 586; Marx 1837h, p. 489; Marx 1837o; Marx 1837p; Marx 1844g, pp. 310–11; Marx 1844h, pp. 550–1; Marx 1856j, p. 54; Marx 1856k, p. 532; Marx 1855ll, p. 558; Marx 1855mm, p. 461; Marx 1862a, p. 252; Marx 1862b, p. 544; Marx 1869e, p. 70; 'Record of Marx's Interview with *The World* Correspondent' 1871, p. 601; Marx 1869l, p. 303; Marx 1869m, p. 331; Marx 1866c, p. 246; Marx 1866d, p. 507; Engels 1844j, p. 438; Engels 1844k, p. 519; Engels 1845d, p. 19; Engels 1845e, p. 18 ; Engels 1846g, pp. 64–5; Engels 1846h, pp. 43–5; Engels 1874, p. 40; Marx (Jenny senior) 1963a, p. 585; Marx (Jenny senior) 1863b, p. 691; Marx (Jenny junior) 1870a, p. 415; Marx (Jenny junior) 1870b, pp. 581–2; Marx (Jenny junior) 1869a, p. 548; Marx (Jenny junior) 1869b, pp. 702–3; Marx (Jenny junior) 1871b, p. 569; Marx (Jenny junior) 1871c, p. 690; Marx-Longuet 1863, p. 586; Engels 1850h, p. 276; Engels 1868e; Engels1868f; Engels 1852c, p. 249; Engels 1852d, p. 524; Engels 1885e, p. 338; Engels 1885f, p. 234; Engels 1851a, p. 280; Engels 1851b, p. 180; Engels 1893c, p. 214; Engels 1893d, p. 152; Marx (Jenny senior) 1868a, p. 581; Marx (Jenny senior) 1868b, p. 692. And a small group that contains items that do not fit any of my categories: Marx 1843o, p. 371; Marx 1843p, p. 361; Marx 1860c, p. 294; Marx 1860d, p. 648; Marx 1844k, p. 141; Marx 1844l, p. 342; Marx 1862e, p. 200; Marx 1862f, p. 500; Marx 1877c, p. 246; Marx 1877d, p. 53; Marx 1851d, p. 323; Marx 1851e, p. 226; Engels 1846a, p. 458; Engels 1846b, p. 389; Engels 1872–3a, pp. 323, 382; Engels 1872–3b, pp. 219, 260–1; Engels 1859f, p. 479; Engels 1859g, pp. 468–9.

For both Marx and Engels theology is like a tobacco-pouch, near at hand. Every now and then, when they need to think something through, one of them reaches out and stuffs a pipe full, taps it down, lights up and blows out a plume of smoke with distinct relish. We might think of it as a theology-pouch, always ready to provide a satisfying allusion with bite.

Chapter Two

The Leading Article: Theology, Philosophy and Science

> As long as we were occupied with the polemic against the ailing article, it would have been wrong to interrupt him in his work of self-destruction.[1]

From the heights of the synoptic survey, I drop down to the valley below, focusing on the arguments of specific texts by Marx and Engels. The first stop is the innocuously entitled piece, 'The Leading Article in No. 179 of the *Kölnische Zeitung*'.[2] It is a sustained response to a certain Karl Hermes, editor of the journal, conservative Roman Catholic and government-agent. I concentrate on this essay for a number of reasons. To begin with, it is – unfortunately – rarely discussed in the regular treatments of 'Marxism and religion'. Further, it signals Marx's effort to counter and extricate himself from the overwhelming theological context of public debate at the time, a context I have outlined in my Introduction. Even more, we find a rather youthful Marx (he was 24 when it was published) broaching a number of themes that will reverberate through his later texts. Lastly, it is in fact a concentrated example of how Marx engaged thoughtfully and extensively with theology. On that score, four themes turn up: the distinction between theology and scientific research; the interaction between theology and philosophy; the relations of church and state; and Marx's first foray into his ongoing concern with fetishism.[3]

---

1. Marx 1842h, p. 194; Marx 1842i, p. 182.
2. Marx 1842h; Marx 1842i.
3. This goldmine of an essay contains other topics as well, but they are not as interesting. These include the arguments to separate civil and religious concerns in regard to marriage and divorce and Marx's comments on education (that it is really a secular

Theology and scientific research

Marx's sustained effort to step out of the quagmire of public theological debate in Germany takes the shape of two closely related oppositions, one between theology and scientific research and the other between theology and philosophy. I begin with the lesser point concerning scientific research, since it establishes Marx's take on theology, before considering theology and philosophy in more detail. On the matter of theology and scientific research (understood in a distinctly European sense),[4] what incites Marx is a comment by the editor of the *Kölnische Zeitung* to the effect that the further scientific research goes, the more it confirms Christian truths. Unfortunately, it is one we still hear bellowed today from the conservative corner of Christianity.

Three assumptions determine Marx's initial response: scientific research and philosophy are interchangeable; they must be free to pursue their work without hindrance, especially of a theological nature; they are concerned with universal truths.[5] Nothing particularly new here – philosophy is defined by

---

matter for the state rather than the church's concern to inculcate Christian principles from above). As far as marriage is concerned, Marx argues that theological matters, or supernatural authority, should not intrude on the civil and secular nature of marriage. Marx was rather a prude when it came to such matters, insisting on matters of dignity and morality. He prefers to point to the contradictions between the recognition of civil marriage in the Rhine province of South-West Germany (due to the continuation of the 1804 *Code Napoléon* in territories once conquered by the aforesaid emperor), the partial Prussian recognition of civil marriage and the need for the sanction of the church in other parts of Germany (Marx 1842h, pp. 192–3; Marx 1842i, pp. 180–2; see also Marx 1842c, p. 310; Marx 1842d, pp. 289–90). Even if the *Rheinische Zeitung* came under royal disapproval for getting its hands on (from a source it refused to divulge) and publishing a secret bill to make divorce much more difficult for religious reasons, Marx's criticism is that the bill was not really a reform but a patchwork-revision that would not make things any better (Marx 1842e; Marx 1842f; Marx 1842c; Marx 1842d). On the matter of education, Marx argues that education is more about the classics and the sciences than the catechism, as his own experience in the *Gymnasium* shows. Again, there is nothing striking about this: 'the state itself educates its members by making them its members, by converting the aims of the individual into general aims, crude instinct into moral inclination, natural independence into spiritual freedom, by the individual finding his good in the life of the whole, and the whole in the frame of mind of the individual' (Marx 1842h, p. 193; Marx 1842i, p. 181).
    4. Marx 1842h, pp. 190–2; Marx 1842i, pp. 178–80.
    5. 'Philosophy asks what is true, not what is held to be true. It asks what is true for all mankind, not what is true for some people. Its metaphysical truths do not recognise the boundaries of political geography; its political truths know too well where the "bounds" begin for it to confuse the illusory horizon of a particular world or national outlook with the true horizon of the human mind' (Marx 1842h, pp. 191–2; Marx 1842i, p. 179).

the unhindered search for universal truth. With this armoury, Marx can easily pull apart the assertion that scientific research must be beholden to theology. He points out that the type of science that is interesting for theology – one that confirms one's own view, from which one picks up a piece here or there that seems to reinforce Christian truths, policed and kept in line with theological assumptions – is not science at all. In fact, it is a rather feeble and threatened theology that must resort to such tactics before the threats of science and philosophy.

I am less interested in Marx's rather liberal assertions concerning the nature of philosophy, assertions that have been made ever since the secular disciplines of the sciences and then humanities began to extract themselves from theology, nor am I interested in elaborating on the point that these credentials of scientific research are by now rather threadbare (we can hardly claim that scientific research is really 'unhindered' or even 'objective' in its search for 'truth'). No, there are some far more interesting things happening just beneath the surface of Marx's argument: one concerns what he means by 'theology' and the other what a more robust theology might look like.

Theology turns out in Marx's text to be a rather conservative business, more concerned with defending doctrinal purity and the 'truths' of Christianity. Here Marx really assumes what the conservative editor of the *Kölnische Zeitung* understands theology to be. What we end up with, to put it bluntly, is that theology is the distinct ideology of the Christian church. Even if such an ideology has myriad forms depending on which of the many churches one happens to be talking about, it does not change the underlying position.

Marx is on rather shaky ground here, for his assumption concerning the conservative nature of theology immediately raises a question: what would a theology that fully embraces scientific research look like? To begin with, it would not be defensive, fighting against the challenges of the sciences. It would also not be weakened by its dirty little relationship with the church or with petty sectarian interests? Not so much an opening to scientific research, such a theology would embrace and vigorously pursue such research for its own good (or ill, as the case may be). The catch with all of this is that it is not particularly new. Biblical studies for one has, from the time of Marx, asserted (admittedly spasmodically) its 'scientific' credentials. And theology too (understood as a distinct discipline from biblical criticism) has, from time to time, stood by the slogan of free, scientific research. This agenda was, after all, part of the struggle in European universities where theology and biblical studies sought to reconfigure themselves within a university-environment, so much so that these days the churches in many countries have little or no control over what goes on in theology-faculties. It is not for nothing that theologians and biblical scholars have often been viewed with a good deal of suspicion by the various churches, even those employed by the churches to train its clergy. At the same time, and somewhat sadly given the long story of such struggles, these old positions still need to be re-asserted for we still find the assumptions Marx is challenging here touted in our own day.

For all my castigating of Marx for his perception of theology, he does assume that it is an inherently conservative and defensive discipline focused on the world above and in preserving the church against attacks. This assumption underlies his effort to show how his own preferred profession of philosophy is far superior to a theology from which he seeks to extricate himself.

Theology and philosophy

On the matter of theology and philosophy, Marx gleefully dissects the pedantic argument of the editor Karl Hermes. The uneasy dance between philosophy and theology is of course as old as theology itself. As a distinctly Christian system in which religious experience is ordered into a more or (often) less rational system of thought, theology first emerged in the intersection between biblical narratives and Greek philosophy. It will come as no surprise that Hermes, whenever he had a half a chance, took aim at the young Hegelians.[6] As for Marx's response, he first has some fun[7] and then elaborates on some more weighty points.[8]

---

6. The young Hegelians form a constant backdrop to this whole essay. They are also mentioned explicitly in the pieces on Bruno Bauer (Marx 1842t; Marx 1842u) and Sallet (Marx 1843o; Marx 1843p), as well as the note on 'The Free' (Marx 1842a; Marx 1842b).

7. One of the better examples: 'The state, he says, has not only the right but the duty to "put a stop to the activities of *unbidden* chatterers". The writer is obviously referring to opponents of his view, for he has long ago convinced himself that he is a *bidden* chatterer' (Marx 1842h, p. 186; Marx 1842i, p. 174).

8. 'We believe we would be insulting the readers of the *Rheinische Zeitung* if we imagined that they would be satisfied with the spectacle, more comic than serious, of a *ci-devant* liberal, a "young man of days gone by", cut down to his proper size. We should like to say a few words on "*the heart of the matter*"' (Marx 1842h, p. 194; Marx 1842i, p. 182).

There are two main arguments in this section: first, Marx makes the rather lightweight point that the right-wing papers should not fume about philosophy making a belated public appearance in order to pronounce its verdict on matters of religion, for this is what the right-wing papers themselves have been doing for some time.[9] The second argument is far stronger and more interesting: given the organic relation between philosophy and the real world, no-one should be surprised when philosophy does speak in the public arena. Let me dwell with this argument for a little while.

His major point is a nascent materialist one: since philosophy is the 'intellectual [*geistige*] quintessence of its time',[10] it faces a moment when it must come out of its secluded cloister where it likes to hide and carry on its esoteric inquiries. And the reason is not that philosophy is forced every now and then to enter the grubby world of politics and public debate, but, rather, that philosophers are 'products of their time, of their nation, whose most subtle, valuable and invisible juices flow in the ideas of philosophy'.[11] So it is no surprise that philosophy, through its own nature, does from time to time become contemporary, public and worldly. In fact, I sense that Marx would like philosophy to be so all the time (as he saw his own rôle), but he sticks with the idea that philosophy emerges to permeate all walks of life and manners of thought.

This is precisely what is happening now, points out Marx, in these early years of the 1840s. But what is the content of that public engagement by

---

9. See especially Marx 1842h, pp. 196–7; Marx 1842i, p. 184: 'For six years German newspapers have been drumming against, calumniating, distorting and bowdlerising the religious trend in philosophy.... All German newspapers...reverberated with the names of Hegel and Schelling, Feuerbach and Bauer, the *Deutsche Jahrbücher*, etc.... For a long time philosophy had remained silent in the face of the self-satisfied superficiality which boasted that by means of a few hackneyed newspaper phrases it would blow away like soap-bubbles the long years of study by genius, the hard-won fruits of self-sacrificing solitude, the results of the unseen but slowly exhausting struggles of contemplative thought. Philosophy had even *protested against the newspapers* as an unsuitable arena, but finally it had to break its silence: it became a newspaper correspondent, and then – unheard-of diversion! – it suddenly occurred to the loquacious purveyors of newspapers that philosophy was not a fitting pabulum for their readers'.

10. Marx 1842h, p. 195; Marx 1842i, p. 183.

11. Ibid. See also Marx's comment to Ruge in 1843: 'Hitherto philosophers have had the solution of all riddles lying in their writing-desks, and the stupid, exoteric world had only to open its mouth for the roast pigeons of absolute knowledge to fly into it. Now philosophy has become mundane, and the most striking proof of this is that philosophical consciousness itself has been drawn into the torment of the struggle, not only externally but also internally' (Marx 1844k, p. 142; Marx 1844l, p. 344).

philosophy in his time? It is none other than theology. The reason is that religion is the central way in which people live their lives, forming their deepest belief-systems and way of being in the world. In Marx's own terms, the public 'can feel the sphere of philosophical ideas only by means of its ideal antennae, and the only circle of ideas in the value of which the public believes almost as much as in the system of material needs is the circle of religious ideas'.[12] This argument is really one of the first steps towards a more complete materialist system, although he does give the realm of ideas more credit than he will later.

We can push Marx a little further, for it is not merely that religion, or rather Christianity, determines the world-outlook but also that in Germany we find a conjunction of reactionary political moves to bolster a specifically Christian state, the filtered impact of more radical developments from France and England, and the history of struggles between Protestants and Roman Catholics. Marx has one more key-point to make: given that Christianity at that moment in Germany is very much a political matter, indeed that it lays at the heart of the political struggles between a conservative monarch and democratic and liberal movements, it is perfectly natural for a very public philosophy also to engage in politics. In other words, if the way of the world is an entanglement of religion with politics, then philosophy is called upon to comment on both.

Marx goes on to muddy his argument every now and then, such as the point that philosophy is far better suited to deal with politics than theology, since, in contrast to theology, philosophy is the 'wisdom of this world' and not some other world,[13] or the argument that a true theocratic state can have only God (of whichever religion) as its head. These are cheap shots, worth making in a polemic, but of little substance. There are, however, a number of more important issues that come out of this passage. To begin with, the base from which Marx operates is philosophy, which he takes as an organic product of its time. He cannot praise philosophy enough, virtually singing a paean to it.[14]

---

12. Marx 1842h, p. 196; Marx 1842i, pp. 183–4.

13. Marx 1842h, p. 198; Marx 1842i, p. 186. See also Marx 1842l, p. 152; Marx 1842m, p. 140.

14. 'But philosophy speaks about religious and philosophical matters in a different way than you have spoken about them. You speak without having studied them, philosophy speaks after studying them; you appeal to the emotions, it appeals to reason; you anathematise, it teaches; you promise heaven and earth, it promises nothing but the truth; you demand belief in your beliefs, it demands not belief in its results but

From this perspective, he seeks the reason why philosophy has engaged with theology. The problem is that he does not give the same scope to theology; it appears as an external discipline with which philosophy has come into contact at this particular historical juncture in Germany. The question left begging is: what about theology? Is it not possible that it too is an organic product of its time; that it too arises from a particular context? Is theology also not a secluded, if not secret practice that seems to dabble in the magic arts only to emerge into the public arena from time to time?

The catch is that Marx's treatment of theology is riven with a contradiction: theology is sometimes the point of intersection between the conservative press and philosophy, especially since religion forms the basic belief-system for people, while at others it is the opponent of philosophy itself. As far as the first treatment of theology is concerned, it is the subject-matter of the struggle between philosophy and the uninformed ranting of the conservative papers over against philosophy. Indeed, this is the primary opposition – philosophy and the conservative newspapers – of this section of Marx's, especially since he is attacking the *Kölnische Zeitung*. But then, at certain moments, he slips, drawing theology and the reactionary papers into a common front against philosophy. The most telling moment is when Marx contrasts theology as the 'wisdom of the other world' with philosophy as the 'wisdom of the world'.[15] In short, theology takes its orders from God and is really concerned with heaven and not earth.[16] Once this opposition is in place, he goes on to characterise theology as unphilosophical, prejudiced, inconsistent and semi-rational. In other words, Marx has assumed that the way the conservative papers represent theology is actually a faithful representation of the nature of theology. A crucial slippage has taken place: theology and the unphilosophical and semi-rational

---

the testing of doubts; you frighten, it calms. And, in truth, philosophy has enough knowledge of the world to realise that its results do not flatter the pleasure-seeking and egoism of either the heavenly or the earthly world. But the public, which loves truth and knowledge for their own sakes, will be well able to measure its judgment and morality against the judgment and morality of ignorant, servile, inconsistent and venal scribblers' (Marx 1842h, p. 197; Marx 1842i, p. 185).

15. Marx 1842h, p. 198; Marx 1842i, p. 186. See also the reference to 'religion' as the 'theory of the other world' (Marx 1842l, p. 152; Marx 1842m, p. 140).

16. See also his guarded defence of Friedrich von Sallet's anticlerical poetry in Marx 1843o, p. 372; Marx 1843p, p. 362: 'the theologian does not judge the gospel by human reason and morality; on the contrary, he judges these by the gospel'. By contrast, the philosopher has no trouble with the contradictions of theology, for that is what one would expect.

attacks of the conservative press have become one and philosophy finds itself battling against this new foe. This characterisation of theology turns up at another point, when he suggests that theology engages in polemics 'against the philosophy of all particular systems'.[17]

At one level, we can understand why he makes this connection, for when he was writing the conservative theologians and churches rose up on their hind lends and bayed like dogs at the work in theology and biblical criticism by young Hegelians such as Strauss, Bauer and Feuerbach. The problem is that this connection between the conservative papers and theology introduces an unnecessary tension in his discussion between two different senses of theology.

But why is it a contradiction? As I pointed out earlier, Marx describes religion as the 'circle of ideas in the value of which the public believes almost as much as in the system of material needs'.[18] This is a far cry from a bigoted and uninformed theology that sets itself against philosophy; rather, what we have is the fundamental way in which people make sense of their place in the much larger contexts of society and history – the crucial life-shaping ideas that are on par with material needs. Now, we can get around this tension by distinguishing between the narrow-minded view of theology purveyed by the reactionary press and the churches on the one hand and the widespread rôle of religious ideas in popular consciousness. But what I want to do is use this point concerning the vital rôle of religion to come back to my earlier questions concerning theology. For there is a distinct hint that theology too may be seen as an organic way of thinking and living that is a product of its time and place. That hint comes in the midst of Marx's justification for public philosophical debate. Here, he describes 'philosophical and religious matters' as 'questions of the time'.[19] Is this not a distinct echo of his earlier characterisation of philosophers as the 'products of their time, of their nation, whose most subtle, valuable and invisible juices flow in the ideas of philosophy'?[20] All we need to do is substitute 'theologians' and 'theology' for 'philosophers' and 'philosophy'.

---

17. Marx 1842h, p. 196; Marx 1842i, p. 184.
18. Ibid.
19. Marx 1842h, p. 198; Marx 1842i, p. 185.
20. Marx 1842h, p. 195; Marx 1842i, p. 183.

Philosophy and theology draw closer to one another once again. Even more so when Marx describes the relation between philosophy and other forms of human activity: 'philosophy, of course, exists in the world through the brain before it stands with its feet on the ground, whereas many other spheres of human activity have long had their feet rooted in the ground and pluck with their hands the fruit of the world before they have an inkling that the "head" also belongs to the world, or that this world is the world of the head'.[21] So too with theology, I want to say. But then, as he opens this discussion, we come across an image of philosophy that is decidedly monkish, echoing the esoteric world of monasteries. Phrases such as 'professor of magic arts', 'ascetic frock of the priest' and references to incantations that 'sound awe-inspiring because no one understands them' are decidedly theological, or rather evoke theologians as much as philosophers.

So what do we end up with? I am not one to argue for the identity of philosophy and theology, however much they may have danced together for some two millennia – often awkwardly, sometimes more in time. Rather, I prefer an image of two secretive disciplines that try to keep to themselves but cannot always manage to do so. Both are in their own way products of their time, permeating and giving voice to the deeper patterns of thought and life. And every now and then both find themselves in newspapers, before microphones, struggling for ways to express themselves in a public manner on crucial issues – as was the case in Germany in the 1830s and 1840s and as is the case now in our own geopolitical context.

It would seem that Marx has not quite managed to make a clean break with theology after all. It is closer to philosophy than he would like and it refuses to stay in the other-worldly and conservative corner into which he would like to box it. As I proceed, we will see that theology and the Bible remained constant, if at times distant, companions.

Church and state

The next major element of this sustained attack against the editor of the *Kölnische Zeitung* concerns church and state, a matter to which Marx would return on more than one occasion. Marx's basic position is to argue for a

---

21. Ibid.

separation of church and state, but he does so with a characteristic twist: he draws on the Bible and the Christian tradition. There are at least three elements to this argument and they do not sit together very well. The first element is a separation between theology and history, where Marx tries to show that religion is subservient to history and not vice versa. Secondly, he attempts to show that the Christian tradition itself supports the separation of church and state, and, conversely, that there are too many elements in that tradition which undermine any moves towards a Christian state such as the one that the Prussian king, Friedrich Wilhelm IV, sought to produce. I have no problems with such an argument (we will consider the details in a moment). However, his underlying assumption is more problematic: the reason why Christianity is in favour of the separation of church and state is because it deals with spiritual, other-worldly matters, while the state is a distinctly worldly institution. Let me take each in turn.

The effort to put history on top of theology is important not merely for the argument itself but also because he introduces a move that he will repeat on many occasions to come. And that is nothing less than an inversion from an idealist position to a materialist one. Over against his protagonist's point – that the peaks and falls of a national culture depend upon its religious culture – Marx grabs hold of the opposition and gives it a good twist: 'To arrive at the truth, the author's assertion must be directly reversed: he has stood history on its head [*auf den Kopf gestellt*]'.[22] A good metaphor is worth recycling, so we will meet this reverse-Hegelian move a few times more, most famously when he does it to Hegel himself in *Capital*. Here the standing of history on its feet involves the rather simple argument that the downfall of states (his examples are the ancient states of Greece and Rome) brings about the downfall of their religions, not the other way around. In other words, religion is secondary, not primary – that rôle falls to politics and history.

By now, this inversion feels a little well-worn, although I suspect that is because it has become such a commonplace after more than a century and a half. At the same time, the sad truth is that it must still be asserted. Perhaps the tired sage of Ecclesiastes is right – there is nothing new under the sun. All too often, we still come across the assertion that the way to bring about change is through a change in attitudes or ideas. People will change, goes

---

22. Marx 1842h, p. 189; Marx 1842i, p. 177.

the propaganda, if they have the right attitude. No matter how well-used it may be, a materialist response such as the one Marx offers is a necessary, if preliminary, move.

In the characteristic rush of his writing, Marx confuses the issue with a few weaker points. In ancient Greece and Rome, he suggests, religion was in fact replaced by something else at precisely their highest points. In Greece it was art and rhetoric – in the hands of the sophists and Socrates – that replaced religion, while a little later Aristotle (at the time of Alexander the Great) denied the existence of any positive 'God'. As for the Romans, their true religion was the state itself, in part due to the influence of Cicero, as well as the Epicureans, Stoics and Sceptics. Now, this is a different line entirely: religion, he suggests, slips away at precisely the highest points of these ancient states. It is, of course, another refutation of Hermes's argument, but it undermines his materialist inversion. Or at least, any connection remains undeveloped: would it not be possible to argue that in both Greece and Rome religion was by-and-large state-fostered? If so, the decline of these states would naturally lead to a decline in such religions. But then, at this level the situation is no different from any other state-supported religion, such as Christianity from the time of Constantine the Great onwards.

Ever polemical, the second major point – Christianity itself leads to the separation of church and state – piles up problems with the idea of a 'Christian state' in Marx's own time, all of them drawn from various elements of the Christian tradition. So we find, at first, that Augustine's *De Civitate Dei* and the church-fathers stand up to condemn it, followed by the Bible, especially Paul and the Gospels. Then the Pope lines up to add his curse on the Christian state: or rather, one unnamed pope (he was actually Pius VII of 1800–23) who, 'with profound intelligence and perfect consistency',[23] refused to join the Holy Alliance of European states under the banner of Christianity.[24] The

---

23. Marx 1842h, p. 199; Marx 1842i, p. 187.
24. Proposed by Tsar Alexander I of Russia, the Holy Alliance was signed on 26 September 1815. Along with the Tsar it initially included Francis I of Austria and Friedrich Wilhelm III of Prussia, but eventually everyone joined the party, except the Prince Regent of England, Pius VII and the Sultan. Now, we can understand the English and their long history of exceptionalism, and indeed the Sultan, who graciously declined to join a coalition that based itself on 'the sublime truths which the Holy religion of our Saviour teaches', which would be the basis of justice, charity and peace. But the Pope does indeed stand out. It became a coalition of the reactionaries, hell-bent on turning the tide of democratic and republican reform.

Pope's reason: the church and not the secular state is the basis of universal communion between Christians. Finally, a couple of stock points close out the argument, one that a proper Christian state is theocratic, with God as its head, the other that as soon as you have more than one form of Christianity, or indeed more than one form of religion, a Christian state becomes meaningless. Or, rather, the chosen creed becomes the oppressor of all others. On this last point, Marx evokes implicitly the common argument that a secular state is the basis of religious tolerance. This is a more interesting point, especially the comment that Christianity itself separated church and state. I will come back to this question in more detail in Chapter Six.

More problematic, however, is the underlying assumption that Christianity should not bother itself with such mundane matters as politics and the state since its concerns are with heaven and not earth. This argument is consistent with his effort to denigrate theology in favour of philosophy and science, especially with his assumption that theology is a reactionary endeavour. Here, Marx goes further and argues that this heavenly focus of theology is actually the reason for Christianity's own push for the separation of church and state. Now, this argument is a little trickier than it first seems. It rests on a firm basis but then makes the wrong move. That basis is the very definition of secularism, which concerns itself with and draws its terms of reference from this world and this age (the senses of *saeculum* and *saecularis*). By implication, anything that focuses on a world above or one in the future is no business of secularism. So far, so good. Yet in the next move, Marx slips up, for he assumes that Christianity concerns itself wholly with another world and the future. For that reason it has no business in secular matters – hence the derived position of the separation of church and state. Why is this (rather common move) a problem? Quite simply because Christianity is concerned with both this world and this age – as some of its central categories such as creation, anthropology and harmatology (the doctrine of sin) and indeed Christology show all too well – as well as the age to come and the world above. In other words, it is both secular and anti-secular. But then, as I have argued elsewhere, so is Marxism, for its concerns are very much with this age in order to bring it to a close and open up the possibility of a very different one.[25]

---

25. See Boer 2009c.

Let me sum up my points thus far. After we sift out the more liberal elements of Marx's argument concerning church and state, especially those concerning the need for a secular state and the contradictions of the idea of a 'Christian state', we find that he invokes an early form of the famous materialist inversion, flipping idealism over so that it stands on its own feet. All of this is framed in terms of his desire to escape the theological framework of political debate of the 1840s in Germany. As we shall see, these items will appear more than once in his later work.

Fetishism and idolatry

The last item I consider here will also turn up again and again: the question of fetishism.[26] It is actually an addendum to Marx's argument concerning church and state, for it appears in the context of Hermes's assertion that great states depend on the greatness of religion. The discussion of fetishism jumps out of Marx's criticism of Hermes's quasi-evolutionary picture of the development of religion. Hermes argues that religion moves through the phases of sensuous desires and (animal) fetishism to end up with the highest stage (Christianity, of course), which is the source of the state's greatness. Marx counters: how can animal-worship be a form of religion higher than sensuous desires when it makes an animal god over human beings?[27] As for fetishism, it is no better than sensuous desires; in fact, it is the ultimate expression of sensuous desires. What he means here is idol-worship.

The appearance of 'fetishism' in this early piece will immediately catch the eye of anyone vaguely familiar with Marx. It is, of course, central to that famous section of *Capital*, 'The Fetishism of Commodities'. In 1842, he writes:

> And now, indeed 'fetishism'! Truly, the erudition of a penny magazine! Fetishism is so far from raising man *above* his sensuous desires that, on the contrary, it is 'the *religion of sensuous desire*'. Fantasy arising from desire deceives the fetish worshipper into believing that an 'inanimate object' will

---

26. See also Marx 1842n, pp. 262–3; Marx 1842o, p. 136.
27. See also his comment in a letter to Ruge on 20 March 1842: 'the deification of animals is probably the most consistent form of religion, and perhaps it will soon be necessary to speak of religious zoology instead of religious anthropology' (Marx 1842z, p. 384; Marx 1842aa, p. 399).

give up its natural character in order to comply with his desires. Hence the crude desire of the fetish-worshipper *smashes* the fetish when it ceases to be its most obedient servant.[28]

Although Marx would eventually take this idea, rework it and extend it to deal with labour, money, commodities and capital (see Chapter Seven), let me focus on Marx's brief comments for a moment.

The key-sentence is the second one, although Marx confuses the issue with his use of 'fantasy' and 'sensuous desire'. It is difficult to read such terms and banish the senses that Freud was to give them some time after Marx wrote these newspaper-articles. What I suggest we need to do, however, is not merely block out Freud but the whole framework of desire and fantasy. So we have: the fetish-worshipper believes that an 'inanimate object' will give up its natural character. In other words, the object of worship – be it a tree or mountain, a sun or moon, or indeed an object made out of wood or stone or whatever – loses its character as tree or moon or object made of wood and becomes a god. It is therefore full of life and far more powerful than the worshipper, who may then fall on her knees before the god.

The secret to this argument is its inversion (the second one Marx makes in this essay). Let us begin with the perspective of the worshipper. Our fervent and faithful worshipper does not believe he is making a figurine out of stone which he then endows with power and life so that it may be worshipped. Rather, he believes that the figurine, or indeed the sun or moon, is first and foremost a god. Or the features of a landscape, such as a river or rocky outcrop, are infused with mythological life before they are in any sense inanimate objects. Indeed, the awareness that all of these items may well be inanimate objects is really a process of de-sacralisation rather than the sacralisation of what is inanimate.

Now for Marx's perspective: he turns the whole thing over to argue that fetishism actually gives life to and sacralises what is primarily an inanimate object. The moment of de-sacralisation is a second step: the worshipper smashes the fetish in a moment of disillusion. Such de-sacralisation is a case of realising what the object was all along – merely a figure carved out of stone,

---

28. Marx 1842h, p. 189; Marx 1842i, p. 177. Here perhaps we find some of the arguments that may have been in the lost work, 'A Treatise on Christian Art' (see Marx 1842x, p. 382; Marx 1842y, p. 397).

or just a tree. Rather than the movement from sacred to profane, we have in Marx's hands a threefold movement: profane-sacred-profane. The intermediate step really was a fantasy and nothing more.

In this inversion we have one of first appearances of Feuerbach's profound influence on Marx. Feuerbach's *Das Wesen des Christentums* came out in 1841, the year before Marx wrote this piece. Feuerbach famously inverted the understanding of the way human beings related to God. He would have none of the priority of God, an eternal, omnipotent and omniscient being who deigned to create the earth and human beings as some afterthought. No, human beings are the prior ones in this relationship. For Feuerbach, religion projects the best possibilities of human activity – labour and productivity, intelligence, imagination and so on – only to hypostatise them all into an entity or force that is exterior to human beings. That entity becomes a figure, a 'god' who appears to human beings as a being in his own right, one that returns to command, punish and save. For Feuerbach, this is the source of the attraction and continued potency of religion. I will have much more to say on Feuerbach and fetishism later in this book, but here we find the source of the crucial inversion of which Marx makes use in his own points concerning fetishism. Marx's point that fetishism is nothing other than the fantastical and deluded attribution of divine powers to some object or other is one that he would use and extend in subsequent reflections on religion, commodities, labour and money.

Conclusion

This early piece from Marx has enabled me to watch him deal with theology at close quarters. In it he tries to pull one foot and then the other out of the pervasive theological nature of public debate – by asserting the primacy of scientific research, philosophy and even history over against theology. And that context, as I argued in the Introduction, was heavily determined by the young Hegelians and their preference for theology, if not the Bible, as the favoured terrain of battle. While there is a large residue of liberalism in his arguments and while I have found Marx wanting in his assumption that theology is a reactionary discipline, a number of other themes and modes of argument have also emerged: the characterisation of theology as other-worldly, the early appearance of the materialist inversion, and his interest in fetishism.

Chapter Three
Against the Theological Hegelians I: Bruno Bauer

> Bauer the *theologian* takes it *as a matter of course*
> that *Criticism* had to indulge endlessly in *specu-*
> *lative theology* for *he*, 'Criticism', is indeed a theo-
> logian *ex professo*.[1]

After the synoptic survey and the exegesis of a specific early piece by Marx, we now plunge further into
the thicket of theological issues in his work. Over the
next six chapters, I cover all of the major themes and
questions bearing directly on theology that emerge
from Marx's texts. Those chapters deal mostly with
Marx, except where some contributions from Engels
are relevant and where occasionally it is impossible
to separate their contributions to joint works, such
as *The Holy Family* and *The German Ideology*. I have
decided to begin with Bauer, follow with Stirner and
then move on to Feuerbach.

Bauer first? Why not Feuerbach, who is the subject of the first very lucid section of *The German
Ideology*, the section that most people read while
skipping over the dense material on Bauer and
Stirner that follows? Apart from the obvious chrono-
logical priority of Bauer here and in The *Holy Family*, the reason is twofold: the sections on both Bauer

---

1. Marx and Engels 1845a, p. 102; Marx and Engels 1845b, pp. 108–9.

and Stirner have languished in the doldrums of Marxist scholarship for far too long. By bringing them forward, I want to emphasise that these sections too are important. Further, an abyss separates the assessments of the three: Bauer and Stirner come in for sustained and unrelenting criticism, whereas Feuerbach receives more praise than criticism. Marx wants to dispense with Bauer and Stirner and move on. In the process he also tries to dispense with theology and a certain theological reading of Hegel. Not so with Feuerbach, for Marx's response is far more favourable, taking up and developing a central idea from Feuerbach – the inversion. This inversion enables him to deal with Hegel far more creatively, so much so that we can see the influence through a number of further themes.

The main question I want to ask here is why Bauer was Marx's favourite target. The answer is, I suggest, that Bauer developed a radical position through theology and biblical criticism. At the time, Bauer was one of the most radical thinkers in Germany.[2] But he was a complex radical, attacking the *ancien régime*, liberalism and socialism. Marx had to negate Bauer on two counts: his anti-socialist stance and his path to radical-political republicanism through biblical criticism. Neither was acceptable.

In what follows, I trace the way Marx's one-time teacher at the Friedrich Wilhelm University in Berlin became one of his main opponents, at whom he fired salvo after salvo. Marx's connection with Bauer goes back to his university-days in Berlin in 1836–9, where he took a course with the young licentiate on the biblical book of Isaiah in the summer of 1839. So I begin with that, exploring Bauer's own ideas in the process. From there, I move on to consider Marx's ongoing and complex relationship with Bauer, whom he could still call a friend and who visited Marx in London many years later. The first deeply critical response to Bauer comes with the essay *On the Jewish Question*, an extended review of Bauer's book of that name. After that, we find the full-blooded critiques in both *The Holy Family* and *The German Ideology*, where Marx and Engels develop a two-pronged attack: that Bauer is, for all his disavowals, still both a theologian and a conventional Hegelian.

---

2. In an excellent study, Moggach 2003 has restored Bauer as an independent and radical political thinker. In particular, he counters the general position that Bauer retreated from his earlier radical theological criticism to vacuous right-wing social criticism.

The book of Isaiah (with Herr Licentiate Bauer)

There is a small note from Marx's Leaving Certificate from the Friedrich Wilhelm University in Berlin that may easily be missed. It reads as follows:

V. In the summer term 1839

1. Isaiah with Herr Licentiate Bauer, attended.[3]

For all its brevity, this entry threatens to explode with significance. Marx's performance, it must be admitted, is not stellar. All he receives is 'attended'; no 'diligent' or even an 'exceptionally' or 'extremely diligent', the grades (if we may call them that) for nearly all his other subjects. These include a variety of law-subjects, where we also find ecclesiastical law, some in philosophy and the classics (Euripides shows up). On top of all of this, 1839 was a crisis-year for Bauer (not an infrequent occurrence for the man), as he was removed from teaching at Berlin and sent to Bonn for an attack on a colleague.

At their first contact, we find Marx studying one of the key prophetic texts in the Hebrew Bible with one the controversial leaders of the young Hegelians. But why Bauer and why the book of Isaiah? Here, another piece of this curious puzzle falls into place. Bauer was primarily a New Testament scholar and theologian and then later a political commentator. The works that landed him in no end of trouble were those on the Gospel of John and the synoptic Gospels (Matthew, Mark and Luke).[4] Appearing during the first great wave of German critical work on the Bible that would launch German biblical scholars into a position of global leadership which they would only relinquish with the Second World-War, Bauer's work was at the edge of that work and beyond. For a time, he was widely regarded as the leader of the young Hegelians. Bauer's genius was to combine painstaking attention to biblical texts within their historical and cultural context and his own development of Hegel's philosophy. This combination led him to argue that Christianity only emerged in the second century CE; that the Gospels contain virtually no historical records, and indeed no record of a historical Jesus, being primarily the products of religious consciousness embodied in individual authors who composed them freely; that the Gospels are saturated with the spirit and thought of

---

3. *Leaving Certificate from Berlin University* 1841, p. 704.
4. Bauer 1840, 1841, 1842b, 1850–1, 1852.

Hellenism (the key-ideas may be traced to Stoic, Philonic and neo-Platonic ideas); and that the crucial tension was between free self-consciousness and religious dogmatism. He took consistent aim at the ossified established church and the repressive state, especially in light of their dirty and corrupt hold on power – so much so that his book *Das Endeckte Christenthum* [*Christianity Exposed*][5] was banned, hunted down and destroyed until it was reprinted in 1927.

I will come back to the content of *Christianity Exposed* and his treatment of the Gospels in a moment, but let me now backtrack a little. Why was Bauer the radical New Testament scholar teaching Marx a course on Isaiah at the Friedrich Wilhelm University in 1839? It so happened that, in the year before, Bauer had published a two-volume work called *Kritik der Geschichte der Offenbarung: Die Religion des alten Testaments in der geschichtlichen Entwicklung ihrer Prinzipien dargestellt* [*Critique of the History of Revelation: The Religion of the Old Testament Explained According to the Principles of Its Historical Development*].[6] It was the only work he wrote on the Hebrew Bible, for the rest were concerned with the New Testament and politics. In the summer of 1839, Marx would have heard the full brunt Bauer's theories on the Hebrew Bible and Isaiah in particular.[7] In *Die Religion des alten Testaments*, Bauer was developing his argument that religion, or rather, religious experience is the result of (a Hegelian) self-consciousness. Not only was such religious experience a transcendental affair, but one could also trace in a phenomenological fashion the development of the various forms of that experience. Following the assumption that the legalistic priestly material (designated by 'P') was the oldest literary source of the Hebrew Bible, he argued that this material lies at

---

5. Bauer 1843a; Bauer 2002.

6. Bauer 1838. At the time, Bauer was also editing the *Zeitschrift für spekulative Theologie*, which ran to only three issues, and writing for the *Jahrbücher für wissenschaftliche Kritik*. Here he tried to develop an alternative theology that categorised Christian doctrines in terms of logical categories.

7. Marx would have been reasonably well prepared for a course on the Bible, since in a typical *Gymnasium* curriculum of the time he studied German, Latin, Greek, French and Hebrew, as well as the 'sciences' (religious knowledge, mathematics, history, geography and physics). Or rather, he did not study Hebrew, if the absence of any comment on his 'Certificate of Maturity' is any guide. In the other two biblical languages, Greek and Latin, he was quite proficient – as he was in religious knowledge: 'His knowledge of the Christian faith and morals is fairly clear and well grounded; he knows also to some extent the history of the Christian Church' (*Certificate of Maturity for Pupil of the Gymnasium in Trier* 1835, p. 644).

the earliest stage of such a development. Here we find an authoritarian deity who demands a law-bound subordination. In contrast to this largely external relation, the later prophetic books mark a much higher stage: over and against the crass and oppressive particularity of the earlier material, here the universal is immanent in community.

One may be forgiven for thinking that all this was a slightly odd interpretation of the Hebrew Bible, indeed that Bauer was a religious crackpot. Not at all, but some context is required. Two features of this context are important for understanding what Marx encountered in Bauer's course: the rapid developments in biblical criticism at the time and the use of the Bible as the ground on which debates over religion, reason, secularism, democracy, and republicanism were fought out.

As for biblical criticism itself, scholars had begun to undermine, often in the face of much resistance, many of the traditional assumptions concerning the Bible and its authors. They argued against traditional interpretations and appeals to divine authority by focussing on the literal and grammatical sense of the text (in opposition to allegory), the internal evidence of the text, and the desire to reconstruct historical situations in order to understand the Bible. Much of the early energy was focused on the five books of Moses – the Torah or Pentateuch. Critics such as Johann Gottfried Eichhorn, who published his three-volume introduction to the Old Testament in 1780–83, Wilhelm de Wette (1780–1849), Johann Vater (1771–1826), Heinrich Ewald (1803–75) and Hermann Hupfeld (1796–1866) had argued that the Pentateuch was really a compilation of different sources or fragments not written by Moses, if he existed at all. Amid much debate, they gradually came to agree, at least by the time Bauer was writing, that there were four sources that lay behind the Pentateuch – the Priestly (P), the Yahwistic (J), the Elohistic (E) and the Deuteronomic (D). In what was called the documentary-hypothesis, P was felt to be the earliest and responsible for most of the laws (613 of them), the Yahwistic and Elohistic (based on two of the names of God) followed, with slightly higher views of religion, and D was responsible for Deuteronomy and the final editing of the first five books of the Bible. Only later, after Bauer's work, did Julius Wellhausen argue that P was the latest stage.[8] In fact, it was in the second half of the nineteenth century that historical criticism

---

8. Wellhausen 1994.

(as it was eventually called) carried the day in German academic biblical criticism. Bauer came in at the earlier point, assuming that the Priestly material was the crassest and earliest. Religion struggles, they argued, to rise above this state until it reaches the prophets and then the New Testament. For these biblical critics, the prophets themselves comprise the high-point of the Old Testament (Luther's great liking for the prophets as a model for Protestant ministers has an obvious influence here). Rather than predictors of the future, they spoke the will of God to their immediate context. They were, it would soon be argued, forth-tellers and not fore-tellers. And their message was nothing other than 'ethical monotheism', of which Isaiah was one of the greatest exemplars. No longer were these texts of Isaiah concerned with foretelling the arrival of Christ, but they told forth the great ideals of ethical life lived under monotheism. We could not be further from the idea that the prophets were harbingers of the eschaton, that the end was nigh.

How did all this come about? As I laid out in the Introduction, German criticism was never as stridently anti-religious or anticlerical as its Anglophone and Francophone cousins. Part of the reason lay in the proverbial cultural and intellectual backwardness of Germany; another element was the strong element of *sola scriptura*. The result: the struggles over reason and supernaturalism, religion and secularism took place on the territory of the Bible. Instead of dismissing the Bible as a document of outmoded superstition, they worked out their theories with the Bible itself. German critics took up with vigour the various uncoordinated strands of biblical criticism from Spinoza, Richard Simon and Jean Le Clerc and turned them into a sustained approach, full of differences, arguments and advances. By the end of the nineteenth century, German dominance in biblical criticism was almost unassailable. At the time of Bauer and Strauss, German biblical criticism was just emerging as an international force.

This is the volatile context into which Marx entered his university-years. But let us return to the ever-active and fertile mind of Bauer. He gave these developments in biblical studies his own spin. As far as the Hebrew Bible was concerned, he argued that even its prophetic texts have not yet arrived at the moment of overcoming the estrangement of externalised and legalistic religion. That, of course, would come with the New Testament, to which he was to direct all of his critical concerns from the beginning of the 1840s. At this point in his thought, he argued that the difference between the Old and New Testaments was that Christianity managed to free the religious consciousness from its limited and particular form in the Old Testament. What his work on the Hebrew Bible enabled him to do was define his key-idea of religious consciousness, namely the unmediated identity of particularity and the abstract universal, which he translated in terms of the immediate identity of the universal with a particular subject or community.

Now, while this position – the immediate identity of particular and universal – may seem like a positive assessment of Christianity, Bauer was soon to argue that it is in fact the core of the problem. Already in *Herr Dr. Hengstenberg,*[9] published in the year he taught in Berlin, he had come to argue that the oppressive and narrow-minded sectarianism of the church – especially the German Lutheran church – lay in this claim by the particular to the universal. The logical core of his argument, which developed over his various works on the Bible, was that Christianity was a 'hubristic particularism' which made an unmediated identity between a specific subject (in this case, Jesus Christ) or a community (the church) with the universal. What happens then is that the universal becomes completely other, divorced from communal and individual life. God and heaven become alienated and abstracted universals from human existence. This meant that any claim by a specific individual or group to be the exclusive representative of this universal inevitably produced a brutal, sectarian monopoly that excluded any other particular, whether religious or political. In short, Christian monotheism is an exclusive rather than an inclusive universal. This ultimate hubris of particularism, characteristic of the state-church at the time and the reactionary Friedrich Wilhelm IV (1840–61), let alone of both Christianity and Judaism, is in fact the essence of religion as such. The Prussian state was only the latest manifestation of this brutal universal; for Bauer traced it all the way back to the polis of ancient Greece.

This position developed over Bauer's studies of the synoptic Gospels and the Gospel of John (written over an intense period from 1840 to 1842), only to receive full expression in his *Christianity Exposed* of 1843.[10] Through his writing, Bauer eventually recognised his own atheism, arguing that free self-consciousness must be released from the constraints of all religion and that the only way for self-consciousness to realise itself is through historical and social

---

9. Bauer 1839.
10. Bauer 1840, 1841, 1842b, 1850–1. For an excellent discussion that traces the way Bauer's position developed over these works, see Moggach 2003, pp. 59–79. Unfortunately Leopold 2007, pp. 101–5, skips by the importance of Bauer's biblical criticism.

transformation. In regard to the Gospels, they are a long way from histori-cal records, being the products of creative and unknown individuals. Within the restrictions of the religious consciousness, these authors responded to the needs of the Christian communities for an understanding of their own nature and origins. So Mark, the earliest Gospel, presents a basic picture of Jesus's adult life and death, while the later Matthew and Luke fill out that story with birth-narratives, additional material and the resurrection. By the time we get to John we already have the full expression of a dogmatic monopoly. But why are these stories problematic?

> The gospel reports are nothing other than free, literary products, whose soul is the simple categories of religion. What is specific to these categories, how-ever, is that they reverse the laws of the real, rational world. They alienate the universality of self-consciousness, rend it violently away, and restore it in the form of representation as an alien, heavenly, or as an alien, limited, sacred history.[11]

Christianity denied the truth that could come only from self-consciousness by identifying such truth with another being and a heavenly realm alien to that self-consciousness. Even worse, Christianity claimed that its ultimate form of alienation was the absolute and universal truth, thereby exacerbating the prob-lem. It intensifies such alienation until it becomes unbearable, thereby open-ing the way for a final resolution. Thus, in good Hegelian fashion, Christianity was both the best and worst of all religions. It may have provided a revo-lutionary breakthrough, freeing people from the ties of nature, family and spirits, but it was also the highest form of alienation. What was needed, then, was a sublation [*Aufhebung*] of the necessary stage of Christianity in order to see that the truth came from a free self-consciousness. Only 'criticism' (which Marx and Engels will come to lampoon mercilessly) is able to release such a universal self-consciousness. But it also meant that any state or church that laid claim to Christianity would have to go too. Religious monopoly and the restoration under way with the German monarchy merely reinforced Bauer's views, so much so that by 1840–1 he rejected all forms of religious representa-tion in favour of an emancipated philosophical self-consciousness.

---

11. Bauer 1967, p. 61. Cited in Moggach 2003, p. 77.

Needless to say, Bauer's radical biblical criticism and theology went hand in hand with a radical political republicanism. But, in the context, Bauer was an extreme radical, which is why he interested Marx and Engels so much. This one-time favourite of Hegel, who recommended Bauer for a royal prize for an essay on Kant in 1829, was removed from his post as licentiate at the Friedrich Wilhelm University in the same year that he taught Marx. His crime: the aforesaid book, *Herr Dr. Hengstenberg*. Hengstenberg happened to be a leading pietistic theologian, colleague and former teacher. Bauer, it seems, could not suffer fools gladly. Fortune was with him, for the Minister of Culture, Altenstein, was favourable to the Hegelians and moved him out of harm's way – or at least so he thought – to Bonn. But fortune did not smile on Bauer for much longer. Altenstein died in 1840, the same year Friedrich Wilhelm III gave up the ghost. Along with the new king came a new Minister for Culture – or as his title was known in full, for Religious Worship, Education and Medicine – by the name of Eichhorn. This enlightened bureaucrat had no time for the Hegelians and was certainly not going to protect the young radical. Bauer had lasted five years in Berlin (1834–9), but he lasted barely three in Bonn. At the end of March in 1842, his *licentia docendi* was revoked by Eichhorn and he was dismissed by direct order of the new king.[12] With no options left in a university, he purchased a small farm, ran a tobacco-shop and wrote – as prolifically as ever – in the evenings until his death in 1882.

The 21-year-old Marx, then, encountered Bauer at a highly charged time in his career. About to be sent off to Bonn for his polemic against Hengstenberg at Berlin, at the crest of a wave of prolific and original work after he had honed his idea of religion in the 1830s, about to become the intellectual leader of the young Hegelians,[13] we may gain a good idea of what Bauer taught Marx.

---

12. His post at Berlin was closed by the Minister for Religious Worship, Education and Medicine, Eichhorn. The story of his dismissal as Privat-Docent of Theology at Bonn is a little confused. Initially, he was put under investigation for his radical views on the New Testament by a consultation that included the Ministry of Education and the theology-faculties of the six Prussian universities, but the investigation was unable to achieve consensus. In an astute moment of ill-timing (a characteristic, it seems), he attended a banquet in honour of the South-German liberal, Karl Welcker, in 1841. Bauer proposed a toast to the Hegelian concept of the state, but the king decided to sack all those who attended the banquet and who were in state-employment.

13. I hesitate to use the designations of 'left' or 'right' Hegelians, not merely because Bauer refused to see himself in these terms, but above all because the distinction was invented by David Strauss in his *In Defence of My 'Life of Jesus' Against the Hegelians* (Strauss 1980; Strauss 1983). Strauss used it to return fire against Bauer's (and oth-

Apart from bringing Marx up to speed on the rapid developments in that first wave of German biblical criticism at the time, Bauer had already come to hold that all religion was problematic. By definition, religion was a hubristic effort by a certain particularism – be that individual, group or institution – to lay claim to the abstract universal. As soon as it did so, it became a crass sectarian monopoly that brooked no opposition. One should not be surprised that the church had become close-minded and authoritarian. Even Isaiah, who was far better than the priestly material that lay (as scholarship held at the time) at the earliest layers of the Hebrew Bible, succumbed to this problem. Isaiah might have moved past the law-driven externality of the priests, he might even have expressed that ethical monotheism in which the universal was immanent in the community, but he still held to religion as such, and that was the problem.

This was heady stuff. With the young Hegelians causing one controversy after another, no-one could avoid being caught up in the fray. It is not for nothing that a little over four years later Marx would begin his *Contribution to the Critique of Hegel's Philosophy of Law* with the words: 'For Germany the *criticism of religion* is in the main complete, and criticism of religion is the premise of all criticism'.[14]

In closing this section let me make one point clear. There was little, if anything, of the much-touted prophetic eschatology or messianism in the air at the time. Time and again, we hear the common point that Marxism is a secularised eschatology, or perhaps that the themes of alienation and revolution are drawn from the biblical pattern of exile and return,[15] and that Marx took over this element from his Jewish background and Christian context and transformed it into a secular version. Stated as an item of common knowledge, or asserted through vague affinities, it is never backed up with any specific references. I would add the point that German biblical scholarship of the time was emphasising anything but prophetic eschatology. Bruno Bauer was certainly not teaching it to Marx in that summer of 1839 at the Friedrich Wilhelm University of Berlin.

---

ers') criticisms of his original *Das Leben Jesu* (Strauss 1835; Strauss 1902) characterising Bauer as a 'right'-Hegelian and himself as a 'left'-Hegelian.

14. Marx 1844c, p. 175; Marx 1844d, p. 378.

15. For a more Jewish angle, see Fischman 1991, pp. 94–108.

'My friend of many years standing...'

'*Bruno Bauer*, my friend of many years standing – but now rather estranged [*jetzt aber mehr entfremdeter*]...'[16] Perhaps this comment, made in a letter to Feuerbach on 11 August 1844, sums up Marx's complex relationship with Bauer. For a time, Marx's hopes for a university-appointment rested on his close connections with Bauer – at least while Bauer still had a university-post, even if it was only at the Licentiate level. But, when Bauer finally lost his position as Privat-Docent of Theology at Bonn, those hopes disappeared for good. The friendship between Marx and Bauer shows up strongly in Marx's doctoral thesis, joint works that they planned together and Marx's defence of Bauer.

Marx's doctoral thesis, with its frequent invocations of self-consciousness, shows clear enough signs that Bauer had made an impact.[17] I am less interested in the fairly obvious point that we can read its topic – the rescue of Epicurus as a serious thinker in his own right against Democritus – as a code for the intense debates on theology and politics swirling around Marx as he wrote. And we should not be deceived by Marx's loose use of the term 'theology' when he actually means the philosophical system of Epicurus. Instead, its importance lies in the effort to reach back to a time before Christian theology even appeared. The project may be framed as follows: if Bauer is right in his argument that Christianity is inescapably alienating and oppressive, then what happens if we go back before Christianity? Is it possible to find a way for moving beyond theology, not so much by destroying it and leaving it behind, but by searching out what went before? Given the deeply classicist assumptions that dominated education in Marx's time (they are still with us in so many ways), that meant going back to classical Greece.

In order to support my argument, I refer to the sections in both what is left of the thesis and the notebooks. I am particularly interested in the way Marx traces the condemnation of Epicurus all the way back to Cicero's observation that Epicurus copied his system from Democritus. Where Epicurus had deviated, suggests Cicero, he made a huge mess. The next moment in the history of that condemnation came from Plutarch's pen, who offers an utter denigration of Epicurus in the name of religion (the Appendix is devoted to

---

16. Marx 1844q, p. 356; Marx 1844r, pp. 426–7.
17. Although Breckman 1999, pp. 259–71, makes a somewhat speculative case for the dominance of Feuerbach even at this early stage (1840–1).

Plutarch's assessment).[18] In the first chapter of the thesis, Marx shows how Plutarch leads directly to the church-fathers who merely copy the condemnation, especially Clement of Alexandria who draws upon what he thought was Paul's letter in Colossians 2:8, where we find a condemnation of those who speculate on the 'elemental spirits of the universe'[19] – which Clement interprets to mean Epicurus, among others. Clement also observes that according to Acts 7:18 the apostle Paul refuted the Epicurean and Stoic philosophers, which leads Clement to conclude that all philosophy which busies itself with these elemental spirits of the universe rather than Christ is worthless. The notebooks upon which the thesis is based have a massive number of quotations and comments on this history of theological disparagement of Epicurus.[20]

Now Marx seeks to roll back this theological tradition of condemnation, rescue Epicurus and claim for philosophy a place diametrically opposed to theology. In other words, Epicurus is the philosophical champion against all the theologians. Quoting Lucretius, Marx writes:

> When human life lay grovelling in all men's sight, crushed to the earth under the dead weight of religion whose grim features loured menacingly upon mortals from the four quarters of the sky, a man of Greece was first to raise mortal eyes in defiance, first to stand erect and brave the challenge. Fables of the gods did not crush him, nor the lightning flash and growling menace of the sky.... Therefore religion in its turn lies crushed beneath his feet, and we by his triumph are lifted level with the skies.[21]

It is hard to miss the biographical element in all this, but what interests me far more is that Marx attempts to find a thinker – of absolute and free self-consciousness no less – who comes well before Christian theology. Even

---

18. Marx 1840–1a, pp. 102–5; Marx 1840–1b, pp. 88–91. This section leads him to the philosophical arguments for the proof of God's existence, which he describes as 'refutations of all concepts of a God' (Marx 1840–1a, p. 105; Marx 1840–1b, p. 91).

19. Marx 1840–1a, pp. 36–8; Marx 1840–1b, pp. 23–5. See also his comments on the efforts at accommodation between Epicurus and theology in the work of the seventeeth-century philosopher Pierre Gassendi (Marx 1839a, pp. 423–4; Marx 1839b, pp. 58–61).

20. Marx 1839a, pp. 431–2, 442–58, 487–8, 493–506; Marx 1839b, pp. 74–7, 92–127, 202–7, 218–48.

21. Marx 1840–1a, p. 73; Marx 1840–1b, pp. 57–8. Marx quotes the text from Lucretius in Latin.

more, this thinker has to be rescued from later theological condemnation. In one sense, this argument by Marx goes against Bauer, for Bauer saw in Christianity the ultimate contradiction that would eventually free self-consciousness. Marx says no, if you go back before Christianity you will find one who actually expresses this freedom. Unfortunately, Marx did not pursue this line of argument, partly because he began to break away from Bauer, partly because he realised that even Epicurus remained trapped in religious imagination and speculative philosophy, but the effort to find a champion of non-theological thought would stay with him.[22] All the same, despite Marx's later efforts to find another way to move from heaven to earth, I wish he had explored the underlying impulse of the thesis further. It has the potential of showing that many of the terms assumed to be originally theological may actually have a pre-theological life. That would mean, against both the assumptions of his own time and figures such as Carl Schmitt, that theology is not the *fons et origo* of most of our major categories of social and political thought. Instead, it is merely one form they may take.

After the thesis was completed in 1841, Marx held the line for his former teacher throughout the following year, although there were signs of strain. In March, Marx wrote to Ruge to say that his contributions – *A Treatise on Christian Art* and a critique of the Hegelian philosophy of law – to a planned joint work with Bauer had not made it into the text.[23] The second work has appeared as a somewhat different text,[24] but for now I am interested in the *Treatise*. Marx's comments are exquisitely tantalising: a few passing references, a mention of the state of the manuscript, but then the manuscript itself has never turned up. Let us see what we can piece together from the scattered materials.

Bauer and Marx had planned a two-volume work together, although only the second volume was to be a properly collaborative business between the two of them. Through a mix of circumstances, some difference of opinion and Marx's inability to finish works, the second joint-volume never appeared.

---

22. In this respect, I agree with Van Leeuwen 2002b, p. 74, that Epicurus really stands in for Marx himself in the thesis. However, he has a tendency to over-cook his argument, suggesting after five chapters on Epicurus that the thesis is 'a resolute reckoning with the claims of Christian theology' (p. 137).
23. Marx 1842x, p. 382; Marx 1842y, p. 397; Marx 1842z, p. 385; Marx 1842aa, p. 400.
24. Marx 1843c; Marx 1843d.

Or rather, it appeared, but only with the sections written by Bauer. Both were supposed to be called *Die Posaune*, or *Trumpet of the Last Judgement*. In the end, the first volume of 1841 bore that title.[25] The second volume became Bauer's own *Hegels Lehre von der Religion und der Kunst*.[26]

So, we are in a somewhat strange situation: Bauer's side of the conversation went to print and has survived, but Marx's contribution has not. He did have a small hand in the first volume, which we can see in the revolutionary angle that Bauer takes. Published anonymously in 1841 as an attempted spoof, *Die Posaune* takes on the voice of a pietistic and conservative critic of Hegel. It argues that Hegel was a revolutionary and that the full outcome of his system would sweep away church and state and bring on the republic made of free individuals. The key to Hegel, argues Bauer, was the idea of an infinite and free self-consciousness, which would overcome any hindrance, any archaic institution that was not justified by reason, and therefore any existing state, church or social hierarchy. Bauer managed to get to this point by invoking the dialectic: it negates transcendent substance on the path to universal self-consciousness. In more detail: to block the possibility that the particularity of the self might become the basis for a universal position (an invalid move), the first step was to posit (an apparently) transcendent substance. The individual then has to internalise this undifferentiated and transcendent substance in order to discipline the differentiated and particular self. Once this crucial step of stripping particularity has been taken, it then becomes possible for a consciousness to appropriate the infinite. In this way, the infinite could take conscious form. Now we have an infinite self-consciousness that absorbs, controls and moves beyond any transcendent substance. However, since this consciousness is infinite, it does not spend its time gazing upon its own glorious navel. Rather, it manifests itself in history.

But then how does this infinite self-consciousness deal with the concrete alienations of God, the church, inherited privilege and the state (especially when it relies on divine sanction)? These alienations are actually the result of what the infinite consciousness has managed to avoid, namely, universal claims of the basis of a particular self; they are false claims to transcendence.

---

25. The full title is *Die Posaune des jungsten Gerichts über Hegel den Atheisten und Antichristen: Ein Ultimatum* (Bauer 1983).
26. Bauer 1967.

The response of infinite self-consciousness is nothing short of revolution, for in the face of infinite self-consciousness, as an immanent and subjective universality, all of these alienated moments must fall away. Infinite self-consciousness overturns all these alienations in the name of freedom. In *Die Posaune*, this argument was put in the mouth of a pious critic of Hegel; he seeks to warn his readers that Hegel was no defender of the Restoration. In Bauer's hands the book becomes an underhand and rather long-winded justification – Marx calls it 'the irksome constraint of the Hegelian exposition'[27] – for the autonomous individual and the claim to full democratic rights.

The fate of Marx's contribution to the second volume was sealed by the terminal illness of Ludwig von Westphalen, Jenny's father. As Bauer was finishing the manuscript for the volume in early 1842, Marx found himself spending three months in Trier. Just as Herr von Westphalen lay on his deathbed, so also Marx's manuscript lay untouched, awaiting its own death.[28] By the time Ludwig was dead, on 3 March, Bauer had published the second volume on his own without Marx's sections.

Still keen to get some version of the *Treatise* published, Marx wrote to Ruge as soon as he could. Perhaps you can publish a 'modified version' in the proposed *Anekdota*, Marx suggests, although the manuscript still requires 'the rewriting of a fair copy and, in part, some corrections'.[29] A couple of weeks later he updates Ruge on the manuscript. Now he is working on a full revision, to be called *On Religion and Art, with Special Reference to Christian Art*, replete with a supplement on the romantics and an attack on the essence of religion that subjects Feuerbach's conception of religion to critique. Here, the disagreements with Bauer bubble to the surface, for in revising the treatise he tells Ruge he wants to break with the 'tone of the *Posaune*'[30] and replace

---

27. Marx 1842z, p. 385; Marx 1842aa, p. 400.
28. 'The fact is that my future father-in-law, Herr von Westphalen, lay on his deathbed for three months and died the day before yesterday. During this period, therefore, it was impossible to do anything properly.' (Marx 1842x, p. 383; Marx 1842y, p. 397.)
29. Ibid.
30. For all Bauer's atheistic pretence, Marx still finds it pietistic and prophetic. In describing the book, Marx paraphrases three biblical texts: 'Thy *word* is a lamp unto my feet, and a light unto my path' (Psalm 119: 105). 'Thy commandments make me wiser than mine enemies, For they are ever with me.' (Psalm 119: 98.) 'The Lord shall roar from Zion' (Amos 1:2).

it with 'a freer, and therefore more thorough exposition'.[31] At this point, the manuscript is but three weeks from completion, for he promises to send it in by mid-April. A little past that date, Marx mentions the work for the last time, now broken up into two works, *On Religious Art* and *On the Romantics*.[32] That is the last mention. If its earlier failure to appear was due to circumstances (Jenny's father's death) and disagreement with Bauer, now it seems as though Marx's inability to stop working on a piece sounded the death-knell. He comments to Ruge that 'the work has steadily grown into almost book dimensions, and I have been drawn into all kinds of investigations which will still take a rather long time'.[33] Inexperience leads to the death of the manuscript by a thousand revisions.

So what did he argue in that lost, unending manuscript? Here, we find a good deal of speculation and use of circumstantial evidence. Following Mikhail Lifshitz,[34] Margaret Rose suggests that it would have moved from a study of the religious and fetishistic art of Asia and Greece to the Christian art of the Romantics, showing how the two are connected.[35] She goes on the argue that it would have fallen foul of the censorship-decrees against which Marx struggled for the whole time he was involved with the *Rheinische Zeitung*. That is about all Rose can glean from evidence of what Marx was reading (based on excerpts from his notebooks) and some of the other subjects Marx covers at the time, especially his first touches on the matter of fetishism. I would add that we find a hint in Marx's comment to Ruge on 20 March 1842, where Marx mentions that the revised manuscript disagrees with Feuerbach's concept of religion – this disagreement has actually turned up in the *Theses on Feuerbach*. As Marx points out in the letter, he disagrees not with the principle (projection) but the conception. It would seem that Marx was already arguing that religion is a projection of the worst in human beings rather than the best, that religion is an expression of alienation and not hope and love.

We might have expected Marx to give up on Bauer after such an experience. But he did not. They kept up their correspondence,[36] Marx continued

---

31. Marx 1842z, p. 385; Marx 1842aa, p. 400.
32. Marx 1842bb, p. 387; Marx 1842cc, p. 402.
33. Ibid.
34. Lifshitz 1973; Lifshitz 1984.
35. Rose 1984, pp. 61–2.
36. So much so that Bauer wrote directly to Marx when he was dismissed from Bonn; see Marx 1842x, p. 383; Marx 1842y, p. 398.

to read Bauer's books avidly, some of which he found better than others,[37] and Marx publicly defended Bauer on at least one occasion. That occasion was an attack by a certain philosopher, Otto Friedrich Gruppe. Marx came to the defence of Bauer in the young-Hegelian flagship-journal, *Deutsche Jahrbücher für Wissenschaft und Kunst*.[38] The topic was Gruppe's attempt to discredit Bauer's credentials as a critic of the New Testament. So what does Marx say in defence? Apart from the heavy *ad hominem* satire that was quickly becoming Marx's trademark – deriding him for 'weakness of intellect' and 'dilettantist ignorance'[39] – he focuses on a lazy howler in Gruppe's attack. In short, Gruppe accuses Bauer of self-aggrandisement by writing in his own prophetic voice, 'keep away from me, theologian!'. Marx easily shows that Bauer is actually offering a paraphrase of Jesus's words in Matthew 12:38–42, attempting to bring out their meaning. It is a relatively minor business, a misreading by a pedantic critic of a much greater one, the former forgotten but for Marx's polemic and the interest of a very few (like me), the latter a major figure in the history of biblical criticism. But what is interesting here is that Marx slips into the detail of a biblical argument, and that he does so to defend Bauer. The great achievement of Bauer's work on the New Testament was to show how German biblical critics distort and twist the biblical text in order to suit theological agendas. In this case – Jesus's denial of the need to give signs and then the promise of the 'sign of Jonah'[40] – these biblical critics bent over backwards to bring consistency to a contradiction. For they simply could not countenance a contradiction, especially in the mouth of Jesus (it is a problem that unfortunately bedevils biblical criticism still today). Bauer brings them up short. However, Marx does not merely take the wind out of the sails of a critic like Gruppe; he also wishes to defend Bauer's character and

---

37. As he comments to Ruge: 'Bauer on Ammon is delightful. The "Sorrows and Joys of the Theological Mind" seems to me a not very successful rendering of the section of the *Phenomenology*...You have probably already read Bauer's self-defence. In my opinion, he has never before written so well' (Marx 1843q, p. 400; Marx 1843r, pp. 417–18; see Bauer 1842a).

38. Marx 1842t; Marx 1842u. Gruppe's book, *Bruno Bauer und die Akademissche Lehrfreiheit*, took on Bauer's *Kritik der evangelischen Geschichte der Synoptiker* (Bauer 1841). Marx makes a comparable defence of the poet Friedrich von Sallet, whose collection of anticlerical poetry, *Laien-Evangelium*, was attacked by the *Rhein- und Mosel-Zeitung* and then (mischievously?) misread as a defence of Christianity against Strauss, Feuerbach and Bauer by the *Trier'sche Zeitung* (Marx 1843o; Marx 1843p).

39. Marx 1842t, p. 213; Marx 1842u, p. 248.

40. Matthew 12:38–42; Luke 11:29–30 and Mark 8:12–13.

teaching. This skilled biblical critic who argues for atheism from within the Bible had become something of a scandal for the conservative press, university theology-departments and the government. So Marx, along with a string of young Hegelians, lined up in Bauer's defence.

The Jewish question

On the Jewish Question marks the moment when Marx and Bauer fell out badly with one another. This is the first of three major polemical engagements with his former teacher and friend. I am particularly interested in the way in which these criticisms turn on the matter of theology. Perhaps I can characterise it this way: theology is the flint upon which Marx strikes his emerging histori-cal-materialist method. Three of those strikes are the attacks on Bauer – *On the Jewish Question*, *The Holy Family* and *The German Ideology*.

On the Jewish Question is widely regarded as one of the major early state-ments by Marx on emancipation. It is a response to two works by Bauer, *Die Judenfrage* and 'Die Fähigkeit der heutigen Juden und Christen, frei zu werden',[41] although the question of the relaxing of restrictions on Jews had been debated for over half a century beforehand in light of limited conces-sions already granted in response to ongoing petitions from the Jews.[42] Both Bauer and Marx seek emancipation, and both agree that it has not yet been realised, but they disagree on what emancipation means and how to achieve it. For Bauer, what is needed is emancipation from religion and the way to do so is through an as yet unachieved 'real freedom' that entails a universal recognition of common humanity. For Marx, this proposal is wrong-headed, for it erroneously gives priority to religion, which thereby does not deal with the real issue – the abstraction of the state from civil society, and thereby a split between individual human being and citizen, as well as atomistic social relations in which each individual is in conflict with the other. Marx opposes this false freedom with real, human emancipation, which recaptures such

---

41. Bauer 1843b and 1843c. Bauer's 'Die Judenfrage' initially appeared in *Deutsche Jahrbücher für Wissenschaft und Kunst*, numbers 274–82, in November 1842. An English translation may be found in Bauer 1958. A translation of the second piece appeared in English in Bauer 1978 and in French in Bauer 2006.

42. See the outlines of this background in Bensaïd 2006a, pp. 20–2; Fischman 1991, pp. 26–30; and Leopold 2007, pp. 105–7.

alienation into a recovered full human existence. Let us see what they say in a little more detail.

Bauer's two texts manifest quite a tension: on the one hand, Judaism is an exclusive religion which forms the primitive initial stage for the universality of Christianity, which is embodied above all in Protestantism; on the other hand, both Christianity and Judaism, like all religions, suffer from the oppressive and alienating particularity of religion.[43] When he is operating in the first mode, especially in *The Jewish Question*, he wheels out Hegelian and popular anti-Judaic characterisations of the time. They are hypocritical (since they find ways around the impossible law), exclusive (as the 'chosen people' they are hostile to universality), and positive (in the Hegelian sense of submitting to arbitrary laws based on authority). So they are 'conceited', 'arrogant', 'stubborn', 'selfish' and given to the naked cunning of 'material egoism'.[44] It is important to distinguish three overlapping elements in Bauer's characterisation of Jews. First, he picks up a number of popular images of Jews as wilfully different, lacking desire for integration, and bringing their discrimination upon themselves. Second, he is committed to a Hegelian schema in which history is the dialectical unfolding of universality and 'self-consciousness' (Bauer's gloss on 'spirit'). In this respect, the Jews are at an earlier stage to Christian universalism. Third, and most importantly for Marx's criticism that Bauer is very much a theologian, Bauer follows a standard theological line in which Judaism is the forerunner of Christianity, but that the 'Old Testament' has been superseded by the 'New Testament' of love in Christ. In light of this status, the Jews have a far greater difficulty in achieving true freedom – which Bauer saw as recognition of our common humanity and the overcoming of all particularity, especially that of religion. Although Bauer argues that Christianity is far closer to this real freedom, he does not argue that Jews should convert to Christianity, for that would merely involve stepping from one form of alienation into another.

This is where we pass to the other side of the tension in Bauer's texts in which he argues that both Christianity and Judaism are alienating and intolerant.[45] This argument comes out more forcefully in the follow-up article,

---

43. See Leopold 2007, p. 118.
44. Bauer 1958, pp. 5, 36, 42; Bauer 1843b, pp. 4, 33, 39; see also Bauer 1978, p. 139.
45. Bauer 1958, pp. 22, 101, 135; Bauer 1843b, pp. 19, 95–6, 175.

'The Capacity of Present-Day Jews and Christians to Become Free'. The reason is that for Bauer, like the 'new atheists' in the early years of the twenty-first century,[46] religion is the primary cause of human alienation and all the world's ills. If only we could be rid of religion, then the world would be a far better place. As long as we are tied up by religious identity, we will never have emancipation in any form. The key to Bauer's argument is the particularity of religion. As we saw above, in his biblical studies Bauer had developed the argument that religion involves the claim to the universal by a specific and particular group. As a result, it becomes brutal and oppressive, and in the name of this universal religion will not tolerate others. So emancipation and toleration are not possible when religion dominates political and civic life.

This means that a prejudiced Christian state such as the one in Germany will never grant freedom to Jews. It is just as much a Jewish problem as a Christian one: Christians may be a step closer to freedom than the Jews, but as long as they are defined by their religion, they are incapable of receiving freedom. The problem is that the opposition between Jews and Christians is at heart a religious one and therefore as resilient as stone. So the only way forward is to dispense with religion, for then the opposition itself falls away. 'Real freedom' means the overcoming of the particularity and sectional intolerance of religion and the recognition of a common and universal humanity. That can take place only in a state that has utterly dispensed with religion. For Bauer the almost insurmountable path to freedom for the Jews requires not the granting of rights similar to other citizens of the Christian state (the subject of many petitions), or assimilation to Christianity (as many Jews had done), or even a secular disinterest in religion in which rights were granted to all irrespective of religion (as in France), but awareness that the problem is religion itself. The Jews must give up their very essence as Jews to become free.

In light of this second line in Bauer's argument, we can see that his elevation of Protestant Christianity (Roman Catholics are lower down the scale in yet another layer of distinctions) to the highest point in the universalising of religion is a backhanded compliment if ever there was one. What it means is that a universal Christianity has also universalised the illusions, alienations and inhumanity of religion. It is a 'self-strangling Unfreedom to the point

---

46. Dawkins 2006; Dennett 2007; Harris 2005, 2006; Hitchens 2007. See Bauer 1958, p. 101; Bauer 1843b, pp. 95–6.

where everything is at stake' so much so that it is 'the height of the religious hypocrisy'.[47] This is, of course, a Hegelian point, since the moment of radical negativity before the transition to a new stage is the most alienating of all. So Christianity's superior status exacerbates the need for a transition to a new post-religious stage.

Marx replies by challenging the idealist focus on religion as the cause of all ills and tackling the question of emancipation head-on. As for emancipation, Marx argues that religious 'emancipation' has already taken place, even political 'emancipation' – this is how he interprets Bauer's 'real freedom' – but not full human emancipation.[48] This is both a historical and a philosophical argument. On the historical register, Marx points out that with the break-up of feudalism (in which the church was the dominant force and religion the glue of society), with the declaration of the rights of man through the French and American Revolutions, and with the emergence of a democratic state, political and religious 'emancipation' has already begun to take place, but the results are far from what Bauer would have expected. Marx argues that especially in the United States, where we find a fully developed secular state, religion has become a private matter, the reserve of the individual citizen. All domains of life are broken up into discrete zones, while the political state is abstracted in an ideal form.[49] In this context, we find that religion has not disappeared, but that there is a right to freedom of conscience and religion. No one religion is to dominate, no religion is to be the religion of the state, and no-one is to tell another how to believe. The upshot: Bauer's 'real freedom' which is realised in such a state would grant religious freedom, not freedom from religion. Here is Marx:

---

47. Bauer 1978, p. 140. Further, 'Christianity is the religion which has promised Mankind the most, namely everything, but it has also denied the most, namely everything' (Bauer 1978, p. 146).

48. See the painstaking exegesis of Marx's text in Leopold 2007, pp. 129–63. Leopold points out that Marx moves away from Bauer's distinction between 'emancipation' (what was being proposed) and 'real freedom' (an atheistic situation that recognises our common humanity), putting in its place 'political emancipation' and 'real' or 'full emancipation'.

49. As Leopold 2007, pp. 69–74 and 145, points out, Marx credits Hegel with this insight into the modern state.

> Hence man was not freed from religion, he received religious freedom. He was not freed from property, he received freedom to own property. He was not freed from the egoism of business, he received freedom to engage in business.[50]

In other words, political freedom from religion does not mean the abolition of religion; it merely produces a non-privileged form of religion.[51]

Philosophically, Marx's argument is rather rough at the edges, but it does contain the seeds of an extremely important point. He replies with a telling insight into the nature of Bauer's proposed 'political' emancipation: what it really means is a new form of alienation, between the state and civil society, between citizen [Staatsbürger] and citizen.[52] This division produced by the political 'freedom' of the bourgeois state is no improvement, for it is yet another form of alienation. This argument is made by analogy with religious alienation: in the same way that the products of religion are made by real human beings, so also is that bourgeois state an alienated product of the everyday life of 'civil society'. This means that the opposition of religious and political emancipation in Bauer's piece is a false opposition, since they play the same game. In other words, the modern bourgeois state (as in the United States) embodies exactly the same pattern of religious alienation, except now in political form. Indeed, the failure of such a demand for political emancipation is not the fault of the Jews, or indeed of any group, religious or otherwise. It is the fault of the nature of political 'emancipation' itself, which is really nothing of the sort. So if this is all Bauer's political 'emancipation' can produce, it falls far short of a full, human emancipation.

What, then, is this 'real', 'full' and 'human' emancipation? Such emancipation means that people are no longer forced into a separation between the life of a private, individualistic bourgeois and the abstract moral Staatsbürger; they no longer need to separate their human capacities from themselves as 'politics', but instead to reappropriate and reintegrate the abstracted and alienated

---

50. Marx 1844m, p. 167; Marx 1844n, p. 369.

51. Leopold 2007, pp. 144–5, argues that Marx admits that there are gains in such a situation, however limited they might be.

52. It is an argument we also find in a text written at about the same time, *Contribution to the Critique of Hegel's Philosophy of Law* (Marx 1843c; Marx 1843d). See the discussion in Chapter Six.

Staatsbürger into their own social life.[53] In other words, Marx already looks beyond the political 'emancipation' of the bourgeois, parliamentary state which is the form of the state under capitalism. This is not true freedom – far from it. Here, we can see an early form of the argument that true freedom can only be attained in a classless society without political domination.[54]

Arguably, the most critical attention given to *On the Jewish Question* has focused on its characterisation of Judaism. Marx continues to be accused, often vigorously, of anti-Semitism – as a morally culpable form of self-loathing. But he has been defended against the charge with equal vigour.[55] I must admit that, on a superficial reading, I too initially became uncomfortable with Marx's somewhat overblown rhetoric,[56] but Marx is hardly ever one to be read quickly and easily. A more careful reading shows that the charge of anti-Semitism – or, more properly, anti-Judaism, since 'anti-Semitism' does not appear as a term and modern practice until the 1870s[57] – misses the dialectical twists and turns of Marx's argument. Given the tendency of many readers to jump to conclusions, it is worthwhile paying close attention to what is going on.

The discussion appears in the last few pages of *On the Jewish Question*, where Marx responds to Bauer's article, 'Die Fähigkeit der heutigen Juden und Christen, frei zu werden'. In his response, Marx makes an initial

---

53. 'Only when the real, individual man re-absorbs in himself the abstract citizen, and as an individual human being has become a *species-being* in his everyday life, in his particular work, and in his particular situation, only when man has recognised and organised his *"forces propres"* as *social* forces, and consequently no longer separates social power from himself in the shape of *political* power, only then will human emancipation have been accomplished.' (Marx 1844m, p. 168; Marx 1844n, p. 370.)

54. I am thankful to Jan Rehmann for this point (private communication).

55. This literature is immense. As a sample, for those who charge Marx with anti-Semitism, see Maccoby 2006, pp. 64–6; Lewis 1999, p. 112; Flannery 2004, p. 168; Perry and Schweitzer 2005, pp. 154–7; Muravchik 2003, p. 164; Greenblatt 1978; Ray 2006; Misrahi 1972 and 2004; Kaplan 1990; Rose 1990, pp. 296–305; Wolfson 1982, pp. 74–103. As for those who argue that this is a misreading of Marx, see Deutscher 1968; Avineri 1964; McLellan 1980, pp. 141–2; Peled 1992; Brown 1995; Aron 2005; Fine 2006. Fischman 1991 takes a more dialectical approach, arguing that Marx's 'reputation as an anti-Semite obscures the true complexity of his views of Judaism' (Fischman 1991, p. 24), for Marx might have despised Jewish religion (as he does all religion), but he saw Judaism as an extremely important social force. For excellent surveys of many of these positions and detailed defences of Marx, see Bensaïd 2006b and Leopold 2007, pp. 163–80. See also the important statement by Engels 1890c; Engels 1890d.

56. A sense conveyed graphically by Fischman 1991, pp. 12–13.

57. See Bensaïd 2006a, pp. 78–9.

distinction between the religious or 'Sabbath Jew [*den Sabbatsjuden*]' and the 'worldly religion' of the 'real secular Jew [*den wirklichen weltlichen Juden*]'. Bauer's mistake, he writes, is to seek the essence of Judaism in its religion; that is fundamentally mistaken, for the nature of 'Judaism' actually appears in its everyday activity in the real world. This distinction carries much more weight than at first seems to be the case, for Marx challenges the dominant discourse concerning Jews by taking it up and undermining it.

What was that dominant representation of Jews? Here, Marx provides us with the terms. The 'worldly religion' of the 'real Jew' (as against the ideal, 'abstract' or 'Sabbath Jew') is nothing less than 'huckstering'; the 'God' of this religion is 'money'; the basis of 'Jewish religion' is 'egoism'.[58] On the face of it, this looks like an anti-Semitic caricature of Jews, and more than one commentator has taken it as precisely that. However, such a reading makes the mistake of reading these terms in a literal sense, falling into the trap of a realistic hermeneutics.[59] But what Marx actually does is appropriate the widespread depiction of Jews in German, if not European, culture as a whole.[60] This depiction dismissed the uniqueness of Jewish religion as a mere pretext for the pursuit of money and gain. Judaism was seen, in other words, as a crass, materialistic religion concerned only with this world.

Now, we can see how Bauer's argument was also an effort to break with this discourse, for he argued that the real secret to Judaism's grubby commercial practices lay with Jewish religion (which in some way exacerbated the anti-Semitic nature of this discourse). The problem is that Bauer does not succeed, for he continually slides into characterising Judaism itself as a material religion concerned with particular practices and observances. Marx's response takes a very different line: forget the religion and let us get inside that popular discourse – *Jude* and its cognates were used at the time in a derogatory sense

---

58. Marx 1844m, pp. 169–72; Marx 1844n, pp. 372–5. See also Marx and Engels 1845a, p. 109; Marx and Engels 1845b, p. 115.

59. For an insightful discussion of the way such a literal reading fails, see Leopold 2007, p. 165. The point concerning 'realistic hermeneutics' comes from Jan Rehmann (private communication).

60. For a discussion of the various senses of 'Jew' and 'Judaism' as widely held stereotypes and literary terms of art, see Leopold 2007, p. 167; Fischman 1991, pp. 30–1, and Bensaïd 2006a, pp. 100–2. Leopold 2007, pp. 165–7, argues that Marx uses *Judentum* in a metaphorical sense, while McLellan 1980, p. 142, suggests that Marx's response is 'an extended pun at Bauer's expense'.

to indicate disreputable forms of 'commerce'[61] – and subvert it from within. What you take as the 'true' nature of 'real Judaism' – given over to monetary gain, usury and self-interest – is, in fact, the nature of the Christian world. Here, Marx draws upon the Christian supersession of Judaism – an assumption upon which Bauer draws heavily – and turns that argument on its head. Christianity might argue that it is the perfection of Judaism, that Christianity has attained spiritual and theoretical superiority, while Judaism remains a practical and materialistic religion, but that actually means that Christianity is the perfection of 'Judaism'. At this point, Marx gives a twist to another feature of Bauer's argument. As we saw above, Bauer argued that Christianity might feel it has attained a higher degree of consciousness than Judaism, but that is no blessing, for it means that Christianity has universalised alienation to all aspects of life. Marx gives this argument a materialist turn: yes, Christianity is a higher level, a 'perfection' of 'Judaism', but only because it is a perfection of the self-serving pursuit of gain. In other words, you might feel that you can externalise all these undesirable features of the grubby world of commerce on the pariah-Jews, but these features are your own essence as Christians. What you take for 'Jewish' is in fact not Jewish but rather the very nature of the bourgeois, capitalist order itself, and that is why this huckstering, money-hungry and egoistic attitude is a deeply Christian attitude.

At last, we can see the connection with Marx's argument for full emancipation. Where do we find this thoroughly Christian attitude? In nothing other than the Christian, bourgeois state where we find that the state is abstracted from 'civil society' and where the human world is dissolved 'into a world of atomistic individuals who are inimically opposed to one another'.[62] True emancipation is to be free of this world, Jews included. Over against Bauer's argument that Jews and Christians must first abandon their religion before they can attain political 'emancipation', Marx argues for a full emancipation that does not require one to become alienated from one's own nature – which means implicitly that the Jews may be emancipated with no strings attached.[63] In other words, if we pursue this line, the various distinctions in Marx's essay become obvious: citizen and human beings; 'Sabbath Jew' and the 'real Jew';

---

61. McLellan 1980, p. 142.
62. Marx 1844m, p. 173; Marx 1844n, p. 376.
63. In a careful analysis, Leopold 2007, pp. 150–63, shows that Marx argues that religious commitment is no reason to exclude people from the 'rights of man'.

Roman Catholic and Protestant. Even more, in the achieved bourgeois state, we find a radical splintering of human beings not merely into atomistic individuals but also into discrete segments given over to religion, property, business, leisure, sport, family, work, and so on. Emancipation, therefore, means the recapture and reappropriation of all these realms into a whole and unalienated social being. Needless to say, this is a tall agenda, but it does provide the basic reference-point for a radical programme of liberation.[64]

Apart from Marx's insights into the nature of emancipation and the alienation inherent in the so-called political freedom of the bourgeois state, what else can we find on a more theological note in this essay? To begin with, we first encounter the argument that Bauer is still too much of a theologian. The charge is relatively muted in *On the Jewish Question*; later, it would become a centrepiece to Marx's argument, as we will see soon enough. As Marx puts it, 'We are trying to break with the theological formulation [*die theologische Fassung*] of the question'.[65] Bauer's problem, at least according to Marx, is twofold: he is beholden to theological schemas such as the supersessionist distinction between Judaism and Christianity; and, more substantially, the fact that Bauer wants to dispense with religion means that his programme privileges religion. Marx does grant that in Germany, where theology dominates public debate – so much so that the state itself is a theologian – criticism of the state must of necessity be theological criticism. But that is also the reason for Bauer's limitation, for he extracts from this situation and universalises his theological solution. The real problem, argues Marx, lies elsewhere.

Further, this essay is one of Marx's first – if somewhat untried and rough – deployments of an argument analogous to the one concerning religious alienation: in the same way that religion and its objects are signs of an alienated condition, so also is the bourgeois state the signal of alienation. That is, the separation between civil society and the political state actually points to the fact that we are alienated, that there is a separation between citizen and human being. In the clutch of texts written while he was at Kreuznach – of which *On the Jewish Question* is but one – Marx would work through this analogous

---

64. For a careful effort to determine what Marx meant by full emancipation, see Leopold 2007, pp. 150–78.
65. Marx 1844m, p. 169; Marx 1844n, p. 372.

argument, apply it and refine it and then add it to his critical store. We will return to it on many occasions below.

Holy families

By the time we get to *The Holy Family* and *The German Ideology* – which really form a pair as far as Bauer is concerned – the polemic has gone into top gear. Here, the satire weighs a little too heavily and the dense writing points to Marx's hand in much of the material. I must admit I found great difficulty in settling into it.[66] Large slabs of these books offer us polemic at close quarters – detailed comments on style, delighting in contradictions whether real or not, ridicule, satire, attacking and mocking Bauer's style, expression, arguments and literary ability, personal attacks that accuse him of a sense of superiority, servile dependence, malice and cowardice, teases about losing his posts as university-lecturer in theology, line after line quoted, dissected and hung out to cure, a tit-for-tat response by Marx to Bauer's response to the critics (Marx included) of Bauer's original *Die Judenfrage*. It is the usual convoluted style to which one becomes accustomed after reading Marx's early journalistic efforts.[67]

In the midst of that stylistic excess and close polemic, a number of themes emerge. *The Holy Family* is ostensibly a response to the first eight issues of *Allgemeneine Literatur-Zeitung* and the key young Hegelians who wrote for the journal, but the main target is the editor of the journal, namely Bruno Bauer himself. Marx and Engels (who contributes a few pages and countless biblical references) recognise that Bauer is the ablest thinker of the lot and so they give him the most textual space, but only so that they can give him an intense

---

66. One can well understand why *The German Ideology* could not find a publisher. It reads like a very rough first draft of an important argument. As far as the *Holy Family* is concerned, Engels too had his misgivings. In a letter to Marx on 17 March 1845, he writes that, while he finds it funny and well written, it is too long and will be incomprehensible to the public at large (Engels 1845f, p. 28; Engels 1845g, pp. 25–6). By contrast, Marx thought highly of *The Holy Family*, since he urges one publisher after another to do it quickly and tells Börnstein that '*every* word counts' (Marx 1844o, p. 8; Marx 1844p, p. 430). As Kouvelakis points out (Kouvelakis 2003, p. 283 and p. 410, n. 169), one response to Prussian repression was to become prolix, as Bauer notably did. Indeed, Engels felt that *The Holy Family* was all too close to the verbosity of the young Hegelians.

67. On style, see Leopold 2007, p. 8.

battering.[68] By comparison, the section on Bauer in *The German Ideology* is quite short, no more than a score of pages.[69] In light of the endless section on Stirner in that work, I can only wonder whether they planned a further draft, extending Bauer or perhaps dropping him entirely in order to even out a very lopsided work. The overwhelming impression is that both Marx and Engels have said what needs to be said about Bruno Bauer in a string of earlier works.

The underlying drive of the attack on Bauer is to show that his path to radical politics through theology is a no-go zone. In fact, Bauer's politics is not really radical after all. Bauer's writings may look radical, Bauer himself may have lost his posts at Berlin and Bonn because of them, he may even be the pin-up boy of the radical liberals, but he is really a speculative and idealist conservative. The linchpin of the attack on Bauer's radical credentials is that he is inescapably a theologian.[70] For all his later efforts to show that religion is at odds with his notion of a free and infinite 'self-consciousness', that the church is a pernicious and small-minded effort to universalise the particular, and that the New Testament already embodies this process, Bauer is still a theologian, at least in Marx's opinion.[71] He may have lost his faith in God, but he has merely shifted that faith onto something else, whether that is the state or even 'Criticism' itself. His much-vaunted atheism is merely the 'last stage of *theism*, the *negative* recognition of God'.[72] And, if he is a theologian, he must ultimately be a reactionary even if he appears to be a radical.

In *The German Ideology*, this charge that Bauer is at heart a theologian focuses on the form of his arguments. For example, Bauer's strategy in the struggle between Feuerbach and Stirner is to present his own position as a higher unity that resolves their differences. But this is to make the Hegelian dialectic into a form of Trinitarian theology: Bauer's resolution is nothing other than the

---

68. Marx and Engels 1845a, pp. 78–143; Marx and Engels 1845b, pp. 82–151. A run of lesser young Hegelians also take a beating for their theological pretensions, such as Edgar Bauer and 'Parson Szeliga' (Marx and Engels 1845a, pp. 61–9, 168–80; Marx and Engels 1845b, pp. 63–72, 178–91).

69. Marx and Engels 1845–6a, pp. 97–116; Marx and Engels 1845–6b, pp. 81–100.

70. See also the comment on Edgar Bauer, Bruno's brother, in Marx and Engels 1845a, p. 34; Marx and Engels 1845b, p. 35. Elsewhere Engels suggests that Bauer and Stirner are the only serious opponents of communism (Engels 1844–5, pp. 240–1).

71. Engels, in the couple of pages he contributed to this section, argues that Bauer is obtuse enough to continue as a theologian despite Feuerbach's devastating criticisms (Marx and Engels 1845a, pp. 93–4; Marx and Engels 1845b, pp. 98–9).

72. Marx and Engels 1845a, p. 110; Marx and Engels 1845b, p. 116.

Holy Spirit.[73] In *The Holy Family* the argument is far more developed: Bauer sucks everything up into theology – whether law, politics, society or philosophy. The result is that Bauer's whole analysis is skewed and often contradictory. Marx, who wrote nearly the whole section on Bauer, throws virtually everything at him: the accusation that he is a sloppy thinker and an élitist; the use of epithets and adjectives to colour the treatment of Bauer's political work; the argument that Bauer is really the caricature and logical extreme of Hegel; the link between idealism and theology; the search for a materialist base to Bauer's idealist categories; and then a direct engagement with Bauer's arguments. All of these dizzying moves turn on the pivot of Bauer's inescapable theology.

The main task of the first few pages of *The Holy Family* is to show that, for all his talk of 'history' and 'the mass', Bauer is an élitist who has little idea of what these terms really mean. According to Marx, Bauer caricatures the 'mass', castigating it for its stupidity and inability to act in history. So Marx takes the opportunity to juxtapose his own position to that of Bauer, or rather what he calls the position of all communist and socialist thinkers. Perhaps because of his élitism, Bauer is also a sloppy thinker.[74] In *The German Ideology*, they accuse him of plagiarising and then misunderstanding what he has just appropriated. It may be Feuerbach, it may be Marx and Engels themselves, it may be Hegel or it may even be Stirner. In *The Holy Family*, they accuse Bauer of either appropriating an idea as his own and throwing it back at the same author as a criticism, or of throwing it at someone else in a way that misses the mark. He takes what is obsolete and assumes it is current and then sets out to refute it by taking what is current and making it out to be a new insight of his own. A similar effect to this charge of sloppy thinking is generated by the mass-epithets and adjectives at Bauer's expense. So we find the text laced with biblical allusions and quotations, invariably used against Bauer in an ironic fashion.[75] 'St. Bruno's' thought ('pure criticism') operates in terms of a

---

73. Marx and Engels 1845–6a, p. 96; Marx and Engels 1845–6b, p. 80.
74. A similar criticism turns up in Marx 1844g, p. 232; Marx 1844h, p. 468.
75. I have discussed these in the chapter on 'The Subterranean Bible', but they begin to appear with far more frequency in the sections that Engels wrote. As a few examples among many: '*Real humanism* has no more dangerous enemy in Germany than *spiritualism* or *speculative idealism*, which substitutes "*self-consciousness*" or the "*spirit*" for the *real individual man* and with the evangelist teaches: "It is the spirit that quickeneth; the flesh profiteth nothing."' (Marx and Engels 1845a, p. 7; Marx and Engels

'heavenly motion' and a 'divine dialectic', he has a 'holy zeal', offers 'Critical prophecy', his 'theological mind' offers the 'latest revelations from the Kingdom of God',[76] and Bauer's journal, the *Literatur-Zeitung*, is the 'Critical Redeemer of the World' and so on.[77] While the effect is to belittle Bauer, much in the style Marx adopted with his early journalism, as well as to hammer home the main point concerning Bauer's inescapable theological perspective, what strikes me is the vast distance that now separates these one-time friends and collaborators.

Further, Marx sets out to show that Bauer is such a faithful disciple of Hegel that he 'chews the old *Hegelian* cud' and 'keeps on warming up a few crumbs dropped by Hegel'.[78] Given that Bauer thought of himself as the creative next step beyond Hegel, the line would no doubt have rankled Bauer (at the least, it certainly would not have repaired their friendship). Marx repeatedly points out that Bauer's categories, like those of Hegel, are *a priori*, abstract and ethereal, out of touch with their material base and, since they are purely theoretical, unable to offer any genuine emancipation. He argues that, like Hegel, Bauer is standing on his head; we need to flip him over and stand him on his feet.[79] In more detail, Marx suggests that Bauer has learnt all too

---

1845b, p. 7) – the quotation is from John 6:63; 'Critical Criticism, however superior to the mass it deems itself, nevertheless has boundless pity for the mass. And Criticism so loved the mass that it sent its only begotten son, that all who believe in him may not be lost, but may have Critical life. Criticism was made mass and dwells amongst us and we behold its glory, the glory of the only begotten son of the father' (Marx and Engels 1845a, p. 9; Marx and Engels 1845b, p. 9) – this time it is the well-known John 3:16 and John 1:14; 'The *world* is a manifestation of the life of self-consciousness which has to *alienate* itself and take on *the form of a slave*, but the difference between the world and self-consciousness is only an *apparent difference*.' (Marx and Engels 1845a, p. 140 – from Philippians 2.)

76. Marx and Engels 1845–6a, p. 98; Marx and Engels 1845–6b, p. 82.

77. Marx and Engels 1845a, pp. 78, 80, 81, 89, 95–6, 98.

78. Marx and Engels 1845a, p. 103; Marx and Engels 1845b, p. 109. Or, as Engels puts it in his short contribution, Bauer has never freed himself from 'the cage of the Hegelian way of viewing things' (Marx and Engels 1845a, p. 92; Marx and Engels 1845b, p. 97). In a lengthy assessment of Bauer's theological works, Marx argues that Bauer does 'not even show any verbal divergence from the Hegelian approach' (Marx 1844g, pp. 326–7; Marx 1844h, pp. 568–9).

79. On Bauer: 'He stands the world *on its head* and can therefore *in his head* also dissolve all limitations, which nevertheless remain in existence *for bad sensuousness*, for *real* man [Er stellt die Welt auf den *Kopf* und kann daher auch im *Kopf* alle Schranken auflösen, wodurch sie natürlich *für die schlechte Sinnlichkeit*, für den *wirklichen* Menschen bestehenbleiben]' (Marx and Engels 1845a, p. 192; Marx and Engels 1845b, p. 204). At about the same time, we also find the following: '(Hegel, who stands every-

well from Hegel the art 'of converting *real objective* chains that exist *outside me* into *merely ideal*, merely *subjective* chains, existing merely *in me* and thus of converting all *external* sensuously perceptible struggles into pure struggles of thought'.[80]

Even more, Bauer reveals the *reduction ad absurdum* of Hegel's own thought. So Marx accuses Bauer of overcoming two of Hegel's hesitancies and in doing so becomes a caricature. Firstly, Hegel argues that even though philosophy is the way in which Absolute Spirit expresses itself, he backs down at the last minute in identifying any one individual as the embodiment of this Spirit. Where Hegel feared to tread, Bauer strides forward in utmost confidence: he is, says Marx, the embodiment of Absolute Spirit, or what he and his close associates call 'Criticism', or what Bauer himself also calls 'infinite self-consciousness'. In other words, Bauer has a huge messiah-complex, for he sees himself as the incarnation of Hegel's Absolute Spirit or his own 'infinite self-consciousness'.[81] Secondly, Hegel would allow the philosopher a rôle only after the fact; Absolute Spirit would become conscious through the philosopher of its world-historical rôle when everything had happened. So the philosopher could reflect only on what was past. Once again, Bauer steps into the breach left open by Hegel: Bauer becomes nothing less than the conscious Absolute Spirit in the act of creating history. As the incarnation of a historically conscious Absolute Spirit, all Bauer need do is think. In other words, he

---

thing on its head, turns the executive power into the representative, into the emanation, of the monarch. Since in speaking of the idea the existence of which is supposed to be the monarch, he has in mind not the real idea of the executive authority, not the executive authority as idea, but the subject of the absolute idea which exists *bodily* in the monarch, the executive authority becomes a *mystical extension of the soul which exists in his body, the body of the monarch*.)' (Marx 1843c, p. 87; Marx 1843d, p. 291). As is well known, Hegel would have the honour of being stood on his feet in *Capital*.

80. Marx and Engels 1845a, pp. 82–3; Marx and Engels 1845b, p. 87.

81. See Marx and Engels 1845a, pp. 142–3; Marx and Engels 1845b, pp. 150–1. The text of *The Holy Family* is full of these types of comments. As a few examples among many: 'just as God is all that *man is not*, *Criticism* bears witness to itself that: "It has achieved a clarity, a thirst for learning, a tranquillity in which it is *unassailable* and *invincible*."' (Marx and Engels 1845a, p. 160; Marx and Engels 1845b, p. 169.); 'In short, the Critic is free from all *human passions*, he is a *divine person*...Critical Criticism has at last succeeded in achieving its *solitary, god-like, self-sufficient, absolute* existence...as a second triumphant *Christ* [can] accomplish the *Critical last judgment* and after its victory over the dragon ascend calmly to heaven.' (Marx and Engels 1845a, p. 161; Marx and Engels 1845b, pp. 170–1.)

is a caricature of Hegel.[82] I am not quite sure what to make of this argument. Is it a way of saying, in Hegelese, that Bauer is too full of himself? Of course, there are more than a few academics with second-rate minds and first-rate egos who think that they are the greatest stars since Plato. I suspect Marx did not think so of Bauer, for he devotes immense energy to refuting him at all levels.

More significant is a further feature of Marx's argument against Bauer, namely that idealism and theology are the same thing, or, as Marx prefers to put it, that speculative, idealist thinking is really theology in disguise. In its simplest form, the argument is that Bauer brings out the truth of Hegel. Or, in more detail: Bauer seeks to develop Hegel for use in his own fields of theology and New Testament criticism. The catch is that this effort is like bringing coals to Newcastle, for Hegel merely provides a speculative shape to what are really still theological concepts and modes of arguing. Bauer throws this facet of Hegel into sharp relief. All of the comments concerning the ethereal, abstract nature of both Bauer's and Hegel's thought tend in this direction, as do those that suggest they are out of touch with reality. Above all, Marx argues that the very terms Bauer uses in his dialectic – 'spirit' and 'mass' – are really caricatures of Hegel's theory of history, for whom they were speculative forms for God and matter. We have completed a full circle: Hegel's idealism is secularised theology; Bauer seeks to apply Hegel's idealism to theology.

I have already slipped into the next criticism of Bauer, which is the search for a materialist base to Bauer's theological and idealist categories.[83] This is a strategy that Marx would sharpen a little more every time he used it: theology is a form of idealism, which is hopelessly out of touch with a material basis, which in turn can explain that idealism and therefore leave it high and dry. But let us follow Marx's steps: he builds on the argument that Bauer is an abstract, theological thinker, but now he goes further. The problem is not merely that Bauer is too Hegelian, that he favours empty categories such as 'spirit', 'progress' or even 'mass', or that he generates speculative oppositions

82. 'Finally, it goes without saying that whereas Hegel's *Phänomenologie*, in spite of its speculative original sin, gives in many instances the elements of a true description of human relations, Herr Bruno and Co., on the other hand, provide only an empty caricature' (Marx and Engels 1845a, p. 193; Marx and Engels 1845b, p. 205). See also Engels 1846c, p. 642; Engels 1846d, p. 607.
83. The next two paragraphs are a critical exegesis on the important pages 83–4 of Marx and Engels 1845a, pp. 83–5; Marx and Engels 1845b, pp. 87–9.

such as 'spirit' and 'mass', but that he does not bother to ask what the material basis of 'spirit' or 'progress' or 'mass' might be. After all, that basis belongs to the real world which 'is excluded as being the *un-Critical hell*' in contrast to the 'Critical heaven' of this society.[84] At this point, Marx makes an astute move: for a moment, he grants Bauer's opposition of 'spirit' and 'mass', positions Bauer clearly with the 'spirit' and then takes up the position of the 'mass'. He will not stay with the opposition for long, but what it enables him to do is set himself up in direct contrast to Bauer.

But, now, he moves on beyond this opposition: Marx grasps Bauer's terms and gives them a communist twist. Here, he makes a move repeated again and again throughout his work: any point in communist-theoretical work has an organic connection with the workers' movement. In this case, he cites Fourier and Owen to show that progress is entirely abstract and inadequate (so much for Marx as a thinker of progress!), indeed that the progress of Spirit has led to even greater misery for the mass of humanity. But, then, he connects these arguments to the experiences of the workers' movement, the real 'mass' rather than the abstract entity favoured by Bauer. Now, while this is a good materialist response to Bauer – investigating the source of idealist terms in their materialist base – I cannot help but sense that Marx too has idealised the real 'great mass' in his effort to characterise the workers as studious, craving knowledge, full of moral energy and desire for development. It is good propaganda and much needed in the élite-ranks of German intellectual life (nothing much has changed), and also needed to counter Bauer's characterisation of the 'mass' as the embodiment of indolence, superficiality and self-complacency, but it runs the risk of coming closer to Bauer than Marx would have liked.

This search for a materialist base signals a shift in Marx's criticism of Bauer, for now he is coming to grips with Bauer's arguments. Marx has tried to locate himself within organic, working-class politics while characterising Bauer as hopelessly lost in the speculative Hegelian heaven. What has happened to Bauer the radical political commentator, to Bauer the democrat and ideologue of republican politics? Marx has conveniently boxed him into the idealist and theological corner of Spirit. Yet he still has to deal with the fact that Bauer

---

84. Marx and Engels 1845a, p. 98; Marx and Engels 1845b, p. 103. See also the point that Bauer 'separates history from natural science and industry and sees the origin of history not in vulgar *material* production on the earth but in vaporous clouds in the heavens.' (Marx and Engels 1845a, p. 150; Marx and Engels 1845b, p. 159.)

spends a good deal of time discussing domestic and international politics, was a keen observer of historical events and was never afraid to draw the consequences.[85] He squarely faces up to Bauer's arguments and tries to pick him off in different ways. First, since Bauer's politics is really theology, it means that he has the equation wrong: it is not that theology is the core in relation to which everything else is secondary (politics, social questions, and economics), but that theology is in fact camouflage for social and political questions. It is the shell that needs to be cracked open and discarded so that the kernel may be revealed. Once you have done this, you can get your teeth into the real, social and political issues.[86]

Second, he pursues a number of variations on the basic idea that the gap between Bauer and the crowd cannot be bridged no matter how hard he tries. So Marx traces the way Bauer tries (vainly for Marx) to abolish the gap, to explain how he became engaged in politics, how he blames the masses for misunderstanding his support, admits that he may have been incomprehensible and unnoticeable and therefore unable to be understood by the mass, suggests it is a temporary breach, and tries to sympathise with and take the mass seriously. All of these Marx tries to shoot down: 'In its involvement with the prejudices of the Mass, Criticism was not *really* involved in *them*'.[87] It really is an all-out effort to put a huge wedge between Bauer and radical politics.

Third, Marx repeats an argument he first made in *On the Jewish Question*: he counters Bauer's arguments concerning religion and the state.[88] Against Bauer's wish that the state should abolish religion as a condition for full emancipation, Marx replies that the liberal state and the rights of man allow freedom of worship. Against Bauer's argument that the removal of privilege for religion is equivalent to the abolition of religion (for it would not survive), Marx points out that such removal is actually the condition for the flowering of religion. Marx goes on to argue that the modern, liberal state has only arrived when it declares religion not to be a public, political matter but a private one into which it will not pry. I have discussed these arguments earlier

---

85. See Bauer 1847–50, 1964, 1965, 1969a, 1969b, 1969c, 1970, 1846b, 1972a and 1972b. Marx long continued to respond to Bauer's commentary on international political matters – see Marx 1857a.

86. See especially Marx and Engels 1845a, pp. 108–9; Marx and Engels 1845b, pp. 114–15.

87. Marx and Engels 1845a, p. 102; Marx and Engels 1845b, p. 108.

88. Marx and Engels 1845a, pp. 110–18; Marx and Engels 1845b, pp. 116–25.

(they still stand, it seems to me, even if they have not been realised in full even now), but we should note here that Marx must at last come to grips with Bauer's actual arguments. It is a tacit recognition that they do have some substance, that Bauer may well represent an alternative position with which he must struggle.

Conclusion

In wrapping up, let me elaborate on a couple of items that are important for the larger theological context of my discussion. To begin with, Bauer was one of the means by which Marx came to terms with Hegel, for Bauer was recognised as a leading proponent of Hegelian thought. What was taking place, I suggest, is that Marx wanted to cut down Bauer's take on Hegel, argue that it was a travesty of Hegel and claim that towering yet ambiguous figure for himself. And it was not as though Bauer represented a mainstream-position, comfortably ensconced in a cushy university-professorship. No, Hegel was out of favour, a reactionary Schelling had been brought to Berlin to counter the Hegelian influence, and Bauer suffered as a result. What was at issue, then, was an out-of-favour mode of thought over which Bauer and Marx struggled for their radical credentials.

Above all, the repeated criticism of Bauer is that 'even the *critical* theologian remains a *theologian*'.[89] This is the unforgivable sin against the Holy Spirit. But why is it such a problem to remain a theologian? Instead of repeating the myriad forms of Marx's response found in his various texts on Bauer, let me turn to the *Economic and Philosophic Manuscripts of 1844*. Here, Marx accuses theology of being inescapably abstract, authoritarian, living in the past, and of being 'philosophy's spot of infection'.[90]

On the first point – theology is unavoidably abstract – we can see Marx turning Bauer's position on theology against him. Through his studies on the Gospels, Bauer had come to conclude that Christianity was a hubristic universal, a claim by a particular group to have exclusive access to the universal. In the process, it alienated self-consciousness by abstracting it and placing it in the heavens instead of realising that it is within human beings. If this is the

---

89. Marx 1844g, p. 232; Marx 1844h, p. 468.
90. Marx 1844g, p. 233; Marx 1844h, p. 469.

case, and if the Christian churches are brutal and intolerant institutions, then the discipline of theology itself is suspect and must be discarded. Not so with Bauer, argues Marx, for he still plays the theological game.

In other words, theology itself is an act of estrangement or abstraction from real, sensuous human beings. Understood in this sense, theology cannot be anything other than an affair of the head and of imagination, in short, of heaven. As Marx developed his own approach, which took its stand with flesh-and-blood human beings here on earth, he came to feel that any position that based itself on theology was hopelessly lost. It traded in abstraction, was aloof and arrogant, and had absolute disdain for the masses; it had no interest in people as they actually lived their lives; it preferred to withdraw into itself and become 'pure' criticism.[91] In short, because theology is abstract, alienated and concerned with heaven, anyone who bases her thought on theology will suffer the same fate.

Further, Marx suggests that theology must accept certain presuppositions as authoritative. We can readily roll out the list: belief in God, in Jesus Christ as the son of God, in Christ's rôle in redemption, in the fact that all good comes from God, and so on. But Marx's point is a little more subtle, for Bauer uses the same approach to philosophy: here too he accepts certain philosophical positions as fixed in stone. It is, to borrow St Anselm's phrase, *fidens quaerens intellectum*, but now with a subservient bow to philosophy.

At one level, Marx's description of theology's underlying subservience to authority is true enough, but, unfortunately for Marx, Bauer is not such a theologian. The tense relationships between the churches and their ideologues, the theologians, are fraught with tensions as the churches have sought to keep them on the straight and narrow path.[92] But this is small-minded theology, not capable of standing on its own legs and walking boldly where it needs and wishes to go. What we have in Bauer's case is anything but a timid and cowering theology, for here is a robust theologian who strode confidently into whatever conclusion his research led him. Even Marx admits that Bauer was willing to overturn any and all of the givens of theology.

---

91. Marx 1844q, p. 356; Marx 1844r, p. 427.
92. I can vouch for that, since when I once taught in a theological college they flayed me again and again for the type of teaching and writing I did.

Bauer, then, was by no means a conventional biblical scholar and theologian, one who would explore the minutiæ of textual variants or the history of theology in order to bolster the church and support the faithful. He was a radical scholar, ending up as a proponent of atheism through biblical study and marking the beginning of a century of global dominance of German biblical scholarship. The reason why Marx keeps returning to Bauer is that Bauer was able to develop a radical position *through the Bible and theology*. For Marx, this was anathema, especially in light of Bauer's own arguments regarding the Bible and theology. He might admit that religion is a protest against suffering, or the heart of a heartless world, but it was certainly not going to offer any practical changes for that heartless and soulless world. Marx felt that Bauer (and Feuerbach, as we will see) had put an end to the viability of anything remotely religious; the task now was to get on with analysing and changing the world of which religion was the twisted expression. He never tires of pointing out that Bauer 'remains a theologian'[93] and that this is the source of his shortcomings. By contrast, Bauer developed an increasingly radical position by means of his theological work. His atheism, polemic against theological dogmatism and narrowness, radical republicanism, democratic tendencies and argument that Christianity was a revolutionary challenge to the Greco-Roman world and provided liberation for the excluded and oppressed elements of that world – all of these grew out of his militant biblical research.

On top of all this, Marx argues that theology lives in the past. This criticism has various shapes: it may be that Bauer's critical theology has not really advanced past Hegel, so that it is nothing more than 'the old *philosophical*, and especially the *Hegelian, transcendentalism*, twisted into a *theological caricature*'.[94] Or it may be that it has not yet settled its accounts with German philosophy and Hegel, from which any worthwhile criticism has emerged as if from some primeval swamp. The bottom line for Marx is that theology has been superseded, as Bauer's own work on the Bible shows. The new age of criticism has begun in a dialectical leap forward, so anyone who still plies the theological trade must by definition be locked into the past. For Marx, the post-theological world has already begun and Bauer has missed the opening ceremony.

---

93. Marx 1844g, p. 232; Marx 1844h, p. 468.
94. Ibid.

Finally, there is the wonderful phrase, 'philosophy's spot of infection [*der faule Fleck der Philosophie*]'. Marx goes on to describe theology as the 'negative dissolution of philosophy' or the 'process of its decay [*Verfaulungsprozeß*]'.[95] Disease, death, burial and decay are the images here, as though theology is the blight of philosophy, that infection which turns out to be cancer and certain death. Again, this is another way of saying that the moment for theology is past. Anyone who sticks with theology may as well dine with the grim reaper. But the images also say more than that: the long and difficult relationship between theology and philosophy, which began when the early theologians brought the tradition of Greek philosophy into contact with the stories of the Bible and especially those of Jesus of Nazareth, has been fatally flawed from the beginning. This is a much gloomier picture of philosophy, one in which philosophy has been hobbled almost from the beginning. The only answer, then, is to discard theology, and therefore Bauer's thought.

Now, all of these are the explicit reasons why Marx cannot see anything valuable in Bauer's critical theology. The crucial problem is that Bauer was able to attain some radical positions through his theological and biblical work. For Marx, this was simply unacceptable. He and Engels were fighting daily battles against the theologically-inspired socialists such as Weitling, who argued that Jesus was the first socialist and who was no better than the air-headed utopian socialists. Even more, Marx had already closed off that path to any sort of radical analysis and action. Bauer's effort to continue to pursue such a path had to be blocked.

Yet there is one telling moment, a slip, in *The Holy Family* where Marx threatens to undo all of his hard work. In all these obscure struggles with Bauer, there is an extraordinarily important sentence that jumps out: 'See by what a complicated detour Absolute Criticism arrives at the present historical movement – namely by the *detour of theology* [*Umwege der Theologie*]'.[96] That phrase – the detour of theology – sums up how Marx (and to a lesser extent Engels) wants to trump Bauer. But it is a slip of Freudian proportions: what Marx is trying to say is that the materialist and even communist categories of analysis and action do not arise from theology, indeed that theology travels in the opposite direction. Theology is not even a crucial stage in their develop-

95. Ibid.
96. Marx and Engels 1845a, p. 98; Marx and Engels 1845b, p. 104.

ment; it is a detour, a side-road used while the main road is being repaired. You, Marx says to Bauer, represent that detour and your problem is that you think the detour is the main road. But now Marx says too much, for a detour is not a dead-end, for it actually connects one from point-of-origin to the end of the journey by another path. It may not be the road chosen by all, especially those who want to get to the destination as quickly as possible, but it will still get you there even if it does wind its way through the hills. Without doing the metaphor to death, I suggest that Marx unwittingly recognises that Bauer's path to radical politics may well be a valid one, if somewhat circuitous.

Like any marriage, the relationship with Bauer was long, complex and troubled. Running through from those early days in Berlin to the sustained polemic of *The Holy Family* and *The German Ideology*, one does not have to be the most astute sleuth to discover that the friendship was not what is used to be. Yet, despite this sea of polemical ink, it does not seem to have severed all ties. I can still recall my surprise when I read in a letter from Marx to Engels on 14 December 1855 that Bruno had been in London for a visit. Marx's own surprise shows through: 'The day before yesterday evening I had a visit, you'll never guess from whom. Edgar Bauer – whom I hadn't seen for about a year – came to see me, and with him – Bruno'.[97] Over the next year or so, we find comments that Marx and Bruno Bauer continued to meet while the latter was in London.[98] Even until the end his life, Marx cannot help himself, commenting on Bauer's latest antics, his characteristic turns of phrase and even his writings.[99] In early January of 1857, Marx heard that Bauer had finally bought some land outside Berlin and wanted to farm it.[100] Marx thinks he is crazy, but Bauer seems to have survived better than Marx himself.

---

97. Marx 1855nn, p. 562; Marx 1855oo, p. 466.
98. Marx 1856d, p. 4; Marx 1856e, p. 6; Marx 1856f, p. 11; Marx 1856g, p. 15.
99. Marx 1859e, p. 403; Marx 1859f, p. 411. Engels 1856a, p. 7; Engels 1856b, p. 10. Marx 1856l, p. 68; Marx 1856m, p. 72. Marx 1857l, p. 127; Marx 1857m, p. 131; Marx 1859g, p. 453; Marx 1859h, p. 445; Marx 1882e, p. 339; Marx 1882f, p. 100; Marx 1869p, p. 343; Marx 1869q, p. 360; Marx 1868b, p. 549; Marx 1868c, p. 44.
100. Marx 1857h, pp. 90–1; Marx 1857i, pp. 93–4. Although Marx expresses concern over Bauer's misfortunes, he dismisses Bauer's farming venture in the 'miserable hole' of Rixdorf (Marx 1861i, p. 288; Marx 1861j, p. 167).

Chapter Four

Against the Theological Hegelians II: Max Stirner and the Lever of History

> I knew Stirner well and we were on *Du* terms; he
> was a good sort, not nearly as bad as he makes
> himself out to be in his *Einzige*...[1]

The sprawling chapter on Max Stirner (a pseud-
onym for Kaspar Schmidt) is the engine-room of *The
German Ideology*. The reason: in response to Stirner's
effort to reinterpret world-history in light of the
ego, Marx and Engels gradually build up their own
historical-materialist schema. So why would I be
interested in spending time in this endless and often
tedious section? It is because the effort to produce a
key to history, to rewrite the whole of history in that
light, is analogous on a formal level with theological
arguments concerning history.

That claim will take some substantiating, but I
have the rest of the chapter in which to do so. Let
me outline my answer briefly before laying it out in
more detail. There were a number of questions that
kept prodding me as I laboured my way through
the hundreds of pages on Stirner: why is this chapter soaked in biblical references and theological satire? Indeed, why is the whole section structured in
terms of the Bible? And why is this canonical biblical

---

1. Engels 1889d, p. 393; Engels 1889e, p. 292.

structure overlaid with a mock imitation of the structure of Stirner's book. On a more general level, it is a question that applies to the whole of *The German Ideology*: if that work is such a crucial text in marking the first clear statement of Marx and Engels's historical materialism, then why is it so full of theology?

The answers to these questions lie in the overlaps between Hegel, Stirner, Marx and Engels, and the Bible. The chapter is structured in terms of the Bible, from Old Testament to New Testament, from Genesis to Revelation. Now, the canonical structure of the Bible has a coherence about it that shows the hand of the last editors, namely those responsible for the canonical ordering of the books of the Bible (the very last of these, working on the New Testament, completed their task in the fourth century CE). It offers nothing less than a story that moves from the creation of the world to the end of history. And it is a canonical ordering that has locked itself into the way we think about the world, an ideological feature of existence that seems almost impossible to dislodge. More specifically, the canonical structure of the Bible is an effort to produce a reasonably coherent narrative of world-history and a theory of the lever of that history.

Does not Hegel also produce such a lever, now understood in terms of the dialectical unfolding of Spirit? And does not Marx charge Hegel with having a barely-concealed theological structure to his thought? In its effort to provide a comprehensive theory of and narrative concerning world-history, Hegel's effort remains part of that vast biblical schema that moves from creation to eschaton. As for Stirner, he attempts a re-reading of world-history in the name of the ego, which now provides an alternative key to that history. Like Bauer's infinite self-consciousness, Stirner's ego is an adaptation of Hegel's world-spirit. With the ego at centre-stage, Stirner offers a loose reconstruction of history in terms of multiple versions of three ages – child-youth-adult, Negro-Mongol-Caucasian, and ancient-modern-ego – all the while spearing opponents who challenge the ego.

So what do Marx and Engels do with all of this? They want to show that, for all his protests, 'Saint Max' is still a Hegelian and that his schema of world-history is therefore deeply theological. For this reason, we find the perpetual biblical texts, usually with an ironic twist, as well as the endless theological references. They want to make sure we do not miss the massive theological stone blocking the entrance. What they set out to do is produce something entirely different: a thoroughly non-theological and materialist theory of history, one that does not depend on a world-spirit, or an infinite self-consciousness or an ego. In many respects, it is, of course, distinct, beginning with the material reality of human existence to build a theory of history. The motor they find – contradiction – is as distinct as the narrative that emerges from it. Yet, at one very deep level, they still share an assumption with Stirner: that it is possible to produce a world-history in the first place. But they also share this with Hegel and with the iconic narrative of the Bible. In other words, for all the difference in content, their alternative world-history arises from and is analogous to this theological form.

In a letter to Marx on 19 November 1844, Engels mentions that he is holding in his hands the specimen-sheets of Stirner's new book from the publisher, Wigand. While outlining the argument of the book and noting suggestions as to what they should do with it, he makes the following comment: 'We must not simply cast it aside, but rather use it as the perfect expression of present-day folly and, *while inverting it*, continue to build on it'.[2] Let us see how they do indeed invert and build on it.

Stirner's ego, or, the lever of history

Towards the end of Stirner's *The Ego and His Own*, there is the following sentence: 'That the individual [*Einzelne*] is of himself a world's history [*Weltgeschichte*], and possesses his property [*Eigentum*] in the rest of world history, goes beyond what is Christian'.[3] This is not a bad summary of what Stirner tries to achieve in this rambling work. To be sure, Stirner rambles, confessing that the book is really an inconsistent collection of his various notes and immediate responses to books and that he has simply gathered them loosely together. But then messy people are not really disorganised; they merely have a different way of organising things. The same applies to Stirner. He organises his text into a number of loose historical stages: child through youth to man; Negro, Mongol and Caucasian; ancients (really the ancient Greeks and Romans), the moderns (roughly from the arrival of Christianity to the struggles between Roman Catholics and Protestants), and then the discovery of the ego in the present

---

2. Engels 1844n, p. 11; Engels 1844o, p. 11.
3. Stirner 2005, p. 365; Stirner 1845, p. 428.

(which boils down to German philosophy in his own time). These various threefold schemas overlap and run into one another. All of this is really the first half of the book – what Marx and Engels dub the 'Old Testament'. The second, called simply 'I', becomes 'New Testament'.

While their response to the 'Old Testament' is largely polemical, by the time they get to the second part, the 'New Testament', Marx and Engels begin to supply more and more constructive comments and suggestions. Part of the reason is that, in this second part, Stirner whirls off diatribes against property, competition, labour and money, precisely those topics where Marx and Engels cannot resort to satire and heavy criticism. Stirner's critiques continue, taking on all manner of topics, such as revolution, love and freedom of the press. Above all, what comes through again and again is a sustained attack on any form the collective might take. It might be the closed-in circle of the family, or the collaborative hold on power by the aristocracy, or the rise in his own time of the party, or indeed the state itself. The list goes on: fatherland, common weal, mankind… No wonder that later, when Stirner's forgotten book was rediscovered, it would be claimed by anarchism as one of its precursors.[4] In this light, it should come as no surprise that Stirner has little time for the communists.

Astonishingly, the liberals too (whether political or humane) suffer in Stirner's hands. The problem, he argues, is that the various liberalisms really retain society and the state. One may argue for responsible citizenship, for the need to respect the rights of one another. Another may say that the state and society are undesirable, but then slips them in the back door anyway. Why? Because the state is needed to ensure that liberal values are upheld. Marx and Engels will seize on these arguments, pointing out that Stirner is in fact the true liberal, for he is a champion of the inviolable private individual.

In all of this, there are a couple of features on which I want to focus. When reading Stirner's book, it becomes quickly obvious that theology is a major topic – not surprising, given the context in German public debate. Most of the time, Stirner points to yet another failing of Christianity, especially when it teaches us how to live with our fellow human beings (in love), but every

---

4. Engels comments in a letter to Max Hildebrand on 22 October 1889: 'Stirner enjoyed a revival thanks to Bakunin…I saw his [Stirner's] wife in this country on one occasion; while here she took up with – *ah que j'aime le militaire!* – ex-Lieutenant Techow and, if I'm not mistaken, accompanied him to Australia.' (Engels 1889d, p. 394; Engels 1889e, p. 293.)

now and then he seeks to appropriate an element for his own project. For example, he claims Christian love for himself. He has little time for the unselfish and sacrificial love preached by Christian theology, love that denies itself for the sake of others. But he does claim a selfish love, one that is his own [*Eigentum*].[5] Here, we glimpse the vision Stirner had for the future of his programme: unlike religious or romantic love, which brutally destroys what it seeks to possess, selfish love is able to love others without seeking to claim anyone, for we are all pure egos. In this way, it can overcome the pain and suffering caused by unselfish love.

Much more significant is his appropriation of the incarnation:

> Christ is the I of the world's history, even of the pre-Christian; in modern apprehension it is man, the figure of Christ has developed into the *figure of man*: man as such, man absolutely, is the 'central point' of history. In 'man' the imaginary beginning returns again; for 'man' is as imaginary as Christ is. 'Man' as the I of world history closes the cycle of Christian apprehensions.[6]

Stirner has neatly identified the logic of Christology, for, in Christ, God becomes a human being. So far, so good, but now it becomes interesting: Christ is not a half-man, half-God, taking on a human body with a divine soul. No, in Christ, God becomes a complete human being. Of course, this is where the logic breaks down, for according to orthodox theology, Christ is also fully divine. But what Stirner does is zero-in on the human dimension – Christ is a man, man as such, man absolutely. This human Christ is what Stirner wants to appropriate for the ego. Further, the complete man known as Jesus Christ is also the 'central point' of history, the pivot on which history turns. What is good enough for Christ is even better for the ego. After all, Christ is the paradigmatic ego.

A few lines later, Stirner tackles the other side of the Christological equation. Christ may have been fully human, but he is also completely God. Human and divine meet in the one person, so Stirner can claim:

> They say of God, 'Names name thee not'. That holds good of me: no *concept* expresses me, nothing that is designated as my essence exhausts me; they are only names. Likewise they say of God that he is perfect and has no calling to strive after perfection. That too holds good of me alone.[7]

---

5. Stirner 2005, pp. 291–2; Stirner 1845, pp. 340–2.
6. Stirner 2005, p. 365; Stirner 1845, p. 427.
7. Stirner 2005, p. 366; Stirner 1845, p. 429.

Christology opens up a two-way street: Christ may have become human, but that means human beings may go in the other direction and become divine. Stirner's ego joins the ride, but with a twist: it is not that the ego wishes to join God or attain God's status. The simple truth is that God has never existed, so when the ego arrives at wherever God is supposed to be, he finds that he is the only one there. That means that, whenever we have been talking about God – his perfection, the inability to name him and so on – we have, in fact, been talking about the individual human being all along.

There are all manner of questions I would to put to Stirner, such as the danger of the personality-cult, since it relies on the logic of Christology.[8] A few too many tyrants and despots (including those elected 'democratically') have made rather similar claims to those made by Stirner. Further, it seems that Marx and Engels's charge that Stirner is still a theologian is correct. For all Stirner's diatribes against Christianity, his thought is still far too theological. But, let me close this discussion of Stirner with the turning point of history. Like Christ, the ego is the lever of history. Here is Stirner again: 'That the individual [*Einzelne*] is of himself a world's history [*Weltgeschichte*], and possesses his property [*Eigentum*] in the rest of world history, goes beyond what is Christian. To the Christian, the world's history is the higher thing, because it is the history of Christ or "man"; to the egoist only his history has value, because he wants to develop only himself'.[9] Not only is the egoist's history the only one that has value, not only is it the principle by which Stirner offers his reinterpretation of the ages of world-history, but he does so in response to the Christian schema of that history whose lever is Christ. However much he may protest, he is playing the same game.

The engine-room of historical materialism

'Whose faith moves all the mountains of world history' – this passing comment is far more than a mere biblical allusion.[10] It pinpoints the underlying feature of the critique of Stirner by Marx and Engels, namely that he offers a reinterpretation of history which is heavily indebted to theology. Not for

---

8. Horkheimer and Adorno 2002, pp. 145–6; Horkheimer and Adorno 2003, pp. 201–3. See also Boer 2007a, pp. 434–5.
9. Stirner 2005, p. 365; Stirner 1845, p. 428.
10. 1 Corinthians 13:2 and Matthew 17:20.

nothing is the label 'theologian' pinned to Stirner's chest. But it is an appropriate label, for he talks about the Bible and Christianity a little too much to avoid it. Even if much of his effort is directed at dispensing with Christianity, we do find the crucial move whereby he appropriates Christology for his own programme. All of this hardly distinguishes 'Saint Max' from 'Saint Bruno'; the same applies to the argument that Stirner is still too beholden to Hegel. But what is distinctive and critically important for my argument is that Stirner dares to produce a new narrative of world-history. The lever (or faith) that will move those vast mountains is, as I have argued above, nothing less than the ego.

As with the criticisms of Bauer, the polemical style dominates one's impression when reading the text. It is as though the style that Marx developed when working on the *Rheinische Zeitung* – in his effort to liven-up public debate, prod at the state-censorship and conservative press, and entertain his readers – flowed over into criticisms of those closer to him politically. In fact, the propensity for sharp language would stay with Marx and, in fact, Engels, showing up every now and then in their later texts. In Stirner's case, they castigate him for his inability to escape from theology. As with the discussion of Bauer, we find the use of myriad epithets and digs. One or two examples will suffice, although they can be found on every one of the hundreds of pages. Alluding to Philippians 2, they write that Stirner's book '*fell* from the heavens towards the end of 1844 and took on the shape of a servant'.[11] In this book, the 'holy author' known as the 'very pious [*recht gläubige*] Saint Max' presents a history of the kingdom of the unique which 'follows a wise plan fixed from eternity'.[12] A little later, they proclaim that 'the holy warrior has now conquered history'.[13]

Further, like the treatment of Bauer, there is a deluge of biblical quotations and allusions. On a page-by-page comparison, there are even more in the section on Stirner. Overall, they run into the hundreds, so I cannot help seeing Engels's hand in this feature of the text. Marx may have known his Bible well enough, but not that well. And if the comparison with some of Engels's other writings is anything to go by (see my discussion in Chapter Nine), he was

---

11. Marx and Engels 1845–6a, p. 116; Marx and Engels 1845–6b, p. 101.
12. Marx and Engels 1845–6a, pp. 123, 130, 134; Marx and Engels 1845–6b, pp. 107, 113, 117.
13. Marx and Engels 1845–6a, p. 191; Marx and Engels 1845–6b, p. 174.

capable of writing a complete text that was a web of biblical phraseology and direct quotations. He seems to have known much of the Bible from memory, a habit that forms when it is read to you regularly from early childhood.

More distinctive about the Stirner chapter is the way in which it is structured like the canonical (*kanon* means 'measure' or 'rule') sequence of the Bible. So we find, as I pointed out earlier, that the first part is called 'The Old Testament: Man' and it includes chapters on 'The Book of Genesis' and 'The Economy of the Old Testament'. Not unexpectedly, the second part is entitled 'The New Testament: Ego' and contains chapters called 'The Economy of the New Testament' and 'The Revelation of John the Divine'. Or, as Marx and Engels put it, the division is between 'the unique history of man (the Law and the Prophets) and the inhuman history of the unique (the Gospel of the Kingdom of God)'.[14] It is of course a very effective way of connecting Stirner at a formal level with the canonical structure of the Bible.

That biblical structure was in its own way the result of an ideological and political struggle which waned and waxed over six or seven centuries (from the third century BCE to the fourth century CE). Although there was a strong element of political control in the various decisions concerning which books were to be included and how they were to be arranged,[15] it is better perhaps to see it in terms of a conflict of ideologies – prophets versus kings, lawgivers versus priests, ruling class versus the disadvantaged, Jew and Greek, law and grace, and so on. Ultimately, these struggles may be understood in terms of

---

14. Marx and Engels 1845–6a, p. 120; Marx and Engels 1845–6b, p. 103.
15. 'The fact is that we do not know why a canon...of religiously authoritative books was created, though we may reasonably assume that its establishment was a political act, intended to create consensus, counter deviance and establish authority' (Davies 1998, p. 182). For a semiotic argument along this line, see Aichele 2001. Reconstructions of the history of the canonisation of the Bible continue to appear at a steady pace. As a sample, see Sundberg 1964, Brettler 1994, Carr 1996, Davies 1998, and Aichele 2001. The status of the debate is covered rather well in McDonald and Sanders (eds.) 2002, but they all operate within certain limits. They oscillate within three oppositions: diversity versus unity, conflict versus consensus, and rupture versus organic or evolutionary development. If you begin from the side of unity and consensus, then the problems arise with diversity and conflict, and vice versa. Often, such reconstructions come up with ingenious and overlapping combinations of these three oppositions, with, for instance, an organic development broken by a rupture or two, or a consensus as the resolution of conflict, or a final unity out of diversity that is yet plagued by diversity. For the Hebrew Bible (Old Testament), the dates vary between the supposed time of Ezra and Nehemiah (sixth century BCE), through the era of the Hasmoneans (third to second century BCE) to the rabbinic efforts in the first centuries of the Common Era. For the New Testament and reordering of the books in the Hebrew Bible by the early Christians, it is generally agreed that the fourth century CE is the *terminus ad quem*.

mode of production and the tensions found therein. In other words, the biblical canon is a product of a dialectical process which enables multiple readings and justifications for conflicting political positions.

One element in these struggles was the search for an overriding narrative into which the disparate biblical books would fit. That narrative had been developing slowly as some books gained authoritative status through community-use, but the final decisions were made only in the fourth and fifth centuries CE. Largely due to continuing disagreements, these final agreements were made at a remarkably late point – three centuries after the New Testament was written and even more after the Hebrew Bible came together – and really only followed in the wake of Constantine's efforts to bring about consensus among the squabbling bishops of the religion he had just decided was to be the religion of the Roman Empire. After Constantine's death, the two ecumenical councils of Carthage in 397 CE and 419 CE placed the final imprimatur on what was to be the canon. Those decisions involved not merely what books were to be accepted or rejected, but also the ordering of the books. Thus, the Hebrew Bible took on the order of the Septuagint (the Greek translation of the Hebrew Bible), beginning with Genesis and finishing with the book of Malachi which promises a redeemer, while the New Testament opens the new age with the four Gospels and then completes the picture with the final battle at the end history and the arrival of the New Jerusalem. I hardly need to point out that this overarching narrative framework within which the various books of the Bible fit has become an inescapably powerful one. I cannot emphasise enough how it is a theological story that moves from the creation of the world to its end and turns on the figure of Christ. This is the narrative that Marx and Engels invoke in their treatment of Stirner.

Before I consider the way Marx and Engels respond with their own narrative, let me make a few comments on the way they criticise Stirner for being beholden to Hegel. Thus they point out that Stirner tries to do what Hegel did, albeit with much less finesse. For example, in dealing with Stirner's phases of Mongol, Christianity (Roman-Catholic and Protestant), and the French Revolution they keep referring him back to Hegel's statements on the same matters.[16] Stirner actually provides a bowdlerised version of Hegel's Absolute Spirit, copying directly here and there, and caricaturing in the process. This

---

16. Marx and Engels 1845–6a, pp. 168–77, 266; Marx and Engels 1845–6b, pp. 151–61, 249.

argument is closely tied in with the criticism that Stirner merely expresses the particular world-view of the petty bourgeoisie, or more specifically the German burgher. All Stirner does is provide an ideology of the individual with no sense of the way social and physical changes affect such an individual. Hegel at least made his individual German burgher 'the servant of the world around him'.[17] Not so Stirner, who abstracts this individual into a solipsistic world of his own, an abstract history of 'ghosts'.[18] In other words, there is no break whatsoever with the tradition of speculative German philosophy or indeed with the theological schema of history that comes with Christianity. No wonder *Don Quixote*, who lived in an imaginary world of his own, entirely divorced from reality, makes regular appearances.

One of the most revealing features of the Stirner section is the way Marx and Engels construct the bits and pieces of their alternative history replete with its lever. As their criticism proceeds they gradually begin to insert more constructive sections. It may be in response to Stirner's comments on property, or money, or labour or competition, but we find increasingly complex and alternative presentations of a materialist approach to these and other matters. The interventions are most persistent in the last hundred pages, where Marx and Engels begin to clarify matters in their own heads.

It is important to note the way in which Marx and Engels edited the work as they proceeded. As the constructive pieces began to take on coherence, they moved some of them in the second draft to the beginning of the manuscript, which is where we now find the first coherent statement of historical materialism. That is, this relatively clear opening statement was actually produced in the workshop known as the chapter on Stirner. So, the tendency of so many readers and commentators to isolate the section on Feuerbach, dismissing the remainder and putting the book down when that section has been read, misses some of the most important material in the whole book. As Fredric Jameson once commented, 'we don't have to go back to Stirner, do we?'. I am afraid that we do.[19]

---

17. Marx and Engels 1845–6a, p. 129; Marx and Engels 1845–6b, p. 112. See also Marx and Engels 1845–6a, pp. 119, 128; Marx and Engels 1845–6b, pp. 102, 111.

18. Although Stirner's spooks and spirits are the trigger for these ghosts, Marx developed a distinct liking for *diese Gespenster*, so much so that Derrida picked this up in his own engagement with Marx (Derrida 1994).

19. Among the scarce literature on Marx and Stirner, see Comstock 1976, pp. 336–8; Thomas 1975; Lobkowicz 1969.

Let us see how Marx and Engels proceed with their constructive responses to Stirner. Early on, they zero-in on the fact that Stirner is trying to present an alternative history, one they feel is not so unique after all. He merely trots out the hoary three-stage idealistic theory of history, although now decked out in new names: it may be child-youth-man, or Negro-Mongol-Caucasian, or indeed (among the Caucasians) ancients-moderns-ego.[20] The problem with this neat schema is that it says nothing about real, everyday history. However, in the early pages of the response to Stirner we find little in the way of an alternative, except for occasional hints that Christianity has no history apart from empirical history, that religion must be explained in terms of material causes and mode of production, or that it 'was not their Christianity that made them vagrants, but their vagrancy that made them Christians'.[21]

We need to wade through many pages of detailed critique of nearly every single one of Stirner's observations and wait until the later stages of the chapter to dig out the more substantial contributions (although not before we come across that favoured metaphor of standing Stirner's ideal history on its feet). Then they begin to appear – at first snippets on the material, economic and relational factors in the 'family', the political factors that led to the collapse of the Roman Empire, the nature of worker-rebellions and of revolutionary communists, the nature of private property, and the Christian dialectic of flesh and desire in relation to food.[22] Apart from one notable exception, to which I will return in a moment, these scattered comments begin to fill out, especially in the section designated 'New Testament'. But then this is where we would expect something to happen, since in the comparable section in his book Stirner covers topics such as competition, revolution and property. It is as though Marx and Engels are getting both wound up and clearer in their own heads about how to respond to Stirner. For example, when they tackle the topic of law, they begin to weave in more and more materialist replies into their argument with Stirner. And then, at certain moments, there is need for a larger comment on law, which ends up being a brief history full of modes of

---

20. See the detailed table with its many overlaps in Marx and Engels 1845–6a, pp. 131–4; Marx and Engels 1845–6b, pp. 114–17.

21. Marx and Engels 1845–6a, p. 136; Marx and Engels 1845–6b, p. 120.

22. Marx and Engels 1845–6a, pp. 180–1, 187–8, 220, 226–7, 230–1, 247, 254–5; Marx and Engels 1845–6b, pp. 163–5, 170–1, 201, 207–8, 211–13, 229, 237–8.

production, class, economics and politics.[23] Before long, this practice becomes standard: in the context of their materialist critique of Stirner, we find ever more expansive explanations. One after another, they tumble out: crime, society, private property, competition, revolution, labour, money, exploitation, class, contradiction, as well as language, railways and food. In a sense, Stirner has forced this out of them, for they cannot abide the way he deals with these matters and need to come up with something coherent in reply.

It would be a little tedious to go through each topic in detail (the reader may well be driven to stubbing cigarettes out on her arm just to stay awake), so let me focus on the most important ones: exploitation, class, and contradiction. Stirner's treatment of 'usefulness' is the trigger for a full-blooded discussion of exploitation.[24] Marx and Engels point out that Stirner is deluded if he thinks his theory is at all new. For Stirner, 'usefulness' is the only way human beings actually relate to one another: you, as an object, may be useful to me or you may not. Marx and Engels leap in and point out that this theory of mutual exploitation has a decent pedigree. But the theory does not appear in a vacuum, the product of pure speculation. No, it comes into its own with the growth of the bourgeoisie and commercial social relations. Before spinning out the historical narrative of how the theory of exploitation grew in relation to the bourgeoisie and the spread of capitalism, Marx (for it really is his section) outlines the way in which the theory first came to life.

In this birth of the theory of exploitation there is a dual process: abstraction and reduction. The theory of utilitarian or exploitative relations is in fact an abstraction. It may appear like an actual relation, but it is already a second-order activity, for primary are the social relations between people. From these relations, one abstracts the idea and gives it the name of exploitation. Once you have the category, you can then begin to fill it with the content of the actual concrete relations between people so that it appears to be a real thing, an actual relation. As for reduction, the theory of exploitation brings the multiform relations between people and forces upon them the straightjacket of a single universal relation. All relations hitherto – bond and free, serf and lord, patrons and client, parents and children – are now explained in terms of utili-

---

23. Marx and Engels 1845–6a, pp. 328–30, 335–6; Marx and Engels 1845–6b, pp. 311–13, 318–19.
24. Marx and Engels 1845–6a, pp. 408–14; Marx and Engels 1845–6b, pp. 393–9.

sation or exploitation. Above all, it becomes an ideological position, a bold programme for the bourgeoisie in its long campaign against feudalism.

With the mechanism described, Marx can go on to track the way the theory of exploitation grew in relation to the bumpy ride of the bourgeoisie. He tracks his way through Hegel, Hobbes, Locke, Helvétius, d'Holbach, Bentham and Mill, contrasts the situations in Germany, France and England, identifies the importance of the French Revolution and Dutch mercantile expansion – all in order to show how the theory gradually filled up with content. While the English gave it a particular economic content, the French were able to universalise the theory so that it could absorb all other forms of social relations. Everything was subordinated to this one overriding universal economic concept and at the same time political economy became a distinct science. This process took place as the bourgeoisie presented itself no longer as a particular class, but as the universal class which determined all others. When it had achieved this status, the abstract and universalising theory became an explanation and apology for the capitalist relations which were spreading their roots rapidly throughout Europe.

All I have been doing is expositing Marx for a few moments, but, now, I would like to pick out a particular feature of the explanation of exploitation, namely the way in which Marx connects it, in a brilliant deployment of dialectical thinking, with a distinct class, the bourgeoisie.[25] In other words, this narrative of the rise of theory could not happen without the assumption of class. One may object that this is as much an abstraction as exploitation (as it indeed is), but it serves Marx again and again in these explanatory sections. For example, it works brilliantly in dealing with the way personal and distinctly individual interests develop into the common and general interests of a class.[26] Here, Stirner finds himself dragged, kicking and screaming, into a class-situation. But Marx forestalls his protests by pointing out that this class-connection takes place against the will of individuals. What we have here, he says, is a contradiction between individual and collective interests. Stirner may think he is a pure ego, independent of any class (against which he keeps

---

25. The first substantial analysis of class comes with the comparison between the rise of the bourgeoisie in France and England, followed by a comparison with the proverbial backwardness of German development (Marx and Engels 1845–6a, pp. 193–7; Marx and Engels 1845–6b, pp. 176–80).
26. Marx and Engels 1845–6a, pp. 245–6; Marx and Engels 1845–6b, pp. 227–9.

protesting), but he cannot avoid the fact that his individual interests are in fact characteristic of a whole class, the petty bourgeoisie. Now Marx makes a virtue of his invocation of abstraction, for class is an objectifying and estranging entity that stands over individuals. The explanation for the contradiction may be found in the nature of production: this mode of production is the primary context in which individuals and classes must operate. Even more, in relation to that mode of production the beliefs and protestations of an individual are secondary, imaginary matters. However, this crude argument will not do, for one cannot merely expel the beliefs of an individual as mere ephemera. So Marx suggests that the contradiction between individual and class is but an expression of a deeper contradiction in the mode of production, and that is nothing other than the division of labour. At this point, we must turn back to the full exposition of the division of labour in the chapter on Feuerbach, to where it was moved from the Stirner chapter.

As another example, let me pick up on Marx's later comments on class within a mode of production.[27] Distinguishing between the revolutionary 'vocation' of the oppressed class and the dominating vocation of the ruling class, which tries to impose its ideology on the proletarians, Marx identifies a basic contradiction – that between the bourgeoisie and the proletariat. In other words, contradiction is really an issue of class, which itself arises from the conditions of production. How does this work? A little earlier,[28] Marx describes a proletarian who needs to work 14 hours a day even to survive; he is thereby reduced to a beast of burden, or, even worse, to an article of trade or even a thing. Opposed to this proletarian is a bourgeois who believes that the particular task of domination of the proletarian is in fact a universal human task. In response, the proletarian has, given his circumstances, no option but to revolutionise his own conditions and overthrow the bourgeoisie. Or, as Marx puts it, when 'the bourgeois tells the proletarian that his, the proletarian's, human task is to work fourteen hours a day, the proletarian is quite justified in replying in the same language that on the contrary his task is to overthrow the entire bourgeois system'.[29]

---

27. Marx and Engels 1845–6a, pp. 418–20; Marx and Engels 1845–6b, pp. 403–5.
28. Marx and Engels 1845–6a, pp. 289–90; Marx and Engels 1845–6b, pp. 270–1.
29. Marx and Engels 1845–6a, p. 290; Marx and Engels 1845–6b, p. 271.

What we have is a basic dynamic of class-identity and conflict, one that operates according to a fundamental contradiction which can only lead to a revolutionary-communist position. We are close to that elusive lever of history. But which one is it, class or contradiction? While this may seem like a false dichotomy – the two are inseparable, in one sense – contradiction also works at a more fundamental level. Towards the close of the section on Stirner, Marx finally lays the explanation out before us.[30] Within productive forces there exists a contradiction, one that is based on the insufficiency of those productive forces. That insufficiency meant that a few who were able to satisfy their needs gained control of the limited productive forces while the rest fell under their sway. Inevitably, this tension, or the desire of the oppressed class to satisfy its needs, led to the overthrow of a narrow-minded ruling class that could not see the problem. Marx again: 'Thus, society has hitherto always developed from within the framework of a contradiction – in antiquity the contradiction between free men and slaves, in the middle ages that between nobility and serfs, in modern times between the bourgeoisie and the proletariat'.[31] No-one will miss the echo of the opening lines of *The Manifesto of the Communist Party*.

Here we have the new pivot of history – contradiction within the mode of production. Of course, that contradiction is all too well known, but I cannot stress enough how it emerges in some detail in this lengthy engagement with Stirner. A more systematic account of the division of labour, class, class-conflict and the contradiction at the heart of all modes of production appears in the first section on Feuerbach, but only, as I pointed out earlier, because Marx and Engels pieced that account together from the struggle with Stirner. What are now Sections III and IV of the initial chapter on Feuerbach originally emerged from the treatment of Stirner.[32] They now form part of that famous first statement of historical materialism.

Yet, if we look at those final two sections of the Feuerbach chapter, it soon becomes clear that Marx and Engels present nothing less than the history of the world. The topics run through division of labour (between the sexes, material and mental, town and country and then, with greater and greater

---

30. Marx and Engels 1845–6a, pp. 431–2; Marx and Engels 1845–6b, pp. 417–18.
31. Marx and Engels 1845–6a, p. 432; Marx and Engels 1845–6b, p. 417.
32. Marx and Engels 1845–6a, pp. 59–93; Marx and Engels 1845–6b, pp. 46–77.

complexity, in commerce and industry), private property, ideology (the 'rul-ing ideas'-statement), individual and society (the legacy of Stirner is very clear on this matter), state, law, class and class-conflict. But, above all, the theme of contradiction runs through nearly of this discussion like a bass-rhythm. It becomes that Archimedean point by which history shifts from one epoch to the other, or, as Marx and Engels put it, the contradiction between productive forces and 'form of intercourse' (it would become 'relations of production') reaches a crisis that is nothing other than revolution. This is the answer to Stirner's own lever of history.

Conclusion

The entanglement with Stirner really is the engine-room of the emerging historical-materialist method. In that room, we find the first rough artefacts that would be shaped, filed and polished as time went on. However, when I began this chapter I made the bold statement that the construction by Marx and Engels of a new historical narrative based on a crucial lever – contradic-tion within the modes of production – is analogous on a formal level with theology. The content may be different, the way that history is told from a materialist perspective may be different, even the lever itself may be novel, but the form is analogous.

This observation requires some attention, not least because it remains a contentious issue between Marxists and their bourgeois and apostate-Marxist critics. I will also return to this formal connection at later moments in this book, so it is worthwhile dealing with it here. To begin with, let me sum up my argument. In the Bible, we find the deeply influential ideological con-struct of a narrative that moves from creation to the end of history, turning on the figure of Christ. Stirner protests against that narrative and produces his own version, moving through different and overlapping phases of history by means of his own key, the ego, which is extrapolated from Christ. Marx and Engels subject Stirner to critique, accusing him of being all too Hegelian and theological, and come up with an alternative, a history periodised in terms of modes of production and one that pivots in its turn on the contradictions within those modes of production, contradictions that manifest themselves as class-conflict and revolution.

What is the relation between these narratives? At the risk of stating the obvious, the one developed by Marx and Engels differs widely in terms of content. Still, it is necessary to make this point, since there are still too many uninformed observations that Marx and Engels merely secularise the content of a Jewish and/or Christian narrative – the proletariat is the saviour which will lead us from our fallen state into an eschatological one of paradise. Or perhaps the course of history is seen as a preordained process with the classless communist society as a type of eschatology.

As I argue elsewhere in this book, there is no appropriation of content, even if secularised. But there is a formal relation between these constructions of history. Yet precisely what that formal relation might be requires some careful distinctions. It may be understood as a simple appropriation: Marx and Engels simply go about applying Stirner's (and thereby Hegel's, and ultimately that of the Bible) in a new way. The problem with this suggestion is that it hardly makes sense of the intense and sustained polemic against Stirner. They quite obviously set themselves against Stirner and, in the process, produce the initial pieces of a very different approach to history.

An advance on simple appropriation is that the form of Marx and Engels's approach is 'grafted' from a theological approach, or that it operates in 'parallel' or 'analogous' fashion.[33] Strictly speaking, 'grafting' suggests a direct connection, a blending in which a new fruit is produced. By contrast, a parallel or analogous approach does not necessarily assume such a connection. The constructions of history may have comparable formal features, but there is no need to assume some form of influence or borrowing.[34] However, those who use terms such as 'parallel' or 'analogous' do assume a degree of influence, but that Marx's use of such a form is quite creative and distinct.

In other words, Marx thoroughly transforms the form of historical narrative found in Stirner and even the Bible in a new direction. For this reason, I would rather speak of the *formal crucible* provided by Stirner. That lengthy and intense engagement brought Marx, and Engels after him, to formulate a radically different approach, but it was one that took place through the critique of Stirner. Or, to use a different image, Stirner and his theological-historical schema is the scaffolding that Marx and Engels use to construct their own approach, but when they are done, they can pull it apart and leave it aside.

---

33. These terms are taken from Kouvelakis 2003, p. 189, and Leopold 2007, pp. 142–3, albeit in discussions of Feuerbach where this issue is inescapable.
34. Michael Löwy's 'elective affinity' would also fit into this category. See Löwy 1992, as well as my treatment in Boer 2011, pp. 159–200.

Chapter Five

Against the Theological Hegelians III:
Ludwig Feuerbach's Inversion

> In these writings you have provided...a philo-
> sophical basis for socialism.[1]

Bauer and Stirner may have come in for unrelenting
criticism; not so Ludwig Feuerbach. The reason lies
in what has been called 'transformative criticism',[2]
although since it was mediated to Marx via Feuerbach, I prefer the more specific 'Feuerbachian inversion': the argument that what appear to be the gods
and religion are, in fact, projections made by human
beings. Marx especially took this move and adapted
it for his own use. He applied it to idealist philosophy in general and Hegel in particular, any ideas or
concepts that claimed prior status (as we saw with
Stirner), and of course economics. He also took it a
step further, pointing out that Feuerbach had only
laid the groundwork. What is really needed is an
analysis of this real, human world in order to understand why such projections were made in the first
place. Now all of this is rather well known, not least
because the *Theses on Feuerbach* are among the best
known and most easily digestible of Marx's texts.

---

1. Marx 1844q, p. 354; Marx 1844r, p. 425.
2. For a brief account of the longer trajectory – passing from Aristotle, through
Galileo and to Kant – of this transformative criticism, see Leopold 2007, p. 84.

However, there is one fact about the Feuerbachian inversion that is neglected all too often: it is, at heart, a theological argument. Feuerbach sets out to improve Christianity, which is already the most advanced religion, by revealing its truth.[3] Using this new idea, he explores the full range of theology and practice from creation to immortality, drawing upon unlikely subjects such as celibacy and miracles. All of them end up being distorted expressions of human hopes and aspirations. With this inversion, Feuerbach felt he was able to clear up the murky and confused nature of theology.

Inversion

So what exactly did Feuerbach argue? Religion, or rather Christianity, is actually the projection or abstraction of human subjectivity. It takes what is best in human beings only to hypostatise all those features into an entity or force that is exterior to human beings. That entity becomes a figure, a 'god' who appears to human beings as a being in his own right, one that returns, loves, saves and directs human life through providence. As Feuerbach puts it, theology is actually anthropology: 'the divine being is nothing else than the human being, or, rather, the human nature purified, freed from the limits of the individual man, made objective – i.e., contemplated and revered as another, a distinct being'.[4] One way of putting it is that religion is an expression of the unrealised wishes of self-transcendence that each human being harbours, that we have not quite realised our full potential. With this definition in place, Feuerbach shows how it illuminates one theological topic after another: wisdom, moral being, love, suffering, the Trinity, logos, cosmogony, providence, creation, prayer, faith, resurrection, heaven and, lastly and appropriately, immortality, which is the perfection of unlimited personality. In short, 'the fundamental dogmas of

---

3. On this matter Engels is correct: 'He [Feuerbach] by no means wishes to abolish religion; he wants to perfect it.' (Engels 1886a, p. 374; Engels 1886b, p. 283.) Of course, for Engels this is a sign of Feuerbach's abiding idealism.

4. Feuerbach 1989, p. 14; Feuerbach 1924, p. 18. Similarly, 'In religion man frees himself from the limits of life; he here lets fall what oppresses him, obstructs him, affects him repulsively; God is the self-consciousness of man freed from all discordant elements; man feels himself free, happy, blessed in his religion, because he only here lives the life of genius, and keeps holiday.' (Feuerbach 1989, p. 98; Feuerbach 1924, pp. 121–2; see also Feuerbach 1989, p. 140; Feuerbach 1924, p. 174.) His later work, *The Essence of Religion*, merely extends the insight to all religion and switches the projection from human beings to nature (Feuerbach 2004).

Christianity are realised wishes of the heart'.[5] This, at least, is the argument of the first, positive part of the book. The second part focuses on a series of contradictions that are irresolvable within traditional theology; of course, he claims that his own proposal resolves them. In fact, he suggests that, if one were to read only the second part, the conclusion would be that theology is mere illusion and falsehood. One needs to read the first part too – which is why it is placed first – to see the benefit of theology.

There are a few points I wish to stress in Feuerbach's argument, for they will become important in Marx's analysis. To begin with, the controversial genius of Feuerbach's argument is that we do not realise what is going on. We may think that God is a more powerful and eternal being who creates us and guides our lives, but that assumption only moves from God to ourselves. There is a prior step, namely the projection of the divine from our own subjectivity. So there are in fact three stages: the projection of religion and God by human beings; the assumption that this being is superior to us and that we are beholden to him; the belief that we are secondary and inferior creatures in relation to this God. Or, as Feuerbach writes:

> God is the highest subjectivity of man abstracted from himself; hence man can do nothing of himself, all goodness comes from God. The more subjective God is, the more completely does man divest himself of his subjectivity, because God is, *per se*, his relinquished self, the possession of which he however again vindicates to himself. As the action of the arteries drives the blood into the extremities, and the action of the veins brings it back again, as life in general consists in a perpetual systole and diastole; so it is in religion. In the religious systole man propels his own nature from himself, he throws himself outward; in the religious diastole he receives the rejected nature into his heart again. God alone is the being who acts of himself, – this is the force of repulsion in religion; God is the being who acts in me, with me, through me, upon me, for me, is the principle of my salvation, of my good dispositions and actions, consequently my own good principle and nature, – this is the force of attraction in religion.[6]

---

5. Feuerbach 1989, p. 140; Feuerbach 1924, p. 174.
6. Feuerbach 1989, p. 31; Feuerbach 1924, pp. 39–40.

This quotation raises a further feature of Feuerbach's argument: it is formally Christological. I do not mean his point that the incarnation of Christ is the ultimate expression of the human form of God, but that the way his argument moves is Christological. Feuerbach is quite deliberate on this issue: he writes that in the same way theology lowers God into human form and thereby makes a human being God, so also does he reduce theology to anthropology and thereby raise anthropology into theology.[7] Like Stirner, Feuerbach plays with the form of Christology. What Feuerbach has done is merely reverse the direction of the interaction between human beings and whatever is beyond – 'God' or the 'gods'. Over against the assumption that the Christological path moves from God to human beings, he reverses the direction: human beings create God.

A further point that is often forgotten is that Feuerbach stresses the way belief in a god diminishes human beings. The elevation of God leads to the depreciation of human beings: 'To enrich God, man must become poor; that God may be all, man must be nothing'.[8] Since Marx's reception of Feuerbach has been so dominant, we tend to miss the fact that Marx's argument takes its cue from Feuerbach here as well. Marx would take Feuerbach's point that Christianity diminishes human beings and turn it into the argument that religion is a sign of human alienation in this world. From there, of course, they would diverge: Marx goes on to argue that religion is not the cause of alienation (an idealist position), but that it is the sign of social and economic alienation. They would also differ in terms of the solution: for Feuerbach, it was a case of showing how this feature led to the doctrines of sin and depravity and that we need to realise our full potential through a proper understanding of religion; for Marx, we need to deal with the oppressive and exploitative conditions in which we live.

All the same, for Marx, this theological argument was a vital breakthrough, one in which he saw immense potential. In later years he may have downplayed the importance of Feuerbach in relation to Hegel,[9] but that belies the

---

7. Feuerbach 1989, p. xviii; Feuerbach 1924, p. xxix.

8. Feuerbach 1989, p. 26; Feuerbach 1924, p. 33. He also points out that the illusion of religion is 'profoundly injurious in its effects on mankind' (Feuerbach 1989, p. 274; Feuerbach 1924, p. 349). Breckman 1999, pp. 90–130, argues that Feuerbach is far more politically radical than many take him to be, but then Feuerbach is the real hero of Breckman's book. On Feuerbach's radical politics, see also Leopold 2007, pp. 203–18.

9. In 1865 he writes: 'Compared with Hegel, Feuerbach is certainly poor. Nevertheless he was epoch-making *after* Hegel because he laid *stress* on certain points which

excitement he first felt when he encountered Feuerbach's work. There are two early letters Marx sent to Feuerbach, written on 3 October 1843 and 11 August 1844.[10] They clearly show that Marx admired Feuerbach immensely, betraying an awkwardness that comes from a precocious young man trying to find the best way to approach someone who was widely regarded as the most important philosopher of the time. In the first letter, the ostensible purpose was to invite Feuerbach to contribute to the first issue of the new journal *Deutsch-Französische Jahrbücher* that Marx was planning to edit in Paris. Marx cannot offer Feuerbach enough praise: not only do I know your work, I have read the second edition of *Das Wesen des Christenthums*. You have said that a German-French alliance is needed – we are realising that desire. By the way, did you know that you have many female admirers? And since you have indicated that you are working on Schelling, perhaps you could send us a piece from that work. In the second letter he pursues the same line, mentioning that German artisans in Paris are having lectures on *Wesen*, that the French and English translations are almost out (a premature comment for the English one, it seems), and that Feuerbach's thought is the great step forward for socialist thought. As Marx puts it, 'I am glad to have an opportunity of assuring you of the great respect and – if I may use the word – love, which I feel for you'.[11]

Yet Feuerbach did not send an article on Schelling for the new journal. Indeed, in the face of almost complete silence from Feuerbach, Marx had to ask for 'some speedy sign of life'.[12] In the midst of this rather one-way correspondence, these letters state a crucial truth, especially for Marx: 'Your *Philosophie der Zukunft*, and your *Wesen des Glaubens*, in spite of their small size, are certainly of greater weight than the whole of contemporary German literature put together. In these writings you have provided – I don't know whether intentionally – a philosophical basis for socialism and the Communists have

---

were disagreeable to the Christian consciousness but important for the progress of criticism, points which Hegel had left in mystic *clair-obscur*.' (Marx 1865a, p. 26; Marx 1865b, p. 25.)

10. Marx 1843s; Marx 1843t; Marx 1844q; Marx 1844r.

11. Marx 1844q, p. 354; Marx 1844r, p. 425. Many years later (in 1867) Marx wrote to Engels, saying that he had come across a copy of *The Holy Family* at Ludwig Kugelmann's place, where he found a better collection of both his and Engels's works than they had themselves. Marx writes, 'I was pleasantly surprised to find that we have no need to be ashamed of the piece, although the Feuerbach cult now makes a most comical impression on me.' (Marx 1867g, p. 360; Marx 1867h, p. 290.)

12. Marx 1844q, p. 357; Marx 1844r, p. 428.

immediately understood them in this way'.[13] At around the same time, he writes in *The Economic and Philosophical Manuscripts of 1844*: 'Feuerbach is the only one who has a *serious, critical* attitude to the Hegelian dialectic and who has made genuine discoveries in this field. He is in fact the true conqueror of the old philosophy'.[14] It is nothing less than the great leap forward, the only 'real theoretical revolution' beyond Hegel.[15] What Feuerbach's argument enables Marx to do, at least in his opinion, is leave these old questions of religion and idealism behind. And, since they have been dealt with once and for all, he can proceed in building his own method as though they were no longer problems.

Idealism and theology

In *The German Ideology*, Marx and Engels take up the inversion with gusto, invoking it in the first lines of the Preface. It is the key to the whole work. We the creators, they tell us, have bowed down before our creations, namely our ideas, beliefs, and imaginary beings such as God. It is no wonder that Feuerbach is the subject of the first chapter, for it is his idea that is wheeled out again and again, even against Feuerbach himself (who is accused of having gone only halfway). But they do not restrict themselves to Bauer, Stirner or Feuerbach, or even to the young Hegelians. It applies to humanity as a whole: 'Hitherto men have always formed wrong ideas about themselves, about what they are and what they ought to be'.[16]

A bold claim, is it not? In one sense, the range of uses to which the inversion is put suggests that it does indeed apply to the whole human race. As

---

13. Marx 1844q, p. 354; Marx 1844r, p. 425. See also Engels's enthusiastic declaration that Feuerbach had come clean as a communist, indeed that his writing naturally flowed in that direction (Engels 1844–5, pp. 235–6). See also Engels 1844b, pp. 461–6; Engels 1844c, pp. 543–8. Engels is less than impressed with Feuerbach's *Essence of Religion* (Feuerbach 2004). He finds that it is mostly rehashed older material and a lot of polemic against God and Christianity (see Engels 1846e, pp. 75–9; Engels 1846f, pp. 55–8). Engels is not far off the mark, since Feuerbach repeats and expands many of his arguments from the earlier work.

14. Marx 1844g, p. 328; Marx 1844h, p. 569.

15. Marx 1844g, p. 232; Marx 1844h, p. 468. There are a small number who stress Bauer's greater rôle in Marx's take on religion; see Rosen 1977, pp. 133–47; Clarkson and Hawkin 1978. However, in light of Marx's own comments, I prefer the majority-viewpoint in which Feuerbach is the primary influence.

16. Marx and Engels 1845–6a, p. 23; Marx and Engels 1845–6b, p. 13.

for those first well-known pages on Feuerbach in *The German Ideology*, the inversion becomes the tool with which Marx and Engels dismantle idealist philosophy. These are the famous sections that juxtapose an idealist approach to history with a materialist one. I do not need to wade through each twist of this argument, apart from a couple of crucial points.

To begin with, it seems as though nothing has changed and that this argument is rehearsed with a weary regularity today. Take part in any discussion over religion and you will find at least one person who asserts that the only way to change people is produce change in ideas or attitude. Another will lament in word or print that historical, literary, cultural…(fill in the blank) research has woefully neglected the rôle of religion. Yet another will fall back on the hoary argument that religion is the key-driver of historical conflict – the most recent example being a putative Muslim East and Christian West. The response is just as predictable: religion or beliefs or ideas are secondary phenomena which can only be explained through other causes, such as social organisation and economic systems. In other words, religion is unimportant, a pseudoscience if you will, and what we need is analysis of the real issues at stake. It is as if this first section on Feuerbach has set the script and that people will merely parrot the positions laid out by Marx and Engels. The paradox is that this crucial text did not appear in published form in Marx and Engels's lifetime, turning up in a belated moment in snippets in the 1920s and 1930s, and then in full in 1932 (German) and then in 1968 (English). Further, it really is a rough nugget, recently dug out of the earth of German philosophy and still needing refinement and polishing. In their enthusiasm, Marx and Engels say much about excretions of the brain, ephemera and the like, failing to see that their own thoughts fall into exactly the same category. In the end, it was not their most original move, for at this level it was appropriated wholesale from Feuerbach. Later, Marx in particular would develop a far more complex analysis that took full account of philosophy, beliefs, culture and religion, as well as the crucial realm of economics and social relations.[17]

Taking a leaf out of their own analysis, we should never forget that the context is crucial, for it arose as a polemic against the overriding trend in

---

17. The critique of religion would become the first step to a theory of 'ideology' (see Larrain 1983b, pp. 10–15 and Barrett 1991, pp. 6–7), but that path is not one I pursue in this study, mainly because it draws me too far from theology.

Germany to favour religious explanations above all others. In fact, Marx and Engels point out that German philosophy is dominated by theology.[18] What has happened is that all other philosophical categories have been subordinated to theology. Juridical, moral, political and metaphysical-philosophical branches have been drawn under the umbrella of theology. This is really another way of saying that all of the important public debates in Germany at the time took place on the ground laid out by theology. Given this situation, it is no surprise that the old Hegelians should uphold this situation, while the young Hegelians attack theology as the source of all the problems besetting Germany.

Marx and Engels both agree and disagree. The real problem, they argue, is that theology is not the dominant problem; that honour is taken by idealism of which theology is but a subset. At another level they agree, for theology reveals all too clearly the problem with idealism – the creations of people's minds seem to dominate their real lives. So they face a dilemma: theology both embodies the very essence of idealism (projection from real conditions of life) and yet it provides the argument that reveals the problem in the first place. Given the presuppositions from which Marx and Engels work, it is not all that easy to escape this dilemma.

What intrigues me about their response is that they use a theological argument appropriated from Feuerbach to undermine idealism. But how is it a theological argument? Is not the Feuerbachian inversion a way to overcome theology? Marx certainly thought that it laid the problem of religion to rest once and for all, if not idealism as such. How then can the destruction of theology and religion as a whole be a theological argument? I might answer that theology has provided its own suicide-pill, or rather that a particular philosophical theologian has done so. Once it has taken its own life, it is no longer a problem as to how it may have done so. Apart from pointing to apparent paradoxes such as atheistic theology (or atheology) or indeed materialist theology, there are two problems with this premature death-notice. At the level of content, Feuerbach's inversion is another approach to theology. The position he overturns – that God, Christ, sin, redemption, creation, eschaton and so on are real and determine who we are as human beings – is but one approach to the content of theology. To argue that they are projections of human desires,

---

18. Marx and Engels 1845–6a, pp. 27–30; Marx and Engels 1845–6b, pp. 17–20.

wishes and aspirations is another. It is perfectly plausible for someone to say, yes, God is a projection of mine or indeed of others, but that is what I worship. The divine is no less or more empirically verifiable with either position. Marx and Engels assumed that Feuerbach's argument was the funeral of any real religious content, but that by no means follows. Much hinges on what one understands by 'real'.

The theological springboard

The Feuerbachian inversion becomes another springboard – along with that provided by Stirner – for historical materialism. That method may well be a new development, but it was not possible without this prior step. This next step appears at various moments in *The German Ideology*,[19] *The Manifesto of the Communist Party*,[20] as well as the 'Introduction' to the *Contribution to the Critique of Hegel's Philosophy of Law* (*Kritik* for the sake of brevity), but its clearest expression appears in the *Theses on Feuerbach*, especially the fourth one:

> Feuerbach starts out from the fact of religious self-estrangement [*der religiösen Selbstentfremdung*], of the duplication of the world into a religious world and a secular one. His work consists in resolving the religious world into its secular basis. But that the secular basis lifts off from itself and establishes itself as an independent realm in the clouds...[21]

This much we have already encountered: religion is indeed a projection from this world that is subsequently hypostatised, or as Marx puts it, 'the secular [or "worldly" – *weltliche*] basis lifts off from itself and establishes itself as an independent realm'. But that is merely the first step. Engels clarifies with his editorial addition: 'He [Feuerbach] overlooks the fact that after completing

---

19. See especially Marx and Engels 1845–6a, pp. 36–7; Marx and Engels 1845–6b, pp. 26–7.
20. Marx and Engels 1848v, pp. 503–4; Marx and Engels 1848w, pp. 479–80.
21. Marx 1845b, p. 4; Marx 1845c, p. 6. Or in Engels's edit, 'Feuerbach starts out from the fact of religious self-estrangement, of the duplication of the world into a religious, imaginary world and a real one. His work consists in resolving the religious world into its secular basis. He overlooks the fact that after completing this work, the chief thing still remains to be done. For the fact that the secular basis lifts off from itself and establishes itself as an independent realm in the cloud...' (Marx 1845d, p. 7; Marx 1845e, p. 534).

this work, the chief thing [*die Hauptsache*] still remains to be done'.[22] Feuerbach has made the initial move, providing the proper basis for *die Hauptsache*, for the real task at hand. And that is to focus on the human beings who make such projections and ascertain why they do so in the first place. I have, of course, quoted only the first half of the fourth thesis on Feuerbach. The rest is as follows:

> Thesis 4:...But that the secular basis lifts off from itself and establishes itself as an independent realm in the clouds can only be explained by the inner strife and intrinsic contradictoriness of this secular basis. The latter must, therefore, itself be both understood in its contradiction and revolutionised in practice. Thus, for instance, once the earthly family is discovered to be the secret of the holy family, the former must then itself be destroyed in theory and in practice.[23]

In other words, Feuerbach's analysis is incomplete.[24] As has been repeated many, many times since Marx, the most important step is to show how these projections arise from the 'inner strife and intrinsic contradictoriness' of the conditions of this world, and to undertake a project of uncovering and revolutionising that basis.[25]

Marx senses that he has launched himself well beyond Feuerbach. In doing so he offers a decidedly negative take on Feuerbach's inversion. Instead of the realm of the gods being the projection of the best of human principles, nature and actions, it is for Marx a far more negative business. As we will see in more detail shortly, religion is actually a projection based on 'inner strife [*der Selbstzerrissenheit*]' and this-worldly contradictions, in short, on alienation.

---

22. Marx 1845d, p. 7; Marx 1845e, p. 534.

23. Marx 1845b, p. 4; Marx 1845c, p. 6. Once again, here is Engels's edited version: 'For the fact that the secular basis lifts off from itself and establishes itself in the clouds as an independent realm can only be explained by the inner strife and intrinsic contradictoriness of this secular basis. The latter must itself, therefore, first be understood in its contradiction and then, by the removal of the contradiction, revolutionised in practice. Thus, for instance, once the earthly family is discovered to be the secret of the holy family, the former must then itself be criticised in theory and transformed in practice.' (Marx 1845d, p. 7; Marx 1845e, p. 534.)

24. In *The German Ideology*, they argue that Feuerbach's materialism is an inconsistent one. See Marx and Engels 1845–6a, pp. 38–41; Marx and Engels 1845–6b, pp. 42–5.

25. Theses six and seven carry the analysis in a slightly different direction, pointing out that Feuerbach is fixated on the individual. So rather than locating the essence of religion within each individual, we need consider both the religious essence and the individual as social products (Marx 1845b, pp. 4–5; Marx 1845c, pp. 6–7).

Religion is a signal of a world out of joint, not the cause of that disjunction. Feuerbach argues that the key to alienation may be found in the religious projection itself; as a result these projections diminish human beings, for we believe that our best belongs to another being. Thus Feuerbach feels that if we reintegrate these projected elements of ourselves – they are our best parts, after all – then we can overcome the alienation of religion. For Marx, this is simply wrong-headed, for religious projection is a signal of deeper, socio-economic, alienation – that is what needs to analysed, understood, and changed. As he would put it later in *Capital*,

> Every history of religion, even, that fails to take account of this material basis, is uncritical. It is, in reality, much easier to discover by analysis the earthly core of the misty creations of religion, than, conversely, it is, to develop from the actual relations of life the corresponding celestialised forms of those relations. The latter method is the only materialistic, and therefore the only scientific one.[26]

Let us pause by the road for a moment and consider the journey so far. Seizing on what they see as a breakthrough, Marx and Engels take up Feuerbach's inversion as a way of tackling theologically saturated German philosophy and public debate. But then they also use it as a springboard for developing their own method in response to the overwhelming idealism of that philosophy. The catch is that, in terms of form, Feuerbach's inversion is a theological argument. Without it, the move by Marx and Engels would not have been possible; this theological form is, as I pointed out earlier, the crucible for their own thought. One might be forgiven for thinking that once the theological scaffolding had been packed away there would be no further need to ponder its intricacies. Yet it was not to be, for the inversion had a tendency to drag its theological baggage with it when invoked.

Irreligious criticism, or, completing the criticism of religion

For the remainder of this chapter, I cover some ground worn bare and dusty from countless footsteps. It is the famous statement on religion found in the first couple of pages of the 'Introduction' to the never-completed *Kritik*. The

---

26. Marx 1867a, p. 375, n. 2; Marx 1867b, p. 393, n. 89.

slightly later *Theses on Feuerbach* may contain the most succinct statement of what Marx proposed to do with Feuerbach, but the 'Introduction' explores the implications of the inversion in greater detail.

Yet this relatively short statement has not been taken up by so many without reason, since it is a crucial piece of Marx's thought. For reasons that now go back some way, I am always on the lookout for style, or in more direct terms, sentence-production. And I have pointed out on more than one occasion that Engels is the better writer of the two by a good way. No matter what it is – a description of one of his long walks, the history of the rifle, war-reports or whatever – Engels draws me in. Marx is much more work. But, every now and then, he rises above the dense web and intense flurry of his writing to produce some stunning sentences. This text is one of one those moments.

The sentences ring out one after another: 'the criticism of religion is the premise of all criticism'; 'The basis of irreligious criticism is: *Man makes religion*, religion does not make man'; 'The criticism of religion is therefore *in embryo the criticism of the vale of tears*, the *halo* of which is religion'; 'Religion is only the illusory sun which revolves round man as long as he does not revolve round himself'.[27] The highest point, at least from a literary perspective, is the series of statements that begin simply with 'Religion is …'

> Religion is the general theory of this world, its encyclopaedic compendium, its logic in popular form, its spiritual *point d'honneur*, its enthusiasm, its moral sanction, its solemn complement, and its universal basis of consolation and justification. It is the *fantastic realization* of the human essence since the *human essence* has not acquired any true reality. The struggle against religion is, therefore, indirectly the struggle *against that world* whose spiritual *aroma* is religion.
>
> *Religious* suffering is, at one and the same time, the *expression* of real suffering and a *protest* against real suffering. Religion is the sigh of the oppressed creature, the heart of a heartless world, and the soul of soulless conditions. It is the *opium* of the people.
>
> Criticism has torn up the imaginary flowers from the chain not so that man shall wear the unadorned, bleak chain but so that he will shake off the chain and pluck the living flower. The criticism of religion disillusions man to

---

27. Marx 1844c, pp. 175–6; Marx 1844d, pp. 378–9.

make him think and act and shape his reality like a man who has been disil-
lusioned and has come to his reason, so that he will revolve round himself
and therefore round his true sun. Religion is only the illusory sun which
revolves round man as long as he does not revolve round himself.[28]

Each time I read this text, it still stuns and delights.[29] As with most of what
Marx wrote, the various phrases might have spilled from his pen at a great
rate (it is no wonder his handwriting was so difficult to read), yet each of them
explores another dimension of religion. Every pore of these sentences breathes
with the insight of Feuerbach. Flushed with this insight into the nature of religion and the implications of that insight for his own work, Marx is finally able
to produce a coherent response to the religious turn of German philosophy. It
enables Marx to undo Hegel and declare the criticism of religion complete.

What Marx does is push Feuerbach's insight into religion as far as it will
go. As I pointed out earlier, Feuerbach argued that religion is the projection
of the best in human beings, a projection that then comes back in hypostatised forms. The problem is that theology begins with the projection, with the
hypostasis, and not its moment of origin in human beings. In other words,
we need to take a step back and begin at the beginning. Marx agrees vigorously. So we find him claiming that human beings make religion, that the
'superhuman being in the fantastic reality of heaven' is simply the reflection
[*Widerschein*] or semblance [*Schein*] of ourselves.[30] Instead of a 'super-man
[*Übermenschen*]' there is simply a 'non-man [*Unmenschen*]'. What does religion
do? It projects human self-consciousness [*Selbstbewußtsein* – a Bauerian term!]
and self-esteem [*Selbstgefühl*]. It is, as that famous sentence puts it, 'the general
theory of this world, its encyclopaedic compendium, its logic in popular form,
its spiritual *point d'honneur*, its enthusiasm, its moral sanction, its solemn com-
plement, and its universal basis of consolation and justification'.[31] All of this

---

28. Ibid. Or as he puts it elsewhere, Christianity has displaced the aspirations of
people to the heavens: 'The self-confidence of the human being, freedom, has first of
all to be aroused again in the hearts of these people. Only this feeling, which vanished
from the world with the Greeks, and under Christianity disappeared into the blue
mist of the heavens, can again transform society into a community of human beings
united for their highest aims, into a democratic state.' (Marx 1844k, p. 137; Marx 1844l,
pp. 338–9.)
29. Kouvelakis 2003, p. 316, too is taken with the 'incisive and carefully chiselled
style'.
30. Marx 1844c, p. 175; Marx 1844d, p. 378.
31. Ibid.

is good, solid Feuerbach: religion is the projected and comprehensive ideal of human existence.

As we already saw with the fourth thesis on Feuerbach, Marx thinks that this is a first step. Feuerbach may have felt that he had completed his argument, but Marx argues that it is merely a prolegomenon. Projections, hypostases, returns – these are all very well, but it is the social and political reality of those people who make the projections in the first place that interest Marx far more. The burning question is not the fantastic projection but the person who makes such projections in the first place. For Marx, however, that person is not merely an individual, but one who is situated within a state and society. What is it about such a state and society that generates such fantastic projections? Simply put, any society that needs and produces such religious projections is deeply troubled. It is an 'inverted world'; it is a 'vale of tears' of which religion is the 'halo'; it is, in short, a society riven with 'self-estrangement [*Selbstentfremdung*]'. Attention to the alienation of this world surpasses any consideration of religious alienation: 'Religious estrangement [*Entfremdung*] as such occurs only in the realm of *consciousness*, of man's inner life, but economic estrangement [*Entfremdung*] is that of *real life*; its transcendence [*Aufhebung*] therefore embraces both aspects'.[32]

One way of reading Marx up until this point is that he has been expanding on Feuerbach's argument that religion belittles and degrades human beings. However, their solutions differ: Feuerbach seeks to restore all these lost attributes to us and therefore provide us with fulfilment; for Marx, the solution requires a political act. Once we are aware of how such a society functions, we need to pursue the following course of action: remove the illusion and relieve the causes of the illusion. In the enthusiastic rush of his discovery, Marx does not tire of repeating the same call to action in slightly different ways: sublate illusory happiness to find real happiness; give up illusions in order to give up the situation that requires illusions; shake off the chain and its imaginary flowers in order to pluck the real flowers; religious disillusionment is a coming to one's senses and the basis for reason; establish the truth of this world once the world beyond has gone.

---

32. Marx 1844g, p. 275; Marx 1844h, p. 515.

So we have three steps: show that religion is an illusory projection (borrowed from Feuerbach); turn one's attention to the situation that produces such fantastic illusions; and remove the conditions that generate those illusions. Now, the purpose of this little piece of hagiography is not merely to show how deeply Marx relies on Feuerbach, or even to show in some detail where he uses the man as a springboard for his own position. I also want to raise some points that are problematic: the opposition of illusion and reality; the relation between Marx's emerging materialist method and theological modes of thinking; and what the end of the criticism of religion really means.

Crucial to Marx's catchy sentences is the opposition of illusion and reality. If we look patiently at the rush of his statements, then a basic opposition begins to show its face: the illusory [*illusorisch*], imaginary [*imaginär*] and fantastic [*phantastisch*] versus the real [*wirklich*] and living [*lebendig*] realm of reason [*Verstand*] and truth [*Wahrheit*]. In short, religion is false, this world is true. Marx feels that if he can show that something is a fantasy or an illusion, then, like the emperor's new clothes, it has lost all its power. It does not exist, since it is not 'real'.[33] Needless to say, this is a problematic distinction that has suffered countless attacks, but I will deal with it more extensively in my discussion of Hegel in the next chapter.

My next criticism – the presence of theological forms of thinking – is a double one. Let me put it this way: the moment that we first catch a glimmer of the controversial base-superstructure model, we also draw closer to theology. In these few pages of the 'Introduction' to Marx's *Contribution*, the metaphor of base and superstructure (a metaphor that seems to come from building but also refers to a railway and its rolling stock) begins to show its controversial face. To put it in terms of the preceding paragraph, what is 'real' soon enough becomes the realm of economics, of the means and relations of production; what is an 'illusion' then becomes the domain of ideology, culture, politics, philosophy and religion. But note what has happened: the base-superstructure comes out of a theological argument, namely, Feuerbach's inversion, but Marx turns it on its head, for theology is no longer the determining model but is now subsumed with the new one. This relationship between Marx's argument

---

33. Marx 1844g, p. 337; Marx 1844h, pp. 578–9.

and that of Feuerbach is analogous to the story of the creation of woman in Genesis 2. In the same way that the woman, who would later be called Eve, is taken from the side of Adam, so also is the base-structure model surgically removed from the side of Feuerbach's argument concerning religion. Once removed and re-shaped, it takes on a new life of its own.

In case my point is not clear, let me tackle it in another way. Feuerbach has shown to Marx's satisfaction that religion is a projection of real human beings. That projection is an illusion and is therefore not real. Later, as we shall see, in the discussion of Hegel Marx would bring along the state, the constitution, sovereignty and politics in order keep religion company. As this group grows to become the superstructure, Marx turns his attention to the 'real' human beings who make these projections and produce these illusions (the second and third steps I outlined a little earlier). What is it about their situation that makes them do so? Pursuing this question would lead Marx to the areas of economics and society, of productive means and relations. These 'real' matters will become the concrete stuff of the base.

Now, all of this may have come to life as Marx grappled with Feuerbach, but I have not yet substantiated my claim that it has the form of a theological argument. I do not simply mean that Marx's position gains its impetus from Feuerbach's philosophy of religion. Rather, it is the form of the argument that interests me, a form that both Marx and Feuerbach use. As I pointed out a little earlier in my discussion of Feuerbach, that form is as follows: while systematic theology traditionally moves from God to man, from theology strictly defined [*theo-logos*] to anthropology, Feuerbach and then Marx invert the order; they move from man to God. More specifically, Feuerbach makes this move – God is a projection of man. Marx, however, goes a good deal further. Initially he drops God: since religion is a product of man, an illusion, Marx gives the impression that he is not interested in religion and turns his attention elsewhere. What actually happens is that the space of theology is filled with nothing other than the superstructure – ideology, politics and, of course, religion. Or, as others have argued, the criticism of religion is the first step to a theory of ideology. As with the engagement with Stirner, here the theological form of thinking becomes the crucible in which Marx forges a new method, with the twist that the method in question accounts for and encompasses the old.

Finally, there is the whole matter of completion or ending. In the same 'Introduction', Marx makes the following statements:

For Germany, the *criticism of religion* is in the main complete, and the criticism of religion is the premise of all criticism.[34]

Für Deutschland ist die *Kritik der Religion* im wesentlichen beendigt, und die Kritik der Religion ist die Voraussetzung aller Kritik.[35]

The evident proof of the radicalism of German theory, and hence of its practical energy, is that it proceeds from a resolute *positive* abolition of religion. The criticism of religion ends [*endet*] with the teaching that *man is the highest being for man*, hence with the *categorical imperative to overthrow all relations* in which man is a debased, enslaved, forsaken, despicable being.[36]

Der evidente Beweis für den Radikalismus der deutschen Theorie, also für ihre praktische Energie, ist ihr Ausgang von der entschiedenen *positiven* Aufhebung der Religion. Die Kritik der Religion endet mit der Lehre, daß *der Mensch das höchste Wesen für den Menschen* sei, also mit dem *kategorischen Imperativ, alle Verhältnisse umzuwerfen*, in denen der Mensch ein erniedrigtes, ein geknechtetes, ein verlassenes, ein verächtliches Wesen ist.[37]

Marx's statement that the criticism of religion is complete appears straightforward. Yet it is not so simple, for it carries on a double life in these passages, best captured by the two terms Marx uses: '*enden*' or '*beenden* [*beendigen*]', meaning to finish or complete, and '*Aufhebung*', the famed Hegelian abolition or sublation with the sense that it carries on to another level. The one indicates that we have reached the end of the line, that there is nothing more to be said or done. The other is less final, designating transition, suggesting that it is now time to move onto the next stage or level.[38]

In both statements Marx actually juxtaposes the two senses of completion. In the second statement, we find that the radicalism of German theory is due to the fact that it 'proceeds from a resolute *positive* sublation [*Aufhebung*] of

---

34. Marx 1844c, p. 175; Marx 1844d, p. 378. For a similar comment, backed up by some dubious information on early-Christian practices, see Marx 1847e.
35. Marx 1844d, p. 378.
36. Marx 1844c, p. 182; Marx 1844d, p. 385.
37. Marx 1844d, p. 385.
38. See also Marx's comments on Hegel's effort at *Aufhebung* – in 'which denial and preservation, i.e., affirmation, are bound up together [*worin die Verneinung und die Aufbewahrung, die Bejahung verknüpft sind*]' (Marx 1844g, p. 340; Marx 1844h, p. 581) – of theology through philosophy and Absolute Mind in Marx 1844g, p. 341; Marx 1844h, p. 583.

religion'.[39] Immediately afterwards, he writes that the 'criticism of religion ends [*endet*] with the teaching that *man is the highest being for man'*. And then, in the first statement, he writes of the dual status of the criticism of religion as both 'complete [*beendigt*]' and as a 'premise' or 'prerequisite [*Voraussetzung*]': 'For Germany the *criticism of religion* is in the main complete, and the criticism of religion is the prerequisite of all criticism'.

What are we to make of this tension between completion and sublation, between ending and abolition? As van Leeuwen points out, there is actually a tension here between the suggestion that the critique of religion is over and that he still sees the need to engage in such a criticism.[40] So let us see how Marx deals with that tension. At least it enables him to escape the criticism that he has somewhat rashly proclaimed the death of God, the bankruptcy of theology and the end of religion. These predictions are like predictions of the end of the world, Armageddon, the Last Judgement and so on. We have had and continue to have all manner of predictions and warnings, and yet the end does not quite want to come. So also with the end of religion and religious criticism, except in reverse: at least since the Enlightenment, time and again, we find its end presented as a *fait accompli*. At some point in the relatively recent past – or so goes the story – someone has slipped the knife into religion and quietly disposed of the body. It is an assumption that afflicts someone like Gilles Deleuze: theology is a dead issue, so he can play with it all he likes. Or Alain Badiou, who argues that the One (and thereby God) was put out of its misery by the mathematician Cohen and his set-theory. Since then, it can no longer be an issue. The problem is that the would-be assassin has not done the job properly – whether Voltaire, Nietzsche, Freud, Feuerbach, Cohen, or…Richard Dawkins today.[41]

Marx's claim is a little more modest. In a Hegelian nutshell, the time of religion and its criticism must come to an end in order to be sublated by something more far-reaching. And that moment has arrived in Marx's own time and in his own thought. In other words, there is both a situation-specific dimension to the claim and a personal one. As I have mentioned a few times, through Marx's high-school and university-years, and even into his first

---

39. A little later he writes, 'The *Aufhebung* of religion as the illusory happiness of the people is the demand for their real happiness.' (Marx 1844c, p. 176; Marx 1844d, p. 379; translation modified.)
40. Van Leeuwen 2002b, p. 184.
41. Dawkins 2006.

forays as a journalist, essayist and radical, the overriding context for political struggle in Germany was theology and especially the New Testament. Marx announces here that he will not be constrained by that context, that he will set his own agenda and move on, that others may want to carry on the criticism of religion but that he has other goals. He escapes (but only just) the world-historical claim for his own thought by inserting two small phrases. The first is *'für Deutschland'* and the second *'im wesentlichen'* – the criticism of religion is complete for Germany...in the main. It is basically finished, at least here.

Even this claim may be too much, no matter how much it expresses his own frustration with the nature of criticism in Germany, no matter how much it gives voice to the development of his own thought. Even in Germany at the time, let alone afterwards on a more global scale, the criticism of religion has had and continues to have a vigorous, healthy and rather long retirement.

So I am far more interested in the other side of his statements on religion, that of *Aufhebung*. On one level, negation and sublation mean that theology continues in some form in the new mode of thought. At another level, it raises a fascinating question: what is it about the criticism of religion that gives it privileged status as some type of Hegelian forerunner of Marx's own criticism? Thus far I have been pursuing an answer to this question via Feuerbach. Later in the 'Introduction' there is a far more surprising answer. It comes in the shape of Martin Luther.

The new Luther

Luther? I cannot stress how much of a surprise this is for me, even with my radar carefully on the watch for such things. Luther embodies, for Marx, that earlier stage of criticism. The Lutheran criticism of religion is the forerunner which must do its job before it is abolished and taken up within the new criticism.

> Germany's *revolutionary* past is theoretical, it is the *Reformation*. As the revolution then began in the brain of the *monk*, so now it begins in the brain of the *philosopher*....But if Protestantism was not the true solution it was at least the true setting of the problem.[42]

---

42. Marx 1844c, p. 182; Marx 1844d, p. 385. See also: 'Shortly before and during the period of the Reformation there developed amongst the Germans a type of literature whose very name is striking – *grobian* literature. In our own day we are approaching

We really have two stages, one that begins with Luther the monk and the second that begins with Feuerbach the philosopher. Or is it Marx who begins the new phase? Does he see himself as the new Luther? The 'philosopher' remains unnamed, while the 'monk' is named. It may be Feuerbach, for he is responsible for the breakthrough. Hegel it is not, unless he marks the end of the first phase of revolutionary criticism. Rather than decide one way or another – Feuerbach or Marx? – I prefer to keep the ambiguity of the text. Marx displays both the excitement of Feuerbach's move and his own sense that he is going beyond that discovery. There was one thing that Marx did not suffer and that was lack of confidence in the importance of his ideas. So the new Luther is ready to take up a new phase of revolution.[43]

But what is Luther's contribution, or that of the Reformation itself? In a series of wonderful Hegelian sentences, Marx lays out Luther's achievement: the transition from an external to an internal religious expression.

> *Luther*, we grant, overcame the bondage of *piety* by replacing it by the bond-
> age of *conviction*. He shattered faith in authority because he restored the
> authority of faith. He turned priests into laymen because he turned laymen
> into priests. He freed man from outer religiosity because he made religios-
> ity the inner man. He freed the body from chains because he enchained the
> heart.[44]

---

an era of revolution analogous to that of the sixteenth century.' (Marx 1847f, p. 312; Marx 1847g, p. 331.) On a lighter note, although still with the comparison to Luther: 'My sincere thanks for the wine. Being myself from a winegrowing region, and for-mer owner of a vineyard, I know a good wine when I come across one. I even incline somewhat to old Luther's view that a man who does not love wine will never be good for anything' (Marx 1866g, p. 334; Marx 1866h, p. 536). Marx had a continuing fascina-tion with Luther; see, for example, Marx 1856h, p. 21; Marx 1856i, p. 25, as well as his appreciative comments on Luther's criticism of usury from his *An die Pfarherrn wider den Wucher zu predigen* of 1540. Marx quotes him again and again in his economic manuscripts and *Capital* (Marx 1859a, pp. 364, 448–9; Marx 1861–3d, pp. 531–8, 539–41; Marx 1861–3e, pp. 516–24; Marx 1867a, pp. 146, 203, 314, 588–9, 741; Marx 1867b, pp. 149, 207, 328, 619, 781; Marx 1894a, pp. 329, 345, 391–2, 594, 605–6, 889; Marx 1894b, pp. 343–4, 359, 407, 613, 624–5, 911). As Marx puts it, 'An excellent picture, it fits the capitalist in general [*Allerliebstes Bild, auf den Kapitalisten überhaupt*]' (Marx 1861–3d, p. 539; Marx 1861–3e, p. 525). Note: Marx 1843k is now agreed not to be by Marx but by Feuerbach.

43. Thankfully he was not always so serious, suggesting in a letter to Eleanor that he is the devil and not Luther: 'Sometimes, however, when I commence whistling, Dicky [Eleanor's bird] treats me as Luther treated the devil – he turns his…on me' (Marx 1869f, pp. 270–1; Marx 1869g, p. 601).

44. Marx 1844c, p. 182; Marx 1844d, p. 386. See also Marx 1844g, pp. 290–1; Marx 1844h, pp. 530–1, where he makes a similar point: Luther internalises faith, the priesthood

Against all forms of outer religiosity – piety, authority, priests and the body – Luther pressed for the internalisation of religious commitment, one characterised by conviction, faith, laity and the heart and the inner man. This internalisation or, as I prefer, privatisation becomes the huge step forward, and, for Marx, it is the first stage in radical revolutionary criticism. It is a break-through only because Luther did not retreat into the inner sanctum as in some monastery; instead, he overcame such an other-worldly retreat by – paradoxi-cally – universalising that inwardness so that it was available for all.[45] Yet, it is a backhanded compliment. The first and last sentences in the quotation from Marx bring the catch out all too clearly: Luther might have freed people from external religious forms, but only by bringing about a whole new level of enslavement – that of conviction and the heart.[46]

What, then, can the 'philosopher', the second Luther, achieve? Here, Marx stumbles, becoming unclear and saying a number of things that do not neces-sarily connect with each other. Let me list them: first, he says that the struggle is now internal: since laymen have become priests, the struggle for emanci-pation is internal, against the priest inside. Second, the struggle is external, that is, against all the newly made priests and 'lay popes', namely the princes and squires to whom Germany is enslaved. Third, the next step is a thorough secularisation, since Luther's revolution was still theological. Indeed, it was theology that drove the Peasant Revolt into the mud. Finally, what Luther

---

and external religiosity. Here, however, he uses an analogy with political economy, in which Adam Smith is the one who shows that private property is an internal reality rather than an external condition.

45. The anticipation of Weber is quite remarkable. Marx points out elsewhere that the retreat to the inner self has a long history within Christianity, especially in the monastic cloister where one must turn inward. It is not for nothing, he points out, that blinding was a common punishment during Christendom: 'This punishment was current in the thoroughly Christian empire of Byzantium and came to full flower in the vigorous youthful period of the Christian-Germanic states of England and France. Cutting man off from the perceptible outer world, throwing him back into his abstract inner nature in order to correct him – blinding – is a necessary consequence of the Christian doctrine according to which the consummation of this cutting off, the pure isolation of man in his spiritualistic "ego" is good itself.' (Marx and Engels 1845a, p. 178; Marx and Engels 1845b, p. 189.) If this is the pre-Reformation way in which the ego was 'encouraged' in its pursuit of spiritual knowledge, then the breakthrough by Luther and the reformers was to overturn this inward focus by universalising it and thereby making it public.

46. Michel Foucault would take this point of internalised control much further in his *Discipline and Punish* (Foucault 1979).

was missing was a material, class-basis for the Reformation; that Marx finds for the new, secular revolution in the proletariat.

A number of slippages and dead-ends emerge in this argument. It is not necessary to seek some hidden logic when a writer loses the way. The desperate effort to find some coherence bedevils too much literary criticism, assuming that an author is always clear and consistent, so I much prefer to explore the nature of the breakdown in logic. As for the slippages, Marx tries to move from the internalisation of religion first begun by Luther to the German nobility. In other words, since they have internalised the Lutheran innovation, these princes have made themselves the new bishops and popes (every laymen becomes a priest). And, so, they need to be opposed in the new revolution, one that is now secular. It is a curious, frog-like argument that hops in an erratic fashion from one lily-pad to another. Yet, each stop is worth developing on its own.

So let us pull Marx up from the mad rush of his writing and ask a few patient questions. I begin with the idea that the new bondage is of the heart, that Luther has successfully internalised religious conviction. This idea can run off into bourgeois cant about changing attitudes, the sacrosanct individual and so on. Yet it can also be taken in a very different and highly productive direction. If the tension between layman and priest, between outer religiosity and inner conviction is one that is internal, then the struggle for liberation becomes an internal affair. Each of us carries that contradiction and struggle within us. But then how might that struggle be resolved? One part of me would suggest that it never will be, at least completely; another part wants to ask what the social and economic conditions are that generated this internal tension and turmoil in the first place. Revolution then becomes one of simultaneously transforming those conditions and the internal struggle.

I have already moved into Marx's second point, namely that the new revolutionary phase is directed against the German nobility. All I need to ask at this point is who is responsible for the social and economic conditions in the first place. It is human beings, of course, and especially those in positions of economic and political power. Yet the choice of the princes is an odd one. They may have held power in Germany at the time, but that power was already waning before the onslaught of the bourgeoisie. Marx will turn to the latter soon enough, which makes the presence of these nobles even stranger.

Then there comes a bolt out of the blue: Marx calls for a thorough secularisation. Of course, secularisation is a complex term but let us see what Marx does say, what is implicit in what he says and what is left begging. Given that theology has come to a dead-end and given that the peasants' rebellion of 1525 ran aground due to theology, secularisation would seem to mean removing theology from any revolutionary activity. From here, we must speculate and explore. It seems to me that what he wants to argue is that Luther's revolution also falls short because of theology. Thus, the way forward for the new Luther is to drop theology entirely. A number of other factors crowd the scene. For one, Feuerbach's rôle is implicit, for his inversion would seem to be the great secularising step forward. However, the most problematic element here is the contested status of the term secularisation and what it entails. The question might be put this way: is secularisation the thorough removal of theology for a new stage of revolutionary activity, or is secularisation the removal of theological content from some key-terms (sin, redemption and so on) and their filling with other non-theological content?

Finally, there is Marx's charge that Luther embodies a feature of German revolutions in general: the absence of a mass, popular basis for his own revolution. Luther's revolution remained a matter of faith and knowledge; there was no popular heart for the theologian/philosopher's head. Marx will go on to find it in the proletariat, using those well-known phrases concerning the need for philosophy to 'grip' the masses, the class in radical chains that needs abolition of its status as a class. But the charge against Luther is not quite fair. It is all very well to have the luxury of sitting in the midst of a society that did experience the Protestant shake-up. Outside of that context, in Italy to be precise, Gramsci would see the situation a little differently. Ensconced in his bleak prison-cell, Gramsci expressed in his neat hand the longing that the Reformation had happened in Italy too. Why? The Reformation grasped the whole of society in one large pitchfork and tossed it up into the wind so that when it came down everything had changed, from bottom to top. More specifically, it gripped the masses, to use Marx's own phrase. Or, as Gramsci put it: 'In Italy there has never been an intellectual and moral reform involving the popular masses'.[47] Gramsci goes on to argue that a communist revolution needs to permeate to the deepest roots of society, just like the Reformation.

---

47. Gramsci 1996, pp. 243–4; Q4§75. So also: 'The Lutheran Reformation and Calvinism created a popular culture, and only in later periods did they create a higher culture; the Italian reformers were sterile in terms of great historical achievements' (Gramsci 1996, p. 142; Q4§3). See also Gramsci 1994, p. 365; Boer 2007a, pp. 258–73.

However much the Reformation may have betrayed its initial impetus (but then it would not be the first movement to do so), Gramsci's observation places a question-mark against Marx's assertion that he is the first to discover a truly mass-basis. Let me push this a little further: it may be that Marx is *rediscovering* the secret of the Reformation, namely, its mass-appeal. Where does this leave Marx's ambiguity over 'the philosopher' as the second Luther, the philosopher who may achieve what the monk could not? It means that his own effort is more truly an *Aufhebung* than he would care to admit. The theological baggage of earlier revolutions has not so much been dumped on the side of the road as it has been tipped out, sorted and repacked before continuing the journey. His last sentence is more telling than he perhaps thought: 'When all the inner requisites are fulfilled, the *day of German resurrection* will be proclaimed by the *ringing of the Gallic cock*'.[48] Not a bad benediction. But this connection with Luther cuts both ways: it may point out the sublation of theology within Marx's thought, but it also shows that the Reformation may have been a little more revolutionary than he might have thought.

Conclusion

There is little need to dwell with the point I have belaboured in this chapter, namely that Marx and Engels employed Feuerbach's theological argument both as the means for answering the dominance of theology in German public debate and as the stepping stone to their own method. Instead, I identify a number of trajectories from this crucial engagement with the Feuerbach inversion, trajectories that are actually the subjects of the following three chapters. We might view this chapter as an intersection from which a number of paths diverge, one towards Hegel, the other to fetishism and yet another to a certain ambivalence over theology.

One of the paths leading out of this short text is to a critique of Hegel's philosophy of the state. Hegel is, after all, the subject of the main text that was to follow this 'Introduction', the *Kritik*. But what is the relevance of theology to that treatment of Hegel? Marx had already written his notes on Hegel's *Rechtsphilosophie* before this 'Introduction' and there he was already flushed with the discovery that the deeper structure of thought in Hegel's system was

---

48. Marx 1844c, p. 187; Marx 1844d, p. 391.

analogous to theology. As he puts it in the *Economic and Philosophical Manuscripts of 1844*, one of Feuerbach's great achievements was the 'proof that philosophy is nothing else but religion rendered into thought and expounded by thought, i.e., another form and manner of existence of the estrangement of the essence of man; hence equally to be condemned'.[49] This was not the simplistic argument that Hegel was really a theologian of a somewhat secular variety. It is an argument concerning the structure of thought, the steps taken in an argument and above all the assumptions with which one begins. So, Marx argues that Hegel's theory of the state, or of sovereignty, or of the constitution begins by assuming the prior existence of these items. The task then involves fitting in the prior idea of the state or sovereignty or the constitution to the real situation of flesh-and-blood people. Such a way of arguing is comparable to theology, which begins with a prior idea concerning God, the Trinity and salvation and then tries to make human reality fit. The problem with both is that they begin at the wrong point and then try to work backwards, from abstraction to concrete situations. The key is to begin with concrete, everyday human beings and then see how the state or God, sovereignty or the Trinity, the constitution or salvation are developed from there. For this reason, theology is the starting-point for Marx's discussion of Hegel, to which I turn in the next chapter.

Another path heads in the direction of Marx's ongoing fascination with fetishism. It turns up in his earliest pieces and makes a well-known reappearance in *Capital*. In this case, we find not a direct application of Feuerbach's inversion but an adaptation or mutation. Marx's basic position is that, with fetishism, human interaction and relations take on the nature of things, while inanimate objects begin to relate to one another in an all-too-human manner. It may best be described as a transferral in which human relations switch places with objects. The connection with Feuerbach's argument is obvious, for human beings may project their own properties onto inanimate objects, but it is also an adaptation, for the objects in question are not illusory products of the human mind, but tangible items in the world around us. The reason for that mutation may be found in a couple of points of contact with other lines of thought, one more obvious and the other less so. Marx's economic studies play a rôle here, especially the insights regarding commodities, but another

---

49. Marx 1844g, p. 328; Marx 1844h, p. 569.

is unexpected: a connection with the critique of idolatry that stems from bib-lical narratives. This is where Adorno's *Bilderverbot* comes into play, for he sought a connection between the ban on images in the second and third com-mandments in the book of Exodus and Marx's own critique of commodity-fetishism.

Another path, somewhat overgrown and far less used, directs us towards an ambivalence concerning theology. I traced a hint of this ambivalence in a few of Marx's biblical and theological allusions in Chapter Two, but we also find it in some of his comments on religion in the 'Introduction'. I do not mean that Marx was unsure – far from it! – or that he was hedging his bets in case there was a God and an afterlife.[50] No, what Marx hints is that even as a pro-jection, even as a 'man-made' product, theology may give voice to a rebellious and revolutionary wish. To be sure, the default-position is that theology is reactionary, but not always. So we find that while man makes religion, while religion is an illusion that must be sublated, a halo for an oppressive vale of tears, it is also a protest against suffering.

Every now and then someone will focus on these statements and argue that Marx was far more sympathetic to a rebellious form of Christianity than we might have thought.[51] In almost every discussion of Marx and religion, someone will eagerly say, 'Ah yes, but if you read Marx more carefully, you will see that he was actually sympathetic to religion'. And then this person will recite the usual verses from the 'Introduction' to the *Kritik*. Marx had little sympathy for religion. What he does is hint at a small opening for the ambivalence of theology. Marx leaves a tiny gap open for a sharp opposition between two understandings of religion, one that is reactionary and the other that begins to look revolutionary. In other words, it is a political ambivalence over the uses and effects of religion that I explore in Chapter Eight. By con-trast, Engels was the one would make much more of this tension.

---

50. This observation was actually made to me by someone who on all counts seemed to be intelligent. He included Rosa Luxemburg, Karl Kautsky and other Marxists who have written on theology, the Bible or religion more generally.

51. For example, see Raines 2002, pp. 5–6, 8–10, as well as the collection of essays in Raines and Dean (eds.) 1970. This was a common move in the Marxist-Christian dia-logue of the 1960s and 1970s. See, for example, Aptheker 1968; Aptheker 1970.

Chapter Six

Hegel, Theology and the Secular State

> If you call your state a *general Christian* state, you are admitting with a diplomatic turn of phrase that it is *un-Christian*.[1]

> The Prussian King, who calls himself emphatically 'the Christian King', and has made his court a most ludicrous assemblage of whining saints and piety-feigning courtiers...[2]

The thread that ties this chapter together is the question of the state. Or rather, we might view it as a necklace upon which hang various jewels of different sizes and values. I begin with a critical commentary on the notes called the *Contribution to the Critique of Hegel's Philosophy of Law* (the *Kritik*). I quite deliberately take this central and much-read text not as a step from theology to politics and law (as so many do, including Marx), but as one of Marx's most sustained reflections on theology and the arguments that might be launched against it. The next section shifts to a collection of texts that concern the relations of church and state. Here, I focus on a tension: on the one hand, Marx argues that theology is a particular concern and that it really should have no part in the general matters of the state. On the

---

1. Marx 1843a, p. 118; Marx 1843b, p. 106.
2. Engels 1844m, p. 515.

other hand, he points out that the secular state is born out of the contradictions within the Christian state. Engels agrees and fills out the detail of this argument. Needless to say, this is a far more interesting and dialectical argument, for it recognises the tensions within theology itself.

The formal theologian

The *Kritik*, written in Kreuznach in 1843 before the family moved to Paris, is usually taken as the moment when Marx extended the theological critique of Feuerbach into political philosophy, or perhaps as an appropriation and extension of Feuerbach's scattered reflections on politics.[3] The problem with these approaches is that they miss some crucial theological arguments Marx makes, or rather the arguments he makes against theology. However, in order to come to grips with those arguments, I want to move in reverse, from politics to theology in order to dig out the theological critique.

I do have a confession to make: it took me a while to see the consistent theological criticism in this text. When I first began to read it, I set out to track the theological spoor. It certainly showed up in a consistent pattern, but the references seemed peripheral, illustrations perhaps to the main argument concerning the state. As I read more carefully, I noticed that the theological 'examples' are the only ones given: often when Marx wants to make a point against Hegel, he suggests that it is just like a certain theological argument or doctrine. I wondered whether Marx wanted to bring Hegel and theology together so that he could distance himself from Hegel and set out on his own. Finally, it struck me: the theological argument underpins his argument against Hegel.

However, my obtuseness may be due to the fact that it is a devilishly complex text, for Marx was clarifying matters as he went along. Or perhaps I should say through his hand and pen, for he seems to have written in order to think. So, by the time of the *Economic and Philosophical Manuscripts of 1844*, he could write with much greater clarity: 'Hegel sets out from the estrangement

---

3. Avineri 1968, pp. 8–13; Dupré 1983, pp. 24–5; Breckman 1999, pp. 284–5. However, see Kouvelakis 2003, especially pp. 290–303, and Leopold 2007, pp. 47–99, for careful readings of this text, albeit with an emphasis on the state. Leopold usefully questions whether Feuerbach is the only source for Marx's use of the 'transformative method'. See Leopold 2007, pp. 83–7.

of substance (in logic, from the infinite, abstractly universal) – from the absolute and fixed abstraction; which means, put in a popular way, that he sets out from religion and theology'.[4] So, let me begin in reverse, using this later clarity as a way into Marx's discussion of Hegel's *Philosophy of Law*.[5]

The key to the quotation from Marx is the phrase, 'put in a popular way [*populär ausgedrückt*]'. In this sense, Hegel begins from religion and theology, at least according to Marx. Yet that is not quite true, for Hegel does not really begin with theology. To be more precise, at a *formal* level his arguments are the same as theology if theology is understood in a Feuerbachian sense. That is, we must understand theology as a hypostasised projection of flesh-and-blood human beings. So also with Hegel's thought: he projects from sensuous human beings a world-spirit or abstract thought which becomes a great overriding force of history with its own existence and power. The problem is that, like theology, Hegel also begins mid-stream: he begins with absolute thought and then tries to make human beings fit in. The result is the dominance of absolute thought and the sidelining of human beings. In light of this dominance, Marx suggests that Hegel's dialectic begins with the estranged and abstracted infinite thought, its negation becomes the negation of the infinite and the positing of real, sensuous existence, and the negation of the negation is nothing less than the reassertion of the absolute and the banishment of sensuous existence.

Marx believes that this re-reading of the dialectic has a deadly effect on Hegel's thought and on theology. In short, anyone who maintains a belief in Hegel's absolute mind or the reality of theology is simply engaging in bad faith. Why? Because they know that theology is unreal, that it is a product of alienation and yet they still believe in it and its propositions. For Marx: 'This implies that self-conscious man, insofar as he has recognised and superseded the spiritual world (or his world's spiritual, general mode of being) as self-alienation, nevertheless again confirms it in this alienated shape and passes it off as his true mode of being – re-establishes it, and pretends to be *at home in*

---

4. Marx 1844g, p. 329; Marx 1844h, p. 570.
5. Marx 1844g, pp. 328–32; Marx 1844h, pp. 569–73. Since I am interested in Marx's engagement with theology in the *Kritik*, I leave other elements on the side. See the careful reading by Leopold 2007, pp. 17–99, and especially his assessment (Leopold 2007, pp. 69–74) that Marx appreciates Hegel's empirical acumen in identifying the abstraction (civil society versus the state) and atomism (each individual for him or herself) of the modern state.

his other-being as such. Thus, for instance, after superseding religion, after recognising religion to be a product of self-alienation he yet finds confirmation of himself in *religion as religion*'.[6] How does this work? We must begin with the assumption, which I explored in the previous chapter, that we know and believe that theology is actually a sign of self-alienation, that we project God from ourselves and thereby know it is false. With this preface in place, the Hegelian dialectic becomes ridiculous: even if we begin with God in the first step, we must negate God in the second, in the full knowledge that the first step really was a projection. Then, if we get to the third step and still assert that God has meaning for us, that theology has some weight, then we are simply deluded, trying to grasp something that has been superseded. Or rather, we live in a state of fundamental contradiction and unreason. We cannot simply posit, negate and re-establish theology without ending up mad.

Formally, then, Hegel's thought is the same as theology, as long as we understand theology in Feuerbach's sense.[7] If you begin with the abstract and absolute you end with the abstract absolute, just as if you begin with God... In this schema, nature or the products of human hands will be nothing more than the products of abstract mind, or thought-entities. But, if you begin with human beings, then the whole game changes. And that is precisely what Marx sets out to do. In all of this there is a big assumption, namely that Feuerbach's theory of projection is in fact viable. However, since I bring forward a series of objections in my discussion of the 'theological state', I will not deal with them here.

The theological state

The lever that Marx uses against Hegel's theory of the state is analogous to the one Feuerbach uses for religion: just as religion is a projection from real human beings, so also is the political state a projection or abstraction of what Hegel calls 'civil society', social and economic interactions independent of the state. The whole of the *Kritik* may be seen as an extended application to Hegel of Feuerbach's insight concerning theology. Marx sums it up rather

---

6. Marx 1844g, p. 339; Marx 1844h, p. 581.
7. Marx also accuses Proudhon of being a formal theologian, since his economic categories exist from eternity and only await their unfolding from the lap of God (Marx 1846a, pp. 100–1; Marx 1846b, pp. 456–7).

nicely: he calls it 'the *theological* notion of the political state [*der* theologischen *Vorstellung des politischen Staates*]'.[8]

There are two crucial moves in this collection of notes: the Feuerbachian inversion and then a strenuous effort to set theology and materialism over against each other before dissolving theology into thin air. I will take each in turn, but, as I do so, I will do my best to avoid getting tangled in Hegel's language. It is a little like a thorn-bush: the more you struggle and thrash about the more you are caught. Marx tries his best, wanting to state bluntly what Hegel means without the verbiage, but in the end he too gets drawn in. Let us see if we can keep clear.

There is no need to repeat the explanation of Feuerbach's inversion here (see Chapter Five), but what Marx does is extend it to Hegel's theory of the state. The delusion is that the state exists, like God, as some abstract entity that pre-exists and thereby controls human beings. The truth, Marx argues, is that the state is a projection of those very same flesh-and-blood human beings. The great appeal of Feuerbach's method is that he places human beings in the foreground – historically and logically.

Enthused with his new tool of analysis, Marx makes the same move again and again, piling on example after example – whether sovereignty, the constitution, political life, primogeniture, political estates, social estates, or bureaucracy. In each case, Marx tries to show that Hegel begins with the objectified, abstract 'sovereignty', 'constitution' and so on, and then tries to make human beings fit. The result: we 'meet at every stage an incarnation of God'.[9] In other words, if Hegel's theory of the state is inescapably theological, then Marx's attack is a systematic attack against theology.

One may go through each example in painstaking detail, but that is not really necessary. So let me take the example of sovereignty, which turns out to be deeply Christological in Hegel. That is to say, sovereignty is incarnated in the single person of the monarch: 'Hegel is concerned to present the monarch as the true "God-man [*Gottmenschen*]", as the *actual incarnation* of the Idea'.[10]

---

8. Marx 1843c, p. 119; Marx 1843d, p. 325. Or, as Marx points out in another part of the Kreuznach notebooks, Hegel's theory of the state and his 'philosophical-religious pantheism' operate in exactly the same way: unreason becomes reason and the old reactionary world of metaphysics dominates the new (Marx 1843n, p. 130).

9. Marx 1843c, p. 39; Marx 1843d, p. 241.

10. Marx 1843c, p. 24; Marx 1843d, p. 225. See also the comment: 'As the monarch mediates himself with civil society through the executive power as its Christ, so

Here, we can see in close-up how Marx works to show how Hegel's idealist method is intrinsically theological.

Marx's argument goes roughly as follows: Hegel starts off on the wrong foot. He postulates an abstract, independent entity known as sovereignty. However, it cannot remain floating in the heavenly ether, so this objectified, abstract entity must become a specific subject. In other words, what we have is incarnation, the 'self-incarnation of sovereignty [*Selbstverkörperung der Souveränität*]'.[11] It must become flesh in a distinct entity, which is not merely the state itself, or perhaps the citizens of that state, but the individual person of the monarch.

But how did Hegel's abstract, objectified entity called sovereignty come to be so? Just like Feuerbach's God, Hegel has projected such sovereignty from its actual material base: the flesh-and-blood subjects of a state. Once it has been so objectified (or 'alienated'), it becomes an entity unto itself which then appears to come down and become embodied in a particular person in a particular situation – hence sovereignty in the person of the monarch. As far as Marx is concerned, Hegel has put the objectified cart before the material horse: one must begin with the real people and from there sovereignty is clearly secondary. Hegel moves in exactly the opposite fashion.

Marx deals with all of the major Hegelian categories in the same way: the constitution, political life, primogeniture, political estates, social estates, bureaucracy, the executive, the monarch... Since I have discussed sovereignty in detail, only a summary is needed for the remainder. As for the constitution, Marx argues that, under Hegel's idealist theory, it is objectified and estranged, so much so that up until now 'the *political constitution* has been the *religious sphere*, the *religion* of national life'.[12] By contrast, once we get the relation right, we can state: 'Just as it is not religion which creates man but man who creates religion, so it is not the constitution which creates the people but the people which creates the constitution'.[13] Concerning Hegel's curious argument for the necessity of primogeniture, Marx comments: 'That man becomes monarch

society mediates itself with the monarch through the estates as its priests' (Marx 1843c, p. 86; Marx 1843d, p. 291).

11. Marx 1843c, p. 24; Marx 1843d, p. 225. See Marx 1843c, p. 26, and Marx 1843d, p. 227, where he refers to 'sovereignty incarnate [*menschgewordene Souveränität*]'.

12. Marx 1843c, p. 31; Marx 1843d, p. 233.

13. Marx 1843c, p. 29; Marx 1843d, p. 231.

by birth can no more be made a metaphysical truth than can the immaculate conception of the Virgin Mary'.[14] On political estates and social estates: 'It is an historical advance which has transformed the *political estates* into *social* estates, so that, just as Christians are equal in heaven but unequal on earth, so the individual members of the nation are *equal* in the heaven of their political world, but unequal in the earthly existence of *society*'.[15] On bureaucracy:

> Since this 'state formalism' constitutes itself as an actual power and itself becomes its own *material* content, it goes without saying that the 'bureaucracy' is a web of *practical* illusions, or the 'illusion of the state'. The bureaucratic spirit is a Jesuitical, theological spirit through and through. The bureaucrats are the Jesuits and theologians of the state. The bureaucracy is *la république prêtre*.... The bureaucracy is the imaginary state alongside the real state – the spiritualism of the state.[16]

And, lastly, to link at least some of these items together – the executive, monarch and sovereignty (once again) – in a package that corresponds all-too-closely with Christianity, we have the following: 'When Hegel calls the executive the *objective* aspect of the sovereignty dwelling in the monarch, that is exactly the same sense in which the Catholic Church was the *real presence* of the sovereignty, substance and spirit of the Holy Trinity'.[17]

This long list of items is more than enough to show how much Hegel and theology are lined up on the same side of the fence. Even if their content may differ, their form is remarkably similar. Both are mystical, guilty of taking the projection (God, the state etc.) as the real thing.[18] What they both need is that famous inversion.

---

14. Marx 1843c, p. 33; Marx 1843d, p. 235. See also; '*Primogeniture is private property* become a *religion* to itself, lost in itself, *elated* by its own independence and power.' (Marx 1843c, p. 101; Marx 1843d, p. 306.) And then: 'The *actuality* of the ethical idea here appears as the *religion of private property*. (Because in primogeniture private property regards itself in a religious manner, it has come about that in our modern times religion in general has become a quality inherent in landed property and that all writings on primogeniture are full of religious unction. Religion is the highest form of thought of this brutality.)' (Marx 1843c, pp. 102–3; Marx 1843d, pp. 307–8.)

15. Marx 1843c, p. 79 (translation modified); Marx 1843d, p. 283.

16. Marx 1843c, pp. 46–7; Marx 1843d, pp. 248–9.

17. Marx 1843c, p. 48 (translation modified); Marx 1843d, p. 250.

18. 'This *uncritical approach*, this *mysticism*, is...the mystery of Hegelian philosophy, particularly the *philosophy of law* and the *philosophy of religion*' (Marx 1843c, p. 83, translation modified; Marx 1843d, p. 287). Van Leeuwen 2002a, pp. 158–9, argues that this text sums up Marx's multi-dimensional critique.

The death of theology?

What are the implications for theology? Does Marx's critique of Hegel mean the death of theology? The major strike against theology is part of a central argument in the *Kritik*: the effort to separate idealism and materialism by a bottomless pit over which no bridge can be thrown. This is really an *idée fixe* of Marx's, one that he repeats at various points, but it boils down to the assumption that theology deals with other-worldly matters, while materialism is resolutely this-worldly. With its talk of heaven and God and the eschaton, theology is not concerned with the 'real world', with politics, society and economics.

The most persistent metaphor, one that turns up again and again, is the opposition between heaven and earth. On the one, materialist, side Marx lines up the actual, democracy, flesh-and-blood people, civil society, citizens of states, while on the other, heavenly, side there are generality, monarchy, sovereignty, constitution, bureaucracy, abstraction, alienation, spiritualism, mystification and God. We can see what is at stake in the following text, where Marx begins with the opposition between the sovereignty of a monarch and that of the people.

> But then it is not a question of *one and the same sovereignty* which has arisen on two sides, but two *entirely contradictory concepts of sovereignty*, the one a sovereignty such as can come to exist in a *monarch*, the other such as can come to exist only in a *people*. It is the same with the question: 'Is God sovereign, or is man?' One of the two is an untruth [*eine Unwarheit*], even if an existing untruth.[19]

He ends with the theological point that there is a sharp opposition between God and man. We can read this in a couple of ways. Either Marx is using a theological point to illustrate and reinforce his argument concerning sovereignty: do you not see, he asks, that it is just like theology and the opposition between God and man? In support of this reading, we should remember that the *Kritik* is really an extended collection of notes and comments rather than a watertight argument. So the examples he uses are really ideas that come to

---

19. Marx 1843c, p. 28; Marx 1843d, p. 230.

mind as he writes.[20] However, I suspect that the argument is more polemical than that: Marx wants to tie theology and Hegel's idealist argument as closely together as possible. This is so he can put Hegel squarely in the theological corner and set out on his own in sharp distinction from theology.

I have a number of questions. Perhaps the most important one is, what about the dialectic? Surely Marx is not going to lock in this opposition between heaven and earth, between God and man, and leave it at that. Not quite, so let us see how his argument unfolds over a couple of dense but extremely important pages.[21] In these pages, Marx begins by arguing that true opposites or extremes cannot have any form of mediation since they have nothing in common. There is no common language, no 'essence' (Wesen, to use Marx's favoured term of that time), and no way of communicating. We might think of the impossibility of communication between the human beings – on the observation-station that circles around Solaris (in Lem's novel) – and that sentient planet itself.[22] They are so different there is no hope of ever bridging the gap. The question then becomes: is this the kind of opposition Marx envisages between God and human beings, between heaven and earth?

The answer is no. He presents two types of what we might call pseudo- or apparent oppositions. The first type actually shares a common ground or language (for Marx, Wesen) – hence the saying 'opposites attract'. Like a divorced couple arguing over money or the children, they have something in common

---

20. Marx's argument is certainly not watertight and his examples are not consistent. Just when I think I have him pinned down on this opposition between theology and materialism, he undermines it. That moment comes in a discussion of democracy and monarchy. While it appears that monarchy is aligned with theology (his previous argument certainly suggests so) and democracy with a materialist approach, Marx turns around and compares Christianity with democracy: 'In a certain respect the relation of democracy to all other forms of the state is like the relation of Christianity to all other religions. Christianity is *the* religion, the *essence of religion* – deified man as a *particular* religion. Similarly, democracy is the *essence of all state constitutions* – socialised man as a *particular* state constitution. Democracy stands to the other constitutions as the genus stands to its species; except that here the genus itself appears as an existent, and therefore as one *particular* species over against the others whose existence does not correspond to their essence. To democracy all other forms of the state stand as its Old Testament. Man does not exist for the law but the law for man – it is a *human manifestation*; whereas in the other forms of state man is a *legal manifestation*. That is the fundamental distinction of democracy.' (Marx 1843c, pp. 29–30; Marx 1843d, p. 231.)

21. See Marx 1843c, pp. 88–90; Marx 1843d, pp. 292–4. For some reason that I cannot fathom, Van Leeuwen 2002a, pp. 137–9, is content to paraphrase these crucial pages, whereas elsewhere he enters into great tangential detail.

22. Lem 1971.

that enables them to communicate, however rancorous it might be. Marx's examples are the North and South Poles as well as women and men, but the point is the same. By contrast, a real opposition is qualitatively different. Here he makes a rather simple logical point: the true opposite of pole is non-pole, of human, the non-human.

The second type of pseudo-opposition is far more interesting and trouble-ridden. Let us say that God and human beings are absolutely different – as Marx has said a little earlier and some forms of theology have done for quite some time. If we say that they have nothing in common, is that a proper, qualitative opposition? No, says Marx: an abstraction (like God) is not a real thing. He is not an 'essence [*Wesen*]' like human beings. Thus, despite appearances, the opposition between an essence and an abstraction is not a real opposition.

Once he has made this point, Marx can move on to dissolve theology, God, heaven and the rest of theology. They are all abstractions and therefore not really proper objects. For that reason they cannot be opposed to philosophy, man or earth, all of which are proper objects. And then he delivers the *coup de grâce*: in fact, philosophy shows that religion is an illusion and therefore not a real object.[23]

> Christianity, for example, or religion in general, and philosophy are extremes. But in truth religion does not form a *true* opposite to philosophy. For philosophy comprehends *religion* in its *illusory* actuality. For philosophy, religion is therefore dissolved into itself [*in sich selbst aufgelöst*], insofar as it wants to be something actual [*Wirklichkeit*]. There is no actual dualism of essence [*Wesen*].[24]

This is Marx's take on Hegel's dialectic. Theology is not the other pole to philosophy, and so philosophy cannot actually negate theology and then sweep it up to another level. Instead, philosophy shows that theology is an illusion and so theology, instead of being 'dissolved [*aufgelöst*]' into philosophy, actually 'dissolves' into itself. The relation between theology and philosophy is not

---

23. Soon enough, philosophy itself would not be adequate, for it remains at the theoretical level. Once we shift to the realm of society, the apparent contradictions – subjectivity versus objectivity, spirituality and materialism, activity and suffering – lose their oppositional character. See Marx 1844g, p. 302; Marx 1844h, p. 542.

24. Marx 1843c, p. 89; Marx 1843d, p. 294.

one of *Aufhebung* but *Auflösung*, not sublation but dissolution, cancellation, and elimination. The reason is that philosophy and theology cannot relate on the same plane, since theology is not *eine Wirklichkeit*, a reality. Its contents are illusions, it has no objective existence, and it therefore cannot relate to other objects since it is simply non-being. Or, more bluntly, anything that is abstract, bloodless, non-sensuous, unsuffering and ahistorical simply cannot exist.[25] And if not, it should be ruled out of court in any serious discussion. 'True criticism', argues Marx, does not bother with the niceties of theological contradictions, such as those of the Trinity. It shows how such theological debates arise in the first place. It explains them, attempts to understand their genesis and tracks their necessity.[26]

There are, it must be admitted, a few problems with this argument, especially since it is a core-position that Marx would take. I focus on the following: the nature of a true opposition; the assumption of what is 'real'; and the dismissal of an abstract projection as un-real and not worth considering. To begin with, Marx sneaks in the argument that a true opposition can operate only between items that are real. Even though it is a common point – an opposition can only take place when the items share some common ground[27] – I am by no means sure that Marx's argument is entirely logical. The real and the non-real are perfectly valid logical oppositions – precisely of the sort Marx specifies earlier. They are qualitatively different on that score. Marx wants to argue that they are not valid opposites, since one is determined by the other. Therefore, their common ground is one term of the opposition. For theology (and indeed the state), that common ground is human beings.

But, then, what is 'real'? This is an unfortunate position to take, for it is far too easy to dismantle. 'Reality' is what is empirically verifiable – my foot, the water in the ocean, the bust of Lenin on the bookshelf, the copy of Annie Sprinkle's book *Post-Porn Modernist*, the cathedral I can see from my window,

---

25. Marx 1844g, p. 337; Marx 1844h, pp. 578–9.
26. 'True criticism...shows the inner genesis of the Holy Trinity in the human brain. It describes the act of its birth.' (Marx 1843c, p. 91; Marx 1843d, p. 296.)
27. He makes use of this general argument more than once. For example, 'the orthodox Catholic is more hostile to the orthodox Protestant than to the atheist, just as the Legitimist is more hostile to the liberal than the Communist. This is not because the atheist and the Communist are more akin to the Catholic or Legitimist, but because they are more foreign to him than are the Protestant and the liberal, being *outside* his circle.' (Marx 1844e, p. 190; Marx 1844f, p. 393.)

and so on. The 'real' must be perceptible by the senses, able to suffer and have a historical existence.[28] By contrast, ideas, beliefs, assumptions and world-views are not real; they are illusions. Again and again, he lumps religion in with politics, arts, literature and so on – they are far too abstract.[29]

There are many ways to tackle this opposition between what is 'illusion' and what is 'real', but let me approach it in this way: there are too many borderline-cases even if we grant the initial assumptions. For example, is 'society' real? Can you verify it any more than you can verify my fantasy of the ideal bicycle-ride? Or is a philosophical idea like historical materialism any more real? Let us assume that Marx is right: theology is an abstract projection, a secondary product of human activity, in short, it is a constructed entity. The big problem then is that, even if these various (Feuerbachian) projections are secondary and derivative, that in no way dispels them. For instance, why is a fantasy or an illusion any less 'real' than anything else? Even if my sexual fantasy of . . . is just that, a fantasy produced by my imagination, is that not real in some sense? I may not be able to touch, smell or see them in the same way that I do physical objects, but they are certainly 'real' for me. Marx would respond that this argument is precisely Feuerbach's failing, for Feuerbach may have argued that the various elements of ourselves which we project and turn into the divine are projections, but he does not dispense with them; they are still 'real', except that they actually belong to us. In reply, I would point out that we also have a whole collection of borderline-cases, such as art or writing or films that have tangible, real outcomes in ways very similar to religion. Yet, they are ultimately products of the human imagination. In short, it seems to me that Marx has here succumbed to the fallacy of showing that something is an illusion and thereby establishing that it is no longer real and not worth one's attention. Later, as we will see with his treatment of fetishism in *Capital*, he would develop a completely new approach to the opposition that effectively negates it. However, at this point, he still subscribes to the opposition and succumbs to the fallacy I have been tracing. The danger of such a fallacy is that you assume that a question has been laid to rest, the prayers said and the coffin lowered into the ground. The problem is that the corpse is not dead

---

28. Marx 1844g, p. 337; Marx 1844h, pp. 578–9.
29. See, for example, Marx 1844g, p. 302; Marx 1844h, p. 542.

and is knocking loudly on the coffin-lid. I fear that Marx, for one, has not heard the sound.

The paradox of the secular state

Or perhaps he did hear. These rough notes on Hegel are not the only time Marx dealt with theology and the state. Marx first picks up the question in an earlier piece, 'Comments on the Latest Prussian Censorship Instruction', which ironically did not pass the censor, as well as a crucial observation from *On the Jewish Question*. At this point, I bring Engels into the discussion with an astute journal-article from the same time, 'Frederick William IV, King of Prussia'. What do we find when we throw these texts together? They actually do not sit easily with one another. While we might attribute this to the mad schedule associated with Marx's early journalistic efforts, or indeed to the fact that he was still developing his ideas and responding in the heat of the moment to various organs of the conservative press, there is a more important issue at stake: the dance between theology and the state. I begin by tracking a piece that comes close to his assessment of Hegel – that theology should have nothing to do with the state – but then move on to pick up a far more dialectical and intriguing argument. They end up providing two very different perspectives on the secular state and the basis for religious tolerance.

In his first journalistic article, where he reflects on the revisions to the Prussian censorship-law of 1842,[30] Marx develops an argument that leads to the following conclusion: the only way to allow a plurality of religions within any state is to have a secular state. In other words, religious tolerance is based on a secular indifference to religion. Muslims, Hindus, Greenlandic shamans, Christians and so on can all exist together as long as I am indifferent to them all. Still common today, especially with the increasing presence of religion within politics, this conclusion is in itself quite unremarkable. However, I am more interested in the way the 24-year-old Marx reaches such a conclusion.

The starting point is an old friend, namely the distinction between the general and the particular. Religion is, by definition, a particular beast. Each religion makes a truth-claim, based on the specific nature of its own belief and doctrines, that excludes all others (the echoes of Bauer are strong here). They

---

30. Marx 1843a; Marx 1843b.

are, if you like, complete world-views that cannot tolerate another complete world-view: 'each religion believes itself distinguished from the various other *would-be* religions by its *special nature*, and that precisely its *particular features* make it the *true religion*'.[31] It follows, then, that any idea of religion in general is a contradiction. One cannot talk about the general features of religion, since that involves denying the specific features that make each religion what it is. These features held in common must of necessity discard any positive content of any specific religion. The result: the idea of religion in general is nothing other than a non-religious position.[32] In short, such a general religion is another version of secularism.

What is wrong with this argument? Apart from the use of the generic term 'religion', which should be ruled out by such an argument, the sample-pool is a little restricted. Marx's context has something to do with this, especially in light of the long wars fought between Roman Catholics and Protestants (1618–48). As I outlined in the Introduction, both the Reformation itself and the retaliation by the Roman Catholics, which eventually won back Southern Germany, contributed to a continuing pattern of exclusive intolerance. In fact, Marx goes on to use this difference between Roman Catholics and Protestants to argue against the push for a Christian state under the Prussian king, Friedrich Wilhelm IV. If it is to be a Christian state, then what type of Christianity will be the religion in favour – Roman-Catholic or Protestant? Favouring one would exclude the other as heretical. Why? The 'innermost essence [*innerstes Wesen*]'[33] of one is completely at odds with the other. Even more, all else becomes secondary, for one 'who wants to ally himself with religion owing to religious feelings must concede it the decisive voice in all questions'.[34]

This is not the best argument, despite the fact that it is recited regularly today. Not all religions operate with mutually exclusive world-views, even though many do. The obvious example is Hinduism, which prides itself on the fact that it is inclusive rather than exclusive, that it is perfectly possible to be a Hindu pursuing a potentially infinite range of specific practices and beliefs. The nice catch here is that Hindus will claim that this feature makes

---

31. Marx 1843a, p. 116; Marx 1843b, p. 104.
32. 'This *rationalist point of view*... is so inconsistent as to adopt the irreligious point of view while its aim is to protect religion.' (Marx 1843a, p. 116; Marx 1843b, pp. 103–4.)
33. Marx 1843a, p. 118; Marx 1843b, p. 105.
34. Marx 1843a, p. 118; Marx 1843b, p. 106.

Hinduism superior, all the while neglecting to mention the ingrained caste-system. I could also cite more open-minded forms of Christianity rather than what we would now call fundamentalist exclusivism. Then there is the long story of syncretism, the gradual acquisition of all manner of 'pagan' practices into any religion that found itself expanding – whether Mahayana Buddhism as it moved into China and Japan, or indeed Christianity as it spread from Palestine to Rome and then across Europe, drawing in all manner of fertility and solstice-festivals along with a good collection of spirits.

What is more interesting than these flaws are the ways in which Marx's argument connects and disconnects with his other positions concerning the state and theology. Without too much trouble it may join forces with his heaven-earth distinction. Theology is a heavenly, other-worldly project and so it should have nothing to do with the earthly, this-worldly concerns of the state and politics (see Chapter Two). When this other-worldly concern does enter politics, then its particular and exclusive approach leads to a brutal intolerance of other religions, or even other versions of the same creed. Now there are two reasons for excluding Christianity from the public life of the state.

But, then, we come to a disconnection with these arguments. Over against his separation of heaven and earth, or, indeed, particular and general, Marx makes a much more perceptive dialectical observation in nothing other than *On the Jewish Question*. Here, Marx argues that the fully realised Christian state is not what everyone thinks it is (the 'Christian state' of Friedrich Wilhelm IV); rather, the true Christian state is the negation of Christianity, that is, a secular, atheistic and democratic one.[35] The crucial point here is that the contradictions inherent within the idea and practice of a Christian state can only lead to its dissolution. These contradictions include the tension between other-worldly religion and this-worldly politics, the problems inherent in a political attitude to religion and a religious attitude to politics, the impossibility of actually

---

35. Marx 1844m, pp. 156–8; Marx 1844n, pp. 357–9. Another example of Marx's awareness of the contradictions inherent in the Christian state appears in his long discussion of thefts of fallen wood (his third piece of commentary on the Sixth Rhine Province Assembly). He points out the paradox of the Reformation's abolition of monasteries and secularisation of their property. Although it was a necessary step to get rid an abusive institution, it also had its down side, for nothing replaced the meagre support the poor had received from the monasteries (Marx 1842n, p. 232; Marx 1842o, p. 207).

living out the prescriptions of the Bible for living with one's fellow human beings (turning the other cheek, giving your tunic as well as your coat, walking the extra mile and so on). What is the resolution of these contradictions? It is 'the state which relegates religion to a place among other elements of civil society [*der bürgerlichen Gesellschaft*]'.[36] This is the realised Christian state, that is, one that has negated itself and relegated Christianity to its own, private place among other religions and other parts of society. As we saw earlier, Marx thought that such a state had been realised in North America, with the secular state and the separation of church and state making religion a private affair.

Yet what is intriguing about this argument is that this modern secular state arises from, or is the simultaneous realisation and negation of, the Christian state. This argument is a long way from his efforts to banish theology from any form of the state or even his critique of Hegel for the theological form of his thinking about the state. It might be argued that his characterisation of theology as other-worldly and Christianity as exclusively particular is consistent with this idea of the secular state. But the difference is that such a particular, heavenly Christianity would have no place in a secular state unless it was thoroughly transformed.

Marx's argument – the realisation of the Christian state in the secular state – moves in a different direction, for it connects with a point made today: the secular state arose out of the Christian need for religious tolerance and pluralism.[37] Even more, goes the argument of our own time, the secular state is the only proper basis of religious tolerance. In order to overcome older practices of religious intolerance and in response to the sheer number of different forms of Christianity, the only viable response is a secular state that favours no Christian denomination or indeed no religion at all. Or, as Marx put it, Christianity itself 'separated church and state'.[38]

---

36. Marx 1844m, p. 156; Marx 1844n, p. 357. Or, as he puts it in his debate with Bauer, the 'modern state that knows no religious privileges is also the fully developed *Christian* state' (Marx and Engels 1845a, p. 111; Marx and Engels 1845b, pp. 117–18).

37. For example, see Brett 2009. Despite his love of pursuing all sorts of angles, Van Leeuwen 2002a, pp. 164–9, is content with this section to offer an exposition of Marx's argument. All he suggests is that it is the key to Marx's essay on Hegel's philosophy of law.

38. Marx 1842h, p. 198; Marx 1842i, p. 186. See Breckman (Breckman 1999, pp. 295–6) who argues that when Marx came to the conclusion that the secular state actually has a dialectical basis in theology, he saw the inadequacies of liberal, republican

This position actually has a sting in its tail. Before we feel that sting, I would like to bring Engels into our discussion, for in an early piece he makes a strikingly similar argument to Marx's. Engels tackles the question of church and state in a rather judicious article from 1843 called 'Frederick William IV, King of Prussia'.[39] His main point is that the efforts of the self-described 'Christian king' (always in mocking quotation-marks)[40] to establish a Christian state are doomed to collapse through a series of contradictions. The underlying problem is that the Christian-feudal model the king has in mind is, like theology itself, an ossified relic from the past that will no longer work in a world that has made huge strides in science and free thought, by which I take it he means not merely philosophy but also democracy, representation and republicanism. The result is that the king must make a whole series of compromises that doom the effort from the start.

Engels does not find the Prussian king an obnoxious person as such. He credits the king with having a system, even with being kind-hearted and witty, but he is also a reactionary with an impossible agenda. Engels begins by pointing out that various obvious measures are really the outward manifestation of a deeper problem – encouraging church-attendance, laws strengthening the observance of Sunday rest, tightening of the laws concerning divorce, purging of the theological faculties, changing examinations to emphasise firm belief, and appointing believers to government-positions. The problem is that the Prussian king is caught in a dilemma: the logical outcome of his programme is the separation of church and state, yet he seeks to fuse the two. On the one hand, as the head of the Evangelical Church, as *summus episcopus*, he seeks to subordinate the church to secular power. Even though he wants to combine ecclesiastical and state-power in his own person, to join 'all power, earthly and heavenly' so that he becomes 'an earthly God',[41] he is, in fact, king first and supreme bishop second. On the other hand, such a move runs

---

arguments for such a state. From this point (1843) he became much more determined to explore human emancipation in a way that was entirely outside theological questions. In other words, Marx's problem was how to conceive of a politics that was entirely non-theological.

39. Engels 1843a; Engels 1843b. See also Engels's comments in the late letters on Paul Lafargue's efforts to bring about the separation of church and state in the French assembly; Engels 1891m, p. 320; Engels 1891n, p. 239; Engels 1892b, p. 330; Engels 1892c, p. 248.

40. See, for example, Engels 1844m, p. 515; Engels 1844i, p. 530.

41. Engels 1843a, p. 362; Engels 1843b, p. 431.

directly into the wall of Christian doctrine: one's primary allegiance should be to God and not some temporal power, whether state or king: 'A person who makes his whole being, his whole life, a preparation for heaven cannot have the interest in earthly affairs which the state demands of its citizens'.[42] In other words, a full recovery of Christianity means the separation of church and state.

Engels muddies his argument by two points. He suggests that the Prussian king's approach is a Protestant one, a compromise with secularism, whereas the separation of church and state is a Roman-Catholic position. I am not so sure, since the Roman Catholics have been all-too-interested in temporal power, with land, armies, and an earthly representative in the Pope, all the while proclaiming superiority over any ruler to the extent of anointing one sovereign after another. The Pope, it would seem, is as compromised as the rest of this sordid bunch. Further, Engels argues that state and church both demand absolute commitment. Nothing should come above one's allegiance to God or the state; the two are therefore incompatible. Once again, this is a strange argument. It betrays once again Engels's own background within the Calvinist tradition: it really is an all-or-nothing perception of God versus Mammon. In the same way that he sees Christianity as an unchanging and monolithic entity of more than 1800 years (see Chapter Nine), so also does he perceive its demand as absolute. It requires total commitment and obedience; any engagement with 'the world' becomes compromise and betrayal. And, if that is the case with one's religious belief, then so also with the state. I would add that the problems of cohesion in the Prussian Empire, or indeed the perpetual issue of German unification, also provide a specific situation for Engels. He does, after all, argue consistently for a unified and large republican state as the proper form for revolutionary politics.

Engels's argument intersects quite neatly with Marx's: Christianity itself leads to a separation of church and state, for there is a tendency towards secularisation within Christianity especially in light of the endless divergence within it. Any effort at a Christian state must decide what form of Christianity is to be favoured.[43] Is it to be Orthodox, Roman-Catholic, Anglican, Pres-

---

42. Engels 1843a, p. 363; Engels 1843b, p. 432.
43. He makes a similar point in his discussion of the established Church of England and the English constitution in relation to 'dissenters' and the Roman Catholics. See Engels 1844f, p. 501; Engels 1844g, pp. 580–1.

byterian, Lutheran, Methodist, Congregational, or...? The existence of the Orthodox churches in their multiplicity, as well as the event of the Protestant Reformation put the lie to the claim by the Roman Catholics to be the one 'catholic' church. Even within the history of the Roman-Catholic Church, there were numerous schisms and breakaways that were either absorbed and curtailed or expelled as heretics. According to this argument, any Christian theory of the state must enable and allow for such diversity. The only way that can happen is through a separation of church and state: no one form of Christianity can dominate without making a travesty of theology itself.

It seems to me that this argument is implicit in Engels's exploration of the contradictions in Friedrich Wilhelm IV's programme. For example, this Prussian king not only recognises both Roman Catholic and Protestant, but he had also freed the Old Lutherans from the enforced union in 1817 of Lutherans and Calvinists in the Evangelical Church. With the various Protestant churches now given freedom in their internal affairs, the king struggles to maintain his rôle as the head of the church. Which church? Is one church to submit to the state-imposed authority of another? It is a hopelessly contradictory solution and one unacceptable to the churches themselves. The more Friedrich Wilhelm IV tries to deal with each situation in question, the more confused the whole situation becomes. In the end, these efforts – like those that sought to restore feudal privilege in the context of an Enlightenment-inspired basis of Prussian law – will lead to the collapse of the so-called Christian state through internal contradictions. The solution is a secular state.[44]

A little earlier, I suggested that this argument, shared by the young Marx and the equally young Engels as well as some today, may come back to bite us. Let me put it this way: the more church and state are separated, the more they seem to be entwined. Of course, this twist comes with some hindsight after a reasonable history of the secular state. For example, in the United States, the separation between church and state is enshrined in the First Amendment to the Constitution: 'Congress shall make no law respecting an establishment of religion, or prohibiting the free exercise thereof'. Initially a response to the established Church of England, especially after the American War of Independence, it has come to be interpreted as any act by the Congress and the legislature that

---

44. The separation of church and state would become standard Social-Democratic policy. See Marx and Engels 1848j, p. 4; Marx and Engels 1848k, p. 4; Engels 1891c, p. 229; Engels 1891d, p. 237.

favours one religion over another with the possible outcome that such a religion may become established. In practice, this really means Christianity and shows up with monotonous regularity in the area of state-funded education. The Bible is not to be taught, prayer is not appropriate and one cannot teach religious doctrines in state-schools.

However, in the United States, the separation of church and state has become something of a legal fiction. The more strictly the courts apply the First Amendment, the more pervasive religion becomes in public life. An external observer cannot help noticing that religion saturates public life in the USA: the founding myth of the escape from oppression to a land of freedom is drawn from the story of the Exodus and the 'promised land', presidents must be openly Christian, they make decisions with religious concerns in mind, most recently on the questions of sex-education and stem-cell research, voting patterns follow religious lines, and, especially in the 'Bible Belt', there is a sharp polarisation over religion. One is either passionately Christian or passionately atheist. By comparison, states which still have an established church, such as Denmark, or those with only recently disestablished churches such as Sweden, are among the least religiously observant countries in the world.

One cannot help wondering whether this paradox is the result of the fact that the separation of church and state arose, in part at least, as a Christian response to the plurality of religions. I have argued elsewhere that secularism and religion are really two sides of the same coin. The various derivative forms of secularism – such as the separation of church and state, or the distinction between scientific academic work and theology, or indeed atheism itself – seem to be riddled with the same contradiction.[45] The purpose of secularism is a salutary one – the removal of oppression in the name of religion. Unfortunately, the ways in which secularism has manifested itself have not done a very good job. Perhaps the way forward is to recognise the liberating elements within both religion and secularism and form a politics of alliance in what may be called a 'new secularism'.[46]

---

45. The basic meaning of secularism (from *saeculum*, 'this age' or 'this world') is that it designates a system of thought, indeed a way of living that draws its terms purely from this age and from this world. That is the positive sense of the term. Of course, it has an implied negative, namely that secularism does not draw its reference-point from something beyond this world, whether that is a God or the gods above, or a time in the future, or indeed a sacred text such as the Bible that talks about both. In light of this basic sense, these other forms – separation of church and state, of theology and other academic disciplines, and an anti-religious position – are secondary and derivative.

46. Boer 2007b.

Conclusion

I began with Marx's systematic use of the Feuerbachian inversion to uncover the formal theologian at work in the heart of Hegel's theory of the state. Before long, it became a comprehensive argument on Marx's part to rule theology out of the picture, for theology is illusory and unreal, heavenly, other-worldly and particular. It has no place in the real world, especially that of politics and the state. But then we found him developing a very different argument, namely that one can actually find a logic for the secular state within Christianity, indeed that the secular state is the full realisation of the Christian state and the resolution of its contradictions. At this point, Engels joined the conversation with an astute piece that dovetailed nicely into Marx's argument.

While much of Marx's assessment of Hegel's implicit theology is extraordinarily engaging and well worth re-reading, I am, in the end, much more interested in what can only be regarded as a tension within his thought concerning theology and the state. Is theology to be dismissed as a pseudoscience, dealing with illusory and imaginary entities, or is it a more complex beast, beset with its own contradictions that yield sometimes surprising results?

Indeed, what strikes anyone who reads through the later journalistic pieces by Marx and Engels – let alone Engels's later concerns with early Christianity – is that the complex issue of religion and politics turns up with a persistence that belies their efforts to move beyond that issue. They kept seeing the entwinement of religion and politics everywhere around them. It may be the tensions between the Russians, Turks, British and French around the Crimean War,[47] or it may be the French Revolution and French history,[48] or

---

47. Marx 1856–7, pp. 86–7; Marx 1857g, p. 178; Marx 1876a, p. 120; Marx 1876b, p. 15; Engels 1853c, pp. 284–5; Engels 1853d, pp. 218–19; Engels 1854a; Engels 1854b; Marx 1854q; Marx 1854r; Marx 1854s, p. 492; Marx 1854t, p. 404; Marx 1860b, p. 429; Marx 1853g, p. 541; Marx and Engels 1853, pp. 6–11; Marx 1853i, p. 19; Engels 1853a, pp. 23–6; Engels 1853b, pp. 32, 35–6; Marx 1853r, p. 67; Marx 1853l, p. 111; Marx 1853t, p. 195; Marx 1853w, p. 211; Marx 1853v, p. 257; Marx 1853u, p. 266; Marx 1853y, p. 313; Marx 1853j, pp. 356–7; Marx 1853x, p. 408; Marx 1854n, p. 576; Marx 1854l, pp. 615–17; Marx 1854b, pp. 20–1; Marx 1854i, p. 33; Marx 1854f; Marx 1854d, p. 74; Marx 1854m, p. 86; Marx 1854c; Marx and Engels 1854; Engels 1855, pp. 163–4; Marx 1855t, p. 232; Marx 1855u, p. 258; Marx 1855j, p. 558; Marx 1855k, p. 560.
48. Marx 1850a, pp. 55, 60, 77, 83, 92–3, 118, 124–5, 131, 141; Marx 1850b, pp. 19, 24, 40–1, 47, 56–7, 81, 87–8, 94, 104; Marx 1851a, p. 570; Marx 1852c, pp. 105–6, 110–14, 125–8, 132, 135, 138–42, 150, 169–71, 181–3, 192–4, 196–7; Marx 1852d, pp. 116–18, 121–5, 137–9, 143, 147, 149–56, 162, 181–3, 194–5, 202–4, 206–7; Marx 1871e, p. 501; Marx 1871f, p. 559; Marx 1871a, p. 352; Marx 1871b, pp. 358–9; Engels 1882c, pp. 62–8, 77–9; Engels 1882d, pp. 478–84, 490–2; Engels 1890–1a, pp. 184–5, 190; Engels 1890–1b, pp. 193–4, 198–9.

the English Revolution and England generally,[49] the Revolution of 1848–9 and the history of other struggles in Germany,[50] Russia,[51] or the Holy Alliance,[52] Switzerland,[53] matters pertaining to Poland,[54] the dealings of the Pope in Italy and France,[55] Spain,[56] the whole question of Ireland,[57] Puritanism in the United States,[58] Austria and the Slavic countries,[59] the revolutionary war in Hungary,[60] China,[61] India,[62] Algiers where Marx went for recuperation close to the end of his life,[63] Europe in general,[64] and even Engels's comments on the family.[65] I would suggest that Marx's comment on the 'East' applies to all of these

---

49. Marx and Engels 1850e, pp. 254–6; Marx and Engels 1850f, pp. 210–12; Marx and Engels 1850c, pp. 512–14; Marx and Engels 1850d, pp. 443–5; Marx 1852f, p. 350; Marx 1853e, p. 486; Marx 1853d, pp. 503–5; Marx 1853b, p. 517; Marx 1853m; Marx 1853a, pp. 50–2, 56; Marx 1853h, p. 189; Marx 1853j, pp. 350–1; Marx 1855bb, pp. 390–1; Marx 1855cc, pp. 398–9.

50. Engels 1851–2, pp. 14–15, 23–4, 28, 35; Marx 1853k, pp. 310–11; Engels 1875a, p. 59; Engels 1875b, p. 576; Engels 1882e, pp. 450–3; Engels 1882f, pp. 325–8; Engels 1882c; Engels 1882d; Engels 1895–6a, pp. 509–10; Engels 1895–6b, pp. 460–1; Engels 1890e, p. 8; Engels 1890f, p. 8.

51. Engels 1882i; Engels 1882j; Engels 1866, pp. 160–1; Marx 1867e, p. 197; Marx 1867f, p. 201; Engels 1874–5a, p. 49; Engels 1874–5b, p. 566; Engels 1890a, pp. 15, 18–19, 30–1; Engels 1890b, pp. 15, 18, 30–2.

52. Marx and Engels 1848x; Marx and Engels 1848y.

53. Engels 1848e, p. 146; Engels 1848f, p. 93; Engels 1848j, p. 183; Engels 1849k; Engels 1849i, pp. 42–4.

54. Marx and Engels 1848n, pp. 339, 356–7, 359–61, 370, 380; Marx and Engels 1848o, pp. 321, 338–9, 341–3, 352, 362; Engels 1874–5a, p. 10; Engels 1874–5b, p. 526.

55. Marx 1860b, p. 430; Marx 1855n, pp. 473–4; Marx 1855o, p. 483f; Marx and Engels 1848t, p. 385; Marx and Engels 1848u, p. 366; Engels 1848i.

56. Marx 1854k, pp. 394–5, 402–5, 411, 435–6.

57. Marx 1871g, p. 620; Marx 1871h, p. 654; Marx 1868d, p. 4; Marx 1868e, p. 543; Marx 1867c, pp. 194–8; Marx 1867d, pp. 550–2; Marx 1869b, pp. 215–20, 230–1, 242–4, 247–52, 265, 270–1, 279; Marx 1853s, pp. 119–20; Marx 1855bb, pp. 384–5; Marx 1855cc, pp. 393–4; Marx 1855x, pp. 79–80; Marx 1855y, pp. 118–19; Engels 1870d; Engels 1870e; Engels 1870a, pp. 169, 171, 176–8; Engels 1870b, pp. 483, 485, 490–2; Engels 1869a, pp. 285–6; Engels 1870k, pp. 299–303; Engels 1870g, pp. 308, 314; Engels 1881c; Engels 1881d; Engels 1882m; Engels 1882n; Engels 1868i, p. 165; Engels 1868j, p. 209; Engels 1867a, p. 458; Engels 1867b, p. 373; Engels 1867e; Engels 1867f. Even Jenny (junior) joins the discussion: Marx (Jenny junior) 1870a; Marx (Jenny junior) 1870b; Marx (Jenny junior) 1869a, p. 549; Marx (Jenny junior) 1869b, pp. 703–4.

58. Engels 1892n, p. 74; Engels 1892o, p. 560.

59. Marx 1856h, p. 21; Marx 1856i, p. 25.

60. Engels 1849p, pp. 469–70; Engels 1849h, p. 147.

61. Marx 1853q, p. 93; Marx 1854e, pp. 41–2.

62. Marx 1853c, p. 126; Marx 1853f, p. 222.

63. Marx 1882c; Marx 1882d.

64. Engels and Kautsky 1887, pp. 597–8, 603.

65. Engels 1884a, pp. 160, 173–4, 178, 186–9, 193, 197, 204–6, 211–12, 224, 228–9, 250–3, 275; Engels 1884b, pp. 56, 68–9, 72, 80–4, 88, 91–2, 98–100, 104–5, 118, 122–3, 145–8, 171; Engels 1890–1c, p. 205; Engels 1890–1d, p. 213.

topics: 'So far as religion is concerned, the question may be reduced to a general and hence easily answerable one: Why does the history of the East appear as a history of religions?'[66] At times, they argue that religion is a screen for political and economic matters, but at others they recognise that, even if religion is an abstract and illusory business, it still seems to have a distinct and problematic political presence. It was not for nothing that the 'religious idea' (and its relation to social, political and intellectual development) was important enough to be listed as part of the programme for the 1866 Geneva Conference of the International.[67]

66. Marx 1853bb, p. 332; Marx 1853cc, pp. 251–2.
67. Marx 1865d; Marx 1865e; Marx 1865f; Marx 1865g.

Chapter Seven
Idols, Fetishes and Graven Images

England, that land of Mammon.[1]

When a great social revolution shall have mastered the results of the bourgeois epoch, the market of the world and the modern powers of production... then only will human progress cease to resemble that hideous, pagan idol, who would not drink the nectar but from the skulls of the slain.[2]

Fetishism is another trajectory that proceeds from the insight which Marx gained from Feuerbach. It has had more than its fair share of attention due to the famous section in *Capital*, 'The Fetishism of Commodities and the Secret Thereof'. That should come as no surprise, since it has been one of the most fertile of Marx's ideas. But it is also one of the most consistent. In this chapter, I follow its trail from the first engagement with Charles de Brosses through to its full flowering as an insight into the workings of the whole of capitalism. Yet, what is little known is that, within Marx's own texts, the theory of fetishism has a significant overlap with the critique of idolatry, especially from the Hebrew Bible, albeit inverted so that fetishism absorbs idolatry within itself. It is

---

1. Marx 1877g, p. 283; Marx 1877h, p. 302.
2. Marx 1853f, p. 222.

this connection, which also marks a mutation of the Feuerbachian inversion,[3] that is my underlying concern in this chapter.

Before proceeding, I should point out that the connection between fetishism and idolatry has been made in theological discussions, especially those that took place during the Marxist-Christian dialogue of the 1960s and 1970s and then more recently in liberation-theology.[4] The main development of these appropriations, drawing upon Marx's comments concerning the fetishism of commodities in *Capital* as well as his observations regarding all the dimensions of capital as 'this religion of everyday life [*diese Religion des Alltagslebens*]',[5] is that the idol – capital – is not merely a false god but that it devours its worshippers. I will return to deal with these developments in the conclusion, although an extended engagement with and critique of liberation-theology and the Marxist-Christian dialogue will take place elsewhere.[6] However, these treatments make the jump between idolatry and fetishism on the basis of the well-known texts of Marx on fetishism. What is missing is both a detailed tracking of the idea of fetishism in Marx's work (only then does the richness of the idea become clear) and a sense of the distinction between fetishism and idolatry that would lead to the absorption of the latter by the former.

History of religions

I used to believe that being opinionated and old age went hand in hand, but then I kept meeting younger people and those of my own age who were just as opinionated. Since then, I have always admired a man, a former mentor, who is now almost 90, for he still gets a sparkle in his eye when he comes across a new idea or discovery. So also with Marx. He was fascinated until the end of his life by the emerging study of the history of religions. It first drew him in when was preparing the lost work on Christian art that I mentioned earlier

---

3. In a frustrating work, Ollman 1971, p. 225, fails to distinguish between the Feuerbach-inspired criticism of religion and the different trajectory of fetishism. Of course, they overlap, but they are not the same.

4. Sobrino 2004a, pp. 57, 146, 165–7; Sobrino 2004b, pp. 59, 99; Dussel 1993; Dussel 2001, pp. 298–9; Sung 2007; Löwy 1996, pp. 56–7; Hinkelammert 1986; Assmann and Hinkelammert 1989; Scott 1994, pp. 75–109; Evans 1984, pp. 146–8; Lischer 1973, pp. 554–5; Suda 1978; Thiemann 1985.

5. Marx 1894a, p. 817; Marx 1894b, p. 838.

6. Boer forthcoming.

and then, close to the end of his life, it was one of the subjects he studied over the period from 1880 to 1882. In particular, he was taken by the topic of fetishism. It turns up in his earliest pieces of journalism and then again in the last pages of one of his most curious texts, *The Ethnological Notebooks*.[7] Over the four decades in between, the idea of fetishism became a multi-purpose tool. And that is precisely what I want trace in this chapter – the various modifications and mutations in fetishism from the earliest stages of the history of religions through to capitalism.

I would dearly love to have a copy of that manuscript on Christian art. But I do not, so, in order to see what Marx made of fetishism in his early years of study, let me refer to two instances in his writings of those years. The first is his discussion of the new wood-'theft' laws in his third article on the Proceedings of the Sixth Rhine Province Assembly.[8] The law was directed against the peasants who were now being denied the ancient right of gathering fallen wood in the lord's estate.

> The *savages of Cuba* regarded gold as a *fetish of the Spaniards*. They celebrated a feast in its honour, sang in a circle around it and then threw it into the sea. If the Cuban savages had been present at the sitting of the Rhine Province Assembly, would they not have regarded *wood* as the *Rhinelanders' fetish?* But a subsequent sitting would have taught them that the worship of animals is connected with this fetishism, and they would have thrown the *hares* into the sea in order to save the *human beings*.[9]

Not a bad estrangement-effect, in which the 'savages of Cuba' become the sane and cultured subjects of the passage and the nobles of the Rhine Province

---

7. Marx 1974. Marx's adaptation of fetishism is, of course, one way in which it has been used. In his much-cited essay-trilogy, William Pietz traces its various uses in ethnography and the history of religion, Marxism and positivist sociology, psychoanalysis and the clinical psychiatry of sexual deviance, modernist aesthetics and continental philosophy. Pietz sets out to develop a theory of the fetish, especially in material, historical, social and bodily terms. See Pietz 1985, 1987, 1988.

8. Marx 1842n; Marx 1842o.

9. Marx 1842n, pp. 262–3; Marx 1842o, p. 236. See also my discussion in Chapter One of Marx's treatment of fetishism in his response to the editor of the *Kölnische Zeitung*, where Marx challenges the suggested sequence of sensuous desires, animal-fetishism and then the higher forms of religion (such as Christianity). There is also the comment on the French who are 'still dazzled by the sensuous glitter of precious metals, and are therefore still fetish-worshippers of metal money, and are not yet fully-developed money-nations' (Marx 1844g, p. 312; Marx 1844h, p. 552).

Assembly become the 'savages'. *They* are the strange ones, concerned more with objects such as wood and gold, or perhaps the worship of animals (the reference is to a proposal to bar peasants from hunting hares as well), than human beings. Already, there are two characteristic moves in regard to fetishism that Marx would use time and again. First, he takes the narrative of development from primitive to modern and inverts it, showing how we moderns are even more primitive than 'primitives' such as the Cubans. Second, he points out that what seemed to have passed with a putative 'primitive' stage of human existence is actually still with us in a modern, scientific world. He would use both moves to great effect when he adapted the idea of fetishism to his economic studies.

The reference to Cuba betrays the influence of the emerging study of the history of religions, itself a response to the increasing awareness of the sheer variety of religious practices outside Europe. But, in this text, Marx has already taken up the basic theory of fetishism: an object, often made by human hands, is granted supernatural powers over others and thereby has material and economic consequences. In other words, there is a transferral taking place from human beings to objects. Eventually, this will become the argument that fetishism is the attribution of inherent value or powers to an object which then comes to dominate human beings. So also in the Rhineland Assembly, for their great attention to wood and hares, indeed the attribution of value to them, suggests that they worship them as fetishes.

The second example is actually a criticism of idolatry rather than fetishism. In Marx's comments concerning freedom of the press in response to debates in the Assembly of the Estates in the Rhine Province,[10] he mocks the tendency to 'canonise individuals' and to 'demand that we should bow down before the holy image of certain privileged individuals'.[11] In short, privilege and aristocratic heritage are nothing more than the idolising and worship of some individuals at the expense of others. I could not agree more, especially when we

---

10. This assembly, basically a pseudo-democratic gathering of the nobility of the towns and country, was restricted to debating local matters of economy and administration, although it could offer opinions on wider matters. Marx is commenting on the sixth assembly from 1841.

11. Marx 1842l, p. 169; Marx 1842m, p. 157. See also his comment on Louis Napoleon: 'And the cast-down, broken idol can never be set on its pedestal again. He may recoil before the storm he has raised, and again receive the benedictions of the Pope and the caresses of the British Queen' (Marx 1859b, p. 273).

still find such approaches to privilege. But then we come across a point that draws its impact from the transferral characteristic of fetishism. Marx points out that the aristocratic prince who assumes the right of his inherited position characterises the people as immature, weak, base and sinful, and he demands that the people offer him obeisance and obedience. Marx then turns the tables on such an argument, indicating that these aristocrats actually transfer their own weaknesses onto the people, that they are self-seeking and hypocritical, for they mention God without believing. In the process, they claim for themselves the best attributes of the people, especially their innate natural laws, the omnipotence of the good and their collective strength. Not only is idolatry the preserve of the weak, a reassurance (enforced by arms and ideology) of a baseless superiority, but it also entails a pernicious transference.

Whence does this argument – the transferral characteristic of fetishism and idolatry – come? As far as fetishism was concerned Marx first came across it in one of the books he read in preparation for his work on Christian art, namely a translation by Pistorius of Charles de Brosses's 1760 work, *Du culte des dieux fétiches ou Parallèle de l'ancienne religion de l'Egypte avec la religion actuelle de Nigritie.*[12] A pioneering work in ethno-anthropology and the history of religion, it introduces the use of parallels between what are felt to be contemporary 'primitive' societies (in this case, West Africa) with ancient practices such as those in Egypt. Essentially, the fetish (from the Portuguese *fetisso*) was an object attributed with superhuman and magical powers which directly affected human social interaction. Although de Brosses had little sympathy for these 'ridiculous' and 'stupid' practices, seeing them as sign of earlier barbarism, he sought to widen the use of the term from its particular situation in West Africa to apply to all animate and inanimate objects which were given divine properties.[13]

As Pietz has shown, de Brosses's important work was but one moment in the longer story of fetishism. It begins with the Portuguese colonial

---

12. Brosses 1760. See Marx's notes on de Brosses's text in Marx 1842g, pp. 320–9.

13. Brosses 1760, pp. 10–11. The word has had to fend off a series of efforts to describe its etymology. It is an English translation of the pidgin *fetisso*, connected to the Portuguese *feitiço*, which in the late middle ages designated 'magical practices' or 'witchcraft'. However, efforts have been made to derive the word from the Latin *fatum*, signifying both fate and charm (de Brosses), *factitius*, linking the magic arts and the work of art (Edward Tylor) or *facere*, designating the false representation of things sacred, beautiful, or enchanting. See Pietz 1985, p. 5; Pietz and Apter (eds.) 1993, pp. 3–4.

encounter, as they maintained their presence on the crucial route to the Indies, with African coastal societies in the sixteenth and seventeenth centuries. The term 'fetish' came to be used by the Portuguese as a way of describing the material religious practices encountered there, especially the amulets worn on the body or perhaps consumed. Above all, it was an effort to show that the Africans misunderstood the nature of material objects and to explain their 'irrational' resistance to mercantile activity. The category of the fetish emerges in the intersection of Christian-feudal, African-lineage and merchant-capital-ist social relations; it was the result of the intersection of two cultures which were incomprehensible to one another; it was elaborated by Enlightenment intellectuals in Europe from the late eighteenth century into a general theory of religion;[14] it was even used by Dutch, French and English Protestants to describe Roman-Catholic sacramental objects.

However, the most significant point concerning fetishism is that a new term was needed, since the traditional theological category of 'idol' was not felt to be adequate. Pietz goes to great lengths to trace the way in which 'idolatry' developed as a category in medieval theology, how it designated a false god with identifiable rituals, beliefs and objects of worship, and how its initial application to the Africans did not seem to work. So, we find that 'fetish' was coined in order to take account of the direct material affects of the fetish in terms of physical and psychological well-being. It also was seen to play a central rôle in social ordering, irrational as that order may seem to be. Traders would go as far as to swear an oath on a fetish in order to ensure a deal, much to the chagrin of the church. It was this material and social feature of the fetish that was unique, although it must not be forgotten that the terminology itself was an effort by the Portuguese to make 'sense' of the incomprehensible and to show how these 'primitive' Africans misunderstood the material nature of objects.

What happened to the theological category of idolatry? In a stunning case of theoretical inversion, idolatry was absorbed into this new term, especially when we find complete theories of the earlier stages of religion framed in terms of primitive fetishism. This is where de Brosses enters the picture, for he

---

14. For August Comte, it becomes the first stage (followed by polytheism and mono-theism) of his first great period of human history. Comte used the term in his *Système de politique positive* (1851–4). After the theological age, of which fetishism is the first stage, we have the metaphysical and scientific stages.

developed from an Enlightenment perspective a theory of primitive fetishism into which he incorporated idolatry.[15] In his effort at comparative religion, de Brosses set out to explain ancient Egyptian cultures in terms of fetishism, using the distorted information from Africa as his template. Here, we come to the reason why this text by de Brosses is important for my purposes in this chapter: the primary 'source' for ancient Egypt, at least in de Brosses's time, was the Bible. So we find de Brosses using the Bible as a major source for his information on ancient fetishism, particularly those texts that deal with idol-worship. For de Brosses, the Bible was seen to be reasonably reliable in terms of historical information (he wrote it in the mid-eighteenth century, before the first flowering of critical approaches to the Bible).

In a book liberally sprinkled with biblical quotations and references,[16] the most important passage is an analysis of two types of fetish in ancient Judah, namely the public and the personal or private. In the second group, we find those 'qui sont pour l'ordinaire quelques animal, quelques être animé ou quelque idole grossiérement fabriquée de terre graffe ou d'yvoire'.[17] It is exactly the same definition for idol and fetish. With regard to the more public type of fetish, he outlines four types to which one would offer sacrifice at important occasions: the serpent, the trees, the sea and 'a small, ugly clay idol which presides over the councils'.[18] For de Brosses, then, idolatry in the Bible is one shape that fetishism may take. Indeed, along with other sources, the Bible provides him with a ready source of examples of the practice of fetishism in the ancient world. Did Marx pick up on the connection, or more specifically the subordination of idolatry to fetishism, when he read de Brosses's work? It seems as though he did, for, in his notes on de Brosses's text, he cites the crucial text on four types of fetish in ancient Israel that I quoted above: 'die Schlange, die Bäume, das Meer und ein kleines schmutziges Bild von Thon,

---

15. Brosses 1760, p. 12.

16. For example, he mentions the serpent of Judah, the 'fetish of Evil-Merodah' and that the Babylonians are depicted as worshipping fetishes in Daniel 14 (Brosses 1760, p. 26). Other samples include Ezekiel 21:21 (Brosses 1760, pp. 105–60), 2 Kings 26:29 with its list of idols (Brosses 1760, p. 126), Ezekiel 8 and the list of fetishes worshipped by the Israelites, including the Canaanite Baal (Brosses 1760, p. 131), Genesis 31:13 (Brosses 1760, p. 136), Numbers 13:52ff.; Leviticus 31:1ff., Deuteronomy 4:16 (Brosses 1760, p. 137), Genesis 31 (Brosses 1760, p. 139), and 1 Kings 12:29 (Brosses 1760, p. 143).

17. Brosses 1760, p. 27.

18. Ibid.

das in den Rattsammlungen den Vorstiz hat'.[19] Note how Marx translates de Brosses's *idole* as *Bild*, or 'image', the same word used in German translation of the ban on images from the second commandment in Exodus 20. At this moment, the appropriation has taken place, for Marx too has subsumed idolatry within the broader category of fetishism.

A further piece of evidence comes from *The Ethnological Notebooks*, a collection of Marx's reading notes and comments on the anthropologists L.H. Morgan (the basis for Engels's *Origin of the Family*), John B. Phear, Henry Maine and John Lubbock. These notebooks are an extraordinary read, with sentences that jump around between German, English and French, good slabs of Greek and Latin and occasional terms from Russian, Sanskrit, Ojibwa and so on, endless abbreviations, unfinished sentences, slang, vulgar terms, exclamations and references to current affairs.[20] However, the pages that draw me in are the few on that 'civilised ass' and pious 'wiseacre' Lubbock, for Lubbock deals with the history of religion. As he did in the criticism of wood-'theft' laws, Marx throws Lubbock's arguments back at him. If we take Lubbock's argument that the earliest human societies were atheist, then it is not because the savage mind was too undeveloped to recognise true religion. No, argues Marx, it was because religion is the result of a repressive system that included castes, slavery and monarchy. Those atheistic savages were far better off.

For my purposes, the next 'stage' in Lubbock's model is more interesting. Here, we find an explicit discussion of idols and fetishes. For Lubbock they are a sign of a slightly more developed 'savage' mind, but one that is given to sin. But I want to read between the lines: what is striking is the way Marx interchanges the terms idol and fetish as though they mean the same thing. Marx notes that Lubbock argues that idols/fetishes may be objects, animals or

---

19. Marx 1842g, p. 321.
20. Marx's notes for Volume II of *Capital* were in a similar state, as Engels notes: 'The language was that in which Marx used to make his extracts: careless style full of colloquialisms, often containing coarsely humorous expressions and phrases interspersed with English and French technical terms or with whole sentences and even pages of English. Thoughts were jotted down as they developed in the brain of the author. Some parts of the argument would be fully treated, others of equal importance only indicated. Factual material for illustration would be collected, but barely arranged, much less worked out. At conclusions of chapters, in the author's anxiety to get to the next, there would often be only a few disjointed sentences to mark the further development here left incomplete. And finally there was the well-known handwriting which the author himself was sometimes unable to decipher.' (Engels 1885c, p. 5; Engels 1885d, p. 7.)

human beings. In fact, most of his comments follow through on the last point: 'The *idol* usually assumes *human form*, and idolatry is closely associated with that form of worship which consists in the worship of ancestors'.[21] The examples pile on top of one another, from Siberia through Greece to Australia. But it is when Marx cites Lubbock on sacrifice that the Bible turns up. Marx begins by noting that sacrifice may be either sacrifice *to* the idol or sacrifice *of* the idol. The latter he calls, quoting Lubbock, 'eating the fetish'. Now four biblical texts appear: a reference to the sacrifice of Jephthah's daughter in Judges 11, the prescriptions for Israelite sacrifice of animals in Leviticus 7 (actually the whole of Chapters 1–7 deal with sacrifice), Paul's comments on the origin of idolatry in Romans 1:23, and, last but by no means least, Christ's sacrifice, which is as good an example as any of 'eating the fetish'.

These few pages in *The Ethnological Notebooks* show that Marx did not feel it was at all strange to use 'idol' and 'fetish' interchangeably. The important point is that he assumes they mean the same thing, or at least that, like de Brosses, he subsumed idolatry as a category under fetishism. And, then, in the midst of that easy interaction, the Bible turns up with startling regularity. I hardly need to labour the point: like de Brosses's text which he read some forty years earlier, Marx uses the biblical texts on idolatry as though they were speaking of fetishism. Or, rather, Marx chooses to make notes from Lubbock on precisely these matters.

Idolatry

So far, my search has yielded some telling hints and connections between idolatry and fetishism in Marx's thought. In a text Marx read in the late 1830s or early 1840s, a text on which he made notes, there is an explicit assumption that idolatry is part of the idea of fetishism, and then, in the early 1880s, Marx chooses to makes critical notes on John Lubbock, where the same assumption turns up. Marx, it would seem, has made the connection. He certainly had a liking for Moloch, the idol of the Ammonites which demanded the sacrifice of children.[22]

---

21. Marx 1974, p. 343.
22. Marx 1864a, pp. 10–11; Marx and Engels 1845a, p. 21; Marx and Engels 1845b, p. 21; Marx 1845a, p. 266; Marx 1882a, p. 234; Marx 1882b, p. 54; Marx 1855a, p. 95; Marx 1855b, pp. 132–3; Marx 1859a, p. 294; Marx and Engels 1848f, p. 264; Marx and

I have deliberately left the most delectable morsel out of my earlier discussion of Marx's ethnological notebooks. It is another reference to the Bible in his discussion of Lubbock. Or, rather, it is a full quotation of the Wisdom of Solomon 14:12–20 – a deuterocanonical work. The ostensible point of quoting this text is to deride Lubbock's use of it as the source of the worship of statues as deities. For Lubbock, the argument is both historical and theological: idolatry is a historical development due to an undeveloped 'primitive' mind and the human sin of not worshipping the one true God. Marx is not impressed with such abuse of the Bible; nor am I. But I am also not satisfied, so, once again, I read between the lines. The biblical text that Marx quotes in full reads as follows:

> For the idea of making idols was the beginning of fornication, and the invention of them was the corruption of life;
>
> For they did not exist from the beginning, nor will they last forever.
>
> For through human vanity they entered the world, and therefore their speedy end has been planned.
>
> For a father, consumed with guilt at an untimely bereavement, made an image of his child, who has been suddenly taken from him;
>
> He now honoured as a god what was once a dead human being, and handed on to his dependants secret rites and initiations.
>
> Then the ungodly custom, grown strong with time, was kept as a law, and at the commands of monarchs carved images were worshipped.
>
> When people could not honour monarchs in their presence, since they lived at a distance, they imagined their appearance far away, and made a visible image of the king whom they honoured, so that by their zeal they might flatter the absent one as though present.
>
> Then the ambition of the artisan impelled even those who did not know the king to intensify their worship.
>
> For he, perhaps wishing to please his ruler, skilfully forced the likeness to take more beautiful form,

Engels 1848g, p. 251; Engels 1846a, p. 474; Engels 1846b, p. 405; Engels 1893e, p. 234; Engels 1893f, p. 171; Eichhoff 1868, p. 330.

And the multitude, attracted by the charm of his work, now regarded as an object of worship the one whom shortly before they had honoured as a human being.

The context of Marx's notes is a discussion of human idols, but the context in the Wisdom of Solomon is the worship of objects made with human hands. It is a sustained polemic against idolatry, focusing on how silly and sinful it is. The polemic is not that effective, for it makes the same point again and again: idolatry is simply the worship of false gods over against the one true God. This is why Lubbock quotes it. Yet the point is rather superficial and it does not really get to the heart of idolatry. For that we need to look at the criticism of idolatry in the book of Isaiah on which this text from Wisdom is a less-than-astute expansion.

For some two decades, I have been struck by the way some texts in the book of Isaiah echo the theory of fetishism as Marx was to develop it.[23] For Isaiah, the construction of an idol is nothing less than the deluded effort to attribute divine status to a material object made in the sweat of human labour. Or, as the text of Isaiah has it:

> [9]All who make idols are nothing, and the things they delight in do not profit; their witnesses neither see nor know. And so they will be put to shame. [10]Who would fashion a god or cast an image that can do no good? [11]Look, all its devotees shall be put to shame; the artisans too are merely human. Let them all assemble, let them stand up; they shall be terrified, they shall all be put to shame.

> [12]The blacksmith fashions it and works it over the coals, shaping it with hammers, and forging it with his strong arm; he becomes hungry and his strength fails, he drinks no water and is faint. [13]The carpenter stretches a line, marks it out with a stylus, fashions it with planes, and marks it with a compass; he makes it in human form, with human beauty, to be set up in a shrine. [14]He cuts down cedars or chooses a holm tree or an oak and lets it grow strong among the trees of the forest. He plants a cedar and the rain

---

23. At this point, I step back behind the centuries of theological elaboration to explore what an ancient text itself says (all too cognisant at the same time that this is a useful hermeneutical 'fiction').

nourishes it. [15]Then it can be used as fuel. Part of it he takes and warms himself; he kindles a fire and bakes bread. Then he makes a god and worships it, makes it a carved image and bows down before it. [16]Half of it he burns in the fire; over this half he roasts meat, eats it, and is satisfied. He also warms himself and says, 'Ah, I am warm, I can feel the fire!' [17]The rest of it he makes into a god, his idol, bows down to it, and worships it; he prays to it and says, 'Save me, for you are my god!'

[18]They do not know, nor do they comprehend; for their eyes are shut, so that they cannot see, and their minds as well, so that they cannot understand. [19]No one considers, nor is there knowledge or discernment to say, 'Half of it I burned in the fire; I also baked bread on its coals, I roasted meat and have eaten. Now shall I make the rest of it an abomination? Shall I fall down before a block of wood?' [20]He feeds on ashes; a deluded mind has led him astray, and he cannot save himself or say, 'Is not this thing in my right hand a fraud?'[24]

The detail may be more graphic than Marx's brief notes on fetishism, but the underlying argument is the same: this inanimate product, made with ordinary, everyday-labour out of metal or wood can never be more than the material out of which it is made. The worshipper may claim that it is a god, that it bestows blessings and curses, but it is nothing of the sort. The passage from Isaiah plays up the sheer ordinariness of the idol with a good dose of satire. Indeed, it stresses the everyday materiality of the idol, one that punctures the exorbitant claims made for it. Like Marx, this text points out that the religious belief attached to the idol is a delusion. Like Marx again, it points to the need for an analysis of the material object in question and not the vapid claims made on its behalf.

However, this inversion – the true nature of the idol lies in its profane origins, in the effort to sacralise what is profane – relies on a deeper and more radical inversion. Here, we need to fill in the steps that lie behind and make possible such a position. Rather than belittle the gods who are rivals to

---

24. Isaiah 44:9–20. See also the explicitly political polemic in Isaiah 40:19–20; 41:6–7; 42: 17; 45:16–17 and 46:1–2, 5–7. Not to be outdone, Paul in the New Testament puts the same point in his own way. Thus, Paul argues that due to darkened minds (Romans 1:21), i.e., unconscious blindness, the dead, created thing comes to life and gains the power to rule and dominate human lives instead of God (Romans 1:23, 25).

Yahweh, perhaps placing them in humiliating subordinate positions, the text of Isaiah denies the existence of all of these gods apart from Yahweh. This inversion then has a profound effect on all those signifiers of the gods – precisely the statues, keepsakes, amulets and so on. For, if there are no gods to whom these objects point, then veneration and worship are no longer directed to the gods but to the objects themselves. In short, they become idols.

The underlying logic to this move is actually provided by the late imposition of monotheism.[25] The critique of – indeed, the very identification of idolatry as the worship of an animate or inanimate object – can happen only after the belated arrival of monotheism, which then generates its own critique of the earlier gods who are no more. The logic goes as follows: in order to have some visible and tactile presence to direct you towards and remind you of your god, you find a suitable animal or rock or make an elaborate figure out of wood of stone. Whenever you pass by and look at it, you call to mind your god, perhaps offering a prayer and leaving a little something to ward off danger, ensure rains or offer thanks. Your god is not physically present, so the figure becomes his earthly representative. All the same, it only ever points towards your god; it is never the god itself. However, if you break this link, then your god and the figure cease to have this (signifying) connection. The statue becomes the object of worship in its own right, bestowing favour, punishing and what have you. The image that represents god becomes god itself, for the signifying link has been broken. It is important to keep this threefold distinction – human being, object, and god – in mind when we move to Marx's texts, for he will turn it over, look at it from different angles, add yet another layer and see new possibilities within it.

As far as the Hebrew Bible itself is concerned, I would suggest that the ban on graven images in the second commandment[26] is not so much a concern with replacing Yahweh with some object or other. Rather, it seeks to negate the possibility of such a signifying link in the first place. Without an image, there is no connection between an earthly image and a divinity in the heavens.

---

25. There is more than enough evidence to suggest that an earlier polytheism was gradually overlaid in the texts of the Hebrew Bible by monotheism. Thus, the various references to the veneration and worship of multiple gods become in light of this late overlay myriad examples of waywardness and apostasy. On the subsequent development of the notion of idolatry in Christian theology, see Pietz 1987, pp. 24–31.

26. Exodus 20 and Deuteronomy 5.

And, if there is no signifying link, it cannot be broken; no-one can decide to sever the signifying chain. It is, if you like, a manifestation of a fear that the process will continue inexorably. Once you have denied the existence of all the other gods bar one, then it is but one step further to deny the existence of the last one standing.[27] So, what you do is close down the mechanism by which this might happen: without a signifying connection between image and god, there is no possibility of breaking the connection and ending up with a pure idol.

These are some of the implications of the polemic against idols in the passage from Isaiah, which one may well call a tendency towards atheism except that it would be anachronistic to use such a term. However, the feel of the Isaiah passage resonates with some elements in Marx's writings on fetishism and religion. To start with, it is difficult to avoid the polemical and mocking focus on everyday material items and the puncturing of lofty theological claims. More than that, the spirit of Feuerbach haunts this passage from Isaiah (if I may put it that way). This object of human hands is projected into the heavens and attributed with all manner of superhuman attributes, especially since it is made in human form and with human beauty. However, it does not fit entirely within such an assumption, especially since Feuerbach's argument is predicated on Christian monotheism in the absence of images – the projection comes from within human beings. This is where the distinctive nature of fetishism comes into play: it is the attribution of divine powers to animate and inanimate objects. There is an implied negative that we find in Feuerbach as well as in Isaiah and Marx, for the idol/fetish is a diminution of human beings and an elevation of non-human objects. The two are intimately connected.

To sum up my argument thus far: there is a tantalising convergence between de Brosses's work on fetishism, Marx's notes on Lubbock, his reading of Feuerbach, his early use of the idea of fetishism and the polemic against idolatry in the book of Isaiah. I would, of course, like to have explicit evidence of a link, a definite connection where Marx uses the biblical text. I can only wonder what texts from Isaiah Marx studied in that course with Bruno Bauer in 1839,

---

27. Hence the perpetual assertion, such as: 'Thus says the Lord, the King of Israel and his Redeemer, the Lord of hosts: "I am the first and I am the last; besides me there is no god. Who is like me? Let him proclaim it, let him declare it and set it forth before me"' (Isaiah 44: 6–7a).

especially since Bauer was developing his idea of infinite self-consciousness and the debilitating limits of specific religions. Yet it seems to me that there is enough evidence to suggest that Marx assumed that idolatry was to be understood in the wider sense of fetishism, but he was to take it and rework it in all manner of new directions.

Economy

The most well-known and endlessly discussed feature of fetishism is the adaptation of the theory into the sphere of economics. There is no need to reiterate the details of Marx's argument blow by blow, so what I do here is trace the way such a theological undercurrent breaks through in Marx's texts, especially in light of my earlier discussion of the polemic against idolatry.

Alienation and labour

Our first stop is the treatment of the alienation of labour in the *Economic and Philosophical Manuscripts of 1844*. A couple of passages stand out:

> All these consequences are implied in the statement that the worker is related to the *product of his labour* as to an *alien* object. For on this premise it is clear that the more the worker spends himself, the more powerful becomes the alien world of objects which he creates over and against himself, the poorer he himself – his inner world – becomes, the less belongs to him as his own. It is the same in religion. The more man puts into God, the less he retains in himself [*Es ist ebenso in der Religion. Je mehr der Mensch in Gott setzt, je weniger behält er in sich selbst*]. The worker puts his life into the object; but now his life no longer belongs to him but to the object.... The *alienation* of the worker in his product means not only that his labour becomes an object, an *external* existence, but that it exists *outside him*, independently, as something alien to him, and that it becomes a power on its own confronting him. It means that the life which he has conferred on the object confronts him as something hostile and alien.[28]

---

28. Marx 1844g, p. 272; Marx 1844h, p. 512. Similarly, 'Every self-estrangement of man, from himself and from nature, appears in the relation in which he places himself and nature to men other than and differentiated from himself. For this reason religious self-estrangement necessarily appears in the relationship of the layman to the priest, or

I could not ask for a clearer passage where the critique of idolatry, the transferral characteristic of fetishism and a smattering of Feuerbach all come together. The passage almost reads like a commentary on the text from Isaiah I quoted earlier. So, we find that, in the labour-process, the worker invests more and more of his life in the object produced. As he does so, his own life drains away. The alien world of objects gains a life of its own; the objects produced by my hands become more powerful than me and rule over me. They wax and I wane. The ordinary products of labour become alien and powerful beings (Isaiah) because of this transferral of powers and relations (fetishism). Yet we need to be careful here, since what Marx has done is collapse the three-fold distinction I established earlier. Instead of human being-object-god, what we have is the equivalence of the object produced and the god; they are one and the same. It is as though Marx has assumed the critique of idolatry, especially in terms of the absence of any god to whom the object points, so that the object itself becomes the god – hence it 'becomes a power confronting him…as something hostile and alien'.

There is a touch of Feuerbach in this passage as well: 'The more man puts into God, the less he retains in himself [*Es ist ebenso in der Religion. Je mehr der Mensch in Gott setzt, je weniger behält er in sich selbst*]'. We put all our best into the projected divinity and thereby belittle ourselves in the process. This analogy is by no means accidental, since, as I argued above, the genealogy of the transferred fetish has distinct theological implications for that reserved zone of one's own religion. So it is not for nothing that Marx uses *Gott*, who too becomes equivalent to the fetish/idol produced and is not some other entity to which it points.

Another text from the same work makes a slightly different point:

> If the product of labour is alien to me, if it confronts me as an alien power, to whom, then, does it belong? If my own activity does not belong to me, if it is an alien, a coerced activity, to whom, then, does it belong? To a being *other* than myself. Who is this being? The *gods*? To be sure, in the earliest times the principal production (for example, the building of temples, etc., in Egypt, India and Mexico) appears to be in the service of the gods, and the product belongs to the gods. However, the gods on their own were never the lords

---

again to a mediator, etc., since we are here dealing with the intellectual world.' (Marx 1844g, p. 279; Marx 1844h, p. 519.) See also Marx 1857–8b, pp. 209–10.

of labour. No more was *nature*. And what a contradiction it would be if, the more man subjugated nature by his labour and the more the miracles of the gods were rendered superfluous by the miracles of industry, the more man were to renounce the joy of production and the enjoyment of the product to please these powers.[29]

The reference to Egypt should alert us to de Brosses's book, since one of its main foci was precisely ancient Egypt. But, now, Marx distinguishes between the three items: the labourer (now personified by Marx himself), the product of labour, and the gods. In the first text the object produced and God were elided into one, or, rather, God is merely an object (idol), but here they are distinct. Yet there is a catch, for people might have believed that they were working for the gods (or perhaps nature), but they were no more real then than they are now. Early labour 'appears to be in the service of the gods', but it is not actually so. They are the imaginary lords of labour, for the real lords of labour may be found elsewhere, although in this text they lurk in the shadows.

There is one further feature of this text that echoes the one concerning the 'theft' of wood and hares: the polemical effect of the argument is to show that what people (especially the political economists) thought was the advance of science and industry is in fact a recurrence of the most superstitious and primitive of practices – fetishism. 'And what a contradiction it would be', Marx begins his last sentence. At times, he argues that only in capitalism do we find that all these older trappings of religion and politics have been stripped away and the pure exploitation of the economic relation has been laid bare.[30] At other times, he feels that the contradictory re-emergence of older superstitions is being realised.

So what is the answer to this fetishism or idolatry, to this externalisation that sucks the life out of human existence and social relations? Already in the *Economic and Philosophical Manuscripts of 1844*, Marx is perfectly clear: we

---

29. Marx 1844g, p. 278; Marx 1844h, p. 518.
30. 'The whole content of the relation, and the mode of appearance of the conditions of the worker's labour alienated from labour, are therefore present in their pure economic form, without any political, religious or other trimmings. It is a pure money-relation. Capitalist and worker. Objectified labour and living labour capacity. Not master and servant, priest and layman, feudal lord and vassal, master craftsman and journeyman, etc.' (Marx 1861–3a, p. 131; Marx 1861–3h, p. 123.)

need to get rid of these projections, estrangements and objectifications. They may be the gods, or they may be the external objects produced by our hands that take on the power of the gods. Or, rather, we need a social and economic situation in which they are no longer needed.

The way Marx does this is to tackle the doctrine of creation with a series of dialectical twists.[31] The most difficult thing, he points out, is to believe that we are our own creators. That entails giving up the belief that I am created by another being, a belief that makes me dependent on that other who is the very source of my life and my continued maintenance. Instead of human beings and nature being the creations of a higher being, he argues that they exist on their own account. Or, to push it further, the interaction of human beings and nature means that they are constantly in the process of creation. This reality makes any question about the origin of nature or human beings – who begot the first man or the earth? – abstract and superfluous.

What this argument does is challenge the overriding and vain search for origins that bedevils (to cull three out of a vast field) science, theology and biblical criticism even today. Carrying on from the preceding point, it is above all an early effort to deal with the eternal problem of human existence: where do I come from? Many years ago someone pointed out to me that when religions have some answers, no matter how mythical, to what happens before we are born and after we die, they are meaningful. But, if they give up these crucial domains, then they have lost the plot and may as well close their doors. Marx too finds he must deal with the question sooner rather than later.

Initially, he wants to dismiss it as a false question – we exist and that is it! But, then, he goes on to try a different tack, arguing that the question of the origin of nature and human beings is an abstract question. The better question is to ask why we are asking that question in the first place. Finally, he realises he must actually answer the question, at least to keep his dialogue-partner happy. So he ends by arguing that nature and human beings are in a constant process of creative interaction. He also tries his hand at arguing that we create ourselves but that sounds a little too much like auto-gestation and generation – being pregnant with oneself. In brief, it is not particularly persuasive. I much prefer the other argument of mutual creative interaction, not least because it destroys the nature/nurture argument (since one produces

---

31. See Marx 1844g, pp. 304–6; Marx 1844h, pp. 543–6.

the other), but also because it has enormous possibilities for ecological trajectories out of Marxism. But that is another topic beyond my mandate.

Money and Christology

Our next stop is the commentary, found in the Paris notebooks, on the French translation of James Mill's *Elements of Political Economy* (Marx's English was still not up to scratch). The argument is strikingly similar to the *Economic and Philosophic Manuscripts*, which is not surprising, given that Marx wrote them at around the same time. All the same, Marx experiments with extending and adapting the basic ideas. This time the issue is the mediation of money and his prime analogy is Christ, the mediator between heaven and earth.

The logic is the same: the mediating activity of money 'is *estranged* from man and becomes the attribute of money, a *material thing* outside man'.[32] Again, we find the blend of the Feuerbachian inversion and the transferral characteristic of fetishism/idolatry. Such a move dehumanises and downgrades human beings, yet there is a difference. Apart from the obvious Hegelian terminology (alienation, estrangement and externalisation), the issue in this case is not an object per se, but a relation – between human beings and things as well as those between human beings. For example, if I gather two or three old bicycles and make a working one out of the various parts, I am the one who mediates between myself and the bicycle. But, if I go out and hand over cash for a bicycle, a different relationship ensues in which money is the mediator. Similarly, if the people next door need someone else to give them a hand with repairing their roof, I can spend a few hours with them to get the job done. But they could also pay someone else to do the job for them. Once again, the direct interaction of human beings finds money coming in as a mediator. Money becomes an 'alien mediator',[33] a power over human beings that controls all these relations, sapping them of their once-human power. So, while money 'circulates', while it becomes a common language, while the dollar rises and falls, human relations become ever more utilitarian and exploitative. It is the classic relation of fetishism and idolatry, except that now it is the alien mediator: 'All the qualities which arise in the course of this activity

---

32. Marx 1844a, p. 212; Marx 1844b, p. 446. Van Leeuwen 2002a, pp. 230–1, misses the link here with fetishism.
33. Ibid.

are, therefore, transferred to this mediator. Hence man becomes the poorer as man, i.e., separated from this mediator, the *richer* this mediator becomes'.[34] The theological analogies are not far away. The first reads: 'It is clear that this *mediator* now becomes a *real God*, for the mediator is the *real power* over what it mediates to me'.[35] Once again, Marx has taken the perspective of the critique of idolatry and collapsed two of the basic terms: the object, which has now become money the mediator, is no different from the god. Or, rather, the mediator-object appears to be a god, for it refers to no entity beyond itself. This mediator has its worshippers and cult, it draws more and more power unto itself, it determines how human beings should relate to one another, and only those who represent this mediator (its priests and ministers) have any value or power. And what is its fundamental function? It mediates, becomes the initiator, lubricator and facilitator of human interaction. Yet the analogy is not as clear as it could be, so another follows soon afterwards: 'Christ *represents* originally: 1) men before God; 2) God for men; 3) men to men. Similarly, *money* represents originally, in accordance with the idea of money: 1) private property for property; 2) society for private property; 3) private property for society'.[36] In the same way that Christ is the signal of a relation – what might be called the Christ-relation – so also the money-relation is the key, not money itself as an object. Money, then, functions in an analogous fashion to Christ. But why make the connection in the first place? Marx might just as easily have argued that money is a mediator without the Christological connection. Is he merely having some polemical fun at the expense of theology? Perhaps, but I would suggest that the theological associations of fetishism/idolatry show up

---

34. Ibid. See also the comments in the *Economic and Philosophical Manuscripts*: 'The distorting and confounding of all human and natural qualities, the fraternisation of impossibilities – the *divine* power of money – lies in its *character* as men's estranged, alienating and self-disposing *species-nature*. Money is the alienated *ability of mankind*.' (Marx 1844g, p. 325; Marx 1844h, p. 565.) 'Money, then, appears as this *distorting* power both against the individual and against the bonds of society, etc., which claim to be *entities* in themselves. It transforms fidelity into infidelity, love into hate, hate into love, virtue into vice, vice into virtue, servant into master, master into servant, idiocy into intelligence, and intelligence into idiocy. Since money, as the existing and active concept of value, confounds and confuses all things, it is the general *confounding and confusing* of all things – the world upside-down – the confounding and confusing of all natural and human qualities.' (Marx 1844g, pp. 325–6; Marx 1844h, pp. 566–7.)
35. Ibid. See also Marx 1857–8a, pp. 154, 164; Marx 1857–8c, pp. 148, 158; Marx 1857–8b, p. 216; Marx 1859a, p. 359; Marx 1867a, pp. 142–3; Marx 1867b, pp. 146–7.
36. Ibid. See also Marx 1857–8a, p. 257; Marx 1857–8c, p. 250.

once again. In fact, after pondering this brief passage in Marx's notebook on James Mill, I can no longer read the long section on money in the *Grundrisse* without thinking of this earlier text.

One further point: this analogy throws a large question back at Christology. Recall my earlier comments about the assumptions behind the polemic in Isaiah against idolatry as well as the ban on images in the second commandment, especially the need to block a signifying relation between an object and the deity. Christ opens up that connection, except that he embodies that relation within himself. He is both the image of God on earth and the representative of human beings before God, for he is – as traditional Christology would have it – both divine and human. Even so, he seems to skip by the polemic against idols in Isaiah, for he is not merely a human being who represents God. But, then, Marx's point about money-as-mediator shifts the whole criticism of idolatry: a mediator too can be a fetish.

Commodities and capital

All this may be very well, characteristic of an early and immature Marx, one who was still to undertake his exhaustive and exhausting economic studies. Does he then leave behind the theological analogies along with his youthful vigour and the heavily theological context of debates in Germany? Not so, for they continue to turn up, especially in the *Economic Manuscripts of 1861–63* and *Capital* itself.

The section in *Capital* – 'The Fetishism of Commodities and the Secret Thereof' – is a place worn down with many crossings. Hordes have descended on these few pages, sat for a while, taken a few photographs, argued heatedly and then moved on. The basic argument is all too well-known: commodity-fetishism is an inverse relationship in which the social relations of labour are transformed into apparently objective relations between commodities or money. However, as with the passage on money I discussed above, it is not so much the commodity itself that becomes the fetish but the commodity-form, the notion that so many vastly different products may be exchanged in terms of their value.

This time the extension of the basic logic of fetishism to commodities seems like a small step, yet Marx gives it a whole new meaning. The connections with his earlier argument concerning money are obvious: once again, it involves both transfer and illusion. Commodity-fetishism transfers the properties of inter-human relations in the context of labour to relations between humans and commodities and between commodities themselves – so also with money. To the belittlement of human relations, it transfers human attributes and powers onto the commodity-form – so also with labour, money and indeed idolatry. As Marx puts it, this transferral is a 'mysterious thing, simply because the social character of men's labour appears to them as an objective character stamped upon the product of that labour; because the relation of the producers to the sum total of their own labour is presented to them as a social relation, existing not between themselves, but between the products of their labour'.[37]

As before, my interest is in the theological undercurrent of Marx's discussion. Now the earlier three-fold distinction becomes vitally important, for Marx seeks a new insight which may best be understood in light of the distinction between the labourer, object (now the commodity and then value), and the beliefs concerning it. In this section of *Capital*, he seems to oscillate, sometimes opening up some distance between the object and the divine and at others collapsing them together. At times, Marx distinguishes between the commodity and the illusory beliefs attaching to it; at others, the two seem to become one.

Marx begins the section on commodity-fetishism with the oft-quoted statement: the analysis of the commodity 'shows that it is, in reality, a very queer thing, abounding in metaphysical subtleties and theological niceties [*voll metaphysischer Spitzfindigkeit und theologischer Mucken*]'[38] – hardly a subtle hint that there is a significant theological residue here. Marx is of course no more enamoured with theology than he has been, but it has a distinct use. However, soon enough, we come across a thorny passage:

---

37. Marx 1867a, pp. 82–3; Marx 1867b, p. 86. See also Marx 1861–3g, p. 450. In the midst of all this intriguing complexity, Marx makes the much-cited crass and 'vulgar' argument based on the premise that the 'religious world is but the reflex of the real world'. In contrast to the external forms of Roman Catholicism, which is appropriate for a monetary system, Protestantism is the appropriate reflex of the internalised world of credit and commodities (Marx 1867a, p. 90; Marx 1867b, p. 93). He repeats it in Volume 3 of *Capital* (Marx 1894a, p. 587; Marx 1894b, p. 606) and then Engels follows suit (Engels 1868a, p. 267; Engels 1868b, p. 247). It is, in fact, an old argument, appearing first in the *Economic and Philosophical Manuscripts* (Marx 1844g, pp. 290–1; Marx 1844h, pp. 530–1), where he seeks to develop Engels's comment that Adam Smith was the 'economic Luther' (Engels 1844j, p. 422; Engels 1844k, p. 503).
38. Marx 1867a, p. 81; Marx 1867b, p. 85.

There [with commodities] it is a definite social relationship between men, that assumes, in their eyes, the fantastic form of the relation between things. In order, therefore, to find an analogy, we must have recourse to the mist-enveloped regions of the religious world. In that world the productions of the human brain appear as independent beings endowed with life, and entering into relation both with one another and the human race. So it is in the world of commodities with the product of men's hands. This I call the Fetishism which attaches itself to products of labour, so soon as they are produced as commodities, and which is therefore inseparable from the production of commodities.[39]

The first impression is that Marx has collapsed the distinction between the object itself, which is now the social relationship between human beings, and the beliefs about it. There are at least three possible ways to interpret this passage. One option is to argue that the constant recourse to terminology derived from the leitmotiv of fetishism means that the transferral in question is illusory.[40] Thus, the belief that the commodity-form has an inherent value is as much a superstition and fantasy as the belief that a pretty object made out of iron or wood has supernatural power. The reality of economic and social relations between people is obscured through the mistaken belief that the commodity-form has its own power. Even more, it is not merely that this commodity-form has no value or power, that each commodity is merely a material object, but that human labour is responsible for the creation of this commodity. As with the polemic against idolatry, Marx stresses the human labour that goes into the making of the idol, which is then endowed with superhuman powers. In support of this reading, one might point out that Marx wants to find out how the commodity becomes 'transcendent', how these 'grotesque ideas' are produced in the first place, especially since they justify the degradation and misery of countless labourers.[41] In fact, these few pages rain down such terms – 'mystical character', 'mysterious thing', 'fantastic form', 'mist-enveloped', 'abstraction', 'social hieroglyphic', 'incarnation of abstract human labour', 'magic and necromancy', 'mystical veil',

---

39. Marx 1867a, p. 83; Marx 1867b, pp. 86–7.
40. Pietz 1985, p. 10, takes this line, arguing that the fetish designates false consciousness. Dupré 1983, p. 49, tends in this direction.
41. Marx 1867a, p. 639; Marx 1867b, p. 674.

'unsubstantial ghost', 'superstition', and 'illusions'. In the midst of industrial capitalist society, an ancient superstitious practice is alive and well. In short, Marx uses the terminology of fetishism/idolatry, for he seeks to demystify and debunk these illusory beliefs and show that these various items are nothing more than economic relations constructed by human beings.

Another interpretation is to argue that Marx's use of idea of fetishism is less than helpful. In a widely quoted observation, Norman Geras suggests that 'the analogy is inexact, for the properties bestowed on material objects in the capitalist economy are, Marx holds, real and not the product of the imagination'.[42] I must admit that Marx is a little misleading in the passage I quoted above, for he moves directly from commodity-relations to the gods, as though they were analogous. Geras prefers other terms that Marx uses, such as natural and social: the properties and powers transferred from human social relations to those between commodities appear natural. But that is an illusion: the belief that the powers are in some sense inherent to commodities is false. He goes on to stress that the powers themselves are no illusions. Geras would rather use terms such as mask and disguise, encouraged by Marx's desire to tear off the veil and uncover what is really going on.

We can distinguish between these two readings in terms of the threefold schema I have mentioned a few times now, particularly the relation between the object made and the divinity to which it points. The first (illusory transferral and powers) says that the divinity is not real, nor are the beliefs concerning it; reality pertains to the object and human production of it. Although the second feels it is unhelpful to think of the properties of commodities as fetishes or gods, what he does suggest – if I may put it this way – is that the 'divinity' is real, where 'divinity' refers to the powers transferred to the object. However, Geras is on the right track. His problem is that he does not see that Marx has in fact collapsed the two terms of the fetish – object and belief. And that leads us to a third option: Marx fuses the two in an effort to move to a new level of understanding.

So, Marx argues that the transferral of powers – from social relations between people to relations between things – is indeed real, for they appear to those producers as 'what they really are, material relations between

_____

42. Geras 1983, p. 165.

persons and social relations between things'.[43] This fetishisation is real, since human beings become subjected to things and the alienated labour embodied within them. At the same time, they are illusory and imaginary, since they are understood as natural, as givens of the world; people believe that things relate to one another in and of themselves, rather than realising that these relations have been transferred from human social relations. One way to consider Marx's argument is ask what is real and what illusory. Obviously, the worker and process of material production and social relations are real, as is the product produced. However, now we come across the breakthrough, for the powers transferred and thereby gained by the product are also real and materially grounded, all of which then means that the effects on human beings are equally real. What are illusory, then, are the theories and beliefs about how these powers arose in the first place – this is where Marx's inversion comes into its own, since he shows that the powers of the fetish came to be through a process very different from what people think. Yet here is the crux, for what workers, consumers and, above all, the economic theorists perceive and describe is quite real; they see 'what they are'. So we get the overlap or fusion: the commodity-fetish has real powers which are described and explained in terms that are both mystical and realistic.

In an effort to explain this double-take, Marx tries various formulations (which take him well beyond the opposition of illusion and reality to which he was committed in his treatment of Hegel's *Kritik*). For example, the qualities of the products of labour 'are at the same time perceptible and imperceptible by the senses'.[44] Further, 'the mist' in which the social character of labour appears to belong to the products themselves by no mean 'dissipates'. He tries once again: even though it is possible to reveal the process of transferral and thereby how value appears in the product of labour, that value appears 'just as real and final, as the fact that, after the discovery by science of the component gases of air, the atmosphere itself remained unaltered'.[45] Marx coins the strange phrase, 'socially valid as well as objective thought-forms [*gesellschaftlich gültige, also objektive Gedankenformen*]',[46] in order to express this dual character of social relations and the transferred relations between

43. Marx 1867a, p. 84; Marx 1867b, p. 87.
44. Marx 1867a, p. 83; Marx 1867b, p. 86.
45. Marx 1867a, p. 85; Marx 1867b, p. 88.
46. Marx 1867b, p. 90; my translation.

commodities. In short, what Marx is saying is that the commodity-form and the value of abstracted labour it attracts are both illusory and real, mysterious and concrete, mist-enveloped and actual. The power they have is mystified and mist-enveloped, since people do not realise how it comes about, but it is all too real in terms of the powers commodities have and the alienating effects they have on people's lives.

So, how does this move – which may be read as a dialectical move beyond his earlier formulations of fetishism – relate to the critique of idolatry? At this point, Marx goes beyond the text from Isaiah that I quoted earlier. In that passage, the effort to debunk the belief of the idol-worshipper – that this object directs one to God – seeks to show how ordinary the idol really is. After all, it is merely a piece of wood, metal or stone, for there is no god to whom it points. By contrast, Marx argues that the powers invested in the fetish are very real, for they alienate and diminish human beings. It is as though the one who made the idol in the first place was right in some respect, for the object does have power, but a pernicious and destructive power. In other words, Marx emphasises another dimension of the picture, the one in which the worker who makes the idol is worn out through hunger, thirst, and failing strength – except that now he gives it a whole new meaning.

However, what is illusory is the way the worshipper/labourer understands how the object, or the relations between commodities, gained its alienating power. And that is what Marx seeks to explore, unpick and reveal. So also are the theories of the political economists. They may describe something that is all too real, but their way of accounting for it is mistaken. As Marx's analysis proceeds in the section 'The Fetishism of Commodities and the Secret Thereof', he focuses more and more on the bourgeois political economists with whom he argues. For all their hard work and occasional insights (Marx does build upon them, after all), they still assume that capitalist production – in which the process of production controls human beings – is absolutely natural. By contrast, all preceding economic forms are unnatural and deluded. Or as Marx puts it: 'Hence forms of social production that preceded the bourgeois form are treated by the bourgeoisie in much the same way as the Fathers of the Church treated pre-Christian religions'.[47]

---

47. Marx 1867a, p. 92; Marx 1867b, p. 96.

What is good for labour, money and commodities is good for capital itself. In a delightful passage towards the end of the extraordinary *Economic Manuscripts of 1861–63*, Marx traces the way in which capital itself becomes a fetish. Here we find exactly the same logic: what appear to be forces and powers beyond the worker are in fact produced by free labour. The difference now is that all of the various items I have already covered make an appearance, along with a few extras. He lists all the abstractions from the real, social process of labour, such as the capitalist as a personification of capital, the productive powers of capital, use-value and exchange-value, the application of forces of nature and science, the products of labour in the form of machinery, wealth and so on. They confront the worker as alien, objective presences in advance that rule over him. In short, capital itself becomes a power before which the worker is powerless: all these items 'stand on their hind legs vis-à-vis the worker and confront him as capital'.[48] Indeed, just like the commodity-form, capital 'becomes a very mysterious being'.[49] It is not for nothing that Marx writes of the 'religion of everyday life',[50] elaborated as though it were theological dogma by political economists, when summarising the various parts of capital – wealth, the personification of things, the conversion of production-relations into entities, interest, rent, wages, profit and surplus-value. All of these suffer from the same dual process of fetishism.

Conclusion

As Marx comments in an earlier volume of that same manuscript, the 'transubstantiation, the fetishism, is complete [*Die Transsubstantiation, der Fetischismus ist vollendet*]'.[51] I have followed the trail of the fetish from its first encounter in the book by de Brosses to its final expansion to cover all of the various

---

48. Marx 1861–3g, pp. 457–8. See also the description of wealth as a fetish in Marx 1859a, p. 387.

49. Marx 1861–3g.

50. Marx 1894a, p. 817; Marx 1894b, p. 838. Apart from Walter Benjamin's oft-noted fragment, 'Capitalism as Religion' (Benjamin 1996), the theme has been developed in a very different direction from liberation-theology or Marxism by a group of what may be called 'economic theologians' such as Cobb Jr. 1998, Meeks 1989, and Loy 1996.

51. Marx 1861–3d, p. 494; Marx 1861–3e, p. 485. Van Leeuwen 2002a, pp. 208–10, completely misses the point of fetishism when he argues that the key to Marx's argument on money is transubstantiation.

illusory projections and transferrals of capitalism as a whole. On the way, Marx took up a specific idea and transformed it at each expansion, so that we found it in labour, the money-relation, the commodity-form, and then every other shape it might take. Through all of these twists and turns, the basic argument retained a remarkable consistency. Yet what also kept recurring was the intimate embrace with the critique of idolatry, especially in the book of Isaiah. Finally, in *Capital*, Marx elevates the argument to a whole new level. For many years, I have been struck by the connection, but I never suspected it would be so consistent and remain so close. From the moment Marx encountered in de Brosses's work the subsumption of the idolatry of the Hebrew Bible in his treatment of fetishism, it has been a constant backdrop to Marx's various re-uses of the idea of fetishism, and it reappears in some of the last material Marx wrote, *The Ethnological Notebooks*. I have no need to argue that it is in any way conscious or deliberate on Marx's part. Nor does this theological resonance diminish the insight that the theory of fetishism provided – in fact, it only strengthens Marx's argument. But what it does entail, at least for those like myself who are interested in these matters, is that one could mount a sustained theological critique of capitalism that would negate any theological apologetic one might find.

There are a number of implications of Marx's analysis, which may well be described as the most developed stage of his critique of religion. To begin with, a little earlier (Chapter Six), I took Marx to task for arguing that religion is illusory and therefore not real in any meaningful sense, but, now, he develops a much more interesting argument. For there is a material reality to the illusion of the fetish, a point that emerges from Marx's dialectical effort to show that the fetishes of commodities, wealth, labour-power, interest, rent, wages, profit, and so on, are both materially grounded and illusory, mysterious and concrete. These fetishes and the powers they hold are all too real, yet the way we understand them is problematic, for they are inverted and appear perfectly natural. Marx seeks to dispel the illusion, to burn away the mist enveloping the realities of capitalism, but what he finds once he has uncovered the inversion is that there is a material reality to this religious form – fetishism – for the brutal and destructive powers it holds are all too real. However, this argument has an unexpected outcome: if fetishism (and thereby idolatry) is paradoxically and objectively real, as 'a socially valid and objective thought-form', then religion too has a presence in this sense. I do not think we can shy away from this implication in Marx's analysis, even if it runs against his own firm atheism. In this respect, Marx's analysis goes beyond a position he often held, namely that religion is merely false consciousness, that it is an excrescence of the human brain, which needs to be uncovered so that it may be discarded. Religion may well be inverted, it may perceive the whole situation in a topsy-turvy fashion, but that inversion has a distinct material reality.

It is this kind of argument that has led some liberation-theologians to argue that capitalism as a whole is idolatrous: its many parts, such as the foreign debt, gross domestic product, current-account balance, and growth, are all parts of a destructive cult that worships these idols as gods. And the economic theories that explain, justify and support these idols are false theologies which demand endless sacrifices. They are both false gods that demand blood and destroy their worshippers. There is great value in this argument, but I have one or two misgivings. A consistent feature of liberation-theology is to hold back from criticising the Bible itself as a destructive force. There are myriad texts that one may find which support the generation of wealth, encourage and justify ruling classes, and by no means make them uncomfortable. The Bible is not to be tampered with, for it is contested terrain and liberation-theologians need to claim it from their opponents. This problem leads onto the next, for the critique of capitalism as idolatry operates on the assumption that there is one true God and that the god or gods worshipped by the acolytes of capitalism are not real. Even more, that false god may well be another form of the Christian God, who has been twisted into something evil – there are more than enough theological apologies for capitalism.

On this matter, Marx's own arguments throw up some profound problems for such assumptions. He offers an insightful comparison between theologians and bourgeois economists: for theology, all the other gods are in fact superstitions, except ours. Everyone else may think they are worshipping a god, argue the theologians, but they are really worshipping a wooden object. It is just that they cannot see it, for they are deluded. So also with the bourgeois economists: all that has gone before is mistaken, unable to see the truth. Capitalist relations, in which commodity-relations are real and the forces of production are in control, finally reveal the truth in comparison to these earlier forms of social production. What they do not realise is that their own theory is just as contrived, artificial and delusory as the ones that have gone before. In other words, their own system is just as idolatrous as all the others.

Now there is a theological kick in Marx's argument, although I need to reverse its emphasis in order to be on the receiving end. He uses the analogy with theology to show how the bourgeois economists are deluded about their own theories. However, if we turn the analogy around, then the point is that the logic one uses to dismiss the truth-claims about other religions is an extremely tricky one, for it may also apply to one's own. This point becomes clearer in a footnote, where Marx quotes from his own *Poverty of Philosophy*:

> Economists have a singular method of procedure. There are only two kinds of institutions for them, artificial and natural. The institutions of feudalism are artificial institutions, those of the bourgeoisie are natural institutions. In this they resemble the theologians, who likewise establish two kinds of religion. Every religion which is not theirs is an invention of men, while their own is an emanation from God.[52]

What interests me about this critique is the way it intersects with the risky critique of idolatry in the Hebrew Bible. Once one begins the process of breaking the signifying link between a representation – an idol – of the gods of others, there is no reason to stop reasoning in the same manner when it comes to one's own beliefs. As I pointed out earlier, this is the reason for the ban on images in the second commandment. If you have no images, then there is no signifying link to break. But the fear that anything – a word, a text, a pope, a church, or a theological position – may represent God in some way re-establishes the signifying chain and thereby exposes it to be broken.

---

52. Marx 1867a, p. 92, n. 1; Marx 1867b, p. 96, n. 33.

Chapter Eight

Of Flowers and Chains:
The Ambivalence of Theology

> *Religion is* a register of the theoretical struggles
> of mankind.[1]

Ambiguities, tensions, contradictions – these are
constant features of Marx's analysis of everything
from laws against the theft of wood or divorce-bills
to the workings of capitalism. Yet this sensitivity
towards contradictions seems to escape him when
he comes to theology and the Bible. Most of the time
theology is mere illusion, fixated on heaven, and a
prime instance of idealism. Marx usually found that
theology was eagerly and energetically jumping in
bed with reaction, power and money, that its concerns were other-worldly rather than this-worldly,
and that religion was a prime instance of a false consciousness that concealed the real causes of exploitation and alienation. Yet, every now and then, he lets
slip another perspective – that theology may be more
ambiguous than he usually thinks. It is usually a

---

1. Marx 1844k, p. 143; Marx 1844l, p. 345. See also: 'And the whole socialist principle
in its turn is only one aspect that concerns the reality of the true human being. But
we have to pay just as much attention to the other aspect, to the theoretical existence
of man, and therefore to make religion, science, etc., the object of our criticism. In
addition, we want to influence our contemporaries, particularly our German contemporaries. The question arises: how are we to set about it?' (Marx 1844k, p. 143; Marx
1844l, p. 344.)

glimpse, a passing comment, a puzzled observation, or the implications of an argument such as that concerning fetishism. I have noted one or two of these in my discussion of his theological allusions, where he moves from using the Bible against opponents to appropriating it for his own use. At this moment, there is a hint of the contradictions that run deep in this text.

In this chapter, I explore that hint much further, picking up one last element from my discussion of Feuerbach in Chapter Five, especially in my treatment of the famous 'Introduction' to his *Kritik*. I will have more to say about that text below, especially on the question of opium. However, I also devote a good deal of time to a little-known and often-ignored text on the Gospel of John, 'The Union of Believers', written for his *Gymnasium* examinations in 1835. One must admit that it is not his best piece. However, my interest is not merely because it shows a precocious Marx engaging with a biblical text, but that when he does so he cannot avoid its contradictions and tensions. From there, I move on to consider his polemic against the idea of a Christian state in an essay I discussed in Chapter Two, 'The Leading Article in No. 179 of the *Kölnische Zeitung*'. In a wonderful part of that essay, Marx carries out a more sustained use of the Bible to show up the contradictions in such a state, but as he does so he uncovers a few more pieces of the ambivalence I am seeking. There follows a contextual analysis of what is arguably one of Marx's most well-known sentences, 'It is the opium of the people'. It turns out that opium itself was a multivalent metaphor that carried all manner of positive and negative associations. All in all, it really is a play between two of Marx's most favoured images – flowers and chains.[2]

Theological tension and the Gospel of John

Marx's youthful essay bears the cumbersome title of 'The Union of Believers with Christ According to John 15:1–14, Showing Its Basis and Essence, Its Absolute Necessity, and Its Effects'.[3] Not quite *Capital*, it has lain in obscurity, shadowed by the larger bulk of Marx's work.[4] However, in line with my

---

2. As a few samples among many, see Marx 1842j, p. 205; Marx 1842k, p. 193; Marx 1843a, p. 116; Marx 1843b, p. 104; Marx 1844c, p. 176; Marx 1844d, p. 379.
3. Marx 1835c; Marx 1835d.
4. Van Leeuwen 2002b, pp. 39–42, is the only work I know where the essay is given some attention. Calling it a piece of 'splendid exegesis' with a solid Trinitarian

desire to bring forth oft-neglected material, especially that which deals with theology and the Bible, this essay is the perfect place to begin. It is rarely if ever the subject of critical attention, and if it does get a mention, it is usually written off as the frivolous exercise of a young man (he was 17) answering a set question in his *Gymnasium* examinations. I can well imagine why it is ignored, since Marx talks of God and love and Christ – not quite the Karl we know. However, the fact that it languishes in the doldrums is more than enough reason for me to become interested, but there are other, more important reasons. Since Marx wrote an essay concerned exclusively with the Bible it would be remiss of me not to deal with it. But, above all, it reveals a Marx who stumbles across a series of tensions when he faces a biblical text. Those tensions are my concern.

The essay is an exercise in biblical exegesis. Yet one of the curious features of biblical exegesis is that, all too often, it goes about its task with an absent text. The biblical text is commented upon, but it does not itself appear. It forms a backdrop, brought in every now and then, but otherwise hovers out of sight like some authoritative absence or ego-ideal. Marx is guilty of this too, so I begin with the text itself: John 15:1–14:

[1] 'I am the true vine, and my Father is the vinedresser.

[2] Every branch of mine that bears no fruit, he takes away, and every branch that does bear fruit he prunes, that it may bear more fruit.

[3] You are already made clean by the word which I have spoken to you.

[4] Abide in me, and I in you. As the branch cannot bear fruit by itself, unless it abides in the vine, neither can you, unless you abide in me.

[5] I am the vine, you are the branches. He who abides in me, and I in him, he it is that bears much fruit, for apart from me you can do nothing.

[6] If a man does not abide in me, he is cast forth as a branch and withers; and the branches are gathered, thrown into the fire and burned.

[7] If you abide in me, and my words abide in you, ask whatever you will, and it shall be done for you.

---

structure and Christological focus, van Leeuwen argues that it is enough evidence to show that Marx's Christian convictions were sufficient for confirmation. Van Leeuwen even manages to find a Trinitarian structure in one of Marx's other essays, 'Reflections of a Young Man on the Choice of a Profession' (Marx 1835a; Marx 1835b).

⁸ By this my Father is glorified, that you bear much fruit, and so prove to be my disciples.

⁹ As the Father has loved me, so have I loved you; abide in my love.

¹⁰ If you keep my commandments, you will abide in my love, just as I have kept my Father's commandments and abide in his love.

¹¹ These things I have spoken to you, that my joy may be in you, and that your joy may be full.

¹² This is my commandment, that you love one another as I have loved you.

¹³ Greater love has no man than this, that a man lay down his life for his friends.

¹⁴ You are my friends if you do what I command you'.

A few comments on the text itself before we see what Marx tries to do with it. John 15:14 is part of the Johannine story of the Last Supper during the Passover,[5] where, after washing the disciples' feet,[6] Jesus holds forth for some time. He runs through a calm prediction of his crucifixion, the promise of a Counsellor, the Holy Spirit, being hated by the world, a prediction (again calmly announced) of his resurrection, a call to courage and finally a prayer for the disciples. Immediately afterwards, the whole group heads off to the Garden of Gethsemane where Jesus is to meet his fate – calmly, of course. In the midst of all of this comes our passage, which is really one- and two-third chunks – or pericopes as they are known in biblical criticism – in between the promise of the Holy Spirit[7] and the words concerning hatred by the world.[8] In the section neatly sliced out and presented on its own, we have one section that is halfway between a parable and an allegory – the vine and its branches[9] – and another concerning the commandment of love.[10] The second is somewhat truncated, for the last two verses have been excised.[11] The result: the four

---

5. John 13–17.
6. John 13.
7. John 14.
8. John 15:18–27.
9. John 15:1–11.
10. John 15:12–17.
11. The absent verses read: '¹⁶ You did not choose me, but I chose you and appointed you that you should go and bear fruit and that your fruit should abide; so that whatever you ask the Father in my name, he may give it to you. ¹⁷ This I command you, to love one another.' (John 15:16–17.)

remaining verses on the commandment of love end up being attached to the parable of the vine. While there is some overlap between these pericopes, they really are distinct in John's text. However, with the exam-question posed for Marx and his classmates, they are crammed into one unit, turning the verses on love into a commentary on the extended metaphor of the vine.

So what does the young Karl do with all of this? His attempted answer betrays two tensions, which for now at least I characterise in terms of content and form. As for content, by the end of the essay he ends up contradicting himself: he begins in a rather long-winded way to argue that however much human beings may strive towards God, they can never quite get there. For that, we need Christ, who meets us and helps us over the last steps of the way. However, by the time he comes to wrap up his essay, Marx produces a much more dialectical – and, to my mind, far more interesting – argument. In this case, the only way to achieve a properly human virtue is to fix our eyes solely on God; our singular love for God through Christ will make us fully human. I would like to call these two the argument from mediation and the argument from dialectics.

A second tension, this time in terms of form, appears in the question set for the exam itself: 'The union of believers with Christ according to John 15:1–14, showing its basis and essence, its absolute necessity, and its effects'. A rather mundane, doctrinal task, is it not, especially in comparison to a text that is almost poetic in its concern for love? In fact, that is the formal problem with this whole exercise – the disjunction between the metaphorical poetry of the text and the request to extract some catechetical points from it. I can almost hear the plodding catechism: what is the basis of union with Christ? What is its essence? And so on. We are a long way from vines, branches, fruit and the sacrifice of love. Marx finds himself caught between the catechetical question and the parable-like form of the text; while trying to deal with the question adequately, he continually finds himself seduced by the very different formal temptations of the text from John.

Let me say a little more on each of these tensions. In terms of the actual contradiction within his arguments – one in terms of mediation and the other through dialectics – the question seeks an answer in four categories, namely the necessity, basis, essence and effects of the union with Christ. Having spent more time than I care to admit with catechisms (my father taught us for a whole year the Heidelberg Catechism), I could have answered such a question with mind-numbing precision: the necessity of union with Christ is due to sin, its basis is the sacrifice of Christ on the cross for our sins, its essence is reconciliation with God, and its primary effect is eternal life with God and the fruits one's reconciliation.

Marx does not quite follow such a conventional argument, although he does attempt to do so. Instead, he offers a different response. Thus, the necessity for union lies in the inability of people (due to superstition or sin) to make that final step to God despite all of their striving, the need for redemption due to sin is the basis, a vital communion with and love for God is its essence, and its effects may be seen in a virtue that can be truly human only by means of focusing singularly on the divine. Not a mention of Christ's 'sacrifice' on the cross (John 15:13 may have been used as a proverbial proof-text), nor indeed to the economy of salvation as such, which one might have expected given the Lutheran tradition.

The least interesting parts of the essay are those concerned with basis and essence, so I do not propose to spend much time with them. If the basis gains the briefest of mentions, then essence becomes far too touchy-feely. All he has to say about the basis of union with Christ is that it is due to sin and corruption; everyone knows this and so it needs no further discussion. By bringing sin in at this point (it should really have gone in his discussion of necessity), Marx has rather conveniently slipped by Christ's sacrifice on the cross (the catechetical answer one would have expected for the basis of union with Christ). The outcome is that, when he gets to the matter of the essence or nature of the union with Christ, he moves not into the territory of reconciliation but into the realm of communion and love. Words such as 'loving eyes', 'ardent thankfulness', 'sink joyfully on our knees', 'forgiving father', 'kindly teacher', 'fondly snuggle', 'most intimate, most vital communion', and 'highest love'[12] give a good feel for this stretch of text. It struggles to be sensuous and often tips over into a syrupy evocation of feeling. Not his best work, to say the least.

More intriguing by far are his treatments of the other two categories of the initial question – necessity and effects. Here we have a glaring contradiction. So, in terms of necessity (a longish opening section of the essay), Marx opts for a very different tack than might have been expected. Instead of pointing out the necessity of union with Christ since we have sinned and fallen short

---

12. Marx 1835c, p. 638; Marx 1835d, p. 451.

of the glory of God and that our only hope lies in the grace of God, Marx pursues what may best be described as a rather Roman-Catholic approach: we may strive towards and reach for God, but we can never quite get there. For instance, even the 'divine Plato' expresses 'a profound longing for a higher being'.[13] And Plato is merely a cipher for the highest point of the history of all peoples, for no matter how much a people may struggle towards God, no matter how close they get, they always fall short of a true sense of God through superstition and whatnot. So also, suggests Marx, with individuals, who for all the 'spark of divinity'[14] they may have, for all their yearning, passion and striving for knowledge, truth and goodness, they run out of steam due to greed, lies and sin. In other words, we may get damn close, but not quite close enough. The answer to that problem, at least for Marx, is that the 'benign Creator' was unable to hate his work of creation; instead 'he wanted to raise it up to him and he sent his son'.[15]

One thing that can be said about this type of argument is that it is certainly not Lutheran, where we might have expected a focus on undeserved grace and the complete inability of human beings to do any good work. Rather, it has the scent of that solid medieval Roman-Catholic doctrine that came to be called Molinism. Luis de Molina (1535–1600) was a Jesuit theologian and ideologue of the Counter-Reformation. Over against the reformers' emphasis on human worthlessness and inability to do any good work, let alone come close to salvation, Molina argued in his *Concordia liberi arbitrii cum gratiae donis* (1588) that obedience to the divine commandments and the doing of good works could get you a decent way. Molina's basic position was that freely chosen human cooperation with the gift of grace was the ultimate cause of the efficacy of grace. This effectiveness, which really relies on the ability of human beings genuinely to obey God, comes from the human decision to obey and not grace (an anathema to reformers such as Luther for whom there was no freedom of the will to choose). Thus, in opposition to the reformers, Molinism gives human beings as much a rôle as they can possibly have in the process of salvation. And, in case we suspect that Molinism espoused self-earned salvation, it argues that the freely chosen act of human beings to cooperate with

---

13. Marx 1835c, p. 636; Marx 1835d, p. 449.
14. Marx 1835c, p. 637; Marx 1835d, p. 450.
15. Ibid. At this point Marx cites John 15:3 and 4 (see above).

God is foreknown by God. Thus, the efficacy of grace has its basis not in the gift of divine grace itself, but in the fact that God foreknows we will freely co-operate with the gift of grace. In short, we can reach the gate of salvation, but we need someone to open it for us. By stretching certain elements of theology as far as they will go, we have here a stress on free will versus the reformers' emphasis on determinism and predestination, as well as the removal of grace from centre-stage versus the central platform of Protestant theology. For some, such as the Dominicans, this was too much (it did not help matters that the Jesuits championed Molinism). However, Molinist approaches did influence the approach of Roman Catholics to missions: instead of seeking to convert the hopelessly lost as Protestant missions did in Greenland or the Pacific Islands, Roman-Catholic missions in places such as the Philippines or the Kimberley region of Australia looked for signs of a natural progression to God which they could then extend and offer to complete with Christianity.

Now, Marx is hardly pushing the intricacies of Molinism in this essay, but he comes much closer to the Roman-Catholic tendency to regard human beings as capable of taking some steps to union with Christ. At the last minute, he does try to redeem himself: when he resorts to a third proof of the necessity of union (the word of Christ), he suggests that just as a branch of a vine cannot bear fruit by itself, 'so, Christ says, without me you can do nothing' (at this point he cites John 15:4, 5, 6).[16] Yet, just when we think he is coming back into line, back to a tolerably Lutheran position, he concludes with the following: 'Our hearts, reason, history, the word of Christ, therefore, tell us loudly and convincingly that union with Him is absolutely essential, that without Him we cannot *fulfil our goal*, that without Him we would be rejected by God, that only He can redeem us'.[17]

The problem with this argument is that Marx is by no means consistent, for by the end of the essay, he makes use of a very different argument. Here, in his discussion of the effects of union with Christ, Marx waxes dialectical (for the first time perhaps): the nub of his argument is that the key to a 'milder and more human virtue' lies in what appears to be its opposite, namely a thoroughly pure and divine virtue that comes only through 'love for a divine

---

16. Marx 1835c, p. 637; Marx 1835d, p. 450.
17. Ibid; emphasis mine.

Being'.[18] In other words, it is only through a singular focus (love for Christ) that a properly human virtue arises. Now, the content may be surprising, especially since it comes from Marx's hurried pen, but the form of the argument is much more so. Only through the divine may earthly virtue achieve its true form. Take the earthly on its own and all we get is virtue as 'a dark distorted image', the 'offspring of a harsh theory of duty', filled with 'repulsive aspects' and 'coarseness'.[19] The only way to a more human virtue – one that is both brilliant and mild – is to find the source of virtue in God. The results: the ability to face misfortune with calm assurance, suffering with consolation, deal with the rages of passion, face up to the anger and oppression of the 'iniquitous', and then finally joy (Marx has to bring in John 15:11 somewhere).

I must admit that, up until this last section, I found the essay a little overblown and less than inspiring. However, what he has tapped into here is what may be called a Christological dialectic: the only complete human being is Christ himself. He can be a full human being precisely because – according to orthodox doctrine – he is divine. From this point, all manner of things follow: as the new Adam,[20] Christ undoes the first sin; in his person, he unites both human and divine as a mark of the truly human; that union enables all human beings to attain to union with the divine.

Is this the first and last time Marx would make use of such an argument? In terms of content, the answer must be 'yes'; in terms of form, 'not quite'. We are not going to find him arguing anywhere else that the only way for human fulfilment is by being drawn up into God. The form of the argument is a different matter entirely. As we saw earlier (Chapter Five), Feuerbach explicitly points out that his own argument was analogous to a Christological model. He has merely reversed the flow: instead of moving from God to human beings and back again, he begins with human beings, shows how God is the projection of our minds and aspirations and then returns to human beings. It was this insight that Marx took up enthusiastically, developing it into the argument that religion is the projection of oppressed and alienated human beings. Yet the basic form is still there, drawn from Feuerbach's

---

18. Marx 1835c, p. 639; Marx 1835d, p. 450. The starting-point here is John 15:9, 10, 12–14, especially the greatest commandment – 'that you love one another as I have loved you' (John 15:12).

19. Marx 1835c, pp. 638–9; Marx 1835d, p. 452.

20. 1 Corinthians 15.

own Christological model, a model that we also find in this early essay on John 15. But that is not all, for there is also an echo of that model in a statement I have mentioned a few times already: 'thus the criticism of heaven turns into the criticism of earth'.[21] In this case, it is not merely a passage from one to the other, a time to get on with the real business of earthly criticism. Rather, that step is dialectically connected with the criticism of heaven.

The catch with this last part of Marx's argument is that it runs straight up against his opening depiction of human beings striving to reach God. I do not mean that the problem lies solely with his effort to hold together two somewhat contradictory theological positions, for that seems to be a leitmotif of theology. Rather, his difficulty is that he tries to couple two very different types of argument. On the one hand, there is the argument (in the section on necessity) that human beings and God meet somewhere in the middle: we may strive and strain to do our best and it gets us some of the way there, but then God must meet us halfway and come to our rescue. Only with his help can we attain our goal (union with Christ). On the other hand, he argues (in the section on effects) that the only possibility for a properly human virtue comes from God, to whom we must direct our love. In short, only through the divine may an earthly virtue come to life.

If the first approach to salvation might be called mediation, the second is then dialectical; the first moderates between two extremes (humanity and God), while the second pushes one extreme (God) to bring the other forth (humanity). While the argument for mediation allows a good deal of space for the exercise of human virtue, for all manner of good works, then for the dialectical argument such earthly virtue is repulsive, coarse and a harsh discipline of duty. They really are two very different arguments. It is as though he has the two ends of different pieces of rope in each hand; strain as he might to get their ends to touch one another, the forces pulling each piece of rope in opposite directions is far stronger.

However, this tension in Marx's argument is but the first. Although it tends to slip into form, this tension between the arguments for mediation and dialectics is mostly one of content. The second tension is more strictly formal, and that is the one between the nature of the text from John 15 and the catechism-style question posed against it in the examination. While the Gospel

---

21. Marx 1844c, p. 176; Marx 1844d, p. 379.

text deals in the metaphor of the vine and its branches, pursuing its various possibilities – vinedressers, fruit, pruning, withering, fires and burning, only to make the connection with abiding in Christ, love and friendship – the question seeks a distinctly catechetical response, moving through the various stages of salvation. I know only too well this effort to butcher texts for the sake of some doctrinal point or other; poetry, myth, metaphor, parable and allegory are chopped into very different and unseemly shapes.

Marx, it seems to me, is caught between these two directions: a metaphorical and parabolic text and the ordered steps of Lutheran doctrine. No wonder he barely answers the question correctly, and no wonder he ends up contradicting himself. Even more, it seems to me that Marx lets the text lead him on a different path. Initially, he tries to stick to the guidelines, but before he knows it the essay takes on a life of its own. He is constantly tempted to run with the text and leave the structure of the question behind. Let me give a few examples:

> Thus, penetrated with the conviction that this union is absolutely essential, we are desirous of finding out in what this lofty gift consists, this ray of light which descends from higher worlds to animate our hearts, and bears us purified aloft to heaven…[22]
>
> But, if it could feel, the branch would not only look upwards to the husbandman, it would fondly snuggle up to the vine, it would feel itself most closely linked with it and with the branches which have sprung from it; it would love the other branches if only because the husbandman tends them and the vine gives them strength.[23]
>
> Therefore union with Christ bestows a joy which the Epicurean strives vainly to derive from his frivolous philosophy or the deep thinker from the most hidden depths of knowledge, a joy known only by the ingenuous, childlike mind which is linked with Christ and through Him with God, a joy which makes life higher and more beautiful.[24]

Not the best writing Marx has produced – too flowery and trying just a little too hard. But then, the Gospel of John is not very good writing either. Repetitive (how many times is it necessary to mention a vine and its branches,

---

22. Marx 1835c, p. 637; Marx 1835d, p. 451.
23. Marx 1835c, p. 638; Marx 1835d, p. 451.
24. Marx 1835c, p. 639; Marx 1835d, p. 452.

or the commandment to love for that matter?), somewhat over-confident (Jesus calmly gives his own commandments, just like his Father), pushing the metaphor a little too far so that it falls into a rather wooden allegory – in each case Marx follows suit. But what happens in these excerpts is that Marx lets the text carry him away, especially in his style. His sentences tend to run on, saying the same thing over again with a small variation. He goes on to kill the metaphor of the branch and vine in perhaps the worst section of the essay – on the nature of union with Christ. In all this he follows the impetus of the text of John.

So what we have with this essay are two tensions, one in terms of the arguments themselves (what I have called arguments of mediation and dialectics) and the other between the nature of this text from John and the catechetical question appended to it. On this second tension, some ingenious exegesis was required. Marx did his best, but the text enticed him on a different path. It is no wonder, then, that his teacher's comments betray these tensions all too clearly. Somewhat puzzled, Küpper writes: 'It is profound in thought, brilliantly and forcefully written, deserving of praise, although the topic – the essence of union – is not elucidated, its cause is dealt with only one-sidedly, its necessity is not proved adequately'.[25] Rather perceptive, it seems to me.

All in all, it is not quite the Marx to whom we have become accustomed. Even his use of a dialectical argument owes more to theology than to the Hegel who would become so important soon enough. He may, of course, have been writing what he thought was necessary to pass his examination on religious knowledge – a line that might have been taken had anyone, embarrassed that the founder of historical materialism had actually written a piece of biblical exegesis, bothered to comment on such a text. Yet what is important about this essay is the way in which the contradictions turn up. One of them – the tension between mediation and dialectics, or between Roman-Catholic and Protestant positions – may be seen as a trace or signal of Marx's immediate context. He belonged to a Lutheran minority (his father converted from Judaism soon after his birth) in a predominantly Roman-Catholic town. And the legacy of conflicts between these two branches of Christianity runs deeply in German history. But there is another factor that is just as important. Marx has come across one of the deep contradictions in theology, in this case over

---

25. Marx 1835c, p. 758, n. 198.

grace. Is salvation entirely due to God since human beings are utterly sinful, or is it due to cooperation between God and human beings, who strive to do good and aspire to God? I would argue that theology is, by its very nature, a discipline riven with such tensions. Further, he has stumbled across a tension with the Bible, or rather between a poetic text in the Bible and the genre of catechism. The two sit very uneasily with one another and Marx does not solve the problem. Once again, there is a deeper issue at stake, for the Bible is full of contradictions, as anyone who cares to read it soon finds out. Historical, generic, theological and political, almost every page runs up against these problems. As with this essay on John, Marx occasionally uncovers such contradictions, usually despite himself.

The Bible and class-conflict

Those contradictions would take on a distinctly political tone in an essay I have discussed on a few occasions, 'The Leading Article in No. 179 of the *Kölnische Zeitung*'.[26] In this case, the issue is church and state, but, in the process, Marx mischievously calls on the Bible to rattle ruling-class assumptions about the rock-solid support of its assumed privilege and the validity of a 'Christian state'. In the very act of using against it those who wanted a Christian state, Marx stumbles across this political multivocity of the Bible.

Let me quote him in full:

> Do you consider it wrong to appeal to the courts if you have been cheated? But the apostle writes that it is wrong. If you have been struck on one cheek, do you turn the other also, or do you not rather start an action for assault? But the gospel forbids it. Do you not demand rational right in this world, do you not grumble at the slightest raising of taxes, are you not beside yourself at the least infringement of your personal liberty? But you have been told that suffering in this life is not to be compared with the bliss of the future, that passive sufferance and blissful hope are the cardinal virtues.
>
> Are not most of your court cases and most of your civil laws concerned with property? But you have been told that your treasure is not of this world. Or if you plead that you render unto Caesar the things that are Caesar's and

---

26. Marx 1842h; Marx 1842i.

to God the things that are God's, then you should regard not only golden
Mammon, but at least as much free reason, as the ruler of this world, and the
'action of free reason' is what we call philosophising.[27]

Marx's ostensible purpose in this passage is to show that the idea of a Christian
state is undermined by the sacred text of Christianity itself, indeed that the
proponents are hypocrites if they think that the Bible supports everything
they do. As I pointed out in Chapter One, no doubt the texts used for the
Christian state would be those such as Romans 13:1–7, which begins with the
infamous, 'Let every person be subject to the ruling authorities', going on to
point out that 'he who resists the authorities resists what God has appointed'.[28]
Add the divine sanction for the despotism of Moses, the claim that the kings
of Israel were divinely appointed for ever,[29] the prophetic cry for vengeance
on Israel's neighbours, and the assumption that God would lead the king into
battle, and we already have enough to justify a divinely appointed Christian
ruler and state without even invoking the doctrine that the king was – analogous to Christ – God's representative on earth.

What does Marx do? He chips away at this biblical foundation with a series
of references. So, in opposition to recourse to the civil courts, he alludes to
Paul's advice that such courts are to be avoided: 'To have lawsuits at all with
one another is defeat for you. Why not rather suffer wrong? Why not rather be
defrauded?'[30] Marx neglects to mention that Paul also suggests that the 'saints'
(i.e. the other believers) should be the ones to judge and not the 'unrighteous'.
Here lies the justification for the systems that continue today of the ecclesiasti-

27. Marx 1842h, pp. 198–9; Marx 1842i, p. 186.
28. The full text reads: 'Let every person be subject to the ruling authorities. For
there is no authority except from God, and those that exist must have been instituted
by God. Therefore, he who resists the authorities resists what God has appointed, and
those who resist will incur judgement. For rulers are not a terror to good conduct, but
to bad. Would you have no fear of him who is in authority? Then do what is good,
and you will receive his approval, for he is God's servant for your good. But if you
do wrong, be afraid, for he does not bear the sword in vain; he is the servant of God
to execute his wrath on the wrongdoer. Therefore one must be subject, not only to
avoid God's wrath but also for the sake of conscience. For the same reason you also
pay taxes, for the authorities are ministers of God, attending to this very thing. Pay
all of them their dues, taxes to whom taxes are due, revenue to whom revenue is due,
respect to whom respect is due, honour to whom honour is due'.
29. 2 Samuel 7:8–17.
30. 1 Corinthians 6:7.

cal courts that try to keep themselves separate from the civil system, a practice that has all manner of pitfalls.

He goes on to invoke the famous passage on balanced cheek-slapping: 'if anyone strikes you on the right cheek, turn to him the other also'.[31] If we in our 'Christian state' were to follow this advice, Marx suggests, we would hardly file a suit for assault. Or, whenever one complains about taxes, or the loss of liberty, or – to add a few of the more common complaints – that your neighbour's music is too loud, his lawn is unkempt, that the service at your favourite café is shoddy, or the flight-attendants are rude, then Marx suggests that the faithful member of the 'Christian state' should bear in mind Paul's suggestion 'that the sufferings of this present time are not worth comparing with the glory that is to be revealed to us'.[32] Or, over against the obsession with and bickering over property, Marx reminds his readers of Jesus's saying that he will invoke on more than one occasion: 'Do not lay up for yourselves treasures on earth, where moth and rust consume and where thieves break in and steal, but lay up for yourselves treasure in heaven, where neither moth nor rust consumes and where thieves do not break in and steal. For where your treasure is, there will your heart be also'.[33] Finally, picking up his line concerning the perfectly acceptable public presence of philosophy in political debates, he gives yet another well-known gospel-saying a twist: 'Render unto Caesar the things that are Caesar's, and to God the things that are God's'.[34] Now, this text may be taken in a number ways. The literary context is the tricky question posed by the Pharisees and Herodians concerning the hot political potato of taxes. Jesus asks for a coin, asks whose inscription it is, they reply 'Caesar's' and then he gives his ambiguous advice. The text has been variously interpreted as yet another justification for secular authority, for the divine sanction of taxes (for both church and state), for the separation of the temporal and heavenly spheres, for the argument that everything belongs to God and therefore nothing to Caesar, or even as a rebellious comment in which Jesus's question – 'Whose likeness and inscription is this?' – becomes a scoffing comment at the bad imprint of a notoriously ugly emperor. Marx takes it as a text that espouses the separation of earthly and heavenly domains

---

31. Matthew 5:39; see also Luke 6:29.
32. Romans 8:18.
33. Matthew 6:19–21; see also Luke 12:33–4.
34. Mark 12:17; see also Matthew 22:21 and Luke 20:25.

and then pushes it to point out that, like Caesar's coin and indeed Mammon itself,[35] reason too is of this world. In fact, free reason is the 'ruler of this world' and not Mammon.

I have, perhaps a little pedantically, brought to the fore the biblical texts that lie behind Marx's polemic since they show up again the tensions in those various texts that make up the Bible. And that tension is one between the sanction of the ruling class – sundry despots, kings, judges and priests with whom God seems to side all too often – and a perpetual current of insurrectionary stories. Since these texts, in both their composition and transmission, arose in the context of political and economic tensions, we find far more stories of insurrection than might be expected. Whether it is the rebellion of Eve and Adam who eat from the forbidden tree, or the murmuring and grumbling of the people of Israel as Moses leads them around and around in circles in the wilderness (so much so that at one point the whole people are called 'sons of rebellion' in Numbers 17:10), or the people perpetually disobeying divine commands and finding themselves the victims of pestilence, fire or invading armies (all brought on as punishment), what we have is a consistent pattern where the people simply will not lie down and take it any more. Add to this the theme of chaos over which order attempts to maintain a hold, as in the flood-story, or the sayings of Jesus that undermine any value of property or temporal power, or Paul's theory of grace that breaks in and shakes up everything, or the legendary communism depicted in Acts 2:44–5 and 4:32–5, or the saying that money is the root of all evil, and the vein of insurrection becomes strong indeed.

It would seem that the Bible is inescapably ambivalent in a political sense – this is what Marx has glimpsed, perhaps unwittingly, when he invokes the Bible. In making that argument, I am not about the much-derided task of 'cherry-picking', choosing texts that suit my agenda and leaving the others. The image itself is mistaken, for it assumes that the Bible is like an orchard or perhaps a supermarket in some quiet middle-class suburb. One may walk along and pick and choose what one likes. Much closer to the text is a political divide: either one opts for the rulers and sundry despots, invoking God to their side and suppressing rebellion in the name of punishing sin, or one opts for the rebels themselves.

---

35. The allusion is to Matthew 6:24 and Luke 16:13.

The two sides of opium

Finally, I come to what is by now an over-used text on the ambivalence of Christianity. It comes from those few paragraphs in his 'Introduction' to the *Kritik*. I have already devoted a significant stretch of text to an analysis of this passage (see Chapter Five), tracing the heavy influence of Feuerbach, the way Marx moves beyond him and the theological resonances that underpin the argument. Above all, there is no doubt that Marx's argument sets out to debunk theology and that he has no intention of resuscitating it. Yet, in the midst of that process, he drops a few famous sentences that are probably the clearest recognition of the multivalency of theology.

> *Religious* suffering is, at one and the same time, the *expression* of real suffering but also the *protest* against real suffering. Religion is the sigh of the oppressed creature, the heart of a heartless world, just as it is the soul of soulless conditions. It is the *opium* of the people.[36]
>
> Das *religiöse* Elend ist in einem der *Ausdruck* des wirklichen Elendes und in einem die *Protestation* gegen das wirkliche Elend. Die Religion ist der Seufzer der bedrängten Kreatur, das Gemüt einer herzlosen Welt, wie sie der Geist geistloser Zustände ist. Sie ist das *Opium* des Volkes.[37]

We need to be careful of attributing too much to Marx here, as many do. The juxtapositions can hardly be missed: expression of and protest against suffering; heart and heartless; soul and soulless. However, they are not quite the same. In the second sentence, the subject is 'religion [*Die Religion*]'. Religion is the sigh, heart and soul of an oppressed creature, a heartless world and a soulless condition. In other words, these comments are directly in line with his theory that religion is the expression of oppression and alienation.[38] They are, if you like, the flares fired up from intolerable economic conditions, expressing exasperation and desperate longing. By contrast, the first sentence stands out on two counts. Firstly, 'religious suffering [*Das* religiöse *Elend*]' is the subject, and, secondly, that suffering is 'at one and the same time, the expression

---

36. Marx 1844c, p. 175 (translation modified).
37. Marx 1844d, p. 378.
38. It may be possible, following Dick Boer (personal communication), to connect 'the sigh of the oppressed creature' with Paul's comments in Romans 8:22 – 'we know that the whole of creation has been groaning in travail together until now'. The allusion is somewhat distant and it does connect with a theory of fall and redemption that may be problematic in relation to Marx's text here.

of real suffering and a protest against real suffering [*in einem der* Ausdruck *des wirklichen Elendes und in einem die* Protestation *gegen das wirkliche Elend*]'. Is that suffering due to religion or the stories of suffering (persecution, execution and above all crucifixion)? I suspect the latter, since the underlying theory still dominates: religious, that is, illusory, suffering is nothing compared to real suffering.

Even with all of this careful exegesis, the juxtaposition of expression [*Ausdruck*] and protest [*Protestation*] stands out. Here, indeed, is ambivalence over religious suffering, as more than one commentator has observed. And it is not as though we have one or other option so that we can choose either 'expression' or 'protest'. No, Marx points out that they are so 'at one and the same time [*in einem... in einem*]' – an effort to hold both elements together in dialectical tension. Add to these the earlier comments on religion being both the universal basis of 'justification' and 'consolation' [*ihr allgemeiner Trost- und Rechtfertigungsgrund*] of this troubled world and we gain a fleeting picture of a multivalent rôle for religion.[39]

All of which comes out in the most succinct and quoted statement of Marx concerning religion, 'It is the *opium* of the people [*Sie ist das* Opium *des Volkes*]'. A little basic grammar never goes astray: the feminine pronoun *sie* refers to religion directly, the subject of the sentence preceding. But how is opium ambivalent? As McKinnon points out in an excellent essay,[40] context is the key. In contrast to our own associations of opium with drugs, altered states, addicts, organised crime, wily Taliban insurgents, and desperate farmers making a living the only way they can, opium was a much more ambivalent item in nineteenth-century Europe. Widely regarded as a beneficial, useful and cheap medicine at the beginning of the century, it was gradually vilified by its end by a coalition of medical and religious forces. In between, debates raged. McKinnon traces in detail how opium was the centre of debates, defences and

---

39. Timothy Bewes develops an interesting argument that really goes beyond Marx: if we cannot escape the 'vale of tears' of exploitation and oppression, then, in order to cope, some form of religion becomes imperative (Bewes 2002, pp. 136–7).

40. McKinnon 2006. Kiernan 1983, pp. 413–14, only just hints at this ambiguity by suggesting opium is a painkiller and addictive drug. It is worth remembering that the term 'opium' to describe religion is not Marx's alone. For example, Moses Hess uses the term in a medicinal sense: 'Religion can make bearable...the unhappy consciousness of serfdom...in the same way as opium is of good help in painful diseases' (cited by Löwy 1996, p. 5). Bauer too wrote of the 'opium-like influence' of theology (McLellan 1969, pp. 78–9).

parliamentary enquiries, how it was used for all manner of ills and to calm children, how the opium-trade was immensely profitable, how it was one of the only medicines available for the working poor, albeit often adulterated,[41] how it was a source of utopian visions for artists and poets, and how it was increasingly stigmatised as a source of addiction and illness. In effect, it ran all the way from blessed medicine to recreational curse.

Marx, too, was a regular user, along with those other useful medicines, arsenic and creosote. As he slowly killed himself through a punishing schedule of too much writing and smoking, too little sleep, and an inadequate diet, Marx would use it for his carbuncles, toothaches, liver-problems, bronchial coughs and so on. As Jenny wrote in a letter to Engels in 1857:

> Dear Mr Engels, One invalid is writing for another by *ordre du mufti*. Chaley's head hurts him almost everywhere, terrible tooth-ache, pains in the ears, head, eyes, throat and God knows what else. Neither opium pills nor creosote do any good. The tooth has got to come out and he jibs at the idea.[42]

For Marx, opium was 'an ambiguous, multidimensional and contradictory metaphor'.[43] I am less interested here in the *Aufhebung* of religion (for that discussion, see Chapter Five) as in the unstable metaphor of opium. In the end, it is an excellent metaphor, encapsulating the earlier tension I have been tracing between expression and protest. This is the tension I wish to keep open, at least for a while. For what it does is open up again the ambivalence of theology, especially if we leave that ambivalence or indeed multivalency unresolved.

Yet what does such ambivalence really mean? Quite simply, a religion such as Christianity is caught in a complex tension between reaction and revolution. That tension takes many shapes in terms of both practice and doctrine. It is all too easy to point to the contrasts in the practice of Christianity. To cull a few more notable examples from a very long list, there is the dirty deal

---

41. As Engels writes in *The Condition of the Working Class in England*: 'The food of the labourer, indigestible enough in itself, is utterly unfit for young children, and he has neither means nor time to get his children more suitable food. Moreover, the custom of giving children spirits, and even opium, is very general; and these two influences, with the rest of the conditions of life prejudicial to bodily development, give rise to the most diverse affections of the digestive organs, leaving life-long traces behind them.' (Engels 1846a, p. 399; Engels 1846b, p. 330.)

42. Marx (Jenny senior) 1857a, p. 563; Marx (Jenny senior) 1857b, p. 643.

43. McKinnon 2006, p. 12.

done with the state under Constantine and the resultant effort at 'catholic' orthodoxy, or the 'Holy Roman Emperors' who followed through the middle ages, the uncanny ability of monarchs to be head of state and of the church, the class-status of the church throughout feudalism, Luther calling on everyone and anyone to slaughter any rebel-peasant they might encounter, the *sine qua non* of deep religious commitment by as many presidents of the United States as one cares to remember, and the grovelling support of wealthy and powerful rulers by any number of ecclesiastical bodies. On the other side, one revolutionary group after another has felt the call to revolt voiced in the Bible. As Karl Kautsky showed so well,[44] it includes a range of mystical and ascetic movements, such as the Beguines and Beghards (from the twelfth century in the Netherlands who lived alone or in groups, were self-sustained, lived lives of simple piety and assisted others), Lollards (followers of Wycliffe in the fourteenth century who stressed personal faith, divine election, and the Bible, who were deeply hostile to the church, were involved in a series of uprisings in England, and who provided fertile ground for later dissent), Taborites (a fifteenth-century religious movement that championed asceticism, communal living and the establishment of the kingdom of God by force of arms), the Bohemian Brethren (who believed that the kingdom of God was among them in a communal life and worship and who had a profound influence on Czech literature through the translation of the Bible), the Anabaptists of the Radical Reformation more generally, and of course those around the Peasants' Revolt and Thomas Müntzer, whom Engels has brought to everlasting fame (see Chapter Ten). To these, I would add the seditious and antinomian groups in England throughout the eighteenth and nineteenth centuries,[45] political and liberation-theologies in our own day, as well the organisations of Christian communists and the International League of Religious Socialists, which has over 200,000 members and represents religious-socialist movements in 21 countries and across a number of religions.[46]

That is all very well for practice, since one can argue (as Engels would) that these revolutionary movements use religious language as a way of expressing distinctly political purposes. But then the question must be: why this language

---

44. Kautsky 1947b.
45. See especially Thompson 1993.
46. See <www.ilrs.org>.

and not another? Or rather, out of a range of possible languages why does theology remain on the agenda? Quite simply, theology as doctrine, as a system of thought, is torn with such tensions as well. I do not mean the proverbial paradoxes of theology that remain intellectual affairs, but the way in which those paradoxes arise from and articulate political and economic tensions.

Let me give an example or two, one taken directly from the letters of Paul in the New Testament and the other from none other than John Calvin. As for Paul, there is the politically explosive theme of 'justification by faith through grace'. The letters of Paul, especially Romans and Galatians, throw out sentences such as: 'a man is not justified [*diakaioutai*] by works of the law but through faith in Jesus Christ';[47] 'For we hold that a man is justified [*dikaioust-hai*] by faith apart from works of the law';[48] 'you are not under law but under grace [*charin*]'.[49] One usually finds that the Greek verb, *diakaioō*, is translated in a strictly theological way as 'justify' or 'make right (with God)'. However, its basic sense is 'to show justice', or 'to do justice' to someone. The point of the texts I have just quoted is that God renders justice not through the law but through 'grace' – by means of a favour or as goodwill.

Radical challenges to vested interest and power emerge in these texts, for none of the known structures will redeem you. The judicial system is not going to render justice (but then does it not favour those who establish it in the first place?), education will not save you from ignorance or poverty, privilege and inherited wealth will not protect you, and the government (whether despot, oligarchy or parliamentary democracy) will make no difference to your status in life. Justice and grace are entirely outside the system. Further, the doctrine of justification by faith undermines any privilege due to wealth, class-status or power. This is where Paul's comment in Romans 3:23–4 comes in: 'since all have sinned and fall short of the glory of God, they are justified by his grace as a gift'. The point that we all stumble puts us at the same level – junkie, serial killer, priest or upstanding civic leader. More than one aristocrat has been revolted by the idea of being on the same level as his filthy cowherd or kitchen-servant; more than one bourgeois householder has tried to

---

47. Galatians 2:16.
48. Romans 3:28.
49. Romans 6:14.

dismiss the idea that her industriousness does not make her a wit better than the dope-dealing paedophile on the nightly news.

Now, justification by faith may run in a number of directions, such as Calvinist predestination (since we are completely reliant on God's grace we are also reliant on his decisions as to who will be saved and who damned), the methodist tendency to Arminianism (God's grace is available to all but we can accept or reject it), licence (if we are of the Elect then nothing we do will change that), Puritanism (in response to grace we need to live lives acceptable to God), quietism (it is all up to God), activism (showing the fruits of grace) and political radicalism (grace is after all the theological version of the revolution). All these possibilities show up either in Paul's own letters, since he was not always clear – in fact he is often contradictory – about the consequences of his 'discovery', or in the groups to whom he addresses his letters. For example, the Corinthian and Galatian churches took the idea much further than he anticipated, pushing Christian freedom from the law into all manner of directions such as freedom in regard to sex, worship, Roman law and so on. Underlying it all is a distinct antinomian tendency. Once this became clear to Paul, especially through those who took up justification by faith with gusto, he realised with some shock what he had let loose. So, he tried to rope it in, setting boundaries on what 'freedom' meant – not to insult or injure one's 'brethren', not to dispense with the law entirely, for it is good, arguing that there is another law, the law of Christ, banning the sexual licence that some saw in the idea, limiting the freedom that women were taking in some of the churches and so on. The same person who wrote 'not under the law, but under grace' also counselled people not to cause a ruckus and to obey the authorities. In fact, this tension – between letting loose the idea of justification by faith and then working hard to bring it under control – is one that Paul would bequeath to whoever took up the idea.

Another instance comes from an unlikely quarter indeed – John Calvin. Usually depicted as the dour killjoy from Geneva, one who would suck the air out of the room as soon as he walked in, Calvin actually struggled with the tension bequeathed to him by Paul. Again and again, Calvin opened the theological bag and gave the political cat inside a glimpse of freedom. Equally as often, he clamped the bag shut. This tension turns up in his high view of the Bible (if God tells you to revolt then you must), his view of teachings on Christian freedom (radical freedom is restricted to the private individual), grace (the radical act of God must be channelled along a set course) and politics (if a ruler does not enact God's law then we must overthrow the rat-bag).[50]

My favourite is the tension between his doctrines of depravity and predestination, or what I call the democracy of depravity and the aristocracy of salvation. Calvin argued that we are so utterly sinful and totally depraved that we can do no good on our own. Everything we do turns to evil, so there is no hope in hell that we can save ourselves. For that we need God, who, through His grace, gives us the faith needed as the first step to salvation. The implication of this doctrine is deeply democratic: *all* of us are equally depraved, whether merchant-banker or mafia hit-man, law-abiding and church-going accountant or high-priest of the Church of Satan. My father, who was for many years a minister in a reformed church, would relish telling his well-heeled and highly-regarded parishioners that they were the most despicable and filthy sinners. Needless to say, they felt his people-skills needed some refining, for they much preferred the aristocracy of salvation. Only the elect, determined by God from eternity, would enter into heaven, while the majority had been predestined for damnation in the fires of hell. And there is nothing anyone can do about it. On this count, Calvin backed down, for he did not dare extend the democracy of depravity to the democracy of salvation. But my point is that this tension appears at the heart of his doctrinal work; try as he might, he could not solve it.

These are only a few examples of a basic theological tension between reaction and revolution within theology. Marx catches a glimpse of it at rare moments in his work, most notably with this unstable metaphor of opium. It may seem as though I have overloaded this metaphor, and, indeed, the contradictions I traced a little earlier, with far too much theological baggage. But what I have sought to do is open up the opium-metaphor and pursue its implications a little further. Indeed, it is difficult to avoid such tensions in light of the deep impression left by Lutheranism on German thought as well as the long history of conflicts between Protestants and Roman Catholics that had left their own marks in the shape of a whole range of entrenched oppositions.

---

50. See further Boer 2009b.

Marx's demurrer: on grace

I have been arguing that every now and then there is a shard in Marx's work that suggests a more ambivalent sense of theology. The last few examples – on justification by faith from Paul and the tension over depravity and predestination in Calvin – actually turn on the basic theological notion of grace, namely, God's free gift. So, in conclusion, let me explore a few comments on grace in Marx's own texts, especially since they act as a warning about getting too carried away with the revolutionary possibilities of one or other element of theology.

Marx reminds us that grace is not always such a good thing. In his effort to turn Hegel's flank in the *Kritik*, which I have discussed in detail earlier, Marx points out that grace may well be the appropriate doctrine for the 'haphazard arbitrariness' and 'unfounded decision' that characterises despotism.[51] How so? Once you have an abstract sovereignty incarnated in a monarch who claims divine sanction, then the monarch becomes God's representative on earth – a Christological God-man. Grace shows up at two points: the sanction of the despot by God (divine right, and so on); and the appropriation by the despot of God's arbitrary decisions. The receiver of such a grace becomes its dispenser.

It is a good point, for what on the one hand may well overthrow the status quo in all its privilege, stolen wealth and power, may also be used by that same 'old corruption' to justify its own completely unjustified hold on power.[52] What looks progressive may turn out to be reactionary:

> The social principles of Christianity have now had eighteen hundred years to be developed, and need no further development by Prussian Consistorial Counsellors. The social principles of Christianity justified the slavery of antiquity, glorified the serfdom of the Middle Ages and are capable, in case of need, of defending the oppression of the proletariat, with somewhat doleful grimaces. The social principles of Christianity preach the necessity of a ruling and an oppressed class, and for the latter all they have to offer is the pious wish that the former may be charitable. The social principles of Christianity place the Consistorial Counsellor's compensation for all infamies

---

51. See especially Marx 1843c, pp. 24–6, 35–6, 51–2; Marx 1843d, pp. 225–7, 236–8, 253–4.
52. Marx 1847a, p. 231; Marx 1847b, p. 200.

in heaven, and thereby justify the continuation of these infamies on earth. The social principles of Christianity declare all the vile acts of the oppressors against the oppressed to be either a just punishment for original sin and other sins, or trials which the Lord, in his infinite wisdom, ordains for the redeemed. The social principles of Christianity preach cowardice, self-contempt, abasement, submissiveness and humbleness, in short, all the qualities of the rabble, and the proletariat, which will not permit itself to be treated as rabble, needs its courage, its self-confidence, its pride and its sense of independence even more than its bread. The social principles of Christianity are sneaking and hypocritical, and the proletariat is revolutionary. So much for the social principles of Christianity.

Indeed, there were more theologians and churchmen willing to argue that God's grace manifested itself in the absolute monarchs than those who challenged such a reading as an affront and a travesty. It was, after all, 'by the grace of God' that a monarch ruled at all – a phrase Marx uses with ironic frequency throughout his reporting on the Prussian royal family.[53] 'Gottes Gnaden König von Preussen' is even printed on Marx's passport of 1861.[54] What was the monarch's proper response to God's grace? To rule 'with responsibility to God alone', i.e., without regard to a parliament, especially in the face of the dissolution of the monarchy before democratic and republican forces.[55]

So a theological idea such as grace is ambivalent. But that is precisely my point, for, like rain on a ridge-line, grace may run in two directions. It may fall a little to the left, and before long we are with the antinomian side of grace, the challenge to any institution or power that is. Grace breaks through from an entirely unexpected quarter, shaking everything to its foundations and setting off sparks in all directions. On this understanding of grace, it is a straight line to Alain Badiou's 'event': the extraordinary, supernumerary and

---

53. Marx 1848w, p. 474; Marx 1848x, p. 430; Marx 1848u; Marx 1848v; Marx 1848i, p. 2; Marx 1848j, p. 5; Marx 1848g, p. 16; Marx 1848h, p. 9; Marx 1858b, p. 126; Marx 1856c, p. 157; Marx 1848aa; Marx 1849g, pp. 262–7; Marx 1849h, pp. 190–6; Marx 1849q, pp. 335–6; Marx 1849r, pp. 253–4; Marx 1949o, pp. 50, 54; Marx 1849p, pp. 339, 343; Marx 1849i, p. 430; Marx 1849j, p. 483; Marx 1849m, p. 453; Marx 1849n, p. 505; Marx and Engels 1848p; Marx and Engels 1848q; Marx and Engels 1849e, pp. 48–9; Marx and Engels 1849f, pp. 337–8. See also Engels 1873d, p. 419; Engels 1849a, p. 194; Engels 1849b, p. 396; Engels 1849l, p. 475; Engels 1849m, p. 525.
54. Marx 1861c; Marx 1861d.
55. Marx 1858f, p. 66.

undeserved interruption that sets the revolution on its way. Here, grace is indeed the theological version of revolution.

If it falls to the right, then it runs a very different course down the mountain. Here, it may become the 'miracle' that sanctions the exceptionality of a monarch, despot or the religious right in its quest for power. Beginning with Paul's 'there is no authority except from God',[56] it is a straight line to Carl Schmitt's argument that the 'miracle' underlies any theory of the state and its sovereignty.[57] In other words, the pure exception of grace becomes the sanction for all manner of reactionary programmes that rely on the arbitrary will of God.

More often than not, this was how Marx saw theology, as a reactionary collection of ideas that are particularly unhelpful. But every now and then, as I have argued here, there is a passing sense that theology is more devious than that, for it embodies too many contradictions to sit safely in either camp.

---

56. Romans 13:1.
57. Schmitt 2005.

Chapter Nine
Engels's Biblical Temptations

> Among my own family – and it is a very pious
> and loyal one...[1]

> If I had not been brought up in the most extreme
> orthodoxy and piety, if I had not had drummed
> into me in church, Sunday school and at home
> the most direct, unconditional belief in the Bible
> and in the agreement of the teaching of the Bible
> with that of the church...[2]

The final section of my study turns directly to Engels.
He has been part of the earlier discussions at various
moments, particularly in my treatment of their
combined writings. Often neglected as Marx's lieu-
tenant, we should really reinstate his nickname, 'the
General'.[3] In this chapter, I dig into Engels's reformed
past, dealing with his many youthful writings on
theology and the Bible. Engels's texts overflow with
biblical references and lengthy treatments. He had
obviously devoted a good deal of time to the Bible,
and was able to read the New Testament in Greek.
It was so much a part of his everyday life that it was

---

1. Engels 1844–5, p. 231.
2. Engels 1839v, p. 466; Engels 1839w, p. 413.
3. For an excellent study of Engels which restores the originality of the 'early Engels',
especially of the essays on political economy and the working class in England, see
Kouvelakis 2003, pp. 167–231.

impossible for him to avoid the Bible. These early texts by Engels show us a young man of profound Christian convictions struggling with the implications of the debates swirling around the Bible in Germany at the time. They produce a difficult process of self-exorcism, the initial topic with which I deal. However, the ground on which that struggle took place was the Bible, and so I consider at length his response to the age-old problem of the contradictions of the Bible. Finally, I offer a commentary on his essays on Schelling. They were responses to Schelling's public lectures in Berlin and signal Engels's rejection of the ossified form of theology that he could no longer find redeemable.

Engels's self-exorcism

> May God watch over his disposition, I am often fearful for this otherwise excellent boy.[4]

> I can't eat, drink, sleep, let out a fart, without being confronted by this same accursed lamb-of-God expression.[5]

At one time in his life, Christianity meant a great deal to Engels. The effort to extract himself was a long and difficult one, so much so that we can speak of a process of self-exorcism. While the commitment was very deep, the cuts were longer and scars more livid. They may show up in various ways: as a more doctrinaire atheistic materialism, as awareness that something was indeed lost,[6] or as an abiding interest in matters of religious rebellion or early Christianity.

What was the nature of the early faith that Engels sought to exorcise? Although Marx has 'of Evangelical faith' written on his Certificate of Maturity from the Trier Gymnasium[7] and Engels had learned, according to his school-leaving reference, the 'basic doctrines of the Evangelical Church',[8] it meant

---

4. Engels (senior) 1835, p. 582.
5. Engels 1845f, p. 29; Engels 1845g, p. 27.
6. For example, 'one can see how fortifying and comforting a religion which has truly become a matter of the heart is, even in its saddest extremes' (Engels 1839d, p. 31; Engels 1839e, p. 64).
7. *Certificate of Maturity for Pupil of the Gymnasium in Trier* 1835, p. 643. For the sake of his application for recovery of his German citizenship in 1861, Marx would still write, 'I... profess the Evangelical religion' (Marx 1861a, p. 355; Marx 1861b, p. 635).
8. Hantschke 1837, p. 585.

rather different things to both of them. Marx's father (originally Herschel) was an assimilated Jew in a predominantly Roman-Catholic South (Marx's mother held on much longer before finally being baptised when Marx was 14). But Engels landed at birth in a reformed family living in the twin-towns of Barmen and Elberfeld (Wuppertal).[9] It is not merely the proximity to the Dutch border that stamps Calvinism on Engels, for we find a few other signals. His mother's maiden name is Elisabeth Francisca Mauritzia *van Haar*,[10] a good and popular Dutch name (and perhaps one reason why Engels managed Dutch so easily). Add to this the following facts and we have a solid reformed Christian commitment: his baptism in the Elberfeld Reformed Evangelical Parish; the way his father's letters drip with good reformed observations and his mother's with anxious wishes;[11] and Engels's own confession to Wilhelm Graeber, part of which I quoted in the epigram to this chapter: 'If I had not been brought up in the most extreme orthodoxy and piety, if I had not had drummed into me in church, Sunday school and at home the most direct, unconditional belief in the Bible and in the agreement of the teaching of the Bible with that of the church...'.[12]

Before I know it, Engels comes rather close to my own background. For my parents, too, are of a distinctly reformed background, especially the conservative breakaway group [*Gereformeerde Kerken*] from the Herformde Kerk in the Netherlands. Further, my maternal ancestors (my mother's father's grandparents) come from Schleswig-Holstein – that endlessly contested zone between Prussia and Denmark. To escape those conflicts they moved in the eighteenth century to the Waddenzee island of Ameland, which is about far as you can go into the Calvinist north of the Netherlands. Engels himself would spend a couple of years (1839–41) in Bremen in the North-West of Prussia, sent

---

9. Engels's baptism-certificate comes from the Reformed Evangelical Parish of Elberfeld; see *Baptism Certificate of Friedrich Engels: Extract from the Baptism Register of the Elberfeld Reformed Evangelical Parish* 1821, p. 580.
10. See *Birth Certificate of Friedrich Engels, Barmen, December 5, 1820: Extract from the Barmen Register of Births, Deaths and Marriages* 1820, p. 577. Both 'van Haar' and 'van Haaren' are common Dutch names.
11. Engels (senior) 1820, 1835, 1842. After the warrant for his arrest and the 1848 revolutions, his mother voices her great angst over his path, asks him to return to the path of God, rejoin the family and take up work in a business (Engels (Elisabeth) 1848a; Engels (Elisabeth) 1848b). See the brilliant description of his parents' reaction when Engels returns home for a brief spell in 1845 when they know he is associating with communists (Engels 1845f, pp. 28–9; Engels 1845g, pp. 26–7).
12. Engels 1839v, p. 466; Engels 1839w, p. 413.

there by his father to work hard as a clerk in the trading house of Consul Leupold and to imbibe a more solid dose of Calvinism. In a letter to Friedrich Graeber he finds it much the same as Wuppertal.[13] It was also the place where F.W. Krummacher, the arch-Calvinist and head-minister of the Elberfeld Reformed Parish in which Engels was baptised, grew up.[14] As with their religious convictions, the people of Bremen still speak a Low German that is almost indistinguishable from the Dutch spoken just across the border.

It is not some purely personal interest that has led me to dig up Engels's reformed background; it also makes much sense of his early struggles. They are, as I have suggested, an exercise in self-exorcism. Or, to shift the terminology, it is also an Oedipal response to his parents' deep religious convictions. And what he is reacting to, as a young man with a critical mind, is the asphyxiating environment of narrow Calvinism in what he mockingly describes at Muckertal, the Valley of Bigots.[15]

The curious thing about that response is that it comes at two levels. In the various letters, he mentions occasionally the 'blazing anger' at the pietism and literal Christianity of his home.[16] The new currents of free thought keep him awake at night, leaving him little peace and at times bringing him to tears.[17] Yet, at other times, there is precious little of this existential crisis. Some of the biblical references are light-hearted,[18] others are used to make a satirical point,[19] and others may form part of a biblical landscape as he walks across

---

13. Engels 1839h, p. 416; Engels 1839i, p. 363.

14. See Engels 1840i, p. 126; Engels 1840j, p. 199, where Engels mentions Krummacher visiting his parents.

15. Engels 1839t, p. 457; Engels 1839u, p. 403.

16. Ibid.

17. Engels 1839t, p. 461; Engels 1839u, p. 407.

18. So, for example, to his sister, Marie: 'Yes, you little goose, you shall have four pages but they are according to the saying that with the same measure as you measure will it be measured unto you, and even that is too much for you.' (Engels 1838a, p. 390; Engels 1838b, p. 330.) The allusion is to Matthew 7:2. Then there is the mention of his effort to write a choral for Luther's famous hymn, *Ein feste Burg ist unser Gott* (Engels 1838c, p. 404; Engels 1838c, pp. 346–7).

19. For example, in the occasional satirical comment on Schelling, he writes: 'and finally it appears somewhat like intellectual meanness, like petty – what does one call that well-known, pale-yellow passion? – when Schelling claims each and every thing he acknowledges in Hegel as his own property, nay, as flesh of his own flesh' (Engels 1841a, p. 186; Engels 1841b, p. 261). Here, the allusion is to Adam's saying after Eve is created out of his side: 'This at last is bone of my bones and flesh of my flesh' (Genesis 2:23).

the Alps.[20] Often, his letters are boisterous and playful, and the material published at the time gives the impression that he is enjoying himself, that he takes much delight in his new discoveries and, indeed, in the polemic against his own hometown – whether it is the satirical, anonymous and delightfully-written depiction of his home twin-town in 'Letters from Wuppertal',[21] the various notes on the rhetorically skilful and anti-Enlightenment pastor, F.W. Krummacher,[22] dreadful Calvinist poetry,[23] the reactionary Roman-Catholic nonsense of a certain Joel Jacoby,[24] the equally reactionary efforts of Friedrich Wilhelm IV to wind back the clock to a Christian-feudal monarchy,[25] the zeal of a young pastor who is staying with Engels in Bremen and who believes in direct divine intervention as a result of prayer,[26] or the proposals for a Christian medicine by Professor Leupoldt from Erlangen (illness is the result of the sin of the fathers and needs to be dealt with accordingly).[27] One of my favourites is a comment on a certain minister called Döring, 'whose absent-mindedness is most odd; he is incapable of uttering three sentences with a connected train of thought, but he can make three parts of a sermon into four by repeating one of them word for word without being at all aware of it'.[28] Although he is engaged in the age-old need to leave the narrow confines of home, in physical, emotional and intellectual senses, there seems to be

---

20. For instance: '...here and there snow glistens through the mists which hover round the most distant summits, and Pilatus rises above the mass of peaks as if it were sitting in judgment like the Judaean governor of old who gave it his name – these are the Alps!' (Engels 1840s, pp. 170–1; Engels 1840t, p. 245).
21. Engels 1839f; Engels 1839g. For example, 'Almost outside the town is the Catholic Church; it stands there as if it had been expelled from the sacred walls. It is Byzantine in style, built very badly by a very inexperienced architect from a very good plan' (Engels 1839f, p. 7; Engels 1839g, p. 32).
22. Engels 1839b; Engels 1839c; Engels 1840q; Engels 1840r; Engels 1840i, pp. 126–8; Engels 1840j, pp. 199–201; Engels 1842c, pp. 315, 346; Engels 1842d, pp. 391, 417; Engels 1843a, p. 361; Engels 1843b, p. 428; Engels 1839h, p. 416; Engels 1839i, p. 363; Engels 1839l, p. 427; Engels 1839m, p. 372; Engels 1839x, p. 472; Engels 1839y, p. 420; Engels 1840u; Engels 1840v.
23. Engels 1839d; Engels 1839e; Engels 1839h, pp. 416–17; Engels 1839i, pp. 363–4. Here he writes: 'Out of anger at present-day religious poetry, out of every piety, that is, one might well go over to the devil. Is our time so shabby that it is impossible for anyone to set religious poetry on to new paths?' (Engels 1839h, p. 417; Engels 1839i, p. 364).
24. Engels 1840a; Engels 1840b.
25. Engels 1843a; Engels 1843b.
26. Engels 1839x, p. 472; Engels 1839y, p. 420.
27. Engels 1842e; Engels 1842f. Engels goes on to anticipate from the same man 'a Christian grammar based on the same principles' (Engels 1842e, p. 283).
28. Engels 1839f, p. 16; Engels 1839g, p. 40.

little regret and much anticipation of the journey itself. He speaks of it more often than not as a glorious awakening from a narrow and barren childhood.

For instance, in the allegorical piece, 'Landscapes', his passage by ship along the Rhine through the drab Calvinist landscape of the Netherlands and out into the open sea becomes a passage from his own background to the depths of speculation and free thought that brings him to cry, 'in God we live, move and have our being'.[29] Later, when he had travelled and lived elsewhere (Bremen, Manchester, Berne, Paris and Brussels), he would return home for what was, on the surface at least, a very different cause: the revolution in Elberfeld in 1849.[30] One gains the sense that, in offering himself to reorganise the armed defence of the revolution, he would have been happy to stay had he not been asked to leave by the bourgeois leaders – and had the revolution been successful.[31]

As for the 'Letters from Wuppertal', written when he was 18 (in 1838), the picture he presents is of a wide sea of pietism and mysticism (the terms are interchangeable) that characterises all of the Protestant churches in Wuppertal, whether Lutheran or reformed (Calvinist).[32] Within that broad sweep, pietism appears in greater or lesser degree, but those he knows best are the reformed churches. They take the prize as the most extreme of the lot. The pietists take a good number of hits, whether in terms of pure hypocrisy,[33] the deleterious

---

29. Engels 1840c, p. 99; Engels 1840d, p. 131.
30. See Engels 1849e; Engels 1849f; Engels 1849n; Engels 1849o.
31. In fact, at the conclusion to his reports on the uprising in Elberfeld, Engels writes: 'Let the workers of the Berg Country and the Mark, who have shown such astonishing affection for and devotion to a member of our editorial board, bear in mind that the present movement is only the prologue to another movement a thousand times more serious, in which the issue will concern their own, the workers' most vital interests. This new revolutionary movement will be the result of the present movement and as soon as it occurs Engels – on this the workers can confidently rely – like all the other editors of the *Neue Rheinische Zeitung*, will be at his post, and no power on earth will induce him to forsake it.' (Engels 1849e, p. 449; Engels 1849f, p. 502.) See also his earlier comment, 'But you too have a homeland and perhaps return to it with the same love as I, however ordinary it looks, once you have vented your anger at its perversities.' (Engels 1839d, p. 31; Engels 1839e, p. 64.)
32. Although an initial effort to bring together the Calvinist and Lutheran churches in Prussia had been made by Friedrich Wilhelm III in 1817 under a broader evangelical church, sharp differences remained. The united church still had its Lutheran and reformed parishes and there were independent 'Old Lutherans' and purely reformed churches as well.
33. As some of the better examples: 'But the wealthy manufacturers have a flexible conscience, and causing the death of one child more or less does not doom a pietist's soul to hell, especially if he goes to church twice every Sunday.' (Engels 1839f, p. 10;

effects on education in the schools,[34] as an alternative addiction to alcohol,[35] or as dreadful poets.[36] It is, in short, the 'sprained foot of Christianity'.[37]

But these shots are really an opening gambit, for, when he turns to the reformed wing of German Protestantism, Engels shifts gear. His target is none other than the reformed parish of Elberfeld. In the context of a uniform orthodoxy across all Protestant churches in Barmen and Elberfeld (differing only in terms of the amount of pietism added to the mix), this one stands out as the most conservative of all. Apart from the facts that he was baptised in this church and that his parents were members, one can see, from the vividness and satirical bite of his images (they conjure up all too quickly memories of my own upbringing), that Engels spent a few too many hours locked to the pew of this church as a child and teenager.

Engels knows it all too well from the inside. With a reputation for his 'religious feeling, purity of heart, agreeable habits and other prepossessing qualities',[38] it is no wonder the young Engels published his early writings under pseudonyms such as S. Oswald. Various items draw out his anger: the collective intolerance of the Elberfeld reformers, and both the style and content of its most powerful minister, F.W. Krummacher. I would suggest that what looked like increasing narrowness and intolerance had much to do with

---

Engels 1839g, p. 35.) 'But anyone who really wants to get to know this breed should visit the workshop of a pious blacksmith or boot-maker. There sits the master craftsman, on his right the Bible, on his left – very often at any rate – a bottle of schnapps. Not much is done in the way of work; the master almost always reads the Bible, occasionally knocks back a glass and sometimes joins the choir of journeymen singing a hymn; but the chief occupation is always damning one's neighbour.' (Ibid.).

34. Engels 1839f, pp. 17–18; Engels 1839g, p. 42.

35. 'Those who do not fall prey to mysticism are ruined by drunkenness. This mysticism, in the crude and repellent form in which it prevails there [Elberfeld], inevitably produces the opposite extreme, with the result that in the main the *people* there consist only of the "decent" ones... and the dissolute riff-raff' (Engels 1839f, pp. 9–10; Engels 1839g, p. 34).

36. Engels 1839f, pp. 24–5; Engels 1839g, pp. 50–1.

37. Engels 1840k, p. 103; Engels 1840l, p. 135.

38. Hantschke 1835, p. 585. See also the very orthodox, if somewhat wooden, poem, *Herr Jesu Christe, Gottes Sohn*, probably written when he was 16 (Engels 1837a; Engels 1837b), as well as his comments on his own conversion in a letter of 12–27 July 1839 to Friedrich Graeber: 'I believed because I realised that I could no longer live only for the day, because I repented of my sins, because I needed communion with God. I gladly gave away immediately what I most loved, I turned my back on my greatest joys, my dearest acquaintances, I made myself look ridiculous to everybody everywhere... You know yourself that I was in earnest, in dead earnest.' (Engels 1839t, pp. 460–1; Engels 1839u, p. 407.)

the growing awareness of a rebellious teenager who had begun to think for himself. As for the Elberfeld reformers as a whole, it seemed to Engels that the strict 'Calvinist spirit' had become of late 'the most savage intolerance' in the hands of a bunch of 'extremely bigoted preachers'.[39] The targets: wayward rationalists and those who denied predestination – among whom Engels now numbers himself, at least for a time. Through the vicious gossiping judgement of the Calvinist church-members as well as through the open polemic between rationalists and Calvinists,[40] rationalist preachers were condemned and anti-predestinarians were sent straight to hell, there to join the Lutherans and their close friends, the idolatrous Roman Catholics. Exasperated, Engels erupts: 'But what sort of people are they who talk in this way? Ignorant folk who hardly know whether the Bible was written in Chinese, Hebrew or Greek...'.[41] Most of the polemic is reserved for a certain Dr Friedrich Wilhelm Krummacher, head-minister of the Elberfeld Reformed Parish and influential enough to colour the poetry written in Wuppertal.[42] Although he never says so directly, I would hazard a guess that Dr Krummacher was one of Engels's own ministers. There are too many details, too many comments on sermons for Engels not to have seen the man in action on countless occasions. All the same, the polemic against Krummacher is curiously mixed: Engels gives voice to a sneaking admiration in the very act of criticising him. It is as though we can see at each point a process of disenchantment, for what looks like an admiring observation ends up being a condemnation.

As far as Krummacher's style is concerned, his 'sermons are never boring' and his 'train of thought is confident and natural'. Yet Krummacher ends up overdoing it: 'Then he thrashes about in the pulpit, bends over all sides, bangs his fist on the edge, stamps like a cavalry horse, and shouts so that the windows resound and people in the street tremble'.[43] His appearance too may be strong and impressive, but his 'circumference has increased' since he settled

39. Engels 1839f, p. 12; Engels 1839g, p. 36.
40. See especially the comments on the struggles between Krummacher and the rationalist (although untalented) K.F.W. Paniel, the minister of St Ansgarius church in Bremen (Engels 1840i, pp. 126–8; Engels 1840j, pp. 199–201; Engels 1840g, pp. 155–8; Engels 1840h, pp. 225–8).
41. Engels 1839f, p. 12; Engels 1839g, p. 36.
42. Engels 1839d, pp. 30–1; Engels 1839e, pp. 63–4.
43. Engels 1839f, p. 14; Engels 1839g, p. 39. See also Engels 1840i, p. 126; Engels 1840j, p. 199, where he writes of 'the burning eloquence, the poetic, if not always well-chosen, splendour of imagery for which this richly talented pulpit speaker is famous'.

in Elberfeld, sporting at the same time a most unfashionable way of doing his hair that everyone in the congregation seems to imitate '*à la* Krummacher'.[44]

Apart from collective intolerance (which is by no means restricted to the Calvinists) and the overblown style, Engels rounds on Krummacher's doctrine, all of which was contained in his sermons. Along with general observations on the nature of his sermons, there are a good number of comments relating to specific sermons, ranging from an account of a dispute with Strauss, through Krummacher's attacks on poetry, imagination and art, to the assertion, based on Joshua 10:12–13 and many other passages in the Bible, that the sun moves around a still earth:

> In a recent sermon in Elberfeld on Joshua 10:12–13, where Joshua bids the sun stand still, Krummacher advanced the interesting thesis that pious Christians, the Elect, should not suppose from this passage that Joshua was here accommodating himself to the views of the people, but must believe *that the earth stands still and the sun moves round it*. In defence of this view he showed that it is expressed throughout the Bible. The fool's cap which the world will give them for that, they, the Elect, should cheerfully put in their pockets with the many others they have already received. – We should be happy to receive a refutation of this sad anecdote, which comes to us from a reliable source.[45]

---

44. Engels 1839f, p. 13; Engels 1839g, p. 38.

45. Engels 1839b, p. 29; Engels 1839c, p. 55. So also: 'Krummacher declared recently in a sermon that the earth stands still and the sun rotates around it, and the fellow dares to trumpet this to the world on this April 21, 1839, and then he says that pietism does not lead the world back to the Middle Ages! It is scandalous. He should be expelled, or one day he will yet become Pope before you know, and then may a saffron-yellow thunderstorm strike him dead.' (Engels 1839n, pp. 446–7; Engels 1839o, p. 393.) For the sake of completeness, here are the rest: 'not long ago he regaled his reverent audience with two sermons about a journey to Württemberg and Switzerland, in which he spoke of his four victorious disputes with Paulus in Heidelberg and Strauss in Tübingen, naturally quite differently from Strauss' account of the matter in a letter.' (Engels 1839f, p. 14; Engels 1839g, p. 39.) Further: 'Anyone who did not accept this crass mysticism as absolute Christianity was delivered up to the devil. And with a sophistry which emerged as strangely naive, Krummacher always managed to shelter behind the apostle Paul. "It is not I who is cursing, nay! Children, reflect, it is the apostle Paul who condemns you!" – The worst of it was that the apostle wrote in Greek and scholars have not yet been able to agree on the precise meaning of certain of his expressions. Among these dubious words is the anathema used in this passage, to which Krummacher, without more ado, ascribed the most extreme meaning of a sentence of eternal damnation.' (Engels 1840i, pp. 126–7; Engels 1840j, pp. 199–200.) See the reference to two further sermons in Engels 1840q; Engels 1840r and Engels 1840i, pp. 126–8; Engels

As for the strict Calvinist doctrine – with its predestination as the manifestation of God's grace, the Christ-less heathen serving to fill up hell, and the few who are chosen out of the many called – Engels cannot see how anyone in their right mind could believe such a doctrine, which is based on a 'pretence of logic' and is 'in most direct contradiction to reason and the Bible'.[46]

What is the nature of those doctrines that stand off against one another in Engels's critiques of Krummacher? As becomes clear through the many quotes and allusions, doctrine is really an effort to weave together a series of disparate biblical texts drawn from all over the place into a somewhat coherent and logically watertight position. However, Engels is not an outsider who observes this practice from a distance. He is very much part of it, using the Bible to take sides in a theological debate. At this level, Engels is no different to Krummacher, except that he leans more heavily on other texts that oppose the ones preferred by Krummacher and other strict Calvinists.

In all of this, there is one element that needs some further comment: the sheer number of biblical texts mentioned or alluded to in Engels's pieces on Krummacher. These texts pepper the polemic: John 14:6 ('no one comes to the father, but by me'); Matthew 22:14 ('many are called but few are chosen'); 1 Corinthians 1:20–5 and 3:19 ('the foolishness of God is wiser than men'); 1 Peter 2:2 ('long for the pure spiritual milk').[47] Engels uses them in various ways. The first three are those favoured by Krummacher et al., but the last he claims for himself: 'How all this fits in with the teaching of the apostles who speak of the rational worship of God and the rational milk of the Gospel is a secret beyond human understanding'.[48] Engels has clearly taken sides within a specific debate.

We can view this situation as follows: the Bible provides a language or agreed-upon battleground. While Krummacher focuses on some texts to bolster his position, Engels responds by picking up others that support his own. A host of issues turn up on that battleground: faith versus reason; the small enclave of the righteous elect versus the ways of that world; the claim to mystery or the claim to open scientific research. Engels still sees himself as

---

1840j, pp. 199–201. There is also a quotation from a sermon by Emil Krummacher, the brother of F.W. Krummacher (Engels 1839f, p. 17; Engels 1839g, p. 41).

46. Engels 1839f, pp. 14–15; Engels 1839g, pp. 39–40.

47. *MECW* does its best to pick up the biblical allusions and reference the quotations, but it does not always succeed. Many are not referenced and some are not quite correct.

48. Engels 1839f, p. 15; Engels 1839g, p. 40.

part of the Christian scene, but he takes a very different stand from the Calvinists with whom he grew up. For example, as he passes out of what he regards as the dreary Calvinist landscape of the Netherlands on his way over the channel to England, the newly awakened free-thinker can exclaim:

> ...it was like a breath of fresh sea air blowing down upon me from the purest sky; the depths of speculation lay before me like the unfathomable sea from which one cannot turn one's eyes straining to see the ground below; in God we live, move and have our being! We become conscious of that when we are on the sea; we feel that God breathes through all around us and through us ourselves; we feel such kinship with the whole of nature, the waves beckon to us so intimately, the sky stretches so lovingly over the earth, and the sun shines with such indescribable radiance that one feels one could grasp it with the hand.[49]

Or in his account of a visit to the Roman-Catholic Cathedral at Xanten, which 'looks out in splendid perfection far across the prose of the Dutch sand flats',[50] he writes of the powerful subduing effect of the organ on him as he enters the Cathedral during the high mass. But when it comes to the moment of transubstantiation he tells himself to 'rush out, save yourself, save your reason from this ocean of feeling that surges through the church and pray outside to the God whose house is not made by human hands, who is the breath of the world and who wants to be worshipped in spirit and in truth'.[51]

These early pieces by Engels provide a distinct insight into a practice that would stay with him through much of his writing – the tendency to use 'proof-texts' in all manner of situations. Such a practice owes its origin to his time in the reformed church in Elberfeld, for, in such a context, the Bible is the supreme and final authority. One must be able to justify one position or other by finding a biblical text that would support it (a practice I know only too well in all its twisting and frustrating detail). Of course, Engels would move away from that specific motivation, but the habit of drawing in a biblical text or two stayed with him.

Towards the close of his 'Letters from Wuppertal', Engels uses one more: 'it looks as though even this rock of old obscurantism will not be able to

---

49. Engels 1840c, p. 99; Engels 1840d, p. 131.
50. Engels 1840o, p. 132; Engels 1840p, p. 203.
51. Engels 1840o, pp. 133–4; Engels 1840p, pp. 204–5.

withstand the surging flood of time any longer; the sand will be washed away and the rock will collapse with a great fall'.[52] The allusion is to Matthew 7:24–7[53] with its brief saying concerning the differences between the house built on sand and the house built on the rock. But Engels gives it a twist, for both houses will be washed away, even the house built on the rock that the conservatives in Wuppertal felt they had built.

The challenge of contradictions

> Indeed it's perfectly possible to remain good friends despite political differ-
> ences. But we've all had to go through the same thing, in my case, in my own
> pious ultra-reactionary family.[54]

Biblical contradiction was the rope Engels used to haul himself out of his biblical past. Contradiction is, of course, a staple of Marxist analysis and the usual narrative traces it back to Marx's grappling with Hegel. Marx turned Hegel's idealist method into a materialist one and came up with his well-known argument: the internal contradictions of a mode of production are both creative and destructive. They may initially enable a certain mode of production to rise to dominance, but they also hobble it and eventually bring about its downfall.

However, there is another point at which contradiction emerges, and that is none other than Engels's struggle with biblical criticism. Since this may seem like a strange point, I need to tell that story in a little detail. Contradiction surges to the front in a number of Engels's early texts, namely his narrative poem, *The Insolently Threatened Yet Miraculously Rescued Bible* of 1842 and the various letters he wrote to Friedrich and Wilhelm Graeber between 1839 and 1841.

The poem is structured as a mock tale of the last great battle of history between the pious forces of religious conservatism and the young Hegelians. Apart from the critiques of 'The Free' and especially Ruge as revolutionaries in word but not deed, or the mention of Marx (whom he did not know

---

52. Engels 1839f, p. 17; Engels 1839g, p. 42.
53. See also Luke 6:47–9.
54. Engels 1892l, p. 527; Engels 1892m, p. 459.

personally at the time)[55] or of himself in disguise,[56] or even that Hegel turns out to be an arch-atheist and leader of the devil's hordes, the major question that emerges in the poem is that of biblical criticism. It appears through the central rôle of Bruno Bauer (at one point they lift him up in place of a weakened devil to be their champion),[57] for he was first and foremost a biblical critic. For Engels, this seems to be the crux of the matter. I have already explored (in the Introduction) the reasons why biblical criticism should be in the midst of the furore in Germany at the time, but here it also has a distinctly personal note for Engels.

So let us see how the question of biblical criticism unfolds. When Satan first appears to Bauer, we find him ruminating over the authorship of the first five books of the Bible:

> A house of pious people and a dingy room
>
> Stacked high with books, and Bauer pondering in the gloom,
>
> The Pentateuch in front of him, the Devil behind,
>
> A tug of war twixt Faith and Doubt within his mind.
>
> 'Did Moses write this book, and is it true for sure?
>
> Philosophy, your meaning is so oft obscure!'[58]

For all his research, Bauer still cannot prove that 'the Pentateuch is not a bluff'[59] and so he searches for what 'hides the source of the Pentateuch' from him.[60] In some respects, this is a curious issue on which to focus, although we can

---

55. 'Who runs up next with wild impetuosity? / A swarthy chap of *Trier*, a marked monstrosity. / He neither hops nor skips, but moves in leaps and bounds, / Raving aloud. As if to seize and then pull down / To Earth the spacious tent of Heaven up on high, / He opens wide his arms and reaches for the sky. / He shakes his wicked fist, raves with a frantic air, / As if ten thousand devils had him by the hair.' (Engels 1842c, p. 336; Engels 1842d, p. 408.)

56. 'Right on the very left, that tall and long-legged stepper / Is *Oswald*, [Engels] coat of grey and trousers shade of pepper; / Pepper inside as well, *Oswald* the Montagnard; / A radical is he, dyed in the wool, and hard. / Day in, day out, he plays upon the guillotine a / Single solitary tune and that's a cavatina, / The same old devilsong; he bellows the refrain: / *Formez vos bataillons! Aux armes, citoyens!'* (Engels 1842c, p. 335; Engels 1842d, p. 407.)

57. 'Hegel embraces crazy Bauer: "Yes, 'tis done! / You've comprehended me! You are my own dear son!" / He frees him. Then the wicked ones with great delight: / "Bauer's our hero! He shall lead us to the fight! / The Devil is deposed. What we need is a man!"' (Engels 1842c, p. 349; Engels 1842d, p. 419.)

58. Engels 1842c, p. 322; Engels 1842d, p. 396.

59. Ibid.

60. Engels 1842c, p. 323; Engels 1842d, p. 397.

grant Engels his poetic licence. Bauer did write a double-volume on the Hebrew Bible, but he was far less interested in questions such as Mosaic authorship, preferring to devote most of his energy to New Testament criticism. Yet the Pentateuch was a touchstone for both German critical scholarship on the Bible and the conservative opposition to it, so much so that many of those critical scholars doubted the very existence of Moses. In response, conservatives argued that questioning the reputed authorship of certain books is the first step on the slippery path to atheism – as, indeed, Bauer is to find in the poem when he engages in conversation with the devil. Even though he 'reaches for his Bible, mad with fear',[61] it is of no avail.

In other words, Bauer is vexed in this poem by the contradictions and discrepancies that abound throughout the Bible. Once Bauer, like Faust, has given himself over to the devil, his lectures focus on precisely these problems; except that now the theologians are the ones 'trapped between the Contradictions of the Text'.[62] No matter how much they might twist and dodge, no matter how much they may try to iron-out or drown those contradictions, they cannot escape them.

But what sort of contradictions are at issue? Engels does not really grapple with them in the poem – he mentions the issue of Mosaic authorship and the theological pussy-footing around the Bible's contradictions. If we wish to find a more detailed engagement with these contradictions, we need to pause with Engels's letters to the Graeber brothers, Friedrich and Wilhelm. These letters catch Engels at an extraordinary moment: in a series of epistles between 23 April 1839 and 22 February 1841 we encounter one side of a debate in which he engages passionately with both brothers. With Friedrich, the more orthodox of the two, Engels finds himself in the midst of sustained and serious debates – largely because there was far more with which to disagree. In the end, Engels's falling out with Friedrich is far greater: their increasing distance from one another eventually puts them on either side of the great divide in German theology.[63] With the liberal Wilhelm, there was less to debate, so Engels seems to relax more, discussing literature, theatre, music, beer and

---

61. Ibid.
62. Engels 1842c, p. 326; Engels 1842d, p. 400.
63. See especially the last letter to Friedrich Graeber, where Engels calls on his old theme of apocalyptic battle (Engels 1841c; Engels 1841d).

friends.[64] There is a direct ratio: the greater the theological difference, the more theological debate we find.

So, while he warns Wilhelm that his views on biblical inspiration are too liberal for any preacher in Wuppertal,[65] he urges Friedrich to become more liberal. Give hell to the pietists, suggests Engels, by becoming nothing less than a pastor in the heart of Krummacher territory in Barmen.[66] The key, Engels suggests, lies in Friedrich basing himself on the Bible itself and on reason. Such a combination would drive the pietists mad. It is almost a vicarious wish, for I sense in part that Engels would have loved to become a liberal pastor in Wuppertal and take on the pietists. All the same, he does hope that his friends have not got too much of the pastor in them as yet and that they will come drinking with him when he returns to Wuppertal.[67]

In these letters, Engels puts forward his own evolving arguments, responds, and bares his soul (quite literally) to his friends on matters of religious belief. He writes of the tears that come to his eyes as he struggles, that he is kept awake by the ideas of freedom racing through his head, that he really wishes for some time and peace to think things through and that he cannot put aside what forces itself on him with such strength. In his search, he enthusiastically takes up one approach only to dump it for another that seems far better. So, he moves rapidly through rationalist theology (with its natural explanations for miracles and moralising), Friedrich Schleiermacher's liberal theology, affirming sensuousness over against puritan moral values,[68] David Strauss's breakthrough in identifying the mythical underlay of the Bible in his *Leben Jesu* and then, through Strauss, to a Hegelian pantheism. He is all too aware

---

64. He is also more playful. For example: 'And if you don't write today I shall geld you in thoughts and make you wait as long as you do me. An eye for an eye, a tooth for a tooth, a letter for a letter. But you hypocrites say: Not an eye for an eye, not a tooth for a tooth, not a letter for a letter, and fob me off with your damned Christian sophistry. No, better a good pagan than a bad Christian.' (Engels 1839dd, p. 482; Engels 1839ee, p. 432.)
65. Engels 1839v, p. 466; Engels 1839w, p. 413.
66. Engels 1839j, p. 423; Engels 1839k, pp. 367–8.
67. Engels 1839z, p. 475; Engels 1839aa, p. 423.
68. 'I should like to see a marriage in which the man does not love his wife but Christ in his wife; and is it not an obvious question there whether he also sleeps with Christ in his wife? Where can you find nonsense like this in the Bible? In the Song of Songs it says – "How fair and how pleasant art thou, O love, for delights!" [The Song of Songs 7:6] But, to be sure, any defence whatever of sensuousness is attacked nowadays in spite of David, Solomon and God knows whom. I can get terribly annoyed over this kind of thing.' (Engels 1839h, p. 416; Engels 1839i, p. 363.)

of the seismic shifts taking place in his own beliefs, where last month's break-through turns out to be a 'preconception of which I have freed myself in the meantime'.[69] At one moment, he defends Christianity against its detrac-tors and, at another, he stands up for the free exercise of reason, hoping all the while to remain 'an honest, and in comparison with others, very liberal, super-naturalist'.[70] In his heart, he wants to be a liberal, rational Christian who regards the core-beliefs of Christianity as myth. At times, he feels he has found that quiet space,[71] but, at others, he is less certain. The question is whether he can pull it off.

Now, these shifts in the thoughts and beliefs of a young Engels usually pro-vide plenty of fuel for tracing the way he gradually gave away his religious convictions. Those amazing prefaces to *MECW* are keen on this line: here, we find Engels on the painful but necessary path to revolutionary atheism. For some reason or other, I am not particularly interested in restricting myself to such a narrative. Part of the reason may be that I am not in the business of writing a spiritual biography of either Marx or Engels. Others have done and will continue to do so. Far more important is what emerges from Engels's intense engagement with his Calvinist upbringing, namely the concern with contradiction and an immanent method.

I have already identified contradiction as one of those items. The other bea-con that begins to glow as the letters progress is nothing less than an imma-nent analysis. While the problem of contradiction runs directly into what is supposed to be a consistent text (after all, it did come from God, as Engels's early teachers would have told him, and God must be consistent), the imma-nent analysis emerges from Engels's efforts to deal with those contradictions. In short, he takes the conservative pietists at their word: if they claim that the Bible is the basis of their belief (and his own in the not-too-distant past), then he will have a damn close look at the Bible to see what it really says. Let us see how he deals with both contradiction and immanent analysis in his letters to the Graeber brothers.

---

69. Engels 1839–40a, p. 489; Engels 1839–40b, p. 438.
70. Engels 1839j, p. 423; Engels 1839k, p. 368.
71. 'My religion was – and is – quiet, blessed peace, and if I have it after my death then I shall be satisfied. I have no reason to believe that God will take it from me.' (Engels 1839t, p. 461; Engels 1839u, p. 407.)

In the first letter that broaches these matters (the one of 23 April–1 May 1839), Engels rolls out a long list of contradictions. Strauss's 'irrefutable work'[72] and the rationalists, it seems, had opened his eyes to reading the Bible properly for the first time. And what does he find? When he reads the Gospels closely he encounters all manner of discrepancies: the two genealogies of Joseph (the husband of Mary) in the Gospels of Matthew and Luke do not match up; the narratives of the Last Supper differ; as do the words of the Lord's Prayer; the miracles appear in different orders (the most notable of which is the timing of the water-into-wine episode – in John, it is at the beginning of Jesus's ministry, whereas in the others it is at the end); the stay of the Israelites in Egypt is only four generations in the Old Testament but 430 years in Paul's letter to the Galatians.[73] The list goes on, but that is more than enough for my purpose.[74]

As the discussion continues, the bone of contention becomes the genealogy of Jesus – or, rather, the conflicting genealogies in Matthew and Luke. Here some background is in order: Matthew's genealogy (in Chapter 1) begins with Abraham and ends with Jesus, while Luke's (in Chapter 3:23–38) goes in reverse and works it way back to Adam, the son of God. Apart from this difference, there is a string of discrepancies, beginning with the name of Joseph's father (in Matthew it is Jacob while in Luke it is Heli). From here, the two genealogies follow very different paths back to King David, come a little closer to each other between David and Abraham, and then Luke pushes on alone to work back to Adam.

For Engels, this is an intolerable contradiction, at least in terms of the 'Wuppertal faith' with which he is struggling. But why? To a non-committed observer, such discrepancies hardly constitute a major problem. They might raise questions about the nature of genealogies (they are highly fluid and adaptable) or of literature (which will often have tensions within it) or even

---

72. Engels 1839r, p. 455; Engels 1839s, p. 401; translation modified. In his letter to Wilhelm Graeber of 8 October 1839 he calls himself an 'enthusiastic Straussian' (Engels 1839x, p. 471; Engels 1839y, p. 419).

73. Genesis 50:23 refers to the third generation of his son Ephraim's children, while Paul mentions 430 years in Galatians 3:17. However, Engels fails to note the mention of 430 years in Exodus 12:40. All this reference does is shift the contradiction to the Hebrew Bible.

74. See further Engels 1839l, p. 426; Engels 1839m, p. 371; and Engels 1839bb, pp. 476–7; Engels 1839cc, pp. 425–6.

of history. But the significant differences between the genealogies of Jesus in Matthew and Luke are not a cause for endless and acrimonious debate – unless one happens to be committed. Then the genealogical contradictions, indeed any contradictions in the Bible, raise immense problems.

They do so at two levels, one theological and the other at the level of personal faith (the two are not necessarily connected). Let me put it this way: since God is so closely identified with the Bible in the Calvinist circles Engels knows all too well, any question about the Bible becomes a question about God. The same applies to his religious faith. What we find is a massive struggle with doubt. For all Friedrich Graeber's efforts to argue that a faith without doubt is the freest and calmest, Engels will not have a bar of it. Doubt is necessary, Engels argues back. It is a priority for anyone who wants a thinking faith and it will come to Graeber too. Indeed faith without doubt is hardly faith at all. And, yet, Engels struggles deeply and heartrendingly with those doubts. In the midst of an extraordinary passage he writes:

> I pray daily, indeed nearly the whole day, for truth, I have done so ever since I began to have doubts, but I still cannot return to your faith. And yet it is written: 'Ask, and it shall be given you'. I search for truth wherever I have hope of finding even a shadow of it and still I cannot acknowledge your truth as the eternal truth. And yet it is written: 'Seek, and ye shall find. Or what man is there of you, whom if his son ask bread, will he give him a stone?... how much more shall your Father which is in Heaven?'[75]

I tackle the theological problems first. The initial one concerns trust and it goes as follows: God is consistent, trustworthy and all-powerful. Hence, if God is responsible for the Bible, then it too is trustworthy. And the only way that it may be so is if it is consistent. We can rely on what the Bible says only if it does not deceive us, and likewise with God. In other words, it was a straight path from contradiction to doubting one's faith. The code for this question of trust is inspiration: as 2 Timothy 3:16 would have it, scripture is inspired by God (or 'God-breathed [*theopneustos*]'). Despite the sense that 'inspiration' has taken on in our own day as inerrancy on all matters of history and science, in the

---

75. Engels 1839t, p. 461; Engels 1839u, p. 407. The biblical references are to Matthew 7:7, 9–11.

debates of Engels's time it was really an issue of trustworthiness.[76] Everything becomes problematic when the Bible ceases to be consistent and trustworthy.

An avalanche of problems follows, especially in the two long letters of 12–17 July and 29 October 1839,[77] where Engels picks apart the contradictions of orthodox theology. Here, we find the problems of God's goodness, omniscience, justice, truth, love and impassibility. Is God good, or did He deliberately place contradictions in the Bible to foster disagreements and arguments? Is He omniscient, or did He simply decide to ignore such glaring problems? Is God just, or will He really damn for eternity those who seek to link reason with God (Spinoza, Kant and Gutzkow)? Is God true, or does He disown those who must pass through doubt as they strive for truth? If God loves us, then why does He condemn nine-tenths of humanity to eternal punishment? If it is metaphysically unthinkable for God to suffer, then how can one claim that Jesus is fully God and man?

And on it goes. From the doctrine of God there is a follow-on effect. Sin, salvation and eternal punishment all crumble before his onslaught. As far as sin is concerned, if the rest of the world strives to overcome sin just as much as Christianity, then why does the latter condemn the former? While he can no longer see any sense in the doctrine of original sin – understood as the inherent propensity to sin in the idea of man and as the cause of human disease and deficiency – he is fully aware of his own tendency to sin. After all, he points out, since human beings were created by God as non-divine beings, then we can hardly expect anything else. Yet the idea of substitutionary atonement – that someone else may remit sin on his behalf and thereby save him – he finds ludicrous and a contradiction of divine justice. Indeed, he asks, if someone offers himself up for someone else then why is he not punished like Christ? Finally, eternal punishment collapses from its own inconsistency: if you have eternal damnation, you must have eternal sin, and if eternal sin, then the eternal possibility of repentance and faith and thus the eternal possibility of being saved.

---

76. See the discussion of biblical inspiration in the letter to Friedrich Graeber of 29 October 1839 (Engels 1839bb, pp. 476–7; Engels 1839cc, pp. 425–6). Here, Engels destroys the defence of biblical inspiration put forward by Friedrich, especially where he seeks to limit inspiration to those parts of the Bible that do not contradict one another.
77. Engels 1839t; Engels 1839u; Engels 1839r; Engels 1839s. See Engels 1839r, pp. 454–5; Engels 1839s, pp. 400–1.

For a good while, Engels struggles to hang on to his faith. However, since the Bible and his Wuppertal faith are so closely entwined, a revision of his approach to one must lead to a revision of the other. So, when he blurts out that he no longer blindly believes in the Bible, or that contradictions destroy all faith in the Bible,[78] what does he do? He seeks an expression of faith that dispenses with biblical phrases. And that gives him a sense of a 'close, heartfelt relationship with God', one that results from the consciousness that we are all of divine origin. After all the struggles of this world, we return eventually, freed from our mortality and sin, to rest with God – 'that is my conviction, and I am at rest with it'.[79] What Engels desperately seeks is a reasoned, liberal faith that is not tied to the orthodox Calvinist dogmas with which he grew up.[80] Friedrich Schleiermacher's theology grabs him for a while, and he has enormous respect for this father of liberal theology with his emphasis on the feeling of God's presence.[81] The problem with all of this reasoned, liberal theology is that it failed to hold Engels with the passion of his former convictions. He sought something stronger than an urbane, calm and all-too-middle-class faith.

Thus the problem of contradictions raises questions for a certain type of theology and for a certain type of personal faith. For Engels, it is very much a struggle within himself, and the struggle shows up in two terms that he uses: reason and faith. Reason says that the Bible is not consistent, while faith says that it is. If we picture reason and faith as two cables pulling in contrary directions, then Engels hauls on each cable in an effort to bring the two together. And the point of contact is none other than the Bible. He does his best to hold onto both faith and reason, even taking up what can only be called a univocal position on reason. He writes: 'God's reason is certainly higher than ours, but still not of a different kind, for otherwise it would no longer be reason'.[82]

This last comment opens up a cornucopia of almost irresistible theological debate. Engels is (probably unknowingly) taking sides in a long-running debate that may roughly be stated in these two propositions: 1) God is qualitatively

---

78. Engels 1839r, p. 454; Engels 1839s, p. 400.
79. Engels 1839t, p. 458; Engels 1839u, p. 404.
80. 'Religious conviction is a matter of the heart and is only concerned with dogma insofar as dogma is or is not contradicted by feeling.' (Engels 1839t, p. 461; Engels 1839u, p. 407.)
81. Engels 1839t, p. 462; Engels 1839u, p. 408. See Schleiermacher 1960.
82. Engels 1839t, p. 459; Engels 1839u, p. 405.

different from His creation so any terms that we might use are entirely inadequate and can only approximate His nature; 2) Since God created the universe and especially reason, then the terms or ideas of that created world should be consistent with His own. The first position usually assumes that one speaks of God by analogy (equivocally), whereas the second by univocity. That is, when one speaks of the reason of God, it is either something completely different from human reason and the only resemblance is in the use of the word 'reason', or it is the same as human reason even if it is of a higher degree.

This long-running debate is also a convenient way to sort out the differences between the orthodox Calvinists and Engels himself. Or, as I prefer, between Engels's former position and the one that appears in the letters to Friedrich Graeber, especially those of 12–27 July and 29 October 1839. But why would the orthodox have sympathy with an analogical (equivocal) position? Simply because we human beings are so utterly depraved, so irredeemably sinful that anything we do or think or believe is separated from God by an impassable abyss.[83] By contrast, Engels's assertion of a univocal position means that he has discarded the Calvinist tenet of total depravity. Human beings can reason in ways similar to God, for they have been made in his image.

I must admit that I have always been drawn towards the analogical position (as well as its Calvinist connection with total depravity), but Engels has a point here, even if he was to give it away before long. I do not mean his argument that God's reason must be largely the same as ours, but that theology, by its very nature, should be a reasoned and reasonable exercise. The effort to systematise, to develop a coherent argument, to take a logical position, to make sense – all of these suggest reason is at the heart of theology. Otherwise it would be pure nonsense. Engels is stating the obvious: reason and theology are in a close dance with one another. Or as he puts it: 'whoever rests content and prides himself on his faith, has in reality no basis whatsoever for his faith'.[84] In fact, he would have helped his argument by pointing out that even the orthodox Calvinists use reason; how would they be able to construct a coherent theological position without it?

---

83. Or, as Engels quotes Friedrich Graeber's orthodox position: '"Man is so fallen that of himself he can do nothing good"' (Engels 1839bb, p. 477; Engels 1839cc, p. 426).

84. Engels 1839t, p. 460; Engels 1839u, p. 406.

Despite all of this, Engels was unfortunately surrounded by those who argued that faith and reason cannot be reconciled. While Bauer and a host of lesser lights argued in favour of reason and atheism from the Bible itself, an army of conservatives saw reason as the enemy of faith (or hypocritically made use of reason to a limited extent to bolster their own position).[85] In the middle were a few rationalists who wished to hold reason and faith together. Although Engels pays close attention to the debates, he ultimately finds the rationalists unconvincing.[86]

A good example (from 1841) is the struggle between the rationalists and Calvinists in the reformed church in Bremen. In two of his 'Reports from Bremen',[87] Engels wades into the debate between the two groups, one led by F.W. Krummacher (Bremen was where he grew up) and the other by a certain K.F.W. Paniel. Try as he can to observe from a critical distance, the debate concerns him very personally. It all began when Herr Krummacher was invited to preach in Paniel's church – St Ansgarius – and thundered away against the learning of this world, philosophy and rationalist biblical interpretation. The Reverend Paniel, who had emerged in Bremen as a champion of the rationalists (about seven of the ministers there belonged to his group and about half of the public), fired back with a criticism of Krummacher and the battle was on. Pietism is really pagan in its source, says one; rationalism is unbiblical says another.

As we saw earlier, Engels's response to Krummacher is a mix of admiration for the man's obvious skills as a preacher and opprobrium for his obnoxious theology. He also admires Paniel's pluck for taking up the cudgels on behalf of the rationalists, but the man – at least in Engels's opinion – cannot preach or write quite as powerfully as Krummacher. Engels finds Paniel's arguments 'a mush of sentimentality', full of 'watery digressions' and 'tasteless flabbiness'.[88] And, yet, he is courageous, determined and learned – a mixed

---

85. See his scathing observations on the limited use of education, philosophy or geology, all of which are used when they suit the conservative agenda and condemned when they do not (Engels 1839r, p. 455; Engels 1839s, p. 401).

86. Engels's dissatisfaction with the rationalists did not stop him enjoying their support in turning the Associations for the Benefit of the Working Classes into radical organisations (Engels 1844n, p. 10; Engels 1844o, p. 10).

87. Engels 1840i; Engels 1840j; Engels 1840g; Engels 1840h.

88. Engels 1840g, p. 156; Engels 1840h, p. 226. See also his satirical 'description' of a street-battle between the forces of Krummacher and Paniel (Engels 1840u; Engels

assessment just like that for Krummacher. He really wishes that Paniel could write a little better. But what interests me most is the way in which Engels ponders the position of the rationalists.

Their bind is that they have a foot in both camps: they wish to stay within the church, claiming the Bible and Christianity for themselves; yet the rationalist arguments seem to lead away from both church and faith. So he finds that they twist the Bible to their purpose, giving the concepts of revelation, redemption and inspiration a strained sense. For the underlying drive of a rationalist position, at least at that time, was to provide perfectly normal and scientific descriptions for miraculous elements in the Bible. Thus, if the Israelites crossed the Red Sea on their flight from Egypt, they must have done so through a marshy expanse of water at low tide. Or when Jesus walked on water, he must have been walking along a sand-bank.

In the midst of this assessment, we come across this crucial observation:

> Rationalism has never been clear about its attitude to the Bible; the unhappy half-way stance which at first appeared definitely to imply belief in revelation but in further argumentation so restricted the divinity of the Bible that almost nothing remained of it, this vacillation puts rationalism at a disadvantage whenever it is a question of giving its tenets a biblical foundation. Why praise reason without proclaiming its autonomy? For where the Bible is acknowledged by both sides as the common basis, pietism is always right.[89]

For most of this passage, Engels is still thinking within a pietist framework, especially of the Calvinist shade. He grants its premises – its stand on the Bible as the revelation of God is the faithful one, it carries on a venerable tradition that dates from the New Testament, it has history and faith on its side. From this perspective, rationalism looks like the new kid on the block, trying out new-fangled ideas and stretching the true meaning of the Bible. I am afraid that Engels falls into the conservative-theological trap: either accept it all or reject it all. If you doubt one piece – say the virgin-birth or that God created the world in six days – then the whole pack of cards comes tumbling down. Hence his crucial question: 'Why praise reason without proclaiming its autonomy?' Do not shackle two partners at odds with one another; do not try

---

1840v), as well as the criticisms in a letter to Marx on 19 November 1844 (Engels 1844n, p. 10; Engels 1844o, p. 10).
  89. Engels 1840g, p. 157; Engels 1840h, p. 227.

to marry faith and reason. Let reason have its head. Soon enough he would do so – as he points out a little later: 'theology must either regress to blind faith or progress towards free philosophy'.[90]

This tension between reason and faith draws Engels towards that other item of his letters I flagged a little earlier – immanent analysis. Succinctly put, such an analysis makes a double move: in debating with those who would base themselves purely on the Bible, he uses the Bible itself to show that they come to that text with a prior set of assumptions. Let me unpick this statement for a little while.

Engels's first move is to claim that he has discovered what the Bible actually says. So where does that leave the orthodox Calvinists of Wuppertal? Either they have different versions of the Bible to the one Engels is reading, or they obviously do not read their Bibles very well. And that means they cannot be that orthodox after all. Here, he really homes in on the key-paradox: for a tradition that claimed to base itself solely on the Bible, they actually do not do so.

Engels has really come across the first challenge that any student of the Bible encounters in their introductory course, except that Engels had to teach himself. Indeed, Engels has followed in the steps of any good teacher of the Bible. One begins (as I used to do in a former life) by saying, 'well, let's look at what the Bible actually says'. Then, by focusing on key-passages such as the genealogies in Matthew and Luke, or the different versions of the Last Supper that split the Lutherans and reformers,[91] or the story of the sun standing still for Gideon in Judges, one builds a huge pile of discrepancies and contradictions in the Bible. Eventually, the weight of evidence cracks open the defence of an inerrant Bible,[92] one sees how constricting such an understanding of the Bible really is and the way is cleared for exploring the various approaches to

---

90. Engels 1844j, p. 421; Engels 1844k, p. 502.
91. While the Lutherans preferred an idea of the 'real presence' of Christ in the Eucharist, the Calvinists argued that the Eucharist was the sign and seal of the new covenant. While the former preferred the words recorded in Mark's gospel – 'this is my blood' (Mark 14:24) – the latter tended to look to Luke's report – 'this cup which is poured out for you is the new covenant in my blood' (Luke 22:20). See Engels 1839r, p. 454; Engels 1839s, p. 400. He neglects to point out that the Luke text is probably a later interpolation.
92. 'I cannot understand how one can still try to maintain literal belief in the Bible or defend the direct influence of God, since this cannot be proved anywhere.' (Engels 1839t, p. 457; Engels 1839u, p. 403.)

interpreting the Bible. In other words, these contradictions then become the royal road to various theories about how to deal with such contradictions. All the same, this is a well-known problem: given that the various texts of the Bible came together approximately over a millennium, one would expect tensions and problems. The difficulty then becomes how one deals with them. Medieval exegetes developed their rather complex allegorical exegesis as one response, using the moment of tension as an allegorical key. A historical-critical approach – precisely the one with which Engels was coming to terms – offered a very different explanation, one that relied on postulating various sources (oral or written) that lay behind the text. More recently, narrative theory has begun to focus on the gaps in the text, deconstruction picks up the contradictions to argue for some very different conclusions, psychoanalytic criticism sees the contradictions as a series of ruptures and slips, and Marxist criticism uses the contradictions to argue for the instability of the dominant ideology of the text – to give but a few examples. In other words, most critical attention to the Bible has developed its various approaches in response to anomalies and contradictions. It is a linchpin and Engels has homed right in on it.

Back to Engels: in his first flush of enthusiasm, he assumes that he is the one reading the Bible properly and the conservatives are not. He sees the Bible with new eyes, surprised that he had not seen all of this before. The problem, of course, is that the contradictions on which Engels had seized had not escaped the orthodox. For instance, a quick glance at Calvin's voluminous commentaries on the Bible shows that he spends a good deal of time dealing with precisely these problems. So also Friedrich Graeber, whose reply Engels notes in his own follow-up letter. The issue has become the different genealogies of Jesus in the Gospels of Matthew and Luke. How to deal with these contradictions? Well, writes Friedrich Graeber, one of them follows the line of Joseph's in-laws. Thus, when Luke writes 'the son of Heli',[93] he actually means the 'son-in-law' of Heli; from there the line of Joseph's in-laws runs back to David. Further, Luke was ignorant of this supposed Hebrew custom since he was writing in Greek for Greeks, especially for his close friend Theophilus. Finally, the whole purpose of the genealogies of Jesus is to show that

---

93. Luke 3:23.

he is the fulfilment of prophecy.[94] As for the rest of Engels's objections, they are 'apparent contradictions'[95] and 'miserable hair-splitting'.[96] Engels retorts in his own way, showing how spurious Friedrich Graeber's points are, asking why Jesus has a genealogy at all since God is his father and then pointing out that the smallest textual differences have a knack of dividing the church.[97]

The detail of this argument is rather preliminary in terms of biblical criticism, but it does lead to an important point: like anyone else, the orthodox actually read their bibles in light of a distinct set of prior assumptions. So they claim that the Bible is divinely inspired, but one cannot find that claim in the Bible. Or, they argue that the Bible should be read 'literally', but the Bible does not demand such a reading. Or they condemn reason as sinful and yet Engels cannot see that reason is condemned at all. For Engels, these orthodox exegetes follow the same 'old routine', killing 'the divine in man to replace it with the dead letter'.[98]

While it may seem all too obvious to argue that everyone reads the Bible with a prior set of extra-biblical assumptions, the conservatives obscure their assumptions with a nice little piece of subterfuge: they claim that they have no prior assumptions and read the Bible as it is. Unlike those evil rationalists, or indeed unlike the Roman Catholics who rely on the church, these conservative Protestants do not come to the Bible with any preconceptions. Was this not the import of Luther's *sola scriptura*? We can take this claim in two ways: either the conservatives are incredibly naïve and actually believe the claim. Or they are astoundingly clever and actually mean to say: we will use the Bible to support our prior assumptions and thereby give them an extra, divine boost. This subterfuge of arguing that the Bible is the basis for one's prior assumptions is an old (and somewhat unconscious) trick of bolstering one's own position – 'I have the Bible and God on my side, so do not you dare question me!'.

---

94. Engels 1839r, pp. 453–4; Engels 1839s, pp. 399–400. See also Engels 1839t, pp. 457–8; Engels 1839u, pp. 403–4.
95. Engels 1839t, p. 460; Engels 1839u, p. 406.
96. Engels 1839r, p. 454; Engels 1839s, p. 400.
97. It would seem that Wilhelm Graeber, the brother of Friedrich, was much more willing to entertain critical positions on such matters. As far as the genealogies are concerned, he prefers Matthew's and finds Luke problematic. Engels comments that Friedrich's position depends on 'unnatural possibilities' (Engels 1839v, p. 466; Engels 1839w, p. 413).
98. Engels 1839l, p. 426; Engels 1839m, p. 371.

Engels probes at the borders of many of these thoughts, not quite slipping through. He equivocates between asserting that he is reading the Bible properly and an awareness of the prior assumptions that both he and his opponents bring to these texts. At these moments, he designates his own approach as a mix of reason and supernaturalism, although he comes down eventually on the side of reason: 'I want to tell you quite plainly', he writes to Friedrich Graeber on 15 June 1939, 'that I have now reached a point where I can only regard as divine a teaching which can stand the test of reason'.[99] And he opposes his newly found approach to that of orthodoxy, which he claims to have cast aside. However, just when we think he has hit upon the insight that his own new perspective on the Bible is just that – another perspective – he falls back on to the argument that his approach is a better and more truthful way to read the Bible.

There is another feature of immanent analysis that lurks behind these debates between Engels and Friedrich Graeber, for as I mentioned earlier (in the Introduction), a feature of the biblical criticism that was being established at the time removed God from any biblical analysis. Or, rather, instead of being an external referent and cause, 'God' became a character in the stories, or a feature of the beliefs of ancient peoples which could be uncovered in terms of the history of religions. A biblical critic such as Strauss or Bauer or any of the other historical critics (as they became known) sought out historical cause and effect, which left God out of the picture. This immanent analysis of the Bible posed a huge challenge to the churches and to the state, which relied on a transcendent justification, based upon the Bible, for their own existence and status. It is no wonder that Strauss, Bauer and Feuerbach generated such furious controversy, for they seemed to threaten the foundations of society itself by cutting the signifying link between the 'God' mentioned in the texts and an external being known by the same name. As I have shown, Engels thoroughly immersed himself in this type of immanent biblical criticism. Of course, such immanent analysis was also characteristic of the liberal, republican and democratic movements, but, in Germany, it found its clearest expression in biblical analysis. I would suggest that Engels's intimate engagement with such an immanent biblical criticism was one avenue that led to the immanence of historical materialism.

---

99. Engels 1839r, p. 454; Engels 1839s, p. 400.

Schelling, the philosopher in Christ

> Nor will he ever teach true understanding
> Who tells you all the dogma that he knows.[100]

We find another sustained engagement by a youthfully precocious Engels (he was 21) on matters theological in his response to Schelling's lectures in Berlin. Engels attended the lectures in between his obligatory military service. Given all of the gatherings he attended, all of the material he read and the writing he completed, that military service must not have been all that onerous – or perhaps he did not sleep much during the year in Berlin. As for the lectures, the subject was the philosophy of revelation. The context: Schelling's invitation by Friedrich Wilhelm IV to come to Berlin in order to counter the strength of Hegel's legacy among the young Hegelians. The line taken by Engels in response: to defend Hegel's grave from abuse, especially the dialectic as a 'mighty, never resting driving force of thought',[101] for, at this moment, Engels is fully on side with the *'ecclesia pressa'*,[102] the oppressed church of the young Hegelians.

From his writings we gain a distinct sense of a young man fired up by the debates and controversies swirling around him. As far as Engels is concerned, Schelling has become weak-minded, finding religion and mysticism in his old age. But my interest is not so much Schelling per se but the key-points Engels makes, especially those that might remain useable in some fashion. There are two substantial pieces, *Schelling and Revelation* and *Schelling, Philosopher in Christ*,[103] along with a shorter essay, *Schelling on Hegel*,[104] which is mostly a copy of Engels's lecture-notes. I am more interested in the first two. Much of *Schelling and Revelation* contains Engels's recollections (drawn from notes) of the lectures he attended, although he adds his own comments and occasionally locks horns with the ageing philosopher.[105] *Schelling, Philosopher in Christ*

---

100. Engels 1839a, p. 5.
101. Engels 1842g, p. 236; Engels 1842h, p. 310.
102. Engels 1841a, p. 187; Engels 1841b, p. 263.
103. Engels 1842g; Engels 1842h; Engels 1842i; Engels 1842j.
104. Engels 1841a; Engels 1841b. See Engels 1842a, pp. 294–5; Engels 1842b, pp. 372–3, where he also comments on a certain Alexander Jung's praise of Schelling and Engels's admission that he wrote *Schelling und die Offenbarung*.
105. A little later, Engels claimed that *Schelling and Revelation* was the first work to point out that the young Hegelians were actually atheists. See Engels 1843e, pp. 404–5.

is a sustained satire of how a pietist might see Schelling's conversion to the true gospel in his old age.

The two essays – both published anonymously as independent pamphlets – are a close-knit pair. One presents what we can assume is closer to Engels's own position at the time, with its celebration of reason and free thought, albeit still within a Christian framework, and the other a rather skilful satire of a position that he would have heard a thousand times in the reformed church of Elberfeld.[106] In other words, one is where he has been and the other where he is now. And we can see in these two pieces a double use of the Bible as both a source of satire and as a support for his own positions.

When I first read *Schelling, Philosopher in Christ*, I set out to track all of the biblical quotations (there are 33 explicit ones), allusions and metaphors, such as the sustained ones comparing Schelling's conversion to that of Saul/Paul on the road to Damascus in Acts, or to Paul's sermon on the Areopagus in Athens in the same book. But, since these references run into the hundreds, the task of listing them all would be both pedantic and pointless. It is obvious to anyone who reads this pamphlet that Engels knows his Bible intimately, that he is all too familiar with the doctrines, the way the Bible is used and the senses given to the various passages plucked out and thrown together in a particularly conservative way.

At a pinch, it might have been written by an F.W. Krummacher, whom Engels knew all too well, but it also goes sufficiently over the top to show its true colours as a satire. The main topic of *Schelling, Philosopher in Christ* is the relation between faith and reason. Its argument goes as follows. Given the Calvinist position that we have all sinned and fallen short of the glory of God,[107] indeed that we can do nothing good or worthwhile on our own, then our reason is a poor, limited thing. Dominated by sin, it will hardly get us anywhere. And anyone who thinks reason is the royal road to truth (like Hegel) really engages in idolatry and pride, for he or she sets reason on the throne of God. In his maturity, Schelling – who was once an idolatrous champion of reason – has seen the light (like Saul/Paul) and demoted reason to its true and proper place. So Schelling has become a witness to grace and truth,

106. In this respect, the satirical poem, *The Insolently Threatened Yet Miraculously Rescued Bible* (Engels 1842c; Engels 1842d), comes close to this essay on Schelling.
107. Romans 3:23.

to the Trinity, to the simplicity of the Bible and to the reconciliation offered by Jesus. Schelling gives a faithful rendition of the prophecies that point to Christ from both pagan sources and the Old Testament, Christ's incarnation, life, death and resurrection. Indeed, Schelling's lectures may be compared to Paul facing up to the Greek philosophers on the Areopagus (and Berlin is quite like a pagan Athens), where he gave witness to the Gospel in the face of their scepticism. Not only is he the champion of faith against the pagan Hegel and all his yapping pack, against the false prophets of the end-time who came out of the French Revolution, but he actually points the way forward, beyond the Roman-Catholic church of Peter and the Protestant church of Paul, to the church of love that is established by the beloved disciple, John.

Not quite blasphemy, the essay does make fun of the way that the Bible is used in defence of obscurantism and resistance to any form of rational thought. What Engels does not see is that this type of conservative response is also rational and logically consistent: the texts do seem to work together once you admit the premise (as he admits in his earlier attack on F.W. Krummacher) of sinful depravity and the need for grace. It is really an alternative rational system that is caught in its own paradox. It claims to uphold the true faith as it has been passed on from Christ himself and the apostles, but it is actually a new development in its own way. In other words, this type of attack on the new directions in philosophy would not have taken place if those new ideas had not arisen in the first place.

The other curious feature of this essay is that it actually satirises a practice to which Engels himself resorted on more than occasion: the use of biblical texts and allusions to back up his own position. While he derides the pietists and Calvinists for the way they use the Bible, on occasion he does exactly the same thing. In fact, he oscillates between a positive use of the Bible to express his own position and a negative, satirical use when he wants to make fun of his opponents (and his old self). Both uses of the Bible occur in the other essay with which I would like to pause for while, *Schelling and Revelation*. The opening section of that piece echoes the tone of *Schelling, Philosopher in Christ* and casts Schelling as a rather feeble modern-day Elijah on Mount Carmel[108] where he scatters the pagan priests of Baal with the help of a thunderstorm

---

108. 1 Kings 18.

sent by God.[109] By contrast, the final pages of that essay offer a run of biblical allusions (I must admit I did count them – there are 13 I can recognise) in a much more positive light.[110] Their purpose is to present the dawn of reason and the new directions in philosophy embodied by Hegel and the Young Hegelians as a conversion, as the apocalyptic dawning of a day of battle, and as the emergence of a glorious new age. Here are two examples:

> ...gird the sword round our loins for its sake and stake our lives joyfully in the last, holy war which will be followed by the thousand-year reign of freedom.[111]

> They are coming, they are coming, from all valleys, from all heights they are streaming towards us with song and the call of trumpets; the day of the great decision, of the battle of the nations, is approaching, and victory must be ours![112]

Engels did have a tendency to get carried away with himself, but we can put that down to a mix of youthful enthusiasm and the sheer excitement of all these new possibilities that were opening up for him in his reading (which he had to do on his own).

Reasonably large sections in *Schelling and Revelation* are given over to reporting on what Schelling has said (and they descend into a babble of Schelling-speak), but the most significant parts are those where Engels's own assessment comes through. If Engels may once have subscribed to the views he puts forward in *Schelling, Philosopher in Christ* (although I suspect that he always had some questions for which the Calvinist answers were not sufficient), by now his own opinions are those expressed in *Schelling and Revelation*. As far as Engels is concerned, Schelling's faults are many: he caricatures Hegel, is deceptive, mystical (and therefore illogical), asserts the Christian 'fact' and does not argue for it, and uses the Bible as his ultimate authority. Let me take each one in turn.

---

109. Engels 1842g, pp. 191–2; Engels 1842h, pp. 269–70.
110. Engels 1842g, pp. 238–40; Engels 1842h, pp. 312–14.
111. Engels 1842g, p. 239; Engels 1842h, p. 313. The allusions here are to the sword of the Spirit in Ephesians 3:17 and the thousand-year reign of Christ (the millennium) in Revelation 20:2–4.
112. Engels 1842g, p. 240; Engels 1842h, p. 314. Here the allusions are to the eschatological visions of Isaiah 2:2; 14:2; 17:12; 34:1–3; 43:9; 66:18 and the apocalyptic vision of Revelation 12; 15:4; 16:14–16.

The charge of misunderstanding and caricaturing of Hegel runs through-out the essay, but it comes to the fore when Schelling presents the 'truth' of Hegel's dialectic in relation to God and creation. It goes as follows: God exists; he then posits the world which turns out to be a contrary being, a negation; he must destroy it because it is evil, a status it attains merely through existing.[113] For Engels, this argument turns Hegel into a speculative thinker. Engels is too much of an enthusiast to see that Hegel's system is speculative and ideal-ist, although he does admit a little later that there may well be a connection between Hegel's thought and Trinitarian theology.[114] But, at this moment, anything that hints at theology in Hegel's thought is unacceptable.

Moreover, Schelling is deceptive. He is really engaged in subterfuge, sneak-ing through a secret trap-door 'belief in dogma [*Autoritätsglauben*], sentimen-tal mysticism, [and] gnostic fantasy into the free science of thinking'.[115] At this point, the attack goes in two directions. One path indicates that Schelling at least tries to bring out the need for theology, God and the Bible from within philosophy itself. How? Schelling argues that, for all its achievements, reason is really a limited human faculty that can make sense only of experience. For anything beyond experience, we must rely on God and revelation. Here, I agree with Engels, for this move is really a theological *a priori*: it relies on the assumption that reason is the product of an inescapably sinful humanity. For Engels, this dethroning of 'omnipotent reason' is nothing more than obscu-rantist, illogical, fantastical and a travesty of Hegel. Reason must be defended from this frontal attack: 'It is a sad spectacle to watch Schelling drag thought down – from its lofty, pure ether into the region of sensory perception, strike from its head the true golden crown and make it stagger about, drunk with the fog and mist of the unaccustomed, romantic atmosphere, in a crown of gilded paper, to be the laughing-stock of the street urchins'.[116] Close to 170 years later, this elevation of reason and thought seems all too suspect, even though we still find its champions. We may not cast the criticism of reason in the theological terms of a sinful humanity that can do no good on its own, but we do have the sustained critique of instrumental reason in the hands of

113. See Engels 1842g, p. 223; Engels 1842h, pp. 297–8.
114. See Engels 1842g, p. 225; Engels 1842h, p. 299.
115. Engels 1842g, p. 201; Engels 1842h, p. 276.
116. Engels 1842g, p. 206; Engels 1842h, p. 281.

Adorno and Horkheimer.[117] For reason, too, has its brutal and violent tendencies, put to work in the technological science of killing machines, or in the 'rationalisation' of the market in which human beings are as dispensable as the machines of which they have become a part.

The other path is the one Engels is keen to establish: Schelling does nothing more than provide a weak philosophical screen for a wholesale recovery of theology. Thus, he accepts the 'the historical fact of Christianity' rather than offering any worthwhile argument for the viability of Christianity.[118] In other words, Christianity is a given, so we must proceed from there. Moreover, he accepts the Bible as authoritative and seeks to buttress his arguments by resorting to it. In short, he is really a theologian in philosophical disguise, one who resorts to superhuman principles to make his philosophy work. These criticisms say more about Engels than Schelling. Resorting to theology, arguing that the Absolute Idea is really God, relying on the Bible as revelation is really a no-go zone and a return to obscurantism.[119]

I want to return to this ban on theology or even on covert theology in a moment, but, first, a couple of further points. To begin with, for Engels, Schelling is caught. His arguments are no guarantee for the uniqueness of Christianity. If one assumes the fact of Christianity for the purpose of constructing a positive philosophy, then one must also accept the facts of Judaism and Islam, or even Roman Catholicism and Anglicanism as similar facts that would lead to other positive philosophies. Even more, Schelling's 'unpremeditated being' is not necessarily Christian: it may well, suggests Engels, be Chinese or 'Otaheitan' (Hawaiian).[120] Thus, the move to discuss the Trinity or the incarnation, life, death and resurrection of Christ are non-sequiturs, for they do not necessarily follow from the philosophical arguments.[121] What Schelling ends

---

117. Horkheimer and Adorno 2002; Horkheimer and Adorno 2003.
118. See Engels 1842g, p. 229; Engels 1842h, p. 303.
119. Engels 1842g, pp. 219–20; Engels 1842h, pp. 294–5.
120. Engels 1842g, p. 222; Engels 1842h, p. 297.
121. 'Thus, out of the abyss of unpremeditated being Schelling has conjured up for us into the light of day not only the personal but also the triune God, Father, Son and Holy Ghost, though the third has indeed only been accommodated with difficulty, and then the arbitrarily created world, dependent on arbitrariness and therefore hollow and void; and he has thus the basis of Christianity. It cannot be my intention to show up one by one the inconsistencies, the arbitrary judgments, the rash claims, the gaps, leaps, assumptions and confusions of which Schelling is guilty here.' (Engels 1842g, pp. 225–6; Engels 1842h, p. 300.)

up with is neither philosophy nor theology: the basis of modern theology has become dreadfully weak. It seems to me that Engels is correct here: the move from philosophy to theology has become an impossible leap. The question left hanging is whether philosophy and theology can indeed work together or whether the rift is too great. Engels by this stage prefers the latter.

Indeed, he argues strongly early in the essay that the work of critics such as Strauss, Bauer and Feuerbach indicates that one can no longer stay within a Christian-theological framework. He is fully on side with the radical young Hegelians who have broken through the limit of Christianity: 'So the *"hegelingische Rotte"* no longer conceals that it neither can nor will any longer regard Christianity as its limit. All the basic principles of Christianity, and even of what has hitherto been called religion itself, have fallen before the inexorable criticism of reason, the absolute idea claims to be the founder of a new era'.[122] Later, he, and especially Marx, would not be so sure, especially when someone such as Bruno Bauer kept his radical critique within the realm of theology. The young Hegelians had by no means broken out of that constraint.

But let me come back to the question of covert theology, or secular theology as it is called in our own day. Schelling is not a very good covert theologian, for he comes out far too strongly in favour of God, the Bible and the main elements of Christian doctrine. Yet the point that Engels makes is one that is still made: Schelling smuggles theology in under the pretence of philosophy. Schelling may try to argue that theology is a necessary consequence of philosophy, but Engels will not have a bar of it.

The closest current movement is what has been called the 'theological turn' in French phenomenology. Basing themselves on Heidegger, a number of French philosophers with a distinct Roman-Catholic bent – Michel Henry, Jean-Louis Chrétien, Jean-Luc Marion, Jean-François Courtine – have been arguing that certain phenomena such as prayer, the call, or vocation actually open themselves out to transcendence and thereby God.[123] What they seek to do is argue from within Heidegger's phenomenology to a (rather conservative and mystical) theological position. The key lies in the idea of the excess of a phenomenon, an excess that produces what Marion calls a 'saturated

---

122. Engels 1842g, p. 197; Engels 1842h, p. 273.
123. See Janicaud, Courtine, Chrétien, Henry, Marion and Ricœur 2000.

phenomenon', which is '*invisible* according to quantity, *unbearable* according to quality, but also *unconditioned* (absolved from any horizon) according to relation, and *irreducible* to the *I* (incapable of being looked at) according to modality'.[124] The response to such an argument comes very close to Engels's charge against Schelling. And it appears in the excellent essay by Dominique Janicaud. For Janicaud, the 'theological turn' is a violation of one of the basic postulates of phenomenology that comes through from Husserl, namely the reduction. By closing down transcendence, or, rather, the ecstatic openness to transcendence, phenomenology deals only with the appearing that remains in and for consciousness. It is, in other words, the field of immanence sundered from any transcendence. For Janicaud, then, the newer developments in phenomenology – he lays much of the blame with Levinas – lead to its self-annihilation, for they use phenomenology 'as a springboard in a quest for divine transcendence'.[125] Thus also with Schelling, I would suggest: the immanence of philosophy becomes the basis for the leap to the transcendence of theology.

We might call this the smuggler's version of covert theology. I must admit that I am as unimpressed as Engels (or indeed Janicaud) with its moves. But there is another that is far more pernicious, namely the effort to empty theological terms of their theological content and refill them with political, economic or philosophical content. Here, Adorno's trenchant critique is well worth remembering, especially when it seems as though thinkers on the Left are resorting to various types of secular theology all around us. We cannot shake off the theological associations of terms such as hope, promise, love, authenticity and meaning all that easily, for they trail the dust of their former glory. Adorno is particularly on the watch for the power-structures that have a remarkable knack of persisting.[126] Thus, while overt theology at least has a recognised power-structure that refers to God, the Bible or the church with which we are all too familiar, secular theology does not have such a structure. So what happens is that the authority rests with none other than the philosopher: she is the final arbiter of truth. Here, too, theology sneaks

---

124. Marion in Janicaud, Courtine, Chrétien, Henry, Marion and Ricœur 2000, p. 211. See also Marion 2002.
125. Janicaud in Janicaud, Courtine, Chrétien, Henry, Marion and Ricœur 2000, p. 70.
126. See especially Adorno 1973, 2003. See also Boer 2007a, pp. 422–30.

in through a secret opening, but it may not be obvious to the philosopher in question.

Let us see what Engels urges in response. It is nothing less than an effort to dispense with theology entirely. How do we construct a system of thought and action that is free from the taint of theology? He felt it had already been attained, especially in the work of David Strauss and Ludwig Feuerbach, who had shown that the secret of theology is in fact anthropology, that 'heaven has come down to earth'[127] – the first time that this well-known phrase appears in the work of either Marx or Engels. All we need do is gather up its treasures like stones by the roadside. The judgement was perhaps a little premature, for Marx and Engels had to undertake the task themselves. One way of characterising that programme is that they sought to develop a system that was thoroughly non-theological, a system for which theology did not count in any way, whether overt or covert. Whether they achieved such a goal is another question.

Yet, despite this insight from a 21-year-old Engels, he could still not resist engaging with the little rotund old man, Schelling. It is a strange and deeply ambivalent criticism, focusing on the famous passage of Philippians 2:6–8. It deals with the *kenosis*, or self-emptying of Christ, who gives up his equality with God to become a human being even to the point of death on a cross. To Schelling's argument that the divine Christ gave up of his own free will his equal status with God in order to unite the world with God and thereby become fully God himself, Engels responds that this contradicts 'the entire basic outlook of Christianity'.[128] Christ, he argues, did not do so out of free will, for that would impute the possibility of evil in Christ. He must have done so by natural necessity. And how in the world can someone become God, especially Christ? He either was God or he was not. At this level, Schelling's argument, for all its careful attention to exegetical detail, is not Christian enough. It falls into the trap of using the odd verse to support 'the most abnormal thing'.[129] Here Engels is actually defending a more orthodox reading of the text over against Schelling's innovations. But, then, in the

---

127. Engels 1842g, p. 238; Engels 1842h, p. 312.
128. Engels 1842g, p. 230; Engels 1842h, p. 304.
129. Ibid.

midst of all of that, he turns around and presents a rather ossified picture of Christianity:

> Christianity is nearly two thousand years old and has had time enough to come to itself. Its content is expressed in the church, and it is impossible that any other positive content of significance is still concealed in it, or that its true meaning has only now been understood. In any case it would now be too late.[130]

To my mind, this is an extremely important passage, for Engels both reveals his adherence to a conservative picture of Christian thought and rejects it at the same time. In short, it throws into sharp relief his own ambivalence. He is tied to that picture, for it is the way he had come to know of Christianity in his reformed context. Yet, in holding to such an understanding, it also becomes frozen in time, unable to countenance any radically new direction or insight. Or, rather, that is how he would prefer to see it: he does not want a renovated Christianity, for then his rejection would become all the more difficult. This is why Feuerbach and Strauss present not a revitalised Christianity he would like to accept, but rather a step beyond Christianity itself.

As for Schelling, perhaps the best final word comes from Engels's own pen:

> The old ship dancing joyfully through the waves turned back and entered the shallow haven of faith, ran its keel so fast into the sand that it is still stuck there. There it lies, and nobody recognises in the old, frail wreck the old ship which went out with all sails spread and flags flying. The sails have long since rotted, the masts are broken, the waves pour in through the gaping planks, and every day the tides pile up more sand around the keel.[131]

Conclusion: on the loss of faith

When I first began critical study of the Bible and theology, back in the 1980s at the University of Sydney, I was warned by a legion of conservative Calvinists that it was the first step on the slippery path to losing one's religious faith. At

---

130. Ibid.
131. Engels 1842g, p. 237; Engels 1842h, p. 311.

the time I scoffed at the idea, thinking of them as wimps who could not stand the challenges thrown up by critical study. I still think that they are wimps, but the advice (given with a serious touch on the shoulder and a downward glance) came out of an oral tradition of almost 150 years. For it began in response to the first full flowering of critical-biblical study that took place in Germany at the time Engels was growing up. I have explored the conjunction of factors that led to such a situation in the first half of the eighteenth century in Germany at an earlier point. The work of Strauss, Bauer and Feuerbach (and they are only the most notable) raised a fury of protest, not merely in Germany but abroad as well. The churches felt such critical study was an attack at their very foundations – the Bible. The paths taken by this study's pioneers (Bauer and Feuerbach ended up in atheism) gave no assurance to their pious detractors.

In some respects, the responses of these pioneers was immature. They shared the assumption of their critics that such study would undermine one's faith, and so they gave it up. Since then, biblical criticism has been enriched and modified, but its basic assumption has remained the same: the only responsible way to deal with the Bible is 'scientifically', that is, an immanent approach without the hypothesis of God as cause and agent. Criticism of this type has passed through a number of phases, moving from radical challenge and vilification by its opponents, through a hegemonic position for all biblical study (for about a century) through to dissipation in the face of questions and newer approaches since the 1970s. Yet, for many who begin biblical and theological studies, historical criticism (as it has come to be called) is the first step. And, for many, it throws up the first challenge to religious faith.

We can distinguish four paths such students take. The first option is open only to those who begin biblical and theological study for reasons of curiosity and no religious faith. This option has become far more common in recent decades as the number of those who study the Bible with religious commitment drops away. The remaining three paths relate to those with some religious faith: they may reject the whole approach and reconfirm their previous prejudices, or they may break through the wall and develop a more sophisticated faith that sees the value in such criticism, or they may follow the path of giving up their religious commitment altogether. Engels falls into the last group. But he is in good company. Nietzsche apart, many of my colleagues have found that the challenge of critical approaches is too much and what seems to be the rock of their belief crumbles into sand. But these colleagues do not lose their interest in the Bible or theology. Indeed, many of them earn their bread and butter through biblical criticism and theological reflection. Engels did not become a theologian or biblical critic, perhaps because he never studied formally at university-level. But he did stay very interested in matters theological and biblical.[132]

I would suggest that this is what we can see in Engels's writings on theology and the Bible. An encounter with critical scholarship leads him first to give up his Calvinist beliefs while struggling to retain a more open religious commitment alongside that scholarship. The comment in the short pseudonymous piece, 'From Elberfeld', is really autobiographical: of 'a dead man' he writes, 'a genuine Wuppertal Christian, recalling the happy time when one could still cherish a childlike belief in a doctrine whose contradictions can now be counted on the fingers, when one burned with pious zeal against religious liberalism, a zeal at which people now smile or blush'.[133] The comments are supposed to refer to an unnamed poet, an educated layman, but the melancholy is Engels's own. Eventually, he steps outside that community of faith, as many of his contemporaries did. Although there was no question of returning to the reactionary nonsense he had left behind,[134] he did feel that something had been lost: 'one can see how fortifying and comforting a religion which has truly become a matter of the heart is, even in its saddest extremes' he writes in the same piece.[135] Here still, at the age of 19, he longs for that 'homeland',

---

132. Every now and then he would report to Marx on his latest reading and thoughts. For example, he discusses at length a book called *The Historical Geography of Arabia* by the Reverend Charles Forster. Apart from pointing out that the parson and biblical apologist peep through, he notes the way in which various Arab practices illuminate ancient Israel. Then he writes: 'It is now quite clear to me that the Jews' so-called Holy Writ is nothing more than a record of ancient Arab religious and tribal traditions, modified by the Jews' early separation from their tribally related but nomadic neighbours. The circumstance of Palestine's being surrounded on the Arabian side by nothing but desert, i.e. the land of the Bedouins, explains its separate development.' (Engels 1853g, p. 327; Engels 1853h, p. 246; see the ongoing discussion in Ebach 1982 and Engels 1853i; Engels 1853j.)

133. Engels 1839d, p. 30; Engels 1839e, p. 63.

134. See his polemic against the reactionary Roman-Catholic Joel Jacoby (Engels 1840a; Engels 1840b).

135. Engels 1839d, p. 31; Engels 1839e, p. 64.

which is both Wuppertal and the faith that was passing: 'But you too have a homeland and perhaps return to it with the same love as I, however ordinary it looks, once you have vented your anger at its perversities'.[136] And he would return, once to fight with the Elberfeld revolutionaries in May of 1849[137] and then a few more times to the arena of biblical study, as the essays on Müntzer, the biblical book of Revelation and early Christianity indicate.

---

136. Ibid.
137. Engels 1849e; Engels 1849f; Engels 1849n; Engels 1849o; *From the Indictment of the Participants in the Uprising in Elberfeld in May 1849* 1850.

Chapter Ten
Revelation and Revolution

> Similarly Isaac Newton in his old age busied
> himself with expounding the Revelation of
> St. John.[1]

> That the millennium was here depicted in *earthly*
> *colours* goes without saying. Even *Revelation* can-
> not rest content with such heavenly delights as
> sitting with a bare bottom on a damp cloud,
> twanging a harp with more or less gory hands
> and singing hymns to all eternity.[2]

A vital moment in the Marxist engagement with
Christianity takes place around 1850, if not before:
Engels begins a process of coming to terms with his
conservative Calvinist background. And the end-run
of that process is that Engels, a couple of years before
his death, affirms a distinctly revolutionary element
within Christianity. This chapter is devoted to tracking and analysing that process through a series of
texts that span more than fifty years. There are, in fact,
two tracks to that final argument. One is a persistent
sense of the ambivalence of theology and the Bible,
especially on political matters. While Engels often
was disparaging and championed an atheism as militant as his earlier religious commitment, he keeps

---

1. Engels 1873–82a, p. 345; Engels 1873–82b, p. 337.
2. Engels 1894e, p. 329; Engels 1894f, p. 277.

on commenting on the opposition between reaction and revolution within Christianity.[3] While, in Marx, that awareness is fleeting, in Engels we see it in full force. The other track is quite different: his unflagging interest in the final book of the Christian Bible, Revelation. It runs from his early use of its language to express exuberance at new discoveries, to tease his friends, and satirise the young Hegelians and their opponents. Later, he would change direction, appreciatively taking up Bruno Bauer's argument that it is the earliest Christian text and therefore gives us a window into a Christianity very different from that to which we are accustomed. Both tracks end up converging, first with his argument that Thomas Müntzer and the Peasant Revolt was a revolution that expressed its goals in Christian language and then with his final reconstruction of a revolutionary early Christianity. While the early Christianity essay is far more interesting than the one on Müntzer, in both we find a striking effort to draw parallels with the socialist movement. It was those parallels that led him to the revolutionary argument. Throughout, I am on the lookout for fruitful ideas that I can take further, insights that still have some life in them.

The two minds of Friedrich Engels

There are two ways we can view Engels's later efforts to deal with Christianity. One is to divide that engagement into three or four fairly conventional periods. The first is his time of youthful faith, the second his period of intense questioning and then eventual jettisoning of that faith, the third a period of rather dogmatic materialist atheism, and then the fourth is a process of coming to terms with his biblical and theological past in a way that appropriates some elements and yet moves beyond it.

While there is an element of truth in such a developmental approach – Engels's last essay on Christianity may be read as a return of his Christian repressed – it does not really work, for the stages do not stand up to closer scrutiny. Engels actually has simultaneous contradictory assessments of Christianity which he tries to reconcile. One side of Engels is the staunch and doctrinaire atheist who thinks that Feuerbach has said the last word, that the

---

3. He certainly kept reading on matters related to Christianity. See, for example, Marx and Engels 1850e; Marx and Engels 1850f.

great awakening is one of realising that human beings have actually deified and worshipped themselves in the shape of the gods.[4] At about the same time, Engels also states quite clearly that early Christianity was a revolutionary movement among the lower classes of Roman society.

Two quotations from this period – 1843–4 – give voice to this tension in Engels's engagement with Christianity: 'We too attack the hypocrisy of the present Christian state of the world; the struggle against it, our liberation from it and the liberation of the world from it are ultimately our sole occupation;... But because we know that all this lying and immorality follows from religion, that religious hypocrisy, theology, is the archetype of all other lies and hypocrisy, we are justified in extending the term "theology" to the whole untruth and hypocrisy of the present, as was originally done by Feuerbach and Bruno Bauer...; all the possibilities of religion are exhausted; after Christianity, after absolute, i.e., abstract, religion, after "religion as such", no other form of religion can arise'.[5] But then, a few months earlier, Engels also wrote these words: 'In general, this is a feature of every revolutionary epoch, as was seen in particular in the religious revolution of which the outcome was Christianity: "blessed are the poor" [Matthew 5:3], "the wisdom of this world is foolishness" [1 Corinthians 1:20], etc.'.[6] This is the tension that fascinates me, the one between the 'war on religion and religious ideas'[7] and the appreciation of Christianity as a revolutionary movement.

Doctrinaire atheism

Apart from regular bouts of anticlericalism, Engels's avowed atheism followed various channels. At times, it became an assertion that materialist atheism simply meant that at death we return 'to the bosom of nature' from whence we came – as he points out in the speech at Jenny Marx's funeral.[8] And, at others,

---

4. Engels 1844b, pp. 461–2; Engels 1844c, pp. 543–4.
5. Engels 1844b, p. 462; Engels 1844c, p. 544. There are many, many more comments on the useless superstition of religion, but here is one of the better ones: 'The prisoner in solitary confinement is driven insane; the model gaol in London, after only three months of existence, had already three lunatics to transfer to Bedlam, to say nothing of the religious mania which is still usually regarded as sanity.' (Engels 1844f, p. 510; Engels 1844g, p. 589.)
6. Engels 1843c, p. 380; Engels 1843d, pp. 451–2.
7. Engels 1844b, p. 463; Engels 1844c, p. 545.
8. Engels 1881a, pp. 420–1; Engels 1881b, p. 294.

it was a matter of class-struggle. Having observed that the established forms of Christianity were the preserve of the old aristocracy and the bourgeoisie (especially in England), he keeps commenting on the way the working class is increasingly enthusiastic about atheism. Keenly taking up Strauss's *Das Leben Jesu* in reading-groups with its members occasionally imprisoned for writing and circulating atheistic tracts, the working class's atheism was very much anti-establishment.[9] As Engels puts it: 'Money is the god of this world; the bourgeois takes the proletarian's money from him and so makes a practical atheist of him. No wonder, then, if the proletarian retains his atheism and no longer respects the sacredness and power of the earthly God'.[10] These observations are coupled with his descriptions of the decline of the established Church of England, the indifference of parishioners, and indeed the outright disdain of the church's parsons, who were in lock-step with the ruling class and widely hated.[11] The fact that the church had to resort to measures such as the Apostasy Act (loss of civil rights and imprisonment), the Blasphemy Act (a fine and a year in prison), and penalties for not attending church with no proper excuse (a fine and imprisonment of up to six weeks) only reinforced the widespread sense of decline.[12]

As far as Engels is concerned, these developments are due to the triumphant march of communism – a narrative he invokes often in his enthusiasm for the movement. So we find a potted narrative that goes back to the origins of life, runs through the Greeks and Romans, notes the struggles against Christianity

---

9. Engels 1843c, pp. 385–6; Engels 1843d, pp. 460–1; Engels 1844b, pp. 446–7, 450; Engels 1844c, pp. 527–8, 531; Engels 1844h, p. 212; Engels 1846a, pp. 421, 556, 569; Engels 1846b, pp. 352–3, 480–1, 492–3; Engels 1845c; Engels 1874–5a, pp. 15–16; Engels 1874–5b, pp. 531–2; Engels 1889a, p. 539. See also Marx 1855jj; Marx 1855kk; Marx 1855e, p. 599; Marx 1855f; Marx 1855g; Marx 1855dd, pp. 308–10; Marx 1855ee, pp. 328–30; Marx 1855c; Marx 1855d; Marx 1855hh; Marx 1855ii; Marx 1861h, p. 248; Marx 1861i, p. 289; Marx 1869j, p. 289; Marx 1869k, p. 610. All the same, Engels notes that despite their celebrations of the education, social work and anti-church polemic, their alternative meetings resembled church-gatherings, with choirs, speeches and hymns, often using church-hymns sets to communist lyrics (Engels 1843c, p. 387; Engels 1843d, pp. 462–3).

10. Engels 1846a, p. 412; Engels 1846b, p. 343.

11. Engels 1844f, pp. 501–4, 512; Engels 1844g, pp. 580–3, 591.

12. See Engels 1844f, p. 503; Engels 1844g, pp. 582–3. However, what Engels does not point out is that various dissenting Christian movements appealed to large numbers of the working class, especially Methodism. They may have disdained the Church of England, but they did not always fall away from Christianity entirely.

in the eighteenth century in the name of science and reason, the great strides in the nineteenth century, and then the inevitable victory of materialism and socialist revolution. The most sustained recounting of this narrative appears in those magnificently flawed texts, *Anti-Dühring* and *Dialectics of Nature*.[13] Before such a gathering tide, the Christian church can only sink and disappear. It has reached the end of its development; all that is left is for it to collapse under its own contradictions.[14]

The underlying assumption of this triumphant narrative is that material causes and scientific advances would bring about the swift demise of religion, especially Christianity in Europe. Engels was not alone in this assumption, for it was a hope among a large number of secular campaigners and caused more than a few furrowed brows among ecclesiastical types. Yet, if we look a little closer, Engels's Enlightenment assumptions concerning the progress of reason begin to waver. For example, conscious of the strength of Christianity in England, he hesitates approving a translation of *Anti-Dühring* since it is very hostile to religion.[15] Or, on a more dialectical note, when he depicts the preindustrial weaving-villages of England he laments the loss of a healthy and robust life, but then also observes that these weavers were religious, asleep, vegetative and unaware politically. He would much rather the unsettling effect of capitalism, for all its curses, since it awakens the proletariat to political action.[16] A comparable dialectical observation comes to mind after his visit to the United States, where he relishes the fact that its citizens had not brought with them the medieval institutions of Europe. Unfortunately, what they did bring were myriad medieval traditions, such as religion, superstition and spiritualism – 'in short, every kind of balderdash that was not immediately

---

13. See the liberal sprinkling of comments on 'religion' in Engels 1877–8a, pp. 16, 22, 26, 40–1, 62, 67–8, 79, 86, 93–9, 125–6, 130, 144, 232, 244, 300–4; Engels 1877–8b, pp. 16, 20–1, 25, 39–40, 62, 66–8, 79, 86–7, 93–100, 126–7, 131, 143–5, 230, 239, 294–8; Engels 1873–82a, pp. 318–20, 325, 423, 474, 480–1, 498–500, 551–2, 565; Engels 1873–82b, pp. 311–13, 318, 415, 465, 470–1, 486–9, 535–6, 547; Engels 1876–7a, pp. 591–3, 603–7; Engels 1976–7b, pp. 580–4. See also Engels 1892a, pp. 283–300.

14. See Engels 1844d, pp. 469–76, 486; Engels 1844e, pp. 550–7, 567; Engels 1844l. In a similar vein he points out that the natural path of the young Hegelians is not merely to atheism, but also communism (Engels 1843e, pp. 404–6). Occasionally, his narrative goes back to the animal spirituality of 'primitive' peoples.

15. Engels 1886c, p. 416; Engels 1886d, p. 452.

16. Engels 1846a, pp. 308–9; Engels 1846b, pp. 238–9.

harmful to business and now comes in very handy for the stultification of the masses [*Massenverdummung*]'.[17]

Another, more interesting, reassessment appears in his occasional observations that religion was not always a mere effect or reflection of social and economic conditions. This reassessment shows up sharply in a letter to Conrad Schmidt in 1890, where Engels describes the 'prehistorical fund' of ideological fields such as philosophy and religion as so much rubbish, which has, unfortunately, been taken over in the historical period. But then come two extraordinary sentences. The first reads: 'In so far as these various false conceptions of nature, of the nature of man, of spirits, magic forces, etc., are economically based, it is only in a negative sense; false conceptions of nature are the corollary of the low level of economic development in the prehistorical period, but also on occasion its precondition if not its actual cause'.[18] Initially it looks like an Althusserian argument *avant la lettre* for the semi-autonomy of the various zones of a mode of production, but it actually goes further, for he suggests that religion or philosophy may in fact be a cause or contributing factor to the economic base. But then there is a second prevarication: 'And even if economic necessity may have provided the main incentive for progress in natural science and done so to an increasing extent, it would be pedantic to seek economic causes for all this primitive rubbish [*all diesen ürzustandlichen Blödsinn*]'.[19] For some curious reason, he is keen to avoid attributing economic causes to prehistoric religion and ideology. So we end up in a double bind: in the historical period (whenever that begins), economics is the driving power for progress in science, but, in the prehistoric period, economics is not the cause of prescience. This argument suggests that Marxist categories are not always applicable before the prehistorical/historical divide and that we need to rethink our terms, but also that economics is not necessarily the only motor of history. Or, at least, that motor is far more limited than we might have thought.

Occasionally, Engels goes all the way, attributing to religion the honour of full causation. We find it in the militant broadsides against Christianity as the source of society's hypocrisy, delusions and hollowness, so much so that he proclaims: 'we have once and for all declared war on religion and religious

---

17. Engels 1886g, p. 533; Engels 1886h, p. 579; see also Engels 1886e, p. 491; Engels 1886f, p. 533.
18. Engels 1890g, pp. 61–2; Engels 1890h, p. 492.
19. Engels 1890g, p. 62; Engels 1890h, p. 492.

ideas and care little whether we are called atheists or anything else'.[20] Here, he also makes a clever inversion: against Carlyle's argument that the source of all the horrors of the age is the loss of religious feeling, Engels argues that the prime cause is religion itself. Or, rather, it is due to that liminal state between the awareness that religion is empty and the need for a fully human, socialist form of society.

Revolutionary versus reactionary Christianity

It is precisely this opening – that religion may in fact be active as well as passive – that leads Engels to his exploration of the more revolutionary elements within Christianity. More often than not, Engels wants to assert the primacy of social formations, especially in the way they shape revolutionary Christianity, but, occasionally, he allows radical Christianity a causative rôle. As he does so, we no longer find the blanket-dismissal of Christianity as reactionary, nor even the unending war on religion in the name of emancipation. And this awareness is not a late development in his thought, for in his 'Progress of Social Reform on the Continent' we encounter the first survey of various radical movements and their leaders who were either Christian or inspired by Christianity: Müntzer, Cabet, Weitling and others.[21] It would not be the last time he would offer such a survey.

But how is this possible? Is not Christianity a collection of out-dated superstitions and are not its institutions all too cosy with power, money and the state? Engels is not consistent in his answers. Sometimes, he suggests that communism has nothing to do with Christianity and that those who think so are simply deluded.[22] At other times, he argues that religious beliefs are irrelevant;

---

20. Engels 1844b, p. 463; Engels 1844c, p. 545. See the whole stretch in Engels 1844b, pp. 461–6; Engels 1844c, pp. 542–8.

21. Engels 1843e. Karl Kautsky took up Engels's list and turned it into his multivolume *Vorläufer des neueren Sozialismus* (Kautsky 1947b; Kautsky and Lafargue 1977).

22. At times, he even denies any revolutionary dimension to Christianity at all, as in this attack on Bakunin from 1872: 'And above all, there should be no disciplined sections! Indeed, no party discipline, no centralisation of forces at a particular point, no weapons of struggle! But what, then, would happen to the model of the future society? In short, where would this new organisation get us? To the cowardly, servile organisation of the early Christians, those slaves, who gratefully accepted every kick and whose grovelling did indeed after 300 years win them the victory of their religion – a method of revolution which the proletariat will surely not imitate! Like the early Christians, who took heaven as they imagined it as the model for their organisation, so

what counts is practice, that is, the human realities at the base of Christianity. If people organise a commune, it matters little what ideological reasons they might have. In fact, the sooner they get rid of their theological justifications the better, since they obscure matters with all sorts of mumbo-jumbo.[23]

However, the most interesting answer is that Christianity contains both elements, both radical strains and stifling reaction. Already, in his 'Letters from London' of 1843, he distinguishes between the corrupt status of the established church and the revolutionary origins of Christianity. On the one hand, the Church of England is a 'decaying edifice'[24] full of bigotry, petty hatreds, obtuse theological distinctions, and blind attachment to the aristocracy and Tories. Not a bad assessment, it seems to me. On the other hand, he notes that at times of revolutionary turmoil the 'lower' classes become the most progressive: 'In general, this is a feature of every revolutionary epoch, as was seen in particular in the religious revolution of which the outcome was Christianity'. He cannot resist adding to the Sermon on the Mount:[25] 'blessed are the poor, for theirs is the kingdom of heaven and, however long it may take, the kingdom of this earth as well'.[26]

The clearest statement of this political ambivalence within Christianity appears in an assessment of Etienne Cabet's Icarian communities. Engels

---

we are to take Mr. Bakunin's heaven of the future society as a model, and are to pray and hope instead of fighting. And the people who preach this nonsense pretend to be the only true revolutionaries!' (Engels 1872c, p. 67; Engels 1872d, p. 478). See also Marx 1872b, p. 255; Marx 1872c, p. 160.

23. After a survey of various communal ventures in North America and England – Quakers, Rappites (following Rapp, a minister from Württemburg), the Separatists from Württemburg and Owen – Engels comments: 'The reader will discover that most of the colonies that will be described in this article had their origins in all kinds of religious sects most of which have quite absurd and irrational views on various issues; the author just wants to point out briefly that these views have nothing whatsoever to do with communism. It is in any case obviously a matter of indifference whether those who prove by their actions the practicability of communal living believe in one God, in twenty or in none at all; if they have an irrational religion, this is an obstacle in the way of communal living, and if communal living is successful in real life despite this, how much more feasible must it be with others who are free of such inanities.' (Engels 1845a, p. 215; Engels 1845b, p. 522.) See also Engels 1844b, p. 464; Engels 1844c, p. 546.

24. Engels 1843c, p. 379; Engels 1843d, p. 451. As another example, see his comments on how the Sunday schools and church day-schools focus on sectarian differences at the expense of any useful education (Engels 1846a, pp. 408–11; Engels 1846b, pp. 339–42).

25. Matthew 5:3.

26. Engels 1843c, p. 380; Engels 1843d, p. 452.

begins by noting that, in contrast to English socialists, the French communists tend to be Christian. *Le Christianisme c'est le communisme* is the slogan
of Cabet's movement, which relied on the image of Christian communism in
the book of Acts of the Apostles as a model for their own communities.[27] And
then Engels observes: 'But all this shows only, that these good people are not
the best Christians, although they style themselves so; because if they were,
they would know the bible better, and find that, if some few passages of the
bible may be favourable to Communism, the general spirit of its doctrines is,
nevertheless, totally opposed to it, as well as to every rational measure'.[28] For
my purposes, this is a crucial observation, since it marks Engels's recognition
of political ambivalence in both the practice of Christianity and in the Bible.
Oppression may be the dominant theme, but every now and then another,
revolutionary line emerges. It is, of course, a far more dialectical understanding of the political complexity of theology and the Bible, one that I will trace
through various pieces by Engels in the remainder of this chapter.

The ambivalent Calvinism of F.W. Krummacher

One of these pieces actually goes back to Engels's youthful comments on
none other than the champion of Calvinist orthodoxy, the Reverend F.W.
Krummacher, whom we met in the previous chapter. In order to gain a sense
of how strong the tension really is, let me set the context with Engels's observations concerning the extreme Calvinist.

Despite Engels's protests against Krummacher's doctrine – it is 'in most
direct contradiction to reason and the Bible'[29] – he does actually admit its

---

27. See also Engels 1843e, p. 403; Engels 1888c, pp. 234–5; Engels 1888d, pp. 117–
18. Rosa Luxemburg and Karl Kautsky would develop this argument for Christian
communism along with criticisms of the 'communism of consumption' in the early-
twentieth century. See Luxemburg 1970; Luxemburg 1982; Kautsky 2007; Kautsky
1977; as well as my treatment of them in Boer 2009c.
28. Engels 1843e, p. 399. Marx was less sympathetic, arguing that Cabet's movement as well as the phalansteries of Fourier are signs of the immaturity of the working
class, who have not yet been sufficiently trained by conflict with the bourgeoisie (Marx
1871e, pp. 499–500; Marx 1871f, pp. 557–8; see also Marx 1873a, p. 394; Marx 1873b,
p. 301).
29. The full text reads: 'Krummacher has formulated the doctrine so sharply, following and firmly adhering to all its consequences, that nothing can be refuted once
the basis is accepted, namely, the inability of man on his own to desire what is good,
let alone do it. Hence follows the need for this ability to come from outside, and since

logical consistency: once you accept the premise (the total depravity of human beings, based on original sin), then the rest is irrefutable. So it seems that this doctrine is consistent, or at least watertight, if you grant the premise. In fact, it is standard Calvinist doctrine: since human beings can do no good on their own, they must rely entirely on God, or, rather, God's grace. The next step is to argue that, because human beings have no say in salvation, it all devolves upon God's own apparently arbitrary will. Salvation depends on God alone, so he is the one who decides who will be saved and who will be damned – in short, predestination.

However, Krummacher is more extreme than this standard Calvinist fare:

> Further, the Scriptures say: no man cometh unto the Father, but by me. But the heathen cannot come to the Father by Christ, because they do not know Christ, so they all exist merely to fill up hell. – Among Christians, many are called but few are chosen; but the many who are called are called only for the sake of appearance, and God took care not to call them so loudly that they obeyed him; all this to the glory of God and in order that they should not be forgiven.[30]

The biblical texts pepper the account (John 14:6 and Matthew 22:14 turn up here), but it does end up being a rather crass solution to an unresolved problem in many theological systems. If you take seriously the text from John 14:6 – 'no one comes to the Father, but by me' – then you face the difficulty that, through no fault of their own, most people throughout history have not actually had the chance to hear about Jesus. All manner of solutions have been offered to deal with this exclusive claim to salvation (Christ is manifest in other, very unexpected ways, or they hear about him in purgatory). The simplistic solution that they go straight to hell without passing 'Go' is, I must admit, one of the less sophisticated. I too would find a sermon thundering on about those un-Christianised heathen filling up hell just a little farcical.

---

man cannot even desire what is good, God has to press this ability on him. Owing to God's free will, it follows that this ability is allotted arbitrarily, and this also, at least apparently, is supported by the Scriptures. – The entire doctrine is based on such pretence of logic; the few who are chosen will, *nolentes, volentes*, be saved, the rest damned for ever. "For ever? – Yes, for ever!!" (Krummacher).' (Engels 1839f, pp. 14–15; Engels 1839g, p. 39.)

30. Engels 1839f, p. 15; Engels 1839g, pp. 39–40.

Now we come across a comment whose brevity conceals a wealth of implications: 'Such doctrines spoil all Krummacher's sermons; the only ones in which they are not so prominent are the passages where he speaks of the contradiction between earthly riches and the humility of Christ, or between the arrogance of earthly rulers and the pride of God. A note of his former demagogy very often breaks through here as well, and if he did not speak in such general terms the government would not pass over his sermons in silence'.[31] Here, the sneaking admiration for Krummacher I noted earlier turns up again, for his sermons would, admits Engels, be rather good if he did not spoil them with such doctrines. In fact, when the doctrines fade into the background and are replaced by other themes, Krummacher's sermons take on a more dangerous political tone. Instead of the damned heathen and the waywardness of other Christian groups, the targets are none other than earthly riches and arrogant rulers. Add a specific reference or two – the Prussian king, for instance, or the owners of capital, or the inherited privileges of the nobility, or the names of a rapacious factory-owner or two – and the political edge of these sermons would have been much sharper. You can see Engels relishing the thought of a government-censor, a provincial governor or the police becoming concerned, asking for copies of the sermons, posting spies in the worship-services, all on the lookout for sedition and insurrection.

What exactly was that earlier demagogy? 'As a student he was involved in the demagogy of the gymnastic associations, composed freedom songs, carried a banner at the Wartburg festival, and delivered a speech which is said to have made a great impression. He still frequently recalls those dashing times from the pulpit, saying: when I was still among the Hittites and Canaanites'.[32] Krummacher may have felt that these days of student-protests and incendiary speeches against monarchist landowners and the Metternich régime (17 October 1819 at the Wartburg Festival) were past him, that they belong to a sinful former life which has been overcome by his conversion. Yet, Engels hints otherwise. Even though he seems to say that there is an unconscious return of this earlier life – Engels speaks of the former demagogy breaking through – he leaves open the possibility that there may in fact be some continuity between the earlier political radical and the later Calvinist preacher.

---

31. Engels 1839f, p. 15; Engels 1839g, p. 40.
32. Engels 1839f, p. 13; Engels 1839g, p. 38.

But that is what one would expect for anyone who follows Calvin to some degree, for there is a comparable tension in Calvin's own thought, especially between what I termed earlier the democracy of depravity and the aristocracy of salvation.

This moment in Engels's 'Letters from Wuppertal' is, as far as I can tell, the first glimmer of an awareness that I have been uncovering in this chapter: the political ambivalence of Christianity itself. It will turn up with greater clarity in later works, such as *The Peasant War in Germany* of 1850 and *On the History of Early Christianity* of 1894. Despite all of the dirty deals between the churches and sundry despots and tyrants throughout the centuries, despite all of the reactionary elements within Christian theology, there was also a current that found a more revolutionary line in the Bible and certain key Christian doctrines. It seems to me that Engels is on the verge of a similar insight here: a radical allegiance to God, especially through a doctrine that stresses the sinfulness of human beings and God's grace, has as one possible outcome a radical political agenda that seeks to overthrow corrupt earthly rulers and their vain desire for wealth and power.

A soft spot for apocalyptic

So far, I have been following a track through Engels's works, one that uncovers a series of texts where he shows some awareness that the Bible and theology are complex political beasts. However, at this point, I would like to pick up another track that will eventually join the first one by the time we get to his essays on Müntzer and early Christianity. In this case it is an abiding fascination with the biblical book of Revelation (*Apocalypse* in Greek). Later in life, Engels wrote an essay on the book,[33] the basic argument of which made it into the early-Christianity essay. More of that later, since here I want to pick up on his earlier seduction by this weird and wonderful text.

The book of Revelation has been an eternal favourite of all manner of Christian movements for a good two millennia, many of them quite revolutionary. Full of the rich imagery of the final battle of good and evil, the beast and the whore of Babylon, the four horsemen and the seven scrolls, the lamb and the new Jerusalem, it remains a rich resource for those who expect an imminent

---

33. Engels 1883.

end to the world, who are oppressed, or who are keen to proclaim themselves prophets and gain a follower or two.[34] As far as I know, none of these reasons count for Engels. In fact, the solid Calvinist upbringing of Engels would not have emphasised this text so much. Suspicious of enthusiasm and millenarian frenzy, they preferred to focus on predestination, the task of the elect, the evils of the damned and matters such as justification by faith through grace. Of course, God would eventually destroy the damned and Jesus would return. But they did not need him to do so now in order to save them from an intolerable situation. Yet resort to the Apocalypse Engels did, especially the theme of the final battle between good and evil in all its gory detail, albeit idiosyncratically.

What catches my eye in these texts is that he uses the book of Revelation in a number of ways – playfully, as critical satire, and as the positive celebration of a new era (in his own life and perhaps of Germany). As for the first use, we find a sustained play with Revelation in two letters to Friedrich Graeber, one from the beginning of his correspondence on 19 February 1839, and the other from the last letter to Friedrich Graeber on 22 February 1841.[35] In the first letter, Engels expresses mock horror at the news that his good friend the pastor actually plays cards. Engels throws a few biblical curses at him and then portrays a vision like that of John the Divine (or for that matter the old prophet Ezekiel).[36] What does he see? It is a great final battle between the King of the Orient, the Prince of the Occident and the Prince of the Sea – a rather more homely version of the battle between the Archangel Michael, the Devil and the Beast of the Sea in Revelation 12–13. Seven spirits appear – modelled on the seven angels of Revelation 8–10 and 14 – but they turn out to be a little more earthly: Faust, Lear, Wallenstein, Hercules, Siegfried, Roland and Mio Cid (with a turban). The whole parody becomes even more complex with

---

34. It could be argued that those responsible for the final biblical canon limited the total number of apocalypses to two – Daniel and Revelation – out of the many available did so to limit speculative fervour. Indeed, Revelation was one of the last books to be included in the New Testament canon.

35. Engels 1839h; Engels 1839i; Engels 1841c; Engels 1841d.

36. 'On the nineteenth day of the second month of 1839, on the day when midday is at twelve o'clock, a storm seized me and carried me afar and there I saw them playing cards' (Engels 1839h, p. 414; Engels 1839i, p. 361) is playfully modelled on the beginning of Ezekiel's vision: 'In the sixth year, in the sixth month, on the fifth day of the month... the spirit lifted me up between earth and heaven and brought me in visions of God to Jerusalem' (Ezekiel 8:1 and 3).

the crisscrossing of Old Testament allusions – the children of Anak,[37] letters on the door in Hebrew[38] and being struck dumb.[39] The point of it all: even though they may have brought the world to an end, nothing will stop the card-players in their evil pastime.

All this is good fun. The second letter is different,[40] for its playfulness is a rather poor camouflage for a more serious tone. Engels and his childhood-friend from Wuppertal have become estranged from the time they began their epistolary debates two years earlier, for now they were taking different theological directions. In a curious intersection, where the apocalyptic battle at the end of the age wraps up a friendship, we return in this letter to the final battle between good and evil, between God and the devil. On one side, stand evil Straussians and Hegelians (the side Engels had joined), while, on the other, are the less-capable orthodox – names we hardly recognise now, such as Tholuck, Hengstenberg, Neander, Nitzsche, Bleek and Erdmann (Friedrich Graeber's preferred theologians). And, yet, despite portents of the great battle – such as the earth's eclipse and the storm raging through the forest – Friedrich has not yet stirred himself for battle with the 'critical-speculative devil' and his enormous following.[41] The problem, it seems, is that Friedrich Graeber has already disengaged from their debates. Engels berates him for his 'calm and detached' writing, as if nothing can stir the calm of his orthodoxy. Engels, on the other hand, wants a battle and Strauss is the super-weapon with which he will knock down Friedrich and any other orthodox champion. But Friedrich, it seems, has already declined the struggle.

We have already slipped from the playful use of the final apocalyptic battle to a more polemical use. The next occasion on which Engels engages Revelation is more fully polemical, and the humour starts to have some bite. It is the long poem which I discussed briefly in the previous chapter, *The Insolently Threatened Yet Miraculously Rescued Bible*.[42] For one who decided to give away his aspirations to be a poet in favour of direct political writing and an increasing fascination with martial matters, it is not too bad. It is a narrative poem

---

37. Numbers 13:33; Deuteronomy 2:10.
38. Daniel 5:5, 24–8.
39. Ezekiel 3:26.
40. Engels 1841c; Engels 1841d.
41. Engels 1841c, p. 527; Engels 1841d, p. 479.
42. Engels 1842c; Engels 1842d.

written with Edgar Bauer, brother of Bruno and member of 'The Free', and its satire owes much to the style of young-Hegelian polemic.

The poem sets a cracking pace and the reader is drawn into the story (or, at least, I was). And that story begins with a Job-like opening (although not without some influence from Goethe) in which Satan slinks his way into heaven, upsets the heavenly chorus and demands access to Bruno Bauer. God asserts that, for all Bauer's research into the Bible, for all his doubts, he still remains faithful and will come through to truth as he sees the flaws of philosophy. The devil is not so sure and secures a chance to test Bauer's faith. Unlike the prologue to the book of Job, Bauer does succumb to Satan, although it takes some persuasion. By the time Bauer begins lecturing again, he is a servant of the devil and sets the pious and atheistic students against one another. All of which eventually leads to a final confrontation between Hegel (who is a confidant of the devil), the young Hegelians and some French *philosophes* such as Voltaire on one side and the pious defenders of the faith, including our friend F.W. Krummacher, on the other. Steeped in terminology from the book of Revelation, this final apocalyptic battle sways back and forth. The young Hegelians build a fortress out of the books they have written, using them as missiles against the attacks of the pious believers. Despite many heroics and pinpoint-accuracy with their projectiles, the young Hegelians fare badly until they dump the weak-kneed devil – he is all talk and no action – and call for reinforcements. Voltaire, Danton, Edelman, Napoleon, Marat and Robespierre appear, Bauer takes charge and they rout the pious, who now flee heavenward. Hegel urges them to attack heaven itself and he leads the charge. But, just as they about to succeed, a small piece of paper floats down, coming to rest at Bauer's feet. Its message: he is redundant, having been sacked from his teaching position. In dismay, the forces of chaos flee and the host of heaven pursue them with glee.

Much more developed than the two letters to Friedrich Graeber, this last great battle of Armageddon is a send-up of the conservative reaction to the challenges of the young Hegelians, some of whom called themselves 'The Free'. Now, while all of this light-hearted play with the Bible may seem relatively innocent, for someone with Engels's upbringing, the very act of making fun of the Bible was potentially blasphemous. For Calvinists, the Bible is serious business. There are – apparently – no jokes to be found within the Bible, and one should in no way joke about it. After all, it deals with matters of life, death, sin, salvation and the future of the universe.[43] So also for Engels: what seems like some harmless joking has a more significant undercurrent of protest.

There is still yet a third use of this biblical apocalyptic material that indicates the complexity of his interactions with the Bible. I think in particular of the closing pages of one of his three pamphlets on Schelling – *Schelling and Revelation*.[44] While most of the text is an effort to report on the content of Schelling's lectures in Berlin in 1841, interspersed with some critical commentary, the closing pages comprise a paean to the new directions of theological and philosophical ideas. Engels had just read Feuerbach's *Das Wesen des Christentums* and it obviously set the adrenalin pumping. The framework is, once again, the book of Revelation: heaven has come down to earth;[45] its treasures lie scattered for whoever wishes to pick them up;[46] the great final battle has been fought and won;[47] the thousand-year reign of freedom has begun.[48] Engels evokes the vast celebration in heaven after the victory of Armageddon: 'And this crown, this bride, this holy thing is the *self-consciousness of mankind*, the new Grail round whose throne the nations gather in exultation and which makes kings of all who submit to it, so that all splendour and might, all dominion and power, all the beauty and fullness of this world lie at their feet and must yield themselves up for their glorification'.[49] As is his wont, Engels draws on other texts in building his picture,[50] but the focus has shifted from his previous apocalyptic visions. Now we are in the millennium, after the great battle, and he looks forward to the unfolding of the new age.[51] Yet there

---

43. I remember once doing something similar to Engels, using the story of the martyrdom of Stephen in the book of Acts in a playful way. My father sternly rebuked me, pointing out that any light-hearted toying with the Bible was a sinful matter.

44. Engels 1842g, pp. 238–40; Engels 1842h, pp. 312–14.

45. Revelation 21:1.

46. Revelation 21:18–21.

47. Revelation 18–19; see also 1 Timothy 6:12.

48. Revelation 20:6.

49. Engels 1842g, p. 239; Engels 1842h, p. 313. Compare Revelation 19–20.

50. They include: renouncing the world (John 12:25; 15:18; and the whole of Chapter 17); what was formerly obscure is now clear (1 Corinthians 13:12); the jewel that was found after a long search (Matthew 13:44–6); giving up everything to follow the truth (Luke 9:57–62); it is stronger than everything in heaven and on earth (Romans 8:35–9); it provides a firm confidence that it can never waver or yield (Hebrews 11:1).

51. See also: 'I hope to live to see a radical transformation in the religious consciousness of the world' (Engels 1839r, p. 456; Engels 1839s, p. 402).

is a twist. It is not some heavenly victory that he celebrates, but a distinctly earthly, human one – all of which is cast in biblical terms.

What are we to make of such a passage? It seems as though his eyes have been opened, that a way out of the stifling conservatism of his youth has now shown itself. We can write this enthusiasm off as youthful exuberance, or perhaps too much beer and fine tobacco (of which he was very fond), but I would like to put in a word for Engels. Over against the world-weary cynicism of age, is there not still room for that sparkle in one's eye at a new discovery, a zeal and enthusiasm that really inspires one?

Engels obviously had a soft spot for the glorious apocalyptic language of the book of Revelation. The youthful Engels uses the book in various ways – to make fun of and attack those who would hold him back, to tease his friend Graeber, and to celebrate his own awakening. So it seems that the terms, images and modes of expression provided a distinct component of the framework of Engels's thought, indeed of his way of understanding his own changing place in the world. Eventually, Revelation will become a major feature of his argument for the revolutionary origins of Christianity, especially because he came to regard it as the earliest Christian text.

I will have more to say on that soon enough, but, for now, there are two questions with which I want to close this section. Firstly, is this the origin of the infamous secular apocalypticism of Marxism? I have already argued that Marx did not pick it up from Bauer when he studied Isaiah with Bauer at university in Berlin. What of Engels? The point has gained authority through endless repetition: the Marxist narrative of the end of capitalism through revolution and the beginning of the new social formation of communism is but a secularised version of the Christian-apocalyptic myth of the end of the world. It is nothing less than another version of Armageddon. Detractors and believers continue to make the same point. I am not so sure. For one thing, Engels's explicit use of apocalyptic language peters out by the time of *The Holy Family*, where he uses it in a satirical way to speak of Bauer and Stirner.[52] Further, in

---

52. See the section entitled 'The Critical Last Judgment' (Marx and Engels 1845a, pp. 210–11; Marx and Engels 1845b, pp. 222–3). The other samples come from early pieces, such as the account of the struggle between the Hegelian Michelet and the pious Leo (Engels 1839l, pp. 435–7; Engels 1839m, pp. 380–3), the street-fight between the supporters of the two ministers in Bremen, Krummacher and Paniel (Engels 1840u; Engels 1840v), and his anticipation concerning the overcoming of Hegel (Engels 1844n, p. 13; Engels 1844o, p. 13). He also makes use of the same language laced with biblical

later life, especially in light of the parliamentary success of the German Social Democrats, Engels became more wary of insurrection. It still has a valid rôle to play, but, in his later letters, there are more cautions against untimely acts that would provide the authorities with an excuse to crush all forms of the Left. His own bitter experience in the revolutions of 1848–50 made him think deeply on these matters.

Above all, there is a marked change in his approach to the book of Revelation. Instead of manifesting itself in an apocalyptic Marxism, Engels's interest in Revelation follows another line, one that would eventually contribute to his argument that early Christianity was a revolutionary movement that was co-opted by the Roman Empire. Even more, that revolutionary origin would show up again and again through history, most notably with Thomas Müntzer. However, that line takes an enthralling detour through his new-found skill in war-correspondence.

Engels's fascination with grand battles goes straight into his love of military analysis and journalism. As anyone who has taken the time to work through these pieces soon finds out, Engels penned numerous articles on battles, campaigns, the nature of armies across Europe, strategies, tactics, equipment, uniforms and so on.[53] These are rather well written, clear and engaging, with the occasional reference to the Bible such as Numbers 1:2 and the construction of the camp of the Israelites in the wilderness after their escape from Egypt, or

---

quotations and allusions to blast the close ties between the German nobility and an arrogant Roman-Catholic Church (Engels 1840m, pp. 66–7; Engels 1840n, pp. 98–9). Only passing allusions turn up in later works (see Engels 1871b, p. 376; Engels 1871c, p. 382; Engels 1852a, p. 7; Engels 1852b, p. 474).

53. I will not list them all here since there are scores of them beginning with Volume 11 of *MECW* (as also with *MEW* Volume 11, although with fewer items). They run through assessments of the revolutions of 1848–9, the Crimean War, the Franco-German War, the Indian uprising against the British and so on. A great cluster appears in Volume 18 with articles on 'Attack', 'Bayonet', 'Army', 'Bivouac' and many more for *The New American Cyclopaedia*. My favourites are the pieces on 'Cavalry', 'Infantry' and, above all, 'The History of the Rifle' (Engels 1860), written for the journal with the fantastic name of *The Volunteer Journal, for Lancashire and Cheshire*. Engels also wrote extensively on the connections between social relations and the nature of the army, pointing out that the nature of the military is a good indicator of the nature of social relations. He pushed for a militia as the best form for communist society, argued for the vital rôle of guerrilla-warfare and even saw the value of the clergy becoming involved in such militias and guerrilla-warfare (see Engels 1870j, pp. 198–200).

the fact that the Romans used 300 catapults in the siege of Jerusalem in 68–70 CE, or the allusion to the walls of Jericho in Joshua 6:20 and the siege of Paris in 1870.[54] I found myself enjoying his first articles on the Hungarian Revolution and the way Engels is able to cut through to the key tactical issues. I began to look forward to his next dispatch analysing the Crimean War or the Franco-Prussian War of 1870–1. He had found a distinct niche. That period of voluntary military training in Berlin with the Twelfth Foot Company of the Guards Artillery Brigade in 1842 seems to have borne some intriguing fruit. No wonder he volunteered to join the revolutionary armies of Elberfeld and Barmen in 1848 (however short his stay might have been) and then the armies of the revolutionary movement in the Palatinate and Baden.

This military interest is one of the developments of that early fascination with the biblical apocalyptic. In those texts on military matters, he developed theories concerning the reorganisation of revolutionary armies. This is where we find him arguing that a revolutionary who neglects the state and discipline of his army does so at his peril, that the nature of the military is a good sign of the nature of class and social formation in a society at large, that any revolutionary act requires swift and bold action along with a good army, and that the ideal form for the army is a militia drawn from the whole population. No wonder his nickname became 'the General'. But then even this general later found a place for peaceful agitation, since untimely violent uprising bred violent repression.

This, then, is the detour that Engels's early interest in the apocalyptic texts of the Bible took before he came to reflect on revolutionary movements in Christianity. His interest in the details of military organisation, tactics and battle-plans would soon join the path I have followed earlier – the insight concerning the tension between the revolutionary and reactionary elements of Christianity. Together they brought him to Thomas Müntzer and the Peasants' Revolution.

---

54. Engels 1859a, p. 263; Engels 1859b; Engels 1870f, p. 73. Of course, there are more: '"Providence always is on the side of the big battalions" was a favourite way of *the* Napoleon to explain how battles were won and lost.' (Engels 1870c, p. 104.)

On Thomas Müntzer and the peasants

In *The Peasant War in Germany*,[55] 'the General' offered what is the first thorough historical-materialist analysis of both the Protestant Reformation and its more radical outcome in Thomas Müntzer and the Peasant-War of the sixteenth century. Although the work would continue to resonate through the later studies of Karl Kautsky and Ernst Bloch,[56] it is not Engels's best piece of work.

The immediate context (it was written and published in 1850) was the failed revolution of 1848–50. After his frontline-involvement in that revolution, especially in the Palatinate and Baden, a short stop in his old hometown of Elberfeld, and then his escape to Switzerland, Engels sits back and ponders what went wrong. There was plenty of contemporary analysis underway, so he makes the bold move of looking back some three centuries at an earlier revolution. In doing so, he takes the first step towards identifying a tradition of revolution in which the communists stand as the most recent exemplars. This is a delicate move, since Engels is all too aware that those earlier revolutions were inspired by the insurrectionary texts of the Bible. The advantage clearly lay in showing that the communists were not the new kids on the block, touting some new-fangled theory and practice that undermined the good old tradition. No, suggests Engels, for we have breathed life into the age-old aspirations of the downtrodden.[57] The disadvantage is that such a move would undermine the determined efforts Marx and Engels had made to separate themselves from the theological trappings of earlier expressions of communism, which, as they put it in the *Manifesto*, was nothing 'but the holy water with which the priest consecrates the heart-burnings of the aristocrat'.[58] So, let us see how he navigates between this Scylla and Charybdis.

I am less interested in the treatment of earlier peasant-uprisings, except to point out that it reinforces the sense of a longer tradition of religiously inspired revolution. What Engels does is offer a neat class-analysis, suggest parallels between the Peasant-War of 1525 and the European revolutions of 1848–50

---

55. Engels 1850f; Engels 1850g. There were some earlier hints that Engels would take up the topic at a later date, especially the long comment on Luther and Müntzer in 'Progress of Social Reform on the Continent' (Engels 1843e, pp. 400–1). See also Engels 1880a, p. 287; Engels 1880b, p. 191; Engels 1884c; Engels 1884d.
56. Kautsky 1947c, pp. 7–103; Bloch 1969.
57. In an excellent couple of essays, John Roberts calls this 'invariant communism'. See Roberts 2008a, 2008b.
58. Marx and Engels 1848v, p. 508; Marx and Engels 1848w, p. 484.

(although his final paragraph mentions a few differences),[59] draw out lessons for revolutionary practice, and assess the relationship between Müntzer's theology and politics. The essay is, as we would expect from Engels, exceedingly well-structured. Most notable on this score is the chiasm between the class-assessments – of princes, nobility, clergy, burghers, plebeians and peasants – of the opening pages and then the outline of the effects of the war on those classes in the conclusion. At times, I felt it all a little too neat, especially when we get to Luther, who ends up representing the desires of burgher-reform and like-minded princes, and Müntzer, who is the voice of radical peasants, plebeians and nascent proletarians (the other group is Roman-Catholic reaction). At certain moments, I began wishing for some more complexity, analysis of class-traitors and the shifts and overlaps between the different classes.

The closest we come is when Engels notes the change in Luther's rhetoric and practice. The stormy and belligerent Augustinian monk of peasant-background began as a fiery opponent of the church and its vested interests. But, notwithstanding his early condemnations of the church and revolutionary zeal – which sparked a united front of disaffected peasants, plebeians, burghers, lesser nobility and even some princes – he soon enough sided with the burghers, nobility and princes, his true allies. So, he toned down his fervour, advocated peaceful reform and came down hard on more extreme elements. For Engels, this was the true Luther, the one who ended up being a champion of the burgher-church when his position gained some clarity. His earlier announcements with their revolutionary tinge were the signs of a man who was as yet unclear about his programme. What Luther's shift really entailed was that he fell under the sway of the princes, whose lackey he became. No wonder he came out so hard against the Peasant-Revolt.

What is lacking in this analysis is a sense of the complexity of theology. In effect, Luther had rediscovered a profound tension at the heart of Christian theology, a tension I have discussed earlier. We do not find that the Bible and theology are squarely with the oppressors and powers-that-be, nor do we find it gives voice solely to the aspirations of the downtrodden. Rather, in that vast mix of literature and thought, we find both. Even more, the stories of rebellion are often cast in terms of sin and rebellion, which must be punished by a

---

59. See the more extensive and updated effort at making parallels and drawing out lessons in the Preface to the second edition (Engels 1870h; Engels 1870i).

stern God or some sundry megalomaniac (such as Moses or David or Paul). In other words, it is well-nigh impossible to separate reaction from revolution, support of entrenched power or desires for its overthrow. Luther plays with both, invoking the rebellious parts at one moment and then those that support order and control at another. Perhaps we can view it in this way: Luther glimpsed the radical possibilities of the Bible only to take fright at what he had unleashed. So, he backtracked and disavowed his more radical statements as time went on. Engels's interpretation is less dialectical than it might have been, but then Luther seems not to have enjoyed the ambivalence he exposed in the Bible either.

When Engels turns to Müntzer, he moves into overdrive: he tries to claim Müntzer as a great revolutionary and forerunner of modern socialism while trying to play down the theological roots of Müntzer's politics. In short, Engels wants the revolutionary but not the theologian. I am afraid that he does not do a very good job, resorting to some dubious arguments. The first is that Müntzer clothed his political statements in biblical language, the only language the peasants knew: 'the class-struggles of those days were clothed in religious shibboleths'.[60] All we need to do is strip off the theological garments and find the pure terms of political revolution beneath. Those terms turn out to constitute an anticipation of the programme for the emancipation for the proletariat, a class that was barely emergent in Müntzer's own time. It was radically egalitarian, advocated communal property, abolished private property, and any state-authority that dared oppose it was to be overthrown. Decoded, this is what Müntzer's biblical talk meant: 'This programme demanded the immediate establishment of the kingdom of God on Earth, of the prophesied millennium, by restoring the church to its original status and abolishing all the institutions that conflicted with the purportedly early Christian but in fact very novel church. By the kingdom of God Müntzer meant a society with no class differences, no private property and no state authority independent of, and foreign to, the members of society'.[61] Müntzer was really an atheist deep

---

60. Engels 1850f, p. 412; Engels 1850g, p. 343.
61. Engels 1850f, p. 422; Engels 1850g, pp. 353–4. Marx was not averse to making a similar point concerning the religious language of political movements. For example, he comments that the revolutionary stirrings of the Taipings in China to overthrow a 300-year-old dynasty have a 'religious tinge' (Marx 1862c, p. 216; Marx 1862d, p. 514). See also Marx's comment on Engels's essay (Marx 1856h, p. 21; Marx 1856i, p. 25).

down, or at least he 'approached atheism'.[62] The closer he came to atheism, the closer he came to the ranks of communists in Engels's own day. And Müntzer needed to do so because the church provided the great synthesis and sanction of the feudal order. Engels argues that Müntzer rejected the Bible as the only revelation and argued for the value of reason, that he discarded heaven and earth and denied the divinity of Christ, that his true doctrine was a kind of pantheism, that man can become godlike, and that the kingdom of God was to be established here on earth. Not a bad summary of the beliefs of the young Engels when he was first extricating himself from his Christian commitment. Unfortunately, it is difficult to establish such positions on the basis of Müntzer's writings without some creative reinterpretation.[63] What we find instead is a man who cannot be understood without the Bible, was deeply involved in liturgical reform (he wrote a full liturgy well before Luther), and who believed in the immediate inspiration of the Holy Spirit, which communicated with Müntzer in visions and dreams. These days, we tend to put such a person in an asylum; in those days, he was a radical prophet.

The second argument is that Müntzer operated at two levels, one for the people and another for the inner circle. The former he 'addressed in the only language they could then comprehend, that of religious prophecy', while to the initiated 'he could disclose his ultimate aims'.[64] Unfortunately, this is pure speculation, since all we have are Müntzer's writings and the material from his opponents (who accused him of being from the devil, if not the devil himself). Those texts say nothing about an inner circle of initiates who were told the true, atheistic and revolutionary nature of his teachings. Equally unfortunately, it is a motif that echoes the picture of Jesus in the Gospel of Mark, where he tells the inner group of disciples that everyone else hears things only in parables, but they are given the truth.

Both arguments are less than persuasive, involving a great deal of twisting and turning to claim Müntzer as precursor to the nineteenth-century communist movement. However, there is one moment when Engels does mention the political ambivalence at the heart of Christianity. On Luther's Bible he writes:

---

62. Engels 1850f, p. 421; Engels 1850g; p. 353.
63. Müntzer 1988.
64. Engels 1850f, p. 426; Engels 1850g, p. 357.

> Luther had put a powerful tool into the hands of the plebeian movement by translating the Bible. Through the Bible he contrasted the feudalised Christianity of his day with the moderate Christianity of the first centuries, and the decaying feudal society with a picture of a society that knew nothing of the ramified and artificial feudal hierarchy. The peasants had made extensive use of this instrument against the princes, the nobility, and the clergy. Now Luther turned it against the peasants, extracting from the Bible such a veritable hymn to the God-ordained authorities as no bootlicker of absolute monarchy had ever been able to match.[65]

Engels's intention is to show how Luther betrayed the peasants, but, in the process, he lays bare, despite himself, the multivocality of the Bible. As Ernst Bloch was to show all too well,[66] the Bible has been inspiration for one insurrectionary movement after another just as much as it has provided ammunition for those sought to suppress those movements. Both Luther and Müntzer were able to use it perfectly well to justify their positions. What is needed, then, is not a denial of that biblical language as a whole, but an awareness that one must take sides with a text like this. Do we support the vested powers or do we support those who in story after story seek a better world without those powers?

The opening sentence in the quotation above is telling for another reason: 'Luther had put a powerful tool into the hands of the plebeian movement by translating the Bible'. In other words, part of the reason for the revolts lies at Luther's feet. Once again, Engels says more than he apparently intends. Elsewhere, he is keen to tie Luther in with the burghers and princes and to show that Müntzer was a radical agitator from the moment he first entered public life. It is convenient for Engels's argument, but fails to appreciate that it was Luther who first fired up Müntzer's imagination and anger. In other words, Luther's own teaching and practice set Müntzer on his radical path. I would argue that Müntzer carried to its logical end one side of the political ambivalence Luther himself had discovered and then sought to close down.

Thus we need to read between the lines a little to find some of the more interesting elements of Engels's analysis. The more obviously better parts are those which trace the battle-plans and manœuvres. The long sections on the

---

65. Engels 1850f, p. 419; Engels 1850g, pp. 350–1.
66. Bloch 1972; Bloch 1970; see also Boer 2007a, pp. 1–56.

formation of the peasant-troops, their number of cannon, level of discipline, and on battle-manœuvres give a sense of how well-organised the peasants were. There are also the sections that outline the key-elements of revolutionary activity. To be sure, they are drawn from a somewhat dubious reconstruction of Müntzer's practice, but they stand alone. The key-lesson remains – a need for bold and decisive action and a need for a good army to defend the gains made. All the same, Engels would offer better arguments elsewhere for the earlier heritage of communism. The great achievement of this text is that he made the first step in connecting the communists of his own day with a rich heritage of rebellion and revolution. He would do a superior job in making that connection in his work on early Christianity.

Early Christianity

Although he had been thinking about it for many years (since 1841!), *On the History of Early Christianity* appeared months before Engels died and may well be seen as the final coming to terms with his Christian past.[67] It has also had an abiding influence on New Testament scholarship, especially the argument that the early church appealed to the lower classes of Roman society. It is really the mature form of an argument with which Engels had been toying for years, namely that Christianity began as a revolutionary force. He also carries

---

67. On 28 July 1894, Engels wrote to Kautsky: 'There is no hurry about printing the article. Once I have seen to the proofs you can print it when you wish, in September, say, or even October. I have been mulling over the thing ever since 1841 when I read a lecture by F. Benary on *Revelation*. Since then I have been in no doubt that here we have the earliest and most important book in the New Testament. After a gestation period of fifty-three years there is no great need to hasten its emergence into the world at large.' (Engels 1894e, pp. 328–9; Engels 1894f, p. 276.) He also sent regular updates to Kautsky, who published it in *Neue Zeit* (Engels 1894a, p. 314; Engels 1894b; Engels 1894c, p. 321; Engels 1894d, p. 268). Kautsky and Engels entered into extensive correspondence over matters of the Bible and Christianity. See, for example, Engels 1891k, p. 200; Engels 1891l, p. 114; Engels 1892d; Engels 1892e; Engels 1891e, p. 174; Engels 1891f, p. 88; Engels 1892f, pp. 493–4; Engels 1892g, pp. 422–3. In a letter of 1 February 1892, Engels suggests that Kaustky should write a book on Luther that argues in terms of a bourgeois movement. The idea was to offer a perspective other than Protestant and Roman-Catholic polemic, to compare the nature of the bourgeoisie before and after 1848 and Luther before and after Karlstad when he faced-off against Anabaptists and the Peasants' Revolution. One gains the sense that had Engels the time he would have written it himself, but was passing on the baton – on religion at least – to Kautsky (Engels 1892d; Engels 1892e). See also the comments to Adler and Bebel (Engels 1892h, p. 501; Engels 1892i, p. 431; Engels 1892j, p. 503; Engels 1892k, p. 434).

on a fascinating comparative exercise with the communist movement in his own day, drawing one parallel after another.

However, let me begin with a curious feature about this essay that takes us all the way back to Engels's early enthralment with apocalypticism: the final pages deal with the book of Revelation. It may be exactly the same biblical text, but the way he uses it is vastly different. Basing his research on some contemporary biblical scholarship, especially that of Ferdinand Benary of the University of Berlin and Bruno Bauer, Engels argues that Revelation is the earliest Christian document. Now he can use it as a purely historical source, mining it for information about the beliefs and practices of the early Christians. Above all, he seeks to decode it and show that all those who use it for speculation about the end of history are simply misguided. Yet these arguments are expanded from an essay he wrote and published eleven years earlier called simply 'The Book of Revelation'.[68] So let us have a look at this earlier text.

Published in 1883 in *Vorwärts*, Engels seeks to introduce the still relatively new German critical approach to the New Testament.[69] Today, it goes by the name of historical criticism, for its two main drives are to reconstruct the history of the literature of the Bible as well as the history behind it. And, today, it is a tired orthodoxy, zealously defended by a dwindling number of practitioners. In Engels's day, it had a radical freshness, since it undermined many of the traditional positions regarding the Bible held by the churches. All the same, he is after the most critical work of all, bypassing those who sought to reconcile historical criticism with religious belief. So he settles on the work of none other than Bruno Bauer.[70]

For some strange reason, he does not mention Bauer in the essay on Revelation. Part of the reason was that the year before (1882) he had written a piece called 'Bruno Bauer and Early Christianity'. Written on the occasion of

---

68. Engels 1883.

69. For all the work done in New Testament criticism at the time, Engels laments in an early piece – an analysis of Karl Gutzkow's play *König Saul* (Engels 1840e, pp. 73–80; Engels 1840f, pp. 87–94) – that similar work has not been done on the Hebrew Bible with a figure such as King Saul.

70. Engels's relationship with Bauer moves in the reverse to Marx's. While Marx gradually became estranged from his one-time friend, Engels moved from satire and dismissal to a deep appreciation of Bauer's contribution to biblical and philosophical thought.

Bauer's death, it is an appreciative essay that goes to great lengths to show how the form of Christianity that has come down to us has little, if anything, to do with its earliest forms. Of course, once you have taken such a position, the next step is to account for that well-known final form. Following Bauer, Engels argues that what we know as Christianity now is the result of a combination of vulgar and popularised versions of the neo-Platonism of Philo of Alexandria, Seneca's stoicism and Roman Imperial beliefs about the emperor as son of God. But why did Christianity catch on? Here, Engels moves beyond Bauer to offer a materialist analysis spiced with some Darwinian observations: the class-structure of the Roman Empire (the rich, including the last few patricians, property-less freemen and slaves) along with crumbling cultural and religious options opened the way for a system of belief that answered one's despair by offering an other-worldly solution that was open to anyone and everyone. It was a case of survival of the fittest. By contrast, what lay behind all of this, back at the earliest moment, was very different.

Now, all three essays converge, for Engels takes up Bauer's argument that Revelation is the best window into early Christianity. Assuming a date of composition between late 68 and early 69 CE, it presents a group of Jews (not Christians) who believed the end would come soon. There is no Trinity, for Jesus is subordinate to God, and certainly no Holy Spirit. There is no doctrine of original sin, no baptism or sacrament of communion, no justification by faith, and no elaborate story of the death and resurrection of Christ. And there is no religion of love, for the author preaches 'sound, honest revenge' on their persecutors.[71] The author is unknown (certainly not the legendary disciple by the name of John) and all of the 'visions' find precursors in the Hebrew Bible and other apocalyptic documents that preceded it. As a conclusion, Engels recounts a theory by Ferdinand Benary that the infamous number 666 (or 616 in a textual variant) can easily be deciphered through some deft playing with numbers: given that Hebrew used letters of the alphabet for numbers, all we need do is add up the value of *Neron Kesar* (Greek: *Neron Kaisar*) and we have 666. So Revelation predicts the end of the 'beast', Nero, at the hand of God and ushers in the new age.

How has Engels's reconstruction stood the test of time? It is easy to dismiss it as reliant on out-of-date scholarship, that Bauer was too extreme in his

---

71. Engels 1894–5c, p. 462; Engels 1894–5d, p. 465.

scepticism and that Benary's numerical theory is implausible. We can hardly blame Engels for using the biblical scholarship available at the time. Nor can we accuse him of complete ignorance of biblical criticism, for he recounts at greater length in the early-Christianity essay the positions of the dominant Tübingen school (Ferdinand Christian Bauer, Heinrich Ewald, Friedrich Lücke et al.), where Strauss also began, and the popularising work of Ernst Renan.[72] I would be in a similar situation if someone a century from now were to read a position I take today in relation to contemporary biblical scholarship, especially if I were dependent on that scholarship rather than developing my own position. The strange thing is that the underlying assumptions of Bauer's work – and thereby that of Engels – are the same in the historical-critical scholarship of the Bible today (which no longer has the hegemony it once had). The tides of some forms of scholarship may come and go, but the basic assumptions remain unchanged. One must be very careful with using the Bible for any historical reconstruction, since it is unreliable to some degree (Engels actually opts for a median position between Bauer's scepticism and the Tübingen school's optimism regarding reliability); the overwhelming concern is with origins, whether that of early Christianity or early Israel; archaeology plays a crucial rôle, since it provides evidence external to the text; and one spends an inordinate amount of energy discussing authorship and dates, which, like the fashion in skirts, can go in only one of two directions – up or down. Engels, Bauer, the Tübingen school and historical-critical scholars today all share the same assumptions. Further, some of Bauer's concerns are still very much alive in biblical criticism, such as the influence of stoicism and the relation with Philo.[73] His argument that the letters of Paul predate the Gospels, which come from the second century CE, still holds water, although his theory on Revelation as the earliest document has little credibility. However, his radical scepticism has returned to biblical scholarship, especially through the so-called 'minimalist school' which finds little that is historically reliable in the texts of the Hebrew Bible or the New Testament concerning Jesus.[74]

---

72. Engels is not overly keen on Renan, since he feels that Renan borrowed and distorted German biblical scholarship. See also the short review of Renan's *The Antichrist* (Engels 1873a).
73. For example, see Engberg-Pedersen 2000; Lee 2006; Winter (ed.) 1997; Loader 2004.
74. Lemche 1988, 1998a, 1998b; Thompson 1992, 1999, 2005; Davies 1995, 1998, 2008, 2009; Price 2000; Zindler 2003.

As for Engels's long interest in the book of Revelation, these later studies seem like a complete turnaround. Once he took up and often mocked the speculation concerning the Last Judgement, but, now, the book is useful as a window into the earliest form of Christianity. As he puts it at the close of his essay on Revelation, 'All this has now lost its interest, except for ignorant persons who may still try to calculate the day of the last judgement'.[75] He may no longer estimate the Day of Judgement, but he certainly has not lost his interest. There is also something deeply reformed about this exercise. Luther and Calvin claimed to be restoring the purity of the early church over against its corruption and accretion of apparently pagan elements. It is as though Engels is saying, if you really want to recover the early church, here it is!

Some of the details of Engels's reconstruction may not have grabbed the imagination, but there is one item in all these essays that remains very much part of current debate: the appeal of Christianity to the lower classes, especially slaves. The argument actually undergoes a shift across the three essays. In the first essay, he draws it directly from Bauer, who argued that a part of Christianity's appeal lay in its reversal, for it despised wealth, power and privilege, seeking its disciples among the rejected – the poor and slaves.[76] The catch is that the religion which made such an appeal was, for Bauer, the fully-fledged form of Christianity with all of its borrowed and blended pieces from Philo and stoicism. By contrast, when we turn to the essay on Revelation, Engels shifts ground, arguing that this appeal to the lower classes was actually a feature of earliest Christianity, before all the accretions. In other words, it is what he finds in the picture depicted by the book of Revelation. He would hold the same line in the third essay: 'Christianity was originally a movement of oppressed people: it first appeared as the religion of slaves and freedmen, of poor people deprived of all rights, of peoples subjugated or dispersed by Rome'.[77] Apart from a few general comments about the effect of Roman imperialism, which he argues crushed older social structures of clan and polis, imposed a new juridical system, exacted punishing tribute, and exacerbated the hopeless state of the vast majority of slaves, impoverished peasants and

---

75. Engels 1883, p. 117.
76. Engels 1882a, p. 429; Engels 1882b, p. 299.
77. Engels 1894–5c, p. 447; Engels 1894–5d, p. 449.

desperate urban freemen, there is relatively scarce attention given to the details of this crucial point.

Despite this scarcity, it is the point that has stuck. In fact, Engels is also the source of the idea in New Testament studies and church-history, especially in terms of class-analysis rather than the dominance of ideas such as despising the rich (Bauer's position). Mediated and elaborated by Luxemburg and Kautsky, by the early-twentieth century this had become the consensus-position among New Testament scholars[78] and sociologists,[79] holding sway until the 1960s. From then on, however, reaction set in and more conservative scholars reclaimed the older argument that predates Engels: Christianity drew its membership from the middle- and upper-strata of Roman society.[80] The problem with either position is that there is there is no conclusive evidence – not an uncommon problem in biblical criticism.

So how does Engels reach the position that the early Christianity of Revelation appealed to the lower classes? He cannot rely on direct evidence, since there is very little outside the notoriously unreliable documents from the time. Nor does he draw on any other literature, mainly because it is his own proposal. It comes from an audacious exercise in comparison. Like his essay on the Peasant-Revolt, Engels sets out to show that early Christianity and the communist movement have multiple parallels. They both appeal to the oppressed classes, they both suffer from sectarian squabbles and endless splits, they have countless false prophets who arise and lead people astray, they suffer from a tension between ascetic self-denial and libertinage, they also suffer from persecution and ostracism, and they both hope for a better world that keeps them struggling despite numerous setbacks. Indeed, Engels and Marx were given to making such comparisons, often in relation to various opponents and sectarian tendencies in the communist movement. There are myriad comments in this vein scattered through their works on Proudhon,

---

78. See, for instance, Deissman 1978, 1929.
79. See Troeltsch 1992.
80. See the work of the 'rational-choice' theorist, Rodney Stark (Stark 1996, pp. 29–48). For a critique of the whole 'rational-choice' approach, see Goldstein (ed.) 2006.

Bakunin, Mazzini and many others.[81] As Marx put it in a comment on Lassalle, 'In fact, every sect is religious'.[82]

This comparative exercise is the underlying theme of the essay on early Christianity. For example, just as the author, 'Paul', of the Second Letter to the Corinthians complains that contributions are not coming in, so also with the International: 'How many of the most zealous propagandists of the sixties would squeeze the hand of the author that epistle, whoever he may be, and whisper: "So it was like that with you too!"' When he turns to the book of Revelation, he picks up on the fictional letters to the seven churches in its opening chapters as evidence of sectarian splits – so also with the workers' movement, with its warring factions of Weitling communists, Proudhonists, Blanquists, the German Workers' Party and the Bakuninists.[83] Revelation shows us that such splits are but the sign of an immature revolutionary movement. And on they go.

There are simply too many parallels for Engels to avoid the inevitable conclusion that Christianity was originally a revolutionary movement. As he puts it succinctly in a text written at about the same time:

---

81. So Engels wrote to Bebel: 'Incidentally, old man Hegel said long ago: A party proves itself victorious by *splitting* and being able to stand the split. The movement of the proletariat necessarily passes through different stages of development; at every stage part of the people get stuck and do not participate in the further advance; and this in itself is sufficient to explain why the "solidarity of the proletariat", in fact, everywhere takes the form of different party groupings, which carry on life-and-death feuds with one another, as the Christian sects in the Roman Empire did amidst the worst persecutions' (Engels 1873g, p. 514; Engels 1873h, p. 591.) See also Engels 1846i; Engels 1846j; Engels 1872–3a, pp. 323, 331, 371, 378, 391; Engels 1872–3b, pp. 219, 227, 267, 274, 286; Engels 1872e; Engels 1872f; Engels 1869d, p. 382; Engels 1869e, p. 400; Engels 1872g; Engels 1872h; Engels 1885a, pp. 316–20, 325; Engels 1885b, pp. 210–14, 219; Engels 1882k, p. 278–9; Engels 1882l, pp. 332–3; Engels 1892f; Engels 1892g; Engels 1887a, p. 74; Engels 1887b, p. 669; Engels 1887e; Engels 1887f; Engels 1888a; Engels 1888b; Engels 1887c; Engels 1887d; Engels 1891i, p. 193; Engels 1891j, p. 107; Engels 1889b, p. 313; Engels 1889c, pp. 202–3; Engels 1891g, p. 186; Engels 1891h, p. 101; Marx and Engels 1850c, pp. 528–32; Marx and Engels 1850d, pp. 459–63; Marx 1858c; Marx 1873a, p. 397; Marx 1873b, p. 304; Marx 1869n, p. 326; Marx 1869o, p. 343; Marx 1860h, p. 85; Marx 1860i, pp. 492–3; Marx and Engels 1873a, pp. 470, 498–9, 503–4, 519, 522, 525–6, 553–4; Marx and Engels 1873b, pp. 346, 376–7, 382–3, 400, 403, 407, 437–8. Engels also likes to play up the persecution of the branches of the International, especially at the hands of the police and authorities – see Engels 1872c, p. 64; Engels 1872d, p. 475.

82. Marx 1868h, p. 133; Marx 1868i, p. 569.

83. Engels 1894–5c, p. 449; Engels 1894–5d, p. 453.

> It is now, almost to the year, sixteen centuries since a dangerous party of overthrow was likewise active in the Roman empire. It undermined religion and all the foundations of the state; it flatly denied that Caesar's will was the supreme law; it was without a fatherland, was international; it spread over the whole empire, from Gaul to Asia, and beyond the frontiers of the empire. It had long carried on seditious activities underground in secret; for a considerable time, however, it had felt itself strong enough to come out into the open. This party of overthrow, which was known by the name of Christians...[84]

In a comparable oppressive economic situation, where class-conflict is rife, both movements sprang up not because of great leaders or prophets but because of the masses. No wonder, then, that the revolutionary movements before the socialists arrived on the scene were invariably Christian, at least if one restricts the sample-pool to Europe. Finally, Engels has an answer to Müntzer and the Peasant-Revolt: it was but one instance of a common phenomenon that began with early Christianity.

Before we dismiss Engels's extensive exercise in comparison, I should point out that it is rife today. It seems that every second book dealing with the New Testament has 'empire' somewhere in the title.[85] These works seek not merely to situate the New Testament within the Roman Empire, a somewhat obvious point that is a response to the earlier emphasis on its deeply Jewish nature, but they also argue that these texts are anti-imperial documents. Or, at least, one can find a consistent anti-imperial theme running through them. Invariably, the comparison is made with our own times, whether it is the imperialism of the United States, or the global ravages of transnational corporations or the profound difference between the majority of impoverished peoples of the world and the small number of the obscenely rich. While all of this is salutary, I cannot help but wonder whether it loses touch with the political tensions in the Bible, tensions between power and insurrection that I have mentioned already a few times. Most of these studies call for some fundamental economic change, but few, if any, espouse a revolutionary agenda. However,

---

84. Engels 1894–5a, p. 523; Engels 1894–5b, p. 526. See also Marx 1881c, p. 67; Marx 1881d, p. 161.
85. Horsley 2000, 2002, 2003; Horsley (ed.) 2008; Elliott 1994, 2000; Carter 2001, 2006.

we do find in much of this New Testament scholarship an item that Engels studiously avoids – a revolutionary Jesus. This idea simply will not go away: the opposition we find in the Gospels to wealth, power, and vested clerical privilege returns again and again to inspire one guerrilla after another. Not a few liberation-theologians have heard the call to arms and joined a guerrilla-group. Ernst Bloch was also keen on the idea, but I must admit to being a little sceptical for the simple reason that it is well-nigh impossible to come up with any viable historical Jesus, no matter how many have tried.

Finally, Engels faces a problem, one that we first met in the study on the Peasant-Revolt. Does Christianity provide a motive force for revolution-ary movements? In other words, can an ideological system become a cause for political action? Here, he equivocates. On the one hand, he reiterates his argument from the study of the Peasant-Revolt: Christianity was a cloak for political and economic agitation, providing in a theological *lingua franca* the common aspirations of people before science and materialist socialism. The impetus for revolution came not from Christianity itself but from oppres-sive social conditions. With socialism, the time has come to shed that cloak and speak of the real causes. However, in the essay on early Christianity he argues that Christianity offered a heavenly answer to intolerable conditions: one could look to salvation in an afterlife as an antidote to present suffering. Socialism differs, for it offers a solution in this world.

On the other hand, Engels also toys with the possibility that a system of ideas, beliefs and even myths can influence the way people act. As Georges Sorel argued, such a system is told in narratives (he called them myths) in order to motivate people, to give them hope that things will improve, and to incite them to perseverance in the face of innumerable setbacks.[86] This theme also runs through Engels's study of early Christianity. It seems to me that it is a more dialectical approach to the interaction of theory and praxis, for the beliefs people develop and the narratives they tell are as much a response to pressing social and economic problems as they are reasons for changing it. Does not the revolutionary theory of historical materialism also play such a rôle, at least in part? Of course, such beliefs, narratives and myths never appear in a vacuum, for they are connected in complex ways with social and political movements.

---

86. Sorel 1961.

Conclusion

I have followed a long trail, all the way from Engels's ambivalence over the reactionary and revolutionary elements of Christianity, through his awareness of a tension in his old preacher, F.W. Krummacher, through his lifelong and shifting concern with the last book of the Christian Bible, to his arguments for the revolutionary credentials of Thomas Müntzer and then early Christianity itself, the latter better argued than the former. I suggested that his last essay, written close to his death, is really Engels's effort to come to terms with his Christian past. But the most viable point in all of this is the political ambivalence – between reaction and revolution – at the centre of Christian thought and practice.

Conclusion

> Religious Question: To be left to the initiative of the French.[1]

> As you see, I am as tormented as Job, though not as god-fearing.[2]

> In the words of our old friend Jesus Christ, we must be as innocent as doves and wise as serpents.[3]

In the intense period of time during which I wrote this book, I have become quite intimate with Marx and Engels. In the process, I feel as though the General, Mohr and even Jenny and the girls have become part of the clan. Yet, my task here is not to summarise the arguments of the book. After all, there is a decent summary of each chapter in the Introduction. Alongside the critical commentary, my agenda has been to see what can be retrieved and reworked from their complex engagements with theology and the Bible. That motley collection has slowly grown and now includes: the implications of atheism (via Feuerbach and Bauer), which, in turn, leads into secularism (and the revived debate over church and state), grand historical narratives (from the chapter on Stirner), fetishism, and the political ambivalence of theology.[4]

---

1. Marx 1866a, p. 194; Marx 1866b, p. 199.
2. Marx 1861g, p. 247; Marx 1861h, p. 144.
3. Engels 1867c, p. 467; Engels 1867d, p. 567. The allusion is to Matthew 10:16.
4. These items will form part of the last volume in this series, *In the Vale of Tears*.

The largest question concerns atheism, which actually has some unexpected consequences once we entice and cajole it to divulge a few secrets. They may be put in terms of three distinctions, which I will explore in turn: atheism must be separated from anticlericalism; atheism is neither a prerequisite nor corequisite for socialism; the same applies to the relationship between theism and theology. As for anticlericalism, it never goes astray and Marx and Engels deliver it in truckloads. I have mentioned a few instances in the first chapter, but here is another example:

> During this tour through Belgium, stay in Aachen, and journey up the Rhine, I convinced myself that energetic action must be taken against the clerics, particularly in the Catholic areas. I shall work in this vein in the International. Where it appears suitable, the rogues are flirting with workers' problems (e.g., Bishop Ketteler in Mainz, the clerics at the Düsseldorf Congress, etc.). In fact we worked for them in 1848, but they enjoyed the fruits of the revolution during the period of reaction.[5]

Anticlericalism is very much a part of the socialist platform, as Marx argues and as the rules of the Communist League make clear.[6] Yet anticlericalism does not necessarily include atheism, as Luther and Calvin among many others showed all too well. Indeed, it seems to me that anticlericalism should be very much part of any theology worth its salt.[7]

When we come to atheism itself, the difference between Marx and Christianity can be stated quite simply. Christianity postulates the existence of God, heaven, hell (sometimes), an afterlife and so on. For Marxism, these do not exist, for what counts are the social, economic and political relations that produce such beliefs. As a form of idealism, Christianity has no independent existence and therefore does not have a history.[8] All of this is really the ABC of Marxism's approach to religion, but there are some curious ramifications.

---

5. Marx 1869r, p. 354; Marx 1869s, p. 371.
6. *Rules of the Communist League* 1850, p. 634.
7. This distinction between atheism and anticlericalism is far more useful than arguing that Marx's knowledge of Christianity was limited and that if he had known of the various Christian liberation-movements he would have revised his opinion (thus argues Raines 2002, p. 9).
8. As Engels puts it with his characteristic clarity in a letter to Franz Mehring of 1893, 'What has above all deluded the majority of people is this semblance of an independent history of political constitutions, legal systems and ideological conceptions in each individual sphere. When Luther and Calvin "overcome" the official Catholic

To begin with, the outline I have just provided may run in at least two directions. A well-oiled distinction in discussions of ideology draws the line between a 'critical' approach in which ideology – and thereby religion – is false consciousness (erroneous beliefs about the world that need to be corrected) and a 'descriptive' or functional approach in which ideology is a necessary and inescapable feature of human existence.[9] If we follow this second line, found in Marx's later work as well as a host of others such as Lenin, Althusser and Gramsci, then theology is no different from other types of ideology such as philosophy, art, writing, politics, metaphysics and so on. In the same way that one holds a philosophical position or produces a plot for a novel, one also produces religious beliefs. However, unlike the character of a story or the arguments of a philosopher, a religion such as Christianity (mostly) asserts the independent existence of its key-characters. But then it is not logically impossible for someone to say: I know that God, the spirits, heaven and hell and so on are constructs of our imagination or characters in a story, but that is no barrier to belief, for I find the story as a whole provides a viable myth by which to live. This is rather close to Feuerbach's own position, except that he argued that these abstracted entities need to be returned to us in order to enhance our lives. The number of people who actually hold to this position with regard to religion, however logical it might be, would probably fit in my bathroom. Yet it is not uncommon to find a very similar argument invoked in relation to a philosophical system, or even a novel or a complex computer-game.

All the same, I am not sure the preceding argument will persuade too many people. At this point, let me pick up two of the distinctions I noted earlier: in the same way that atheism is not a necessary correlate with socialism, so also belief in the existence of a god is distinct from the practice of theology. As for theism and theology, Marx was no exception in believing that the two

---

faith, when Hegel "overcomes" Fichte and Kant, or when, with his *Contrat social*, Rousseau indirectly "overcomes" the constitutionalist Montesquieu, the process is one which remains within the confines of theology, philosophy and political science, which represents a stage in the history of these spheres of thought and never emerges from the sphere of thought.' (Engels 1893a, pp. 164–5; Engels 1893b, p. 97.)

9. For example, see Barrett 1991, pp. 18–34; Larrain 1983a; Larrain 1983b; Dupré 1983, pp. 238–44 and McLellan 1995, p. 16.

are coterminous,[10] but it is quite possible and logically consistent to practice theology and not believe in a god. Theology is actually a system of thought, with its distinct myths, stories, terminology, modes of argument and lively debate that can operate perfectly well without any external reference-point. In a sister-discipline to theology – biblical criticism – this is a perfectly viable way to carry on one's work. In fact, for well over a century, biblical criticism has operated as an immanent approach, working from the assumption that one does not include the gods as causes of history or in the production and collation of the biblical texts. At most, the multiple personalities of God are actually characters in the story, as with any other literature. If this is possible with biblical criticism, why not then with theology? After all, the discipline has a wealth of experience discussing and debating crucial issues – such as the universal and particular, the nature of history or the human condition – that it would be foolhardy to discard.

A similar distinction operates in Marx's own writings, although now with atheism and historical materialism. While Marx admitted that he had a particular dislike of Christianity – 'so specific is my aversion to Christianity [*so spezifisch ist mein Widerwille gegen das Christentum*]', he wrote to Lassalle[11] – and even though he is guilty of occasional moments of crass materialism,[12] he also argued that atheism is not a prerequisite for socialism. One reason was theoretical, for as Marx points out already in his response to Bruno Bauer's programme to abolish religion, atheism is 'the last stage of *theism*, the *negative* recognition of God'.[13] In other words, atheism is really a theological position;

---

10. As Janz 1998, p. 9, points out, Marx felt that once you exposed theistic belief as a fantasy, religion itself becomes obsolete.

11. Marx 1862k, p. 377; Marx 1862l, p. 627.

12. 'The figments of his brain assume corporeal form. A world of tangible, palpable ghosts is begotten within his mind. That is the secret of all pious visions and at the same time it is the general form of insanity.' (Marx and Engels 1845a, p. 184; Marx and Engels 1845b, pp. 195–6.)

13. Marx and Engels 1845a, p. 110; Marx and Engels 1845b, p. 116. See also Engels's comment in 1884: '... that atheism merely expresses a negation is an argument we ourselves had already advanced against the philosophers 40 years ago, only with the corollary that atheism, as the *mere* negation of, and referring only to, religion, would itself be nothing without it and is thus itself another religion' (Engels 1884e, p. 173; Engels 1884f, p. 186). See also Marx's comment to Arnold Ruge: 'if there is to be talk about philosophy, there should be less trifling with the *label* "atheism" (which reminds one of children, assuring everyone who is ready to listen to them that they are not afraid of the bogy man), and that instead the content of philosophy should be brought to the people. *Voilà tout*' (Marx 1842ff, p. 395; Marx 1842gg, p. 412).

one needs a god whose existence can be denied. He goes one step further in an astute couple of sentences in the *Economic and Philosophical Manuscripts of 1844*. He begins with this very same argument – atheism is theological since it is a negation of God in order to focus on the existence of human beings (Feuerbach did as much). But then Marx argues that we need to move beyond the opposition of theism and atheism: '*Atheism*... has no longer any meaning, for atheism is a *negation of God*, and postulates the *existence of man* through this negation; but socialism as socialism no longer stands in need of such a mediation... It is man's *positive self-consciousness*, no longer mediated through the abolition of religion'.[14] Abolition here is, of course, *Aufhebung*: the sublation, preservation and lifting to another level of religion. One does not need atheism or even the Aufhebung of religion as a basis for socialism. Or, as Marx put it more prosaically and somewhat quaintly in an interview with the *Chicago Tribune*:

> 'You and your followers, Dr. Marx, have been credited with all sorts of incendiary speeches against religion. Of course you would like to see the whole system destroyed, root and branch'.
>
> 'We know', he replied after a moment's hesitation, 'that violent measures against religion are nonsense; but this is an opinion: as Socialism grows, religion will disappear. Its disappearance must be done by social development, in which education must play a great part'.[15]

Another reason for distinguishing between atheism and socialism was tactical. On one side, Bakunin and the anarchists wanted the International to declare itself atheist, abolish cults and replace faith with science. Marx comments dryly, 'As if one could declare by royal decree abolition of faith!'[16] On the other side, there were plenty of accusations that the International was precisely as Bakunin had wanted. I do not mean the scaremongers of state-repression, but former comrades such as Jules Favre and Mazzini, who stated that the International wanted to make atheism compulsory. Engels repeatedly points out that atheism is not part of the socialist programme.[17] In a similar

---

14. Marx 1844g, p. 306; Marx 1844h, p. 546 (translation modified).
15. Marx 1879, p. 576.
16. Marx 1868a, p. 208. See further Marx 1872a, p. 142; Engels 1872a, pp. 275–6; Engels 1872b, pp. 169–70; Engels 1870l; Engels 1870m; Marx and Engels 1873a, p. 460; Marx and Engels 1873b, p. 335.
17. Engels 1871a, p. 608; Engels 1871d, p. 28; Engels 1871h, p. 164.

vein, Marx in his interview with *The World* replies to the question, 'And as to religion?'

> On that point I cannot speak in the name of the society. I myself am an athe-
> ist. It is startling, no doubt, to hear such an avowal in England, but there is
> some comfort in the thought that it need not be made in a whisper in either
> Germany or France.[18]

Does this mean that the communist movement took the position of freedom of conscience for its members? Here Marx is ambivalent. In his 'Comments on the Latest Prussian Censorship Instruction', he argues that religion is an inviolable and 'subjective frame of mind [*subjectiven Gesinnung*]'.[19] This point is part of a longer argument against religious censorship by the state, suggesting that the state-censor usurps God's sole rôle as judge of the heart. The reasons why such an argument was made in the context of censorship are not difficult to determine – the preservation of at least some domain that is free from censorship (the 'kingdom within'), as well as the characteristic inversion whereby the censor turns out to be the one guilty of defamatory and offensive judgement. It is, of course, a position that is all too common today: religion is a private matter that is no-one else's business. My initial reaction is that he merely buys into the privatisation of religious commitment that is by now almost universal. Religion ceases to have any communal or social presence; all that counts is one's relationship with one's God. So we find one politician after another responding to the latest social comment from church, synagogue or mosque: 'Stop seeking the media-spotlight and mind your own business, which is the cultivation of souls and religious experience!' Is this not a deeply liberal position in which the individual is sacrosanct? We can at least account for Marx's argument by pointing out that it comes from an early text before he had taken up communism.

Later on, be blasts the very idea of freedom of conscience as a tired old liberal catchword. For example, in *Critique of the Gotha Programme*, he writes that what freedom of conscience really means is that 'everyone should be able to attend to his religious as well as his bodily needs without the police sticking their noses in'.[20] What it actually means is the toleration of only certain types

---

18. 'Record of Marx's Interview with *The World* Correspondent' 1871, pp. 605–6.
19. Marx 1843a, p. 121; Marx 1843b, p. 109.
20. Marx 1875a, p. 98; Marx 1875b, p. 31.

of religion, and *that* is nothing less than 'unfreedom of conscience'. It certainly does not include the freedom to be liberated from religion itself. There is actually more here than at first seems to be the case. Marx does appear to dismiss the whole idea of freedom of conscience as an irredeemable liberal position, but then he takes another step. This 'freedom of conscience' is actually not freedom of conscience at all, for, if it were, then one should be able to hold whatever religion one wants or indeed dispense with the witchery of religion completely. It is as if he is saying, you want freedom of conscience, then I will damn well give it to you!

I suspect that Rosa Luxemburg picked up on this radical sense of such freedom. She argued that socialists should embrace freedom of conscience:

> The Social-Democrats, those of the whole world and of our own country, regard conscience [*Gewissen*] and personal opinion [*Überzeugung*] as being sacred. Everyone is free to hold whatever faith and whatever opinions will ensure his happiness. No one has the right to persecute or to attack the particular religious opinion of others. Thus say the Social-Democrats.[21]

Is there a liberal left-over here? Not at all. For Luxemburg, 'liberty of conscience' is two-edged. What lies behind her argument is the following: in challenging the brutal censorship of the Czarist régime in Russia and Poland, which persecuted Roman Catholics, Jews, heretics and freethinkers, and in tackling the efforts of the church to direct what people believe by whatever means available, from state-power to the Inquisition, she must be consistent and argue that the socialists should not exercise the same type of censorship. The logical outcome of this argument is that freedom of conscience also applies to religious belief: 'religion is a private affair [*la religion est une affaire privée*]'.[22]

What intrigues me about Luxemburg's argument (and thereby Marx's own point) is a paradox that goes to the heart of socialism. As a movement whose starting-point is collective experience, one would expect that freedom of conscience would be the least of its concerns. Nothing could be further from the truth, for a fully collective programme does not seek to impose the will of either the one or the many over the other. It is, if you like, the complex effort to allow each one in the collective to express her or his beliefs, foibles and

---

21. Luxemburg 1970, p. 132; Luxemburg 1982, p. 19; translation modified.
22. Luxemburg 2004, p. 2; Luxemburg 1903, p. 28. See further my discussion of Luxemburg in Boer 2009c.

obsessions without the imposition of control and censorship. So I end with a dialectical point: rather than dropping freedom of conscience beside the road along with the rest of liberal ideology, a fully collective programme will enable the full realisation of freedom of conscience. And that applies as much to religious belief as to anything else.

It seems that atheism has many shapes in the writings of Marx and Engels – a personal abhorrence of Christianity (for Marx at least), a matter of personal belief and not party-platform, political pragmatism and philosophical objection. But there is one further type of atheism which is a feature of Marx and Engels's texts and that is what I call protest-atheism.[23] This atheism does not base itself on scientific denunciation (as Engels was wont to do at times and which we find today in the 'new atheists' such as Dawkins, Dennett and Hitchens), but, rather, on an analysis of the social contradictions of religious belief, structures and forms. In this sense, protest-atheism makes an awful lot of sense. In the face of all the abuses justified by theology, all of the oppression for which theology is the theory, all of the reactionary forms that system of thought has taken, and all the craven brown-nosing of power and wealth in which the churches have engaged over time, atheism becomes a protest. The church can be a cruel institution, destroying lives and perverting social relations, so much so that its various branches seem to have a reactionary default. I must admit that the presence of a dog-collar or the gleam in the eye of a zealot makes me exceedingly uncomfortable. In this context, atheism is a necessary protest. It seems to me that the atheism of Marx and Engels had a good deal of this protest-element. But I also suggest that such protest-atheism is indispensable for any theology that is honest with itself. It is as if we can say, yes, in light of all these abuses and demolitions of human lives, atheism is the one viable response. Another is, of course, the emancipatory stream of Christianity which drew Engels, and a host of figures after him, for this too condemns and works against the reactionary forms of Christianity.

This protest-atheism (and indeed revolutionary Christianity) brings me to the next matter I want to retrieve from Marx and Engels. It is the matter of church and state, or, as it tends to be put today, the relation between religion and politics. It has, of course, become a topic of renewed debate in our own time due to the return of religion to the forefront of global politics.

---

23. More than thirty years ago, Lochman 1978 made a similar argument.

The response of the states in the Middle East to imperialism and colonialism as well as the politics of oil are now cast all too often in the terms of Islam versus Christianity. From Denmark to Australia, countries that have for many years sat very loosely with any Christian heritage are now claiming to be 'Christian' states. People who hardly know who Adam and Eve are or who have never touched the threshold of a church begin to claim that they are indeed 'Christian' and that such an identity needs to be defended against the threat of Islam. In this light, Marx and Engels's scattered comments on church and state have a renewed relevance.

As I argued in Chapter Six, Marx in particular is contradictory on the question of church and state. His more common argument is that theology and politics should have nothing to do with one another since theology is heavenly and other-worldly while politics is very much an earthly business. This unholy alliance leads to all manner of impossible contradictions. Which church is to be dominant? Can you really live up to all the ethical guidelines in the Bible? What does it mean to protect 'religion' from attack? But his other argument, backed up by an astute piece by Engels, is far more interesting. The secular state is not the rejection of the Christian state, or even the much-desired separation of church and state. It is actually the realisation of the Christian state. I take this as the argument that the secular state is an effort to resolve the contradictions of the Christian state. Eventually, the internal contradictions of the union of church and state become too much and lead to a secular state. Thus, as Marx points out in his reply to Bruno Bauer's *On the Jewish Question*, a secular state – the outcome of 'political' emancipation – is really an attempt to come to terms with religious pluralism. You can have your beliefs and I will have mine, but we will keep them to ourselves as personal matters and will not let them intrude on public life. This means that the secular state is not freedom from religion but freedom of religion. It is merely another way of being religious.[24]

The underlying issue in all of this is secularism. It seems to me that both atheism and the separation of church and state are derivative and secondary features of secularism itself. Here, I indulge in a little etymology, for if we take

---

24. See further Taylor 2007, who develops this argument in great detail. The rise of secularism is not one story but multiple explorations. Above all, he argues that secularism is really a collection of new ways of being religious rather than the decline of religion.

the Latin terms *saeculum* (adjective *saecularis*) with its meaning of 'this age' and 'this world', then secularism means that we draw our terms from and base our way of life on this age and this world and not some future age or a world beyond. As a derivative step, one could argue that secularism entails atheism and that religion must disappear. Or we could argue that one form such secularism might take is the separation of church and state. But these are not crucial to the definition of secularism itself. Furthermore, we might argue that Christian theology is anti-secular, since its prime concern is the world above and to come. Among many others, Marx does indeed argue this on a number of occasions. But, as I pointed out in my earlier discussion, such an argument misses the fact that theology concerns itself just as much with the here and now, with the plight of human beings and their place in a natural and social world. It is a small step to realise that on this score theology is both anti-secular and secular. However, the surprising outcome of this argument is that any political movement that finds this *saeculum* wanting in terms of economic, social and political justice is also anti-secular. The desires and specific programmes for a better world than the one in which we live is not merely concerned with this world and this age. I hardly need to point out that the political work of Marx and Engels also fits the bill, as Marx's enthusiastic comment on the Paris Commune shows all too well:

> Working men's Paris, with its Commune, will be forever celebrated as the glorious harbinger of a new society. Its martyrs are enshrined in the great heart of the working class. Its exterminators' history has already nailed to that eternal pillory from which all the prayers of their priest will not avail to redeem them.[25]

This last point brings us to the matter of historical narratives. In my discussion of Stirner in Chapter Four, I traced the way both Christian and Marxist narratives of history are linked at a formal level. In their effort to produce a coherent response with a crucial lever of history, Marx and Engels may have come up with a very different story in terms of content – division of labour, class-conflict and modes of production which are all driven by inescapable contradictions – but the form arises in response to a mutated biblical

---

25. Marx 1871a, p. 355; Marx 1871b, p. 362. See further my discussion of Lucien Goldmann in Boer 2009c.

narrative-structure in Stirner's text. Given that most readers quail and turn away at the sight of those monstrous pages on Stirner in *The German Ideology*, I can at least claim that I have provided a distinct argument for the way in which historical materialism relates to the Christian and biblical historical narratives. It is a formal response that was produced in the engine-room of that heated and polemical engagement with Stirner.

This is the appropriate point to say something more on the matter of the formal parallels between theology and some of the arguments developed by Marx and Engels. This matter first appeared in my discussion of Stirner, but then recurred in relation to Feuerbach and then fetishism. In the conclusion to the chapter on Stirner, I distinguished between direct borrowing and application and then what has variously been termed 'grafted', 'analogous' or 'parallel' approaches. I also made a rather conventional distinction between content and form, since it is quite clear that neither Marx nor Engels appropriated theological content concerning history, Christology or eschatology into their work. As far as form is concerned, I settled on the metaphor of a crucible, since the innovations of historical materialism arose from the response to – in part at least – the dominant theological and biblical nature of public debate in Germany at the time.[26] The three overlaid senses of the word 'crucible' – possibly deriving from *crux* ('cross' and then 'trial') – are applicable here. A device for testing purity, mixing chemicals and metals, and, in the industrial revolution, a process of mixing iron, charcoal and other additives in order to make high-quality steel, 'crucible' also has the sense of a severe test or a confluence and concentration of powerful political, social and economic forces that produce something new. So, I would suggest that theology was one of the crucial elements in a formal crucible out of which Marx and Engels produced historical materialism. It is in this sense that the formal analogies and parallels between that method and types of theological argument may be understood.

What Marx and Engels develop is not some secularised version or historical successor of Christianity, as Alasdair MacIntyre argued long ago,[27] nor is it secularised Christian history and eschatology, as more than one cheap

---

26. This historical situation also means that theology does not have an absolute priority but rather one generated by the context. It is worthwhile keeping in mind my comments in the discussion of Marx's doctoral thesis (Chapter Three) concerning the need to relativise theology and negate the assumption of an *a priori* status.

27. MacIntyre 1971, pp. 12–13.

shot has suggested: Marx is a prophet who foresees the New Jerusalem that will be ushered in by the collective redeemer-figure of the proletariat through a final battle.[28] Perhaps the most dreadful version of that argument came in the context of a paper I once gave on Christian communism in the work of Rosa Luxemburg and Karl Kautsky. Someone stood up and argued that, because religious belief was so deeply ingrained at the time, Marx and Engels were hedging their bets in case Christianity proved to be right. As politely as I could (I wanted to say it was utterly wrong), I pointed out that if anyone linked eschatological apocalyptic together with communism it was Moses Hess, whose *Die Heilige Geschichte der Menschheit* and *Europäische Trierarchie* both introduced communism to Germany and gave it a distinctly apocalyptic tone.[29] Hess's widely read *Europäische Trierarchie* proposed that the fusion of the young-Hegelian criticism of theology, French socialist politics and English industrial materialism would bring about the total collapse of the existing order and usher in a new age. In the end, Marx and Engels viewed his apocalyptic fervour rather dimly. I added that the only one with any interest in eschatology and apocalyptic was Engels, and that it was a youthful fascination which manifested itself in jest, satire and as a way to express exhilaration at a new discovery. Even then he never took it all that seriously. Later on, Engels used exactly the same biblical material to pour water on any apocalyptic fervour by arguing that the apocalyptic book of Revelation is merely a historical book that provides a window into early Christianity. Indeed, in his last years, Engels became far more cautious about untimely revolutionary uprisings since they would merely give the authorities pretext to crush the socialists.

More sustained criticism has come from the infamous postmodern ban on master-narratives. We are told that a narrative, in which Marx and Engels engage time and again in various reworkings, is imperialist, colonising and what have you. By its very singularity it excludes vast numbers of people who have no say in how that narrative is constructed. The Christian narrative of history, from creation to eschaton, has also suffered severe criticism for the same reason. The problem with this criticism is twofold. Firstly, even if we assume for a moment that there is one master-narrative, then there is no

---

28. For one of the most influential and misguided statements of this argument, see Kolakowski 1981, pp. 372–5.

29. Hess 1837; Hess 1961; Hess 2004. See the excellent discussion of Hess in Kouvelakis 2003, pp. 121–66.

inherent reason for it to be exclusive. That possibility depends on whether the singular story is catholic (universal) by exclusion or by inclusion. The early battles for a singular 'catholic' church in the fourth and fifth centuries provide a good example (as Gramsci noted). Engaging Augustine as a theological hitman, it claimed to be catholic, but could do so only by excluding those that did not fit the template. Its policy was simple – if you cannot absorb them, crush them. However, there is another possibility: an overarching narrative is the way in which all manner of other stories come to light. In other words, such a singular narrative may well be inclusive rather than exclusive. More philosophically, it is an inclusive universal rather than an exclusive one. Secondly, Marx and Engels do not actually develop a singular narrative of history; they tell multiple stories. Marx, for one, would take a particular topic, such as private property or the division of labour or even religion and put together a story as to how it might have developed and changed over time, only to pick up on another angle on the same topic and tell the story again in a different way.

My final point concerning history is not so original, but it is worth making all the same. The grand narrative(s) of Marxism and Christianity actually provide stories to live by. As Fredric Jameson is fond of saying, they enable the biological individuals that we are to make sense of the almost incomprehensible patterns of the world in which we live. Marxism provides one such story, while Christianity provides another. Elsewhere, I have suggested that we might describe them as political myths.[30] One of the reasons why Marxism and Christianity have been so often at loggerheads is that they offer competing political myths. Yet they can compete because the game is similar.

A further item full of possibilities is Marx's multiple adaptations of fetishism, a relatively simple idea drawn from the early study of the history of religions. Fetishism involves a basic transference, for the object venerated – whether a product made by human labour or an animate or inanimate object – gains at the expense of the worshipper. Or at least it appears to do so, for Marx never tires of pointing out that such transference belongs in the realms of mist, illusion and deception. And Marx certainly worked this fetishistic transferral into many different shapes – political polemic, the alienation of labour, money, commodities, the commodity-form, and even the idea of capital. Yet

---

30. Boer 2009b.

the basic idea remains reasonably consistent throughout. Apart from his constant invocation of religious and theological examples, *The Ethnological Notebooks* indicate that he never lost sight of the religious dimension of fetishism.

However, what strikes me about the many shapes of fetishism is the overlap with the biblical polemic against idolatry. As we saw, Charles de Brosses (from whom Marx initially borrowed the concept) assumed that idolatry was part of fetishism, so much so that many of his examples come from the Bible. Marx assumed the same, as his comments on Lubbock in *The Ethnological Notebooks* indicate. I do not need to repeat my analysis of the critique of idolatry in the book of Isaiah, but I do want to take up my comment that the connection between fetishism and idolatry opens up the possibility of a sustained theological criticism of capitalism. I do not mean here the Roman-Catholic tradition of social criticism of which Marx is scathing and which seeks to ameliorate the harsh edges of any social formation much like a theological version of social democracy. Nor do I mean the warnings against a fuzzy 'materialism' by some ecclesiastical leaders (by which they mean an excessive love of possessions at the expense of one's far more important spiritual concerns). Rather, I mean a theological criticism of precisely those items Marx describes as fetishes, such as the alienation of labour under capitalism, money-relations, the commodity-form, capital, to which may be added the foreign debt, fiscal restraint, the GDP, balance of payments, and so on. Here, Marx's effort to produce a new concept of the fetish, in which both illusion and reality combine, has some mileage (as some liberation-theologians have argued).[31] Marx's innovation was to argue that what seems to workers to be a mist-enveloped apparition – the powers attained by commodities or money or... – is, in fact, real: the destructive powers over human lives and human interaction. The illusion Marx seeks to dispel is the perception of the way in which these powers came to be, for they are not natural attributes or givens of nature, but the result of an alienating transferral. In this way, the fetish gains a reality as an 'objective thought-form'. At this point, theological anticapitalism and Marxism merge, for the only response to idols is to smash them and grind them into dust.

However, capitalism is not the only place where the critique of idolatry has some bite. I would suggest that Adorno's development of the *Bilderverbot*,

---

31. See Chapter Seven.

the ban on images, to become a leitmotiv of his philosophy – targeted against concepts, secularised theology, the personality-cult and utopia, to name but a few – has been the most fruitful and sustained development of the critique of idolatry. The underlying drive is caught best by the phrase, 'pretensions of the finite'.[32] Any finite thing or person that has pretensions to the infinite becomes an idol, a fetish. And that includes theology itself. The problem for theology is as follows: for the various theological traditions of Christianity, idolatry describes what other people do. We do not worship idols, goes the argument, for this image of ours refers to the one true God. Your images, on the other hand, have no reference-point beyond them. So you stupidly worship a destructive object that you have made or perhaps an animal you like. It is an extraordinarily vulnerable position, since it is a small step to realising that my own image has no reference-point either: I, too, am an idolater like all the rest. It is not for nothing that the rigorous ban on images keeps being reasserted, whether in the Decalogue of Exodus 20 or Deuteronomy 5, or in the extreme moments of the Reformation under Calvin. You can still find churches in reformed countries such as the Netherlands that are completely devoid of even the vaguest hint of tinted glass, let alone any images inside. The underlying logic is to block any possibility of cutting that connection between image and referent. With no image, there is no link on which to work those bolt-cutters. This still leaves a number of sticky problems, such as the Bible, or the church, or indeed the question of Christology, for is not Christ God's representative on earth, the incarnate form of God to show us a little of what God is like? Here, too, it seems to me, the ban on images must apply, for otherwise we get the whole problem of the personality-cult and worship of redeemer-figures.[33] Here, too, we must engage idolatry in critique.

Finally, there is the political ambivalence of theology. From some unwitting glimpses by a determined Marx to the flowering of the idea in Engels, this is one of the most promising ideas of all. In Marx, it flashes a little skin in his comment that religious suffering is both the expression of real suffering and the protest against that suffering, as it does in the multivalent image of opium. But Engels explores this ambivalence in some detail, especially with Thomas

---

32. Horkheimer and Adorno 2002, p. 145; Horkheimer and Adorno 2003, p. 201. See further Boer 2007a, pp. 430–9.
33. See further Boer 2007a, pp. 430–9 and 449.

Müntzer and early Christianity. Fortunately, he never lost his anticlericalism and determined atheism, for the presence of both the revolutionary argument and the awareness of how oppressive a religion such as Christianity can be shows up the political ambivalence at the heart of theology. It can be the most reactionary of ideologies but it can also be deeply revolutionary. The two are inseparable. That means those who argue for a revolutionary core in theology and the Bible see only half the picture. I think here of the search for a rebellious core in the Bible by Ernst Bloch, or Terry Eagleton's effort to recycle the old arguments for a revolutionary Jesus, or the figure of a rebel that recurs in political and liberation-theologies, or, more recently, in the quests for the historical Jesus that argue he was a rebellious peasant, or even the position that he was a proto-socialist.[34] I know that many people base their faith and social-justice activism on the position that Jesus was a social, political and moral radical, a friend of anti-imperialists and outcasts, a champion of the poor, the sick and immigrants, and a determined opponent of the rich, clergy and powerful. Apart from the insurmountable problem that it is impossible to know anything with certainty about the historical figure Jesus of Nazareth, it misses the point that even the sayings in the Gospels, let alone the rest of the Bible, have a good deal in them that runs in the other direction.

The reason for such theological tension is, of course, that a religion such as Christianity has its own institutional forms. Anyone who has spent the least amount of time in such an institution knows that they are full of skulduggery, sexual favours and intrigue, backstabbing, party-politics and struggles over money, property and power. In other words, these institutions – one of the best instances of Althusser's ideological state-apparatuses – are sites of ideological struggle. And those struggles are invariably tied up with the complex overlaps of class. To paraphrase Althusser, theology is class-struggle in the realm of theory. Yet the political ambivalence of theology is not tied merely to its institutions, for it also registers in its own way wider economic and social struggles.[35] Indeed, I have argued elsewhere that the massive social upheaval

---

34. For example, see Eagleton 2007; Bloch 1970; Bloch 1972; Bloch 1985; Bloch 1995; Crossan 1993; Crossan 1995.

35. Or as Marx put it, 'In studying such transformations it is always necessary to distinguish between the material transformation of the economic conditions of production, which can be determined with the precision of a natural science, and the legal, political, religious, artistic or philosophic – in short, ideological forms in which men become conscious of this conflict and fight it out.' (Marx 1859a, p. 263.)

brought about by the transitions between modes of production is inseparable from the theological tensions in the writings of someone such as Paul in the New Testament. In his case, the violent intersection between the system the Romans brought with them and an older sacred economy generated all manner of tensions that he registers in his letters. The same applies to someone such as John Calvin, who was repeatedly caught between his innate conservatism and the radical possibilities of topics such as the Bible, grace, Christian freedom and politics. He found that the revolutionary cat kept trying to get out of the theological bag. In Calvin's case, his theological struggles cannot be understood without an awareness of the brutal reality of a fading feudalism and emergent capitalism.[36]

Those who register, articulate and try to respond to these political tensions within theology and the Bible are by far the most interesting. I, for one, find that tension too intriguing to throw out the whole lot. In a somewhat different way, it seems to me that Marx and especially Engels were aware of this political ambivalence in the Bible and theology. And that is to their credit.

---

36. See Boer 2007b and Boer 2009a.

References

A Circular of the First Congress of the Communist League to the League Members, June 9, 1847 1847, in Marx and Engels 1969.

Adorno, Theodor W. 1973 [1964], *The Jargon of Authenticity*, translated by Knut Tarnowski and Frederic Will, Evanston: Northwestern University Press.

—— 2003 [1964], *Jargon der Eigentlich: Zur deutschen Ideologie*, in *Gesammelte Schriften*, Volume 6, Frankfurt am Main: Suhrkamp.

Aichele, George 2001, *The Control of Biblical Meaning: Canon as a Semiotic Mechanism*, Lewisburg: Trinity Press International.

Aptheker, Herbert 1968, 'Marxism and Religion', *Religion in Life*, 37, 1: 89–98.

—— 1970, *The Urgency of the Marxist-Christian Dialogue: A Pragmatic Argument for Reconciliation*, New York: Harper Colophon.

Aron, Jacques 2005, *Karl Marx, antisémite et criminal?*, Brussels: Didier Devillez.

Assmann, Hugo and Franz J. Hinkelammert 1989, *A idolatria do mercado*, Petrópolis: Vozes.

Avineri, Shlomo 1964, 'Marx and Jewish Emancipation', *Journal of the History of Ideas*, 25, 3: 445–50.

—— 1968, *The Social and Political Thought of Karl Marx*, Cambridge: Cambridge University Press.

Baptism Certificate of Friedrich Engels: Extract from the Baptism Register of the Elberfeld Reformed Evangelical Parish 1821, in Marx and Engels 1975b.

Barrett, Michèle 1991, *The Politics of Truth: From Marx to Foucault*, Stanford: Stanford University Press.

Bauer, Bruno 1838, *Kritik der Geschichte der Offenbarung: Die Religion des alten Testaments in der geschichtlichen Entwicklung ihrer Prinzipien dargestellt*, Berlin: Ferdinand Dümmler.

—— 1839, *Herr Dr. Hengstenberg: Ein Beitrag zur Kritik der religiösen Bewußtseins. Kritische Briefe über den Gegensatz des Gesetzes und des Evangeliums*, Berlin: Ferdinand Dümmler.

—— 1840, *Kritik der evangelischen Geschichte des Johannes*, Bremen: Karl Schünemann.

—— 1841, *Kritik der evangelischen Geschichte der Synoptiker*, two volumes, Leipzig: Otto Wigand.

—— 1842a, *Die Gute Sache der Freiheit und meine eigene Ungelegenheit*, Zurich/Winterthur: Verlag des literarischen Comptoirs.

—— 1842b, *Kritik der evangelischen Geschichte der Synoptiker und des Johannes, Dritter und letzter Band*, Braunschweig: Fr. Otto.

—— 1843a, *Das entdeckte Christenthum. Eine Erinnerung an das 18. Jahrhundert und ein Beitrag zur Krisis des 19. Jahrhundert*, Zurich/Winterthur: Verlag des literarischen Comptoirs.

—— 1843b, *Zur Judenfrage*, Braunschweig: Fr. Otto.

—— 1843c, 'Die Fähigkeit der heutigen Juden und Christen, frei zu werden', in *Einundzwanzig bogen aus der Schweiz*, edited by Georg Herwegh, Zurich/Winterthur: Verlag des literarischen Comptoirs.

—— 1847–50, *Der Aufstand und Fall des deutschen Radicalismus vom Jahre 1842*, Berlin: Gustav Hempel.

—— 1850–1, *Kritik der Evangelien und Geschichte ihres Ursprungs*, three volumes, Berlin: Gustav Hempel.

—— 1852, *Die theologische Erklärung der Evangelien*, Berlin: Gustav Hempel.

—— 1958 [1843], *The Jewish Problem*, translated by Helen Lederer, Cincinnati: Hebrew Union College Press.

—— 1964 [1847], *Vollständige geschichte der Parteikämpfe: in Deutschland während der Jahre 1842–1846*, Aalen: Scientia Verlag.

—— 1965 [1843–5], *Geschichte der Politik, Cultur und Aufklärung des 18. Jahrhunderts*, Aalen: Scientia Verlag.

—— 1967 [1842], *Hegels Lehre von der Religion und der Kunst von dem Standpunkte des Glaubens aus beurteilt*, Aalen: Scientia Verlag.

—— 1969a [1849], *Die bürgerliche Revolution in Deutschland; seit dem Anfang der deutsch-katholischen Bewegung bis zur Gegenwart*, Aalen: Scientia Verlag.

—— 1969b [1882], *Disraelis romantischer und Bismarcks sozialistischer Imperialismus*, Aalen: Scientia Verlag.

—— 1969c [1888], *Der Einfluss Frankreichs auf die preussische Politik und die Entwicklung des preussischen Staates, dargestellt an den Bündnissen, Verträgen und gegenseitigen Beziehungen; historische Studie*, Aalen: Scientia Verlag.

—— 1970 [1849], *Der Untergang des Frankfurter Parlaments: Geschichte der deutschen konstituierenden Nationalversammlung*, Aalen: Scientia Verlag.

—— 1972a [1846], *Geschichte Deutschlands und der französischen Revolution unter der Herrschaft Napoleons*, Aalen: Scientia Verlag.

—— 1972b [1853], *Russland und das Germanentum*, Aalen: Scientia Verlag.

—— 1978 [1843], 'The Capacity of Present-Day Jews and Christians to Become Free', *Philosophical Forum*, 2–4: 135–49.

—— 1983 [1841], *Die Posaune des jüngsten Gerichts über Hegel den Atheisten und Antichristen: Ein Ultimatum*, Aalen: Scientia Verlag.

—— 2002 [1843], *Christianity Exposed: A Recollection of the Eighteenth Century and a Contribution to the Crisis of the Nineteenth Century*, translated by Esther Ziegler and Jutta Hamm, Lewiston: Edwin Mellen.

—— 2006 [1843], '«L'aptitude des juifs et des chrétiens d'aujourd'hui à devenir libres', in Marx 2006.

Benjamin, Walter 1996 [1921], 'Capitalism as Religion', in *Selected Writings, Volume 1: 1913–1926*, edited by Marcus Bullock and Michael W. Jennings, Cambridge, MA.: Belknap.

Bensaïd, Daniel 2006a, '«Zur Judenfrage», une critique de l'émancipation politique', in Marx 2006.

—— 2006b, '«Dans et par l'histoire». Retours sur la Question juive', in Marx 2006.

Berdahl, Robert M. 1988, *The Politics of the Prussian Nobility: The Development of a Conservative Ideology*, Princeton: Princeton University Press.

Berlin, Isaiah 1978, *Karl Marx: His Life and Thought*, Fourth Edition, Oxford: Oxford University Press.

Bewes, Timothy 2002, *Reification: Or the Anxiety of Late Capitalism*, London: Verso.

Bhattacharyya, Anindya 2006, 'Marx and Religion', *Socialist Worker*, 4 March, available at: <http://www.socialistworker.co.uk/art.php?id=8373>.

Birth Certificate of Friedrich Engels, Barmen, December 5, 1820: Extract from the Barmen Register of Births, Deaths and Marriages 1820, in Marx and Engels 1975b.

Blanton, Ward 2007, *Displacing Christian Origins: Philosophy, Secularity, and the New Testament*, Chicago: University of Chicago Press.

Blasius, Dirk 2000, *Friedrich Wilhelm IV. 1795–1861: Psychopathologie und Geschichte*, Göttingen: Vandenhoeck & Ruprecht.

Bloch, Ernst 1969 [1921], *Thomas Münzer als Theologe der Revolution*, in *Ernst Bloch Werkausgabe*, Volume 2, Frankfurt am Main: Suhrkamp.

—— 1970 [1968], *Atheismus im Christentum: Zur Religion des Exodus und des Reichs*, Hamburg: Rowohlt Taschenbuch Verlag.

—— 1972 [1968], *Atheism in Christianity: The Religion of the Exodus and the Kingdom*, translated by J.T. Swann, New York: Herder and Herder.

—— 1985 [1938–47], *Das Prinzip Hoffnung*, in *Ernst Bloch Werkausgabe*, Volume 5, Frankfurt am Main: Suhrkamp Verlag.

—— 1995 [1938–47], *The Principle of Hope*, translated by Neville Plaice, Stephen Plaice and Paul Knight, Cambridge, MA.: MIT Press.

Boer, Roland 2007a, *Criticism of Heaven: On Marxism and Theology*, Leiden: Brill.

—— 2007b, *Rescuing the Bible*, Oxford: Blackwell.

—— 2009a, *Political Grace: The Revolutionary Theology of John Calvin*, Louisville: Westminster John Knox Press.

—— 2009b, *Political Myth: On the Use and Abuse of Biblical Themes*, Durham, NC.: Duke University Press.

—— 2009c, *Criticism of Religion: On Marxism and Theology II*, Leiden: Brill.

—— 2011, *Criticism of Theology: On Marxism and Theology III*, Leiden: Brill.

Bottomore, Tom (ed.) 1983, *A Dictionary of Marxist Thought*, Oxford: Blackwell.

Breckman, Warren 1999, *Marx, the Young Hegelians, and the Origins of Radical Social Theory*, Cambridge: Cambridge University Press.

Brett, Mark 2009, 'Theological Secularity: A Response to Roland Boer', in *Secularism and Biblical Studies*, edited by Roland Boer, London: Equinox.

Brettler, Marc 1994, 'How the Books of the Hebrew Bible Were Chosen', in *Approaches to the Bible: The Best of Bible Review*, Volume 1, *Composition, Transmission and Language*, edited by Harvey Minkoff, Washington, DC.: Biblical Archaeology Society.

Brosses, Charles de 1760, *Du culte des dieux fétiches ou Parallèle de l'ancienne religion de l'Égypte*, Paris: n.p.

Brown, Wendy 1995, 'Rights and Identity in Late Modernity: Revisiting the "Jewish Question"', in *Identities, Politics, and Rights*, edited by Austin Sarat and Thomas Kearns, Ann Arbor: University of Michigan Press.

Carr, David M. 1996, 'Canonization in the Context of Community', in *A Gift of God in Due Season*, edited by R.D. Weis and David M. Carr, Sheffield: Sheffield Academic Press.

Carter, Warren 2001, *Matthew and Empire: Initial Explorations*, Harrisburg: Trinity Press International.

—— 2006, *The Roman Empire and the New Testament: An Essential Guide*, Nashville: Abingdon.

Certificate of Maturity for Pupil of the Gymnasium in Trier 1835, in Marx and Engels 1975a.

Clarkson, Kathleen and David Hawkin 1978, 'Karl Marx on Religion: The Influence of Bruno Bauer and Ludwig Feuerbach on His Thought and the Implications for the Christian Marxist Dialogue', *Scottish Journal of Theology*, 31: 533–55.

Cobb Jr., John 1998, *The Earthist Challenge to Economism: A Theological Critique of the World Bank*, Basingstoke: Palgrave Macmillan.

Comstock, Gary 1976, 'The Marxist Critique of Religion: A Persisting Ambiguity', *Journal of the American Academy of Religion*, 44, 2: 327–42.

Crossan, John Dominic 1993, *The Historical Jesus: The Life of a Mediterranean Peasant*, San Francisco: HarperSanFrancisco.

—— 1995, *Jesus: A Revolutionary Biography*, San Francisco: HarperSanFrancisco.

Davies, Philip 1995, *In Search of Ancient Israel*, Sheffield: Sheffield Academic Press.

—— 1998, *Scribes and Schools: The Canonization of the Hebrew Scriptures*, Louisville: Westminster John Knox Press.

—— 2008, *Memories of Ancient Israel: An Introduction to Biblical History – Ancient and Modern*, Louisville: Westminster John Knox Press.

—— 2009, *On the Origins of Judaism*, London: Equinox.

Dawkins, Richard 2006, *The God Delusion*, Boston: Houghton Mifflin.

Deissman, Adolf 1929, *The New Testament in the Light of Modern Research*, Garden City: Doubleday, Doran and Company.

—— 1978 [1908], *Light From the Ancient East*, Grand Rapids: Baker Book House.

Dennett, Daniel C. 2007 [2006], *Breaking the Spell: Religion as a Natural Phenomenon*, Harmondsworth: Penguin.

Derrida, Jacques 1994 [1993], *Spectres of Marx: The State of the Debt, the Work of Mourning and the New International*, translated by Peggy Kamuf, London: Routledge.

Deutscher, Isaac 1968, *The Non-Jewish Jew and Other Essays*, edited by Tamara Deutscher, Oxford: Oxford University Press.

Dupré, Louis 1983, *Marx's Social Critique of Culture*, New Haven: Yale University Press.

Dussel, Enrique 1993, *Las metáforas teológicas de Marx*, Estella: Editorial Verbo Divino.

—— 2001, 'From *Ethics and Community*', in *The Postmodern Bible Reader*, edited by David Jobling, Tina Pippin, and Ronald Schleifer, Oxford: Blackwell.

Eagleton, Terry 2007, *The Gospels: Jesus Christ*, London: Verso.

Ebach, J. 1982, 'Der Blick des Engels. Für eine "Benjaminische" Lektüre der hebräischen Bibel', in *Walter Benjamin: Profane Erleuchtung und Rettende Kritik*, edited by Norbert W. Bolz and Richard Faber, Würzburg: Königshausen & Neumann.

Eichhoff, Wilhelm 1868, 'The International Working Men's Association: Its Establishment, Organisation, Political and Social Activity, and Growth', in Marx and Engels 1985b.

Elliott, Neil 1994, *Liberating Paul: The Justice of God and the Politics of the Apostle*, Maryknoll: Orbis.

—— 2000, 'Paul and the Politics of Empire: Problems and Prospects', in *Paul and Politics: Ekklesia, Israel, Imperium, Interpretation. Essays in Honor of Krister Stendahl*, edited by Richard A. Horsley, Harrisburg: Trinity Press International.

Engberg-Pedersen, Troels 2000, *Paul and the Stoics*, Louisville: Westminster John Knox Press.

Engels, Elisabeth 1848a, 'Elisabeth Engels to Frederick Engels in Brussels, Barmen after 4 October 1848', in Marx and Engels 1982b.

—— 1848b, 'Elisabeth Engels to Frederick Engels in Berne, Barmen, 5 December 1848', in Marx and Engels 1982b.

Engels, Friedrich 1837a, 'Poem, Probably Written Early in 1837', in Marx and Engels 1975b.

—— 1837b, 'Herr Jesu Christe, Gottes Sohn', in Marx and Engels 1985d.

—— 1838a, 'To Marie Engels in Barmen, Sept. 11 1838', in Marx and Engels 1975b.

—— 1838b, 'An Marie Engels 11. September 1838', in Marx and Engels 2008.

—— 1838c, 'To Marie Engels in Barmen, end of December 1838', in Marx and Engels 1975b.

—— 1838d, 'An Marie Engels, Ende Dezember 1838', in Marx and Engels 2008.

—— 1839a, 'Book Wisdom', in Marx and Engels 1975b.

—— 1839b, 'F.W. Krummacher's Sermon on Joshua', in Marx and Engels 1975b.

—— 1839c, 'Friedrich Wilhelm's Predigt über Josua', in Marx and Engels 1985d.

—— 1839d, 'From Elberfeld', in Marx and Engels 1975b.

—— 1839e, 'Aus Elberfeld', in Marx and Engels 1985d.

—— 1839f, 'Letters from Wuppertal', in Marx and Engels 1975b.

—— 1839g, 'Briefe aus dem Wuppertal', in Marx and Engels 1985d.

—— 1839h, 'To Friedrich Graeber, Bremen, February 19, 1839', in Marx and Engels 1975b.

—— 1839i, 'An Friedrich Graeber, 19. Februar 1839', in Marx and Engels 2008.

—— 1839j, 'To Friedrich Graeber, Bremen, April 8, 1839', in Marx and Engels 1975b.

—— 1839k, 'An Friedrich Graeber, 8.–9. April 1839', in Marx and Engels 2008.

—— 1839l, 'To Friedrich Graeber in Berlin, Bremen, about April 23–May 1, 1839', in Marx and Engels 1975b.

—— 1839m, 'An Friedrich Graeber, um den 23. April–1. Mai 1839', in Marx and Engels 2008.

—— 1839n, 'To Wilhelm Graeber in Berlin, Bremen, about April 28–30, 1839', in Marx and Engels 1975b.

—— 1839o, 'An Wilhelm Graeber, um den 28.–30. April 1939', in Marx and Engels 2008.

—— 1839p, 'To Wilhelm Graeber in Berlin, Bremen, May 24–June 15, 1839', in Marx and Engels 1975b.

—— 1839q, 'An Wilhelm Graeber, 24. Mai–15. Juni 1839', in Marx and Engels 2008.

—— 1839r, 'To Friedrich Graeber in Berlin, Bremen, June 15, 1839', in Marx and Engels 1975b.

—— 1839s, 'An Friedrich Graeber, 15. Juni 1839', in Marx and Engels 2008.

—— 1839t, 'To Friedrich Graeber in Berlin, Bremen, July 12–27, 1839', in Marx and Engels 1975b.

—— 1839u, 'An Friedrich Graeber, 12.–27. Juli 1839', in Marx and Engels 2008.

—— 1839v, 'To Wilhelm Graeber in Berlin, Bremen, July 30, 1839', in Marx and Engels 1975b.

—— 1839w, 'An Wilhelm Graeber, 30. Juli 1839', in Marx and Engels 2008.

—— 1839x, 'To Wilhelm Graeber in Berlin, Bremen, October 8, 1839', in Marx and Engels 1975b.

—— 1839y, 'An Wilhelm Graeber, 8. Oktober 1839', in Marx and Engels 2008.

—— 1839z, 'To Wilhelm Graeber in Berlin, Bremen, October 20–21, 1839', in Marx and Engels 1975b.

—— 1839aa, 'An Wilhelm Graeber, 20./21. Oktober 1839', in Marx and Engels 2008.

—— 1839bb, 'To Friedrich Graeber, Bremen, October 29, 1839', in Marx and Engels 1975b.

—— 1839cc, 'An Friedrich Graeber, 29. Oktober 1839', in Marx and Engels 2008.

—— 1839dd, 'To Wilhelm Graeber in Berlin, Bremen, November 13–20, 1839', in Marx and Engels 1975b.

—— 1839ee, 'An Wilhelm Graeber, 13.–20. November 1839', in Marx and Engels 2008.

—— 1839ff, 'To Friedrich Graeber, Bremen, January 20, 1839', in Marx and Engels 1975b.

—— 1839gg, 'An Friedrich Graeber, 20. Januar 1839', in Marx and Engels 2008.

—— 1839–40a, 'To Friedrich Graeber in Berlin, Bremen, December 9, 1839–February 5, 1840', in Marx and Engels 1975b.

—— 1839–40b, 'An Friedrich Graeber, 9. Dezember 1839–5. Februar 1840', in Marx and Engels 2008.

—— 1840a, 'Joel Jacoby', in Marx and Engels 1975b.

—— 1840b, 'Joel Jacoby', in Marx and Engels 1985d.

—— 1840c, 'Landscapes', in Marx and Engels 1975b.

—— 1840d, 'Landschaften', in Marx and Engels 1985d.

—— 1840e, 'Modern Literary Life', in Marx and Engels 1975b.

—— 1840f, 'Modernes Literaturleben. 1. Karl Gutzkow als Dramatiker', in Marx and Engels 1985d.

—— 1840g, 'Reports from Bremen: Ecclesiastical Controversy', in Marx and Engels 1975b.

—— 1840h, 'Korrespondenz aus Bremen: Kirchlicher Streit', in Marx and Engels 1985d.

—— 1840i, 'Reports from Bremen: Rationalism and Pietism', in Marx and Engels 1975b.

—— 1840j, 'Korrespondenz aus Bremen: Rationalismus und Pietismus', in Marx and Engels 1985d.

—— 1840k, 'Reports from Bremen: Theatre. Publishing Festival', in Marx and Engels 1975b.

—— 1840l, 'Korrespondenz aus Bremen: Theater. Buchdruckerfest', in Marx and Engels 1985d.

—— 1840m, 'Requiem for the German Adelszeitung', in Marx and Engels 1975b.

—— 1840n, 'Requiem für die deutsche Adelzeitung', in Marx and Engels 1985d.

—— 1840o, 'Siegfried's Native Town', in Marx and Engels 1975b.

—— 1840p, 'Siegfried's Heimat', in Marx and Engels 1985d.

—— 1840q, 'Two Sermons by F.W. Krummacher', in Marx and Engels 1975b.

—— 1840r, 'Zwei Predigten von Friedrich Wilhelm Krummacher', in Marx and Engels 1985d.

—— 1840s, 'Wanderings in Lombardy', in Marx and Engels 1975b.

—— 1840t, 'Lombardische Streifzüge. 1. Über die Alpen!', in Marx and Engels 1985d.

—— 1840u, 'To Wilhelm Graeber in Barmen, Bremen, November 20, 1840', in Marx and Engels 1975b.

—— 1840v, 'An Wilhelm Graeber, 20. November 1840', in Marx and Engels 2008.

—— 1841a, *Schelling on Hegel*, in Marx and Engels 1975b.

—— 1841b, *Schelling über Hegel*, in *Marx and Engels* 1985d.

—— 1841c, 'To Friedrich Graeber, February 22, 1841', in Marx and Engels 1975b.

—— 1841d, 'An Friedrich Graeber, 22. Februar 1841', in Marx and Engels 2008.

—— 1842a, 'Alexander Jung, "Lectures on Modern German Literature"', in Marx and Engels 1975b.

—— 1842b, 'Alexander Jung, Vorlesungen über die moderne Literatur der Deutschen', in Marx and Engels 1985d.

—— 1842c, *The Insolently Threatened Yet Miraculously Rescued Bible or: The Triumph of Faith, To Wit, the Terrible, Yet True and Salutary History of the Erstwhile Licentiate Bruno Bauer; How the Same, Seduced by the Devil, Fallen from the True Faith, Became Chief Devil, and Was Well and Truly Ousted in the End: A Christian Epic in Four Cantos*, in Marx and Engels 1975b.

—— 1842d, *Die frech bedräute, jedoch wunderbar befreite Bibel. Oder: Der Triumph des Glaubens. Unter Mitwirkung von Edgar Bauer*, in Marx and Engels 1985d.

—— 1842e, 'Polemic Against Leo', in Marx and Engels 1975b.

—— 1842f, 'Polemik gegen Leo', in Marx and Engels 1985d.

—— 1842g, *Schelling and Revelation: Critique of the Latest Attempt of Reaction Against the Free Philosophy*, in Marx and Engels 1975b.

—— 1842h, *Schelling und die Offenbarung. Kritik des neuesten Reaktionsversuchs gegen die freie Philosophie*, in Marx and Engels 1985d.

—— 1842i, *Schelling, Philosopher in Christ, or the Transfiguration of Worldly Wisdom into Divine Wisdom: For Believing Christians Who Do Not Know the Language of Philosophy*, in Marx and Engels 1975b.

—— 1842j, *Schelling, der Philosoph in Christo, oder die Verklärung der Weltweisheit zur Gottesweisheit*, in Marx and Engels 1985d.

—— 1843a, 'Frederick William IV, King of Prussia', in Marx and Engels 1975b.

—— 1843b, 'Frederick William IV, König von Preußen', in Marx and Engels 1985d.

—— 1843c, 'Letters from London', in Marx and Engels 1975c.

—— 1843d, 'Briefe aus London', in Marx and Engels 1985d.

—— 1843e, 'Progress of Social Reform on the Continent', in Marx and Engels 1975c.

—— 1844a, 'The Civil War in the Valais', in Marx and Engels 1975c.

—— 1844b, 'The Condition of England: *Past and Present* by Thomas Carlyle, London, 1843', in Marx and Engels 1975c.

—— 1844c, 'Die Lage Englands. "Past and Present" by Thomas Carlyle', in Marx and Engels 1974a.

—— 1844d, 'The Condition of England. I. The Eighteenth Century', in Marx and Engels 1975c.

—— 1844e, 'Die Lage Englands I. Das achzehnte Jahrhundert', in Marx and Engels 1974a.

—— 1844f, 'The Condition of England II: The English Constitution', in Marx and Engels 1975c.

—— 1844g, 'Die Lage Englands II. Die englische Konstitution', in Marx and Engels 1974a.

—— 1844h, 'Continental Socialism', in Marx and Engels 1975d.

—— 1844i, 'News from Prussia', in Marx and Engels 1975c.

—— 1844j, 'Outlines of a Critique of Political Economy', in Marx and Engels 1975c.

—— 1844k, 'Umrisse zu einer Kritik der Nationalökonomie', in Marx and Engels 1974a.

—— 1844l, 'Parsonocracy in Prussia', in Marx and Engels 1975c.

—— 1844m, 'The Situation in Prussia', in Marx and Engels 1975c.

—— 1844n, 'Engels to Marx in Paris, Barmen, 19 November 1844', in Marx and Engels 1982b.

—— 1844o, 'Engels an Marx 19. November 1844', in Marx and Engels 1973n.

—— 1844–5, 'Rapid Progress of Communism in Germany', in Marx and Engels 1975d.

—— 1845a, 'Description of Recently Founded Communist Colonies Still in Existence', in Marx and Engels 1975d.

—— 1845b, 'Besrebung der in neuerer Zeit enstanden und noch bestehenden kommunistischen Ansiedlungen', in Marx and Engels 1974b.

—— 1845c, '"Young Germany" in Switzerland (Conspiracy Against Church and State)', in Marx and Engels 1975d.

—— 1845d, 'Engels to Marx in Paris, Barmen, 20 January 1845', in Marx and Engels 1982b.

—— 1845e, 'Engels an Marx 20. Januar 1845', in Marx and Engels 1973n.

—— 1845f, 'Engels to Marx in Brussels, Barmen, 17 March 1845', in Marx and Engels 1982b.

—— 1845g, 'Engels an Marx 17. März 1845', in Marx and Engels 1973n.

—— 1845–6, 'The State of Germany', in Marx and Engels 1976c.

—— 1846a, *The Condition of the Working-Class in England*, in Marx and Engels 1975d.

—— 1846b, *Die Lage der arbeitenden Klasse in England. Nach eigner Anschauung und authentischen Quellen*, in Marx and Engels 1974b.

—— 1846c, 'A Fragment of Fourier's on Trade', in Marx and Engels 1975d.

—— 1846d, 'Ein Fragment Fouriers über den Handel', in Marx and Engels 1974b.

—— 1846e, 'Engels to Marx in Brussels, Paris, about 18 October 1846', in Marx and Engels 1982b.

—— 1846f, 'Engels an Marx 18. Oktober 1846', in Marx and Engels 1973n.

—— 1846g, 'Engels to the Communist Correspondence Committee in Brussels, Paris, Wednesday, 16 September 1846', in Marx and Engels 1982b.

—— 1846h, 'Engels an das kommunistische Korrespondenz-Komitee in Brüssel 16. September 1846', in Marx and Engels 1973n.

—— 1846i, 'Engels to the Communist Correspondence Committee in Brussels, Paris, 23 October 1846', in Marx and Engels 1982b.

—— 1846j, 'Engels an das kommunistische Korrespondenz-Komitee in Brüssel 23. Oktober 1846', in Marx and Engels 1973n.

—— 1847a, 'The Chartist Banquet in Connection with the Elections of 1847', in Marx and Engels 1976c.

—— 1847b, 'Das Bankett der Chartisten zur Feier der Wahlen von 1847', in Marx and Engels 1972a.

—— 1847c, 'The Civil War In Switzerland', in Marx and Engels 1976c.

—— 1847d, 'Der Schweizer Bürgerkrieg', in Marx and Engels 1972a.

—— 1847e, 'The Communists and Karl Heinzen', in Marx and Engels 1976c.

—— 1847f, 'Das Kommunisten und Karl Heizen', in Marx and Engels 1972a.

—— 1847g, 'The Decline and Approaching Fall of Guizot: The Position of the French Bourgeoisie', in Marx and Engels 1976c.

—— 1847h, 'The Free Trade Congress in Brussels', in Marx and Engels 1976c.

—— 1847i, 'German Socialism in Verse and Prose', in Marx and Engels 1976c.

—— 1847j, 'Deutscher Sozialismus in Versen und Prosa', in Marx and Engels 1972a.

—— 1847k, 'Protective Tariffs or Free Trade', in Marx and Engels 1976c.

—— 1847l, 'Schutzzoll oder Freihandels-System', in Marx and Engels 1972a.

—— 1848a, 'The German Central Authority and Switzerland', in Marx and Engels 1977b.

—— 1848b, 'Die deutsche Zentralgewalt und die Schweiz', in Marx and Engels 1973c.

—— 1848c, 'The Movements of 1847', in Marx and Engels 1976c.

—— 1848d, 'Die Bewegungen von 1847', in Marx and Engels 1972a.

—— 1848e, 'The National Council', in Marx and Engels 1977b.

—— 1848f, 'Der Nationalrat', in Marx and Engels 1973c.

—— 1848g, 'Personalities of the Federal Council', in Marx and Engels 1977b.

—— 1848h, 'Die Persönalichkeiten des Bundesrats', in Marx and Engels 1973c.

—— 1848i, 'Sitting of the National Council. – The Council of States. – Protest of the Pope. – Imperial Grain Embargo. – The Valaisan Great Council', in Marx and Engels 1977b.

—— 1848j, 'Ursuline Convent. – Recruiting for the Grape-Shot King. – The 'Burghers' Commune. – Commission on a General Customs Tariff', in Marx and Engels 1977b.

—— 1849a, 'The Comedy with the Imperial Crown', in Marx and Engels 1977c.

—— 1849b, 'Die Komödie mit der Kaiserkrone', in Marx and Engels 1973c.

—— 1849c, 'The Debate on the Address in Berlin', in Marx and Engels 1977c.

—— 1849d, 'Die Adreßdebatte in Berlin', in Marx and Engels 1973c.

—— 1849e, 'Elberfeld', in Marx and Engels 1977c.

—— 1849f, 'Elberfeld', in Marx and Engels 1973c.

—— 1849g, 'From the Theatre of War', in Marx and Engels 1977c.

—— 1849h, 'From the Theatre of War. – The Confused State in Serbia', in Marx and Engels 1977c.

—— 1849i, 'The Model Republic', in Marx and Engels 1977c.

—— 1849j, 'Müller. – The Freiburg Government. – Ochsenbein', in Marx and Engels 1977b.

—— 1849k, 'The Priests' Rebellion', in Marx and Engels 1977b.

—— 1849l, 'The Revolutionary Uprising in the Palatinate and Baden', in Marx and Engels 1977c.

—— 1849m, 'Die revolutionäre Erhebung in der Pfalz und Baden', in Marx and Engels 1973c.

—— 1849n, 'The Situation in Elberfeld', in Marx and Engels 1977c.

—— 1849o, 'The Uprising in Elberfeld and Düsseldorf', in Marx and Engels 1977c.

—— 1849p, 'The War in Hungary', in Marx and Engels 1977b.

—— 1850a, 'The Campaign for the German Imperial Constitution', in Marx and Engels 1978.

—— 1850b, 'Der deutsche Reichsverfassungskampagne', in Marx and Engels 1973d.

—— 1850c, 'The English Ten Hours' Bill', in Marx and Engels 1978.

—— 1850d, 'Die englische Zehnstundenbill', in Marx and Engels 1973d.

—— 1850e, 'Letters From Germany', in Marx and Engels 1978.

—— 1850f, *The Peasant War in Germany*, in Marx and Engels 1978.

—— 1850g, *Der deutsche Bauernkrieg*, in Marx and Engels 1973d.

—— 1850h, 'The Ten Hours' Question', in Marx and Engels 1978.

—— 1850i, 'Two Years of a Revolution: 1848 and 1849', in Marx and Engels 1978.

—— 1851a, 'Engels to Marx in London, Manchester, 5 February 1851', in Marx and Engels 1982b.

—— 1851b, 'Engels an Marx 5. Februar 1851', in Marx and Engels 1973n.

—— 1851c, 'Engels to Marx in London, Manchester, Thursday, 13 February 1851', in Marx and Engels 1982b.

—— 1851d, 'Engels an Marx 13. Februar 1851', in Marx and Engels 1973n.

—— 1851e, 'Engels to Marx in London, Manchester, Friday, 9 May 1851', in Marx and Engels 1982b.

—— 1851f, 'Engels an Marx 9. Mai 1851', in Marx and Engels 1973n.

—— 1851g, 'Engels to Marx in London, Manchester, 17 July 1851', in Marx and Engels 1982b.

—— 1851h, 'Engels an Marx um den 17. Juli 1851', in Marx and Engels 1973n.

—— 1851i, 'Engels to Marx in London, Manchester, about 20 July 1851', in Marx and Engels 1982b.

—— 1851j, 'Engels an Marx um den 20. Juli 1851', in Marx and Engels 1973n.

—— 1851k, 'Engels to Marx in London, Manchester, about 10 August 1851', in Marx and Engels 1982b.

—— 1851l, 'Engels an Marx um den 10. August 1851', in Marx and Engels 1973n.

—— 1851m, 'Engels to Marx in London, Manchester, about 27 October 1851', in Marx and Engels 1982b.

—— 1851n, 'Engels an Marx um den 27. Oktober 1851', in Marx and Engels 1973n.

—— 1851–2, *Revolution and Counter-Revolution in Germany*, in Marx and Engels 1979a.

—— 1852a, 'Engels to Jenny Marx in London, Manchester, 14 January 1852', in Marx and Engels 1983a.

—— 1852b, 'Engels an Jenny Marx 14. Januar 1852', in Marx and Engels 1973o.

—— 1852c, 'Engels to Marie Blank in London, Manchester, 22 November 1852', in Marx and Engels 1983a.

—— 1852d, 'Engels an Marie Blank 22. November 1852', in Marx and Engels 1973w.

—— 1853a, 'The Turkish Question', in Marx and Engels 1979b.

—— 1853b, 'What is to Become of Turkey in Europe?', in Marx and Engels 1979b.

—— 1853c, 'Engels to Marx in London, Manchester, 10 March 1853', in Marx and Engels 1983a.[1]

—— 1853d, 'Engels an Marx 9. März 1853', in Marx and Engels 1973o.

—— 1853e, 'Engels to Joseph Weydemeyer in New York, Manchester, 12 April 1853', in Marx and Engels 1983a.

—— 1853f, 'Engels an Joseph Weydemeyer 12. April 1853', in Marx and Engels 1973o.

—— 1853g, 'Engels to Marx in London, Manchester, before 28 May 1853', in Marx and Engels 1983a.[2]

—— 1853h, 'Engels an Marx um den 26. Mai 1853', in Marx and Engels 1973o.

—— 1853i, 'Engels to Marx in London, Manchester, 6 June 1853, evening', in Marx and Engels 1983a.

1. The date for this letter is listed as 9 March 1853 in *MEW*.
2. The date for this letter is listed as 'um den 26. Mai 1853' in *MEW*.

—— 1853j, 'Engels an Marx 6. Juni 1853', in Marx and Engels 1973o.

—— 1854a, 'Engels to Marx in London, Manchester, 1 May 1854', in Marx and Engels 1983a.

—— 1854b, 'Engels an Marx 1. Mai 1854', in Marx and Engels 1973o.

—— 1855, 'The European Struggle', in Marx and Engels 1980b.

—— 1856a, 'Engels to Marx in London, Manchester, 7 February 1856', in Marx and Engels 1983b.

—— 1856b, 'Engels an Marx 7. Februar 1856', in Marx and Engels 1973p.

—— 1856c, 'Engels to Marx in London, Manchester, 23 May 1856', in Marx and Engels 1983b.

—— 1856d, 'Engels an Marx 23. Mai 1856', in Marx and Engels 1973p.

—— 1859a, 'Camp', in Marx and Engels 1982a.

—— 1859b, 'Catapult', in Marx and Engels 1982a.

—— 1859c, 'The War – No Progress', in Marx and Engels 1980c.

—— 1859d, 'Engels to Ferdinand Freiligrath', in London, Manchester, 25 January 1859', in Marx and Engels 1983b.

—— 1859e, 'Engels an Ferdinand Freiligrath 25. Januar 1859', in Marx and Engels 1973p.

—— 1859f, 'Engels to Marx in London, Manchester, 3 August 1859', in Marx and Engels 1983b.

—— 1859g, 'Engels an Marx 3. Augustus 1859', in Marx and Engels 1973p.

—— 1860, 'The History of the Rifle', in Marx and Engels 1982a.

—— 1862a, 'Engels to Carl Siebel in Barmen, Manchester, 4 June 1862', in Marx and Engels 1985c.

—— 1862b, 'Engels to Marx in London, Manchester, 15 November 1862', in Marx and Engels 1985c.

—— 1862c, 'Engels an Marx 15. November 1862', in Marx and Engels 1972g.

—— 1865a, 'The Prussian Military Question and the German Workers' Party', in Marx and Engels 1985a.

—— 1865b, 'Die preußische Militärfrage und die deutsche Arbeiterpartei', in Marx and Engels 1973g.

—— 1866, 'What Have the Working Classes to do with Poland?', in Marx and Engels 1985a.

—— 1867a, 'Engels to Marx in London, Manchester, 1 November 1867', in Marx and Engels 1987c.

—— 1867b, 'Engels an Marx 1. November 1867', in Marx and Engels 1973q.

—— 1867c, 'Engels to Ludwig Kugelmann in Hanover, Manchester, 8 and 20 November 1867', in Marx and Engels 1987c.

—— 1867d, 'Engels an Ludwig Kugelmann 8. und 20. November 1867', in Marx and Engels 1973q.

—— 1867e, 'Engels to Marx in London, Manchester, 29 November 1867, 7 Southgate', in Marx and Engels 1987c.

—— 1867f, 'Engels an Marx 29. November 1867', in Marx and Engels 1973q.

—— 1868a, 'Synopsis of Volume One of *Capital* by Karl Marx', in Marx and Engels 1985a.

—— 1868b, 'Prospekt über „Das Kapital" von Karl Marx, Erster Band', in Marx and Engels 1973p.

—— 1868c, 'Engels to Jenny Marx in London, Manchester, 3 January 1868', in Marx and Engels 1987c.

—— 1868d, 'Engels an Jenny Marx 3. Januar 1868', in Marx and Engels 1973r.

—— 1868e, 'Engels to Marx in London, Manchester, about 14 August 1868', in Marx and Engels 1988c.

—— 1868f, 'Engels an Marx um den 14. August 1868', in Marx and Engels 1973r.

—— 1868g, 'Engels to Marx in London, Manchester, 14 October 1868', in Marx and Engels 1988c.

—— 1868h, 'Engels an Marx 14. Oktober 1868', in Marx and Engels 1973r.

—— 1868i, 'Engels to Marx in London, Manchester, 20 November 1868', in Marx and Engels 1988c.

—— 1868j, 'Engels an Marx 20. November 1868', in Marx and Engels 1973r.

—— 1868k, 'Frederick Engels: Confession, London, Early April 1868', in Marx and Engels 1988c.

—— 1869a, 'Notes on Goldwin Smith's Book *Irish History and Irish Character*', in Marx and Engels 1985b.

—— 1869b, 'Engels to Marx in London, Manchester, 21 March 1869', in Marx and Engels 1988c.

—— 1869c, 'Engels an Marx 21. März 1869', in Marx and Engels 1973r.

—— 1869d, 'Engels to Marx in London, Manchester, about 19 November 1869', in Marx and Engels 1988c.

—— 1869e, 'Engels an Marx 19. November 1869', in Marx and Engels 1973r.

—— 1870a, 'The History of Ireland', in Marx and Engels 1985b.

—— 1870b, 'Die Geschichte Irlands', in Marx and Engels 1973g.

—— 1870c, 'How to Fight the Prussians', in Marx and Engels 1986b.

—— 1870d, 'Notes for the Preface to a Collection of Irish Songs', in Marx and Engels 1985b.

—— 1870e, 'Bemerkungen für das Vorwort zu einer Sammlung irischer Lieder', in Marx and Engels 1973g.

—— 1870f, 'Notes on the War – XIII', in Marx and Engels 1986b.

—— 1870g, 'Plan for The History of Ireland', in Marx and Engels 1985b.

—— 1870h, 'Preface to the Second Edition of *The Peasant War in Germany*', in Marx and Engels 1985b.

—— 1870i, 'Vorbemerkung zum Zweiten Abdruck (1870) „Der deutsche Bauernkrieg"', in Marx and Engels 1973g.

—— 1870j, 'Prussian Francs-Tireurs', in Marx and Engels 1986b.

—— 1870k, 'Varia on the History of the Irish Confiscations', in Marx and Engels 1985b.

—— 1870l, 'Engels to Marx in London, Manchester, 21 April 1870', in Marx and Engels 1989c.

—— 1870m, 'Engels an Marx 21. April 1870', in Marx and Engels 1973r.

—— 1871a, 'Account of Engels's Speech on Mazzini's Attitude Towards the International', in Marx and Engels 1986b.

—— 1871b, 'The Address *The Civil War in France* and the English Press', in Marx and Engels 1986b.

—— 1871c, 'Die Adresse „Der Bürgerkrieg in Frankreich" und die englische Presse', in Marx and Engels 1973h.

—— 1871d, 'On the Progress of the International Working Men's Association in Italy and Spain', in Marx and Engels 1988a.

—— 1871e, 'The Position of the Danish Members of the International on the Agrarian Question', in Marx and Engels 1988a.

—— 1871f, 'Engels to Wilhelm Liebknecht in Leipzig, London, 4 May 1871', in Marx and Engels 1989c.

—— 1871g, 'Engels an Wilhelm Lienknecht 4. Mai 1871', in Marx and Engels 1973s.

—— 1871h, 'Engels to Carlo Cafiero in Barletta, London, 1–3 July 1871', in Marx and Engels 1989c.

—— 1871i, 'Engels to Wilhelm Liebknecht in Leipzig, London, 15 December 1871', in Marx and Engels 1989c.

—— 1871j, 'Engels an Wilhelm Lienknecht 15. December 1871', in Marx and Engels 1973s.

—— 1872a, 'The Congress at The Hague (Letter to Enrico Bignami)', in Marx and Engels 1988a.

—— 1872b, 'Der Haager Kongreß [Brief an Bignami]', in Marx and Engels 1973i.

—— 1872c, 'The Congress of Sonvillier and the International', in Marx and Engels 1988a.

—— 1872d, 'Der Kongreß von Sonvillier und die Internationale', in Marx and Engels 1973h.

—— 1872e, 'Engels to Carlo Terzaghi in Turin, London after 6 January 1872, 122 Regent's Park Road', in Marx and Engels 1989c.

—— 1872f, 'Engels an Carlo Terzaghi um den 6. Januar (1. Entwurf) 14/15. Januar (2. Entwurf) 1872', in Marx and Engels 1973s.

—— 1872g, 'Engels to Carlo Cafiero in Naples, London, 14 June 1872', in Marx and Engels 1989c.

—— 1872h, 'Engels an Carlo Cafieri 14. Juni 1872', in Marx and Engels 1973s.

—— 1872–3a, *The Housing Question*, in Marx and Engels 1988a.

—— 1872–3b, *Zur Wohnungsfrage*, in Marx and Engels 1973i.

—— 1873a, 'Note on a Review of E. Renan's *L'Antéchrist*', in Marx and Engels 1988a.

—— 1873b, 'On the Articles in the *Neuer Social-Democrat*', in Marx and Engels 1988a.

—— 1873c, 'Zu den Artikeln im „Neuen Social-Demokrat"', in Marx and Engels 1973i.

—— 1873d, 'The Republic in Spain', in Marx and Engels 1988a.

—— 1873e, 'Varia on Germany', in Marx and Engels 1988a.

—— 1873f, 'Varia über Deutschland', in Marx and Engels 1973i.

—— 1873g, 'Engels to August Bebel in Hubertusburg, London, 20 June 1873', in Marx and Engels 1989c.

—— 1873h, 'Engels an August Bebel 20. Juni 1873', in Marx and Engels 1973s.

—— 1873–82a, *Dialectics of Nature*, in Marx and Engels 1987a.

—— 1873–82b, *Dialektik der Natur*, in Marx and Engels 1973k.

—— 1874, 'Engels to Marx in Karlsbad, London, 5 September 1874', in Marx and Engels 1991a.

—— 1874–5a, 'Refugee Literature', in Marx and Engels 1991a.

—— 1874–5b, 'Flüchlingsliteratur', in Marx and Engels 1973i.

—— 1875a, 'Semi-Official War Cries', in Marx and Engels 1991a.

—— 1875b, 'Offiziözes Kriegsgeheul', in Marx and Engels 1973i.

—— 1876–7a, 'From Engels' Preparatory Writings for *Anti-Dühring*', in Marx and Engels 1987a.

—— 1876–7b, 'Aus Engels' Vorarbeiten zum „Anti-Dühring"', in Marx and Engels 1973k.

—— 1877–8a, *Anti-Dühring: Herr Eugen Dühring's Revolution in Science*, in Marx and Engels 1987a.

—— 1877–8b, *Herr Eugen Dührings Umwälzung der Wissenschaft (Anti-Dühring)*, in Marx and Engels 1973k.

—— 1880a, *Socialism: Utopian and Scientific*, in Marx and Engels 1991a.

—— 1880b, *Die Entwicklung des Sozialismus von der Utopie zur Wissenschaft*, in Marx and Engels 1973j.

—— 1881a, 'Draft for the Speech over the Grave of Jenny Marx', in Marx and Engels 1991a.

—— 1881b, 'Rede am Grabe von Jenny Marx', in Marx and Engels 1973j.

—— 1881c, 'Engels to Jenny Longuet in Paris, London, 24 February 1881', in Marx and Engels 1992.

—— 1881d, 'Engels an Jenny Longuet 24. Februar 1881', in Marx and Engels 1973u.

—— 1882a, 'Bruno Bauer and Early Christianity', in Marx and Engels 1991a.

—— 1882b, 'Bruno Bauer und das Urchristentum', in Marx and Engels 1973j.

—— 1882c, *The Frankish Period*, in Marx and Engels 1990a.

—— 1882d, *Fränkische Zeit*, in Marx and Engels 1973j.

—— 1882e, 'The Mark', in Marx and Engels 1991a.

—— 1882f, 'Die Mark', in Marx and Engels 1973j.

—— 1882g, 'The Vicar of Bray', in Marx and Engels 1991a.

—— 1882h, 'Der Vikar von Bray', in Marx and Engels 1973j.

—— 1882i, 'Engels to Eduard Bernstein in Zurich, London, 22 and 25 February 1882', in Marx and Engels 1992.

—— 1882j, 'Engels an Eduard Bernstein 22.–25. Februar 1882', in Marx and Engels 1973u.

—— 1882k, 'Engels to Friedrich Adolph Sorge in Hoboken, London, 20 June 1882', in Marx and Engels 1992.

—— 1882l, 'Engels an Friedrich Adolphe Sorge 20. Juni 1882', in Marx and Engels 1973u.

—— 1882m, 'Engels to Eduard Bernstein in Zurich, London, 26 June 1882', in Marx and Engels 1992.

—— 1882n, 'Engels an Eduard Bernstein 26. Juni 1882', in Marx and Engels 1973u.

—— 1882o, 'Engels to August Bebel in Leipzig, London, 28 October 1882', in Marx and Engels 1992.

—— 1882p, 'Engels an August Bebel 28. Oktober 1882', in Marx and Engels 1973u.

—— 1883, 'The Book of Revelation', in Marx and Engels 1990a.

—— 1884a, *The Origin of the Family, Private Property and the State in Light of the Researches by Lewis H. Morgan*, in Marx and Engels 1990a.

—— 1884b, *Der Ursprung der Familie, des Privateigentums und des Staats*, in Marx and Engels 1973l.

—— 1884c, 'On the Peasant War', in Marx and Engels 1990a.

—— 1884d, 'Zum „Bauernkrieg"', in Marx and Engels 1973i.

—— 1884e, 'Engels to Eduard Bernstein in Zurich, London, July 1884', in Marx and Engels 1995.

—— 1884f, 'Engels an Eduard Bernstein Juli 1884', in Marx and Engels 1973v.

—— 1884g, 'Engels to Eduard Bernstein in Zurich, London, 11 November 1884', in Marx and Engels 1995.

—— 1884h, 'Engels an Eduard Bernstein 11. November 1884', in Marx and Engels 1973v.

—— 1885a, 'On the History of the Communist League', in Marx and Engels 1990a.

—— 1885b, 'Zur Geschichte des Bundes der Kommunisten', in Marx and Engels 1973l.

—— 1885c, 'Preface to the First German Edition of *Capital: A Critique of Political Economy, Volume II*', in Marx and Engels 1997a.

—— 1885d, 'Vorwart an „Das Kapital. Kritik der politischen Ökonomie. Zweiter Band Buch II. Der Zirkulationsprozeß des Kapitals"', in Marx and Engels 1973m.

—— 1885e, 'How Not to Translate Marx', in Marx and Engels 1990a.

—— 1885f, 'Wie man Marx nicht übersetzen soll', in Marx and Engels 1973l.

—— 1885g, 'Engels to Laura Lafargue in Paris, London, 16 June 1885', in Marx and Engels 1995.

—— 1885h, 'Engels an Laura Lafargue 16. Juni 1885', in Marx and Engels 1973v.

—— 1885i, 'Engels to Wilhelm Liebknecht in Berlin, London, 1 December 1885', in Marx and Engels 1995.

—— 1885j, 'Engels an Wilhelm Liebknecht 1. Dezember 1885', in Marx and Engels 1973v.

—— 1886a, *Ludwig Feuerbach and the End of Classical German Philosophy*, in Marx and Engels 1990a.

—— 1886b, *Ludwig Feuerbach und der Ausgang der klassischen deutschen Philosophie*, in Marx and Engels 1973l.

—— 1886c, 'Engels to Florence Kelley-Wischnewetsky in Zurich, London, 25 February 1886', in Marx and Engels 1995.

—— 1886d, 'Engels an Florence Kelley-Wischnewetsky 25. Februar 1886', in Marx and Engels 1973v.

—— 1886e, 'Engels to Friedrich Adolphe Sorge in Hoboken, 16–17 September 1886', in Marx and Engels 1995.

—— 1886f, 'Engels an Friedrich Adolphe Sorge 16./17. September 1886', in Marx and Engels 1973v.

—— 1886g, 'Engels to Friedrich Adolphe Sorge in Hoboken, London, 29 November 1886', in Marx and Engels 1995.

—— 1886h, 'Engels an Friedrich Adolphe Sorge 29. November 1886', in Marx and Engels 1973v.

—— 1887a, 'Engels to Laura Lafargue in Paris, London, 7 June 1887', in Marx and Engels 2001a.

—— 1887b, 'Engels an Laura Lafargue 7. Juni 1887', in Marx and Engels 1973v.

—— 1887c, 'Engels to Friedrich Adolph Sorge in Hoboken, London, 18 June 1887', in Marx and Engels 2001a.

—— 1887d, 'Engels an Friedrich Adolphe Sorge 18. Juni 1887', in Marx and Engels 1973v.

—— 1887e, 'Engels to Friedrich Adolph Sorge in Rochester, London, 16 September 1887', in Marx and Engels 2001a.

—— 1887f, 'Engels an Friedrich Adolphe Sorge 16. September 1887', in Marx and Engels 1973v.

—— 1888a, 'Engels to Florence Kelley-Wischnewetsky in New York, London, 2 May 1888', in Marx and Engels 2001a.

—— 1888b, 'Engels an Florence Kelley-Wischnewetsky 2. Mai 1888', in Marx and Engels 1974g.

—— 1888c, 'Engels to August Bebel in Berlin, London, 25 October 1888', in Marx and Engels 2001a.

—— 1888d, 'Engels an August Bebel 25. Oktober 1888', in Marx and Engels 1974g.

—— 1889a, 'The Ruhr Miners' Strike of 1889', in Marx and Engels 1990a.

—— 1889b, 'Engels to Paul Lafargue at La Perreux, London, 11 May 1889', in Marx and Engels 2001a.

—— 1889c, 'Engels an Paul Lafargue 11. Mai 1889', in Marx and Engels 1974g.

—— 1889d, 'Engels to Max Hildebrand in Berlin, London, 22 October 1889, 122 Regent's Park Road, N.W.', in Marx and Engels 2001a.

—— 1889e, 'Engels an Max Hildebrand 22. Oktober 1889', in Marx and Engels 1974g.

—— 1890a, 'The Foreign Policy of Russian Tsardom', in Marx and Engels 1990b.

—— 1890b, 'Die auswärtige Politik des russischen Zarentums', in Marx and Engels 1972e.

—— 1890c, 'On Anti-Semitism (from a Private Letter to Vienna)', in Marx and Engels 1990b.

—— 1890d, 'Über den Antisemitismus (Aus einem Brief nach Wien)', in Marx and Engels 1972e.

—— 1890e, 'What Now?', in Marx and Engels 1990b.

—— 1890f, 'Was nun?', in Marx and Engels 1972e.

—— 1890g, 'Engels to Conrad Schmidt in Berlin, London, 27 October 1890', in Marx and Engels 2001b.

—— 1890h, 'Engels an Conrad Schmidt 27. Oktober 1890', in Marx and Engels 1974g.

—— 1890–1a, 'Introduction to Karl Marx's *The Civil War in France*', in Marx and Engels 1990b.

—— 1890–1b, 'Einleitung zu Karl Marx' „Bürgerkrieg in Frankreich" (Ausgabe 1891)', in Marx and Engels 1972e.

—— 1890–1c, 'To the Early History of the Family (Bachofen, McLennan, Morgan): Preface to the Fourth German Edition of *The Origin of the Family, Private Property and the State*', in Marx and Engels 1990b.

—— 1890–1d, 'Vorwort zur vierten Auflage (1891) des „Ursprung der Familie, des Privateigentums und des Staats"', in Marx and Engels 1972e.

—— 1891a, 'In the Case of Brentano Versus Marx Regarding Alleged Falsification of Quotation, the Story and Documents', in Marx and Engels 1990b.

—— 1891b, 'In Sachen Brentano contra Marx wegen angeblicher Zitatsfälschung Geschichtserzählung und Dokumente', in Marx and Engels 1972e.

—— 1891c, 'A Critique of the Draft Social-Democratic Programme of 1891', in Marx and Engels 1990b.

—— 1891d, 'Zur Kritik des sozialdemokratischen Programmentwurfs 1891', in Marx and Engels 1972e.

—— 1891e, 'Engels to Kark Kautsky in Stuttgart, London, 30 April, 1891', in Marx and Engels 2001b.

—— 1891f, 'Engels an Karl Kautsky 30. April 1891', in Marx and Engels 1968.

—— 1891g, 'Engels to Laura Lafargue at Le Perreux, London, 4 May 1891', in Marx and Engels 2001b.

—— 1891h, 'Engels an Laura Lafargue 4. Mai 1891', in Marx and Engels 1968.

—— 1891i, 'Engels to Paul Lafargue at Le Perreux, London, 29 May, 1891', in Marx and Engels 2001b.

—— 1891j, 'Engels an Paul Lafargue 29. Mai 1891', in Marx and Engels 1968.

—— 1891k, 'Engels to Karl Kautsky in Stuttgart, London, 13 June 1891', in Marx and Engels 2001b.

—— 1891l, 'Engels an Karl Kautsky 13. Juni 1891', in Marx and Engels 1968.

—— 1891m, 'Engels to Laura Lafargue at Le Perreux, London, 19 December 1891', in Marx and Engels 2001b.

—— 1891n, 'Engels an Laura Lafargue 19./20. Dezember 1891', in Marx and Engels 1968.

—— 1892a, 'Introduction to the English Edition of *Socialism: Utopian and Scientific*', in Marx and Engels 1990b.

—— 1892b, 'Engels to Laura Lafargue at Le Perreux, London, 6 January 1892', in Marx and Engels 2001b.

—— 1892c, 'Engels an Laura Lafargue 6. Januar 1892', in Marx and Engels 1968.

—— 1892d, 'Engels to Karl Kautsky in Stuttgart, London, 1 February 1892', in Marx and Engels 2001b.

—— 1892e, 'Engels an Karl Kautsky 1. Februar 1892', in Marx and Engels 1968.

—— 1892f, 'Engels to Karl Kautsky in Stuttgart, Ryde, 12 August 1892, The Firs, Brading Road', in Marx and Engels 2001b.

—— 1892g, 'Engels an Karl Kautsky 12. August 1892', in Marx and Engels 1968.

—— 1892h, 'Engels to Victor Adler in Lunz, Ryde, 19 August 1892, The Firs, Brading Road', in Marx and Engels 2001b.

—— 1892i, 'Engels an Victor Adler 19. August 1892', in Marx and Engels 1968.

—— 1892j, 'Engels to August Bebel in St Gallen, Ryde, 20 August 1892, The Firs, Brading Road', in Marx and Engels 2001b.

—— 1892k, 'Engels an August Bebel 20. August 1892', in Marx and Engels 1968.

—— 1892l, 'Engels to Conrad Schmidt in Zurich, London, 12 September 1892', in Marx and Engels 2001b.

—— 1892m, 'Engels an Conrad Schmidt 12. September 1892', in Marx and Engels 1968.

—— 1892n, 'Engels to Adolph Sorge in Hoboken, London, 31 December 1892', in Marx and Engels 2004.

—— 1892o, 'Engels an Friedrich Adolphe Sorge 31. December 1892', in Marx and Engels 1968.

—— 1893a, 'Engels to Franz Mehring in Berlin, London, 14 July 1893', in Marx and Engels 2004.

—— 1893b, 'Engels an Franz Mehring 14. Juli 1893', in Marx and Engels 1973w.

—— 1893c, 'Engels to Laura Lafargue at Le Perreux, London, 18 October 1893', in Marx and Engels 2004.

—— 1893d, 'Engels an Laura Lafargue in Le Perreux, 18. Oktober 1893', in Marx and Engels 1973w.

—— 1893e, 'Engels to Natalie Liebknecht in Berlin, London, 1 December 1893', in Marx and Engels 2004.

—— 1893f, 'Engels an Natalie Liebknecht 1. Dezember 1893', in Marx and Engels 1973w.

—— 1894a, 'Engels to Karl Kautsky in Stuttgart, London, 26 June 1894', in Marx and Engels 2004.

—— 1894b, 'Engels an Karl Kautsky 26./27. Juni 1894', in Marx and Engels 1973w.

—— 1894c, 'Engels to Karl Kautsky in Stuttgart, London, 16 July 1894', in Marx and Engels 2004.

—— 1894d, 'Engels an Karl Kautsky 16. Juli 1894', in Marx and Engels 1973w.

—— 1894e, 'Engels to Karl Kautsky in Stuttgart, London, 28 July 1894', in Marx and Engels 2004.

—— 1894f, 'Engels an Karl Kautsky 28. Juli 1894', in Marx and Engels 1973w.

—— 1894–5a, 'Introduction to Karl Marx's The Class Struggles in France', in Marx and Engels 1990b.

—— 1894–5b, 'Einleitung zu Karl Marx's „Klassenkämpfe in Frankreich 1848 bis 1850" (1895)', in Marx and Engels 1972e.

—— 1894–5c, On the History of Early Christianity, in Marx and Engels 1990b.

—— 1894–5d, Zur Geschichte des Urchristentums, in Marx and Engels 1972e.

—— 1895a, 'Engels to Paul Lafargue at Le Perreux, London, 26 February 1895', in Marx and Engels 2004.

—— 1895b, 'Engels an Paul Lafargue 26. Februar 1895', in Marx and Engels 1973w.

—— 1895–6a, The Role of Force in History, in Marx and Engels 1990a.

—— 1895–6b, Die Rolle der Gewalt in der Geschichte, in Marx and Engels 1973l.

Engels, Friedrich and Karl Kautsky 1887, 'Lawyers' Socialism', in Marx and Engels 1990a.

Engels, Friedrich (senior) 1820, 'Friedrich Engels Senior to Karl Snethlage in Berlin, Barmen, December 1, 1820', in Marx and Engels 1975b.

—— 1835, 'Friedrich Engels Senior to His Wife Elise in Hamm, Barmen, August 27, 1835', in Marx and Engels 1975b.

—— 1842, 'Friedrich Engels Senior to Karl Snethlage in Berlin, Barmen, October 5, 1842', in Marx and Engels 1975b.

Evans, Stephen C. 1984, 'Redeemed Man: The Vision Which Gave Rise to Marxism', Christian Scholar's Review, 13, 2: 141–50.

Feuerbach, Ludwig 1924 [1841], Das Wesen des Christentums, Leipzig: Friedrichs & Bley.

—— 1989 [1841], The Essence of Christianity, translated by George Eliot, Amherst: Prometheus Books.

—— 2004, The Essence of Religion, translated by Alexander Loos, Amherst: Prometheus Books.

Fine, Robert 2006, 'Karl Marx and the Radical Critique of Anti-Semitism', Engage Journal, 2 May, available at: <http://www.engageonline.org.uk/journal/index.php?journal_id=10&article_id=33>.

Fischer, Karl Philipp 1839, Die Idee der Gottheit: Ein Versuch den Theismus speculativ zu begründen und zu entwickeln, Stuttgart: Liesching.

Fischman, Dennis 1991, Political Discourse in Exile: Karl Marx and the Jewish Question, Amherst: University of Massachusetts Press.

Flannery, Edward H. 2004, The Anguish of the Jews: Twenty-Three Centuries of Antisemitism, Marwah: Paulist Press.

Foucault, Michel 1979 [1975], Discipline and Punish: The Birth of the Clinic, translated by Alan Sheridan, New York: Vintage.

From the Indictment of the Participants in the Uprising in Elberfeld in May 1849 1850, in Marx and Engels 1978.

Geras, Norman 1983, 'Fetishism', in Bottomore (ed.) 1983.

Goldstein, Warren S. (ed.) 2006, Marx, Critical Theory and Religion: A Critique of Rational Choice, Leiden: Brill.

Gramsci, Antonio 1994, Letters from Prison, Volume 1, translated by Raymond Rosenthal, New York: Columbia University Press.

—— 1996 [1975], Prison Notebooks, Volume 2, translated by Joseph A. Buttigieg, edited by Lawrence D. Kritzman, New York: Columbia University Press.

Greenblatt, Stephen J. 1978, 'Marlowe, Marx, and Anti-Semitism', Critical Inquiry, 5, 2: 291–307.

Gruppe, Otto Friedrich 2010 [1842], Bruno Bauer und die Akademische Lehrfreiheit, Whitefish: Kessinger Publishing.

Hantschke, J.C.L. 1837, 'School-Leaving Reference for Primary Pupil Friedrich Engels (No. 713)', in Marx and Engels 1975b.

Harris, Sam 2005, *The End of Faith: Religion, Terror and the Future of Reason*, New York: W.W. Norton.

—— 2006, *Letter to a Christian Nation*, New York: Knopf.

Hess, Moses 1837, *Die Heilige Geschichte der Menschheit*, Stuttgart, n. p.

—— 1961 [1841], *Die Europäische Trierarchie*, in *Philosophische und sozialistische Schriften, 1837–1850*, edited by Auguste Cornu and Wolfgang Müncke, Berlin: Akademie Verlag.

—— 2004 [1837], *The Holy History of Mankind and Other Writings*, edited by Shlomo Avineri, Cambridge: Cambridge University Press.

Hinkelammert, Franz J. 1986, *The Ideological Weapons of Death: A Theological Critique of Capitalism*, Maryknoll: Orbis.

Hitchens, Christopher 2007, *God Is Not Great: How Religion Poisons Everything*, New York: Twelve Books.

Hook, Sidney 1994 [1936], *From Hegel to Marx: Studies in the Intellectual Development of Karl Marx*, New York: Columbia University Press.

Horkheimer, Max and Theodor W. Adorno 2002 [1947], *Dialectic of Enlightenment: Philosophical Fragments*, translated by Edmund Jephcott, Stanford: Stanford University Press.

—— 2003 [1947], *Dialektik der Aufklärung* in *Gesammelte Schriften*, Volume 3, Frankfurt am Main: Suhrkamp.

Horsley, Richard A. 2000, 'Rhetoric and Empire – and 1 Corinthians', in *Paul and Politics: Ekklesia, Israel, Imperium, Interpretation. Essays in Honor of Krister Stendahl*, edited by Richard A. Horsley, Harrisburg: Trinity Press International.

—— 2002, *Jesus and Empire: The Kingdom of God and the New World Order*, Minneapolis: Augsburg Fortress.

—— 2003, *Religion and Empire: People, Power, and the Life of the Spirit*, Minneapolis: Augsburg Fortress.

—— (ed.) 2008, *In the Shadow of Empire: Reclaiming the Bible as a History of Faithful Resistance*, Louisville: Westminster John Knox.

Hunt, Richard N. 1974, *The Political Ideas of Marx and Engels. I. Marxism and Totalitarian Democracy, 1818–1850*, Pittsburgh: University of Pittsburgh Press.

Janicaud, Dominique, Jean-François Courtine, Jean-Louis Chrétien, Michel Henry, Jean-Luc Marion and Paul Ricœur 2000, *Phenomenology and the 'Theological Turn': The French Debate*, New York: Fordham University Press.

Janz, Denis R. 1998, *World Christianity and Marxism*, Oxford: Oxford University Press.

Kaplan, Francis 1990, *Marx antisémite?*, Paris: Imago/Berg International.

Kautsky, Karl 1947a [1888], *Thomas More und seine Utopie: mit einer historischen Einleitung*, Berlin: Dietz.

—— 1947b [1895–7], *Vorläufer des neueren Sozialismus*, Volume 1, Berlin: Dietz.

—— 1947c [1895–7], *Vorläufer des neueren Sozialismus*, Volume 2, Berlin: Dietz.

—— 1977 [1908], *Der Ursprung des Christentums: Eine Historische Untersuchung*, Stuttgart: Dietz.

—— 2003 [1888], *Thomas More and His Utopia*, translated by Henry James Stenning, Whitefish: Kessinger Publishing.

—— 2007 [1908], *Foundations of Christianity*, translated by H.F. Mins, London: Resistance Books.

Kautsky, Karl and Paul Lafargue 1977 [1922], *Vorläufer des neueren Sozialismus*, Stuttgart: J.H.W. Dietz.

Kiernan, J.G. 1983, 'Religion', in Bottomore (ed.) 1983.

Kolakowski, Leszek 1981, *Main Currents of Marxism*, Volume 1, translated by P.S. Falla, Oxford: Oxford University Press.

Kouvelakis, Stathis 2003, *Philosophy and Revolution: From Kant to Marx*, translated by G.M. Goshgarian, London: Verso.

Kroll, Frank-Lothar 1990, *Friedrich Wilhelm IV. und das Staatsdenken der deutschen Romantik*, Berlin: Copress.

Larrain, Jorge 1983a, 'Ideology', in Bottomore (ed.) 1983.

—— 1983b, *Marxism and Ideology*, Basingstoke: Macmillan.

Leaving Certificate from Berlin University 1841, in Marx and Engels 1975a.

Lee, Michael 2006, *Paul, the Stoics, and the Body of Christ*, Cambridge: Cambridge University Press.

Lem, Stanisław 1971 [1961], *Solaris*, translated by Joanna Kilmartin and Steve Cox, London: Faber.

Lemche, Niels Peter 1988, *Ancient Israel: A New History of Israelite Society*, Sheffield: Sheffield Academic Press.

—— 1998a, *Prelude to Israel's Past: Background and Beginnings of Israelite History and Identity*, translated by E.F. Maniscalco, Peabody: Hendrickson.

—— 1998b, *The Israelites in History and Tradition*, London: SPCK.

Leopold, David 2007, *The Young Karl Marx: German Philosophy, Modern Politics, and Human Flourishing*, Cambridge: Cambridge University Press.

Lewis, Bernard 1999, *Semites and Anti-Semites: An Inquiry into Conflict and Prejudice*, New York: W.W. Norton.

Lifshitz, Mikhail 1973 [1933], *The Philosophy of Art of Karl Marx*, translated by Ralph B. Winn, London: Pluto.

—— 1984, *Collected Works*, Moscow: Progress Publishers.

Lischer, Richard 1973, 'The Lutheran Shape of Marxian Evil', *Religion in Life*, 42, 4: 549–58.

Loader, William 2004, *The Septuagint, Sexuality, and the New Testament: Case Studies on the Impact of the LXX in Philo and the New Testament*, Grand Rapids: Eerdmans.

Lobkowicz, Nicholas 1969, 'Karl Marx and Max Stirner', in *Demythologising Marxism*, edited by Frederick J. Adelmann, The Hague: Martinus Nijhoff.

Lochman, Jan Milič 1978, 'The Place for Prometheus: Theological Lessons from the Christian-Marxist Dialogue', *Interpretation*, 32, 3: 242–54.

Löwy, Michael 1988, *Marxisme et théologie de la libération*, Amsterdam: IIRE, available at: <http://gate.iire.org/cer/PDF%20CER%2010.PDF>.

—— 1992 [1988], *Redemption and Utopia: Jewish Libertarian Thought in Central Europe: A Study in Elective Affinity*, Stanford: Stanford University Press.

—— 1996, *The War of the Gods: Religion and Politics in Latin America*, London: Verso.

Loy, David 1996, 'The Religion of the Market', *Journal of the American Academy of Religion*, 65, 2: 275–90.

Luxemburg, Rosa 1903, 'Enquête sur l'anticléricalisme et le socialisme', *Le Mouvement Socialiste*, 9, 111: 28–37.

—— 1970 [1905], *Socialism and the Churches*, in *Rosa Luxemburg Speaks*, edited by Mary-Alice Waters, translated by Juan Punto, New York: Pathfinder.

—— 1982 [1905], *Kirche und Sozialismus*, Frankfurt am Main: Stimme-Verlag.

—— 2004 [1903], 'An Anti-Clerical Policy of Socialism', *The Social Democrat*, August: 1–8.

Maccoby, Hyam 2006, *Antisemitism and Modernity: Innovation and Continuity*, London: Routledge.

MacIntyre, Alasdair 1971, *Marxism and Christianity*, Harmondsworth: Penguin.

Marion, Jean-Luc 2002, *In Excess: Studies of Saturated Phenomena*, translated by Robyn Horner and Vincent Berraud, New York: Fordham University Press.

Marx, Eleanor 1876a, 'Eleanor Marx to Carl Hirsch in Paris, London, 25 November 1876, 41 Maitland Park Road, N.W.', in Marx and Engels 1991c.

—— 1876b, 'Eleanor Marx an Carl Hirsch 25. November 1876', in Marx and Engels 1973t.

Marx, Heinrich 1837, 'Heinrich Marx to son Karl, December 9, 1837', in Marx and Engels 1975a.

Marx, Jenny (junior) 1869a, 'Jenny Marx (daughter) to Ludwig Kugelmann in Hanover, London, 27 December 1869', in Marx and Engels 1988c.

—— 1869b, 'Jenny Marx (Tochter) an Ludwig Kugelmann 27. December 1869', in Marx and Engels 1973r.

—— 1870a, 'Articles by Jenny Marx on the Irish Question', in Marx and Engels 1985b.

—— 1870b, 'Artikel von Jenny Marx zur irischen Frage', in Marx and Engels 1973g.

—— 1871a, 'Jenny Marx's Letter to the Editor of *Woodhull & Claflin's Weekly*', in Marx and Engels 1986b.

—— 1871b, 'Jenny Marx (daughter) to Ludwig and Gertrud Kugelmann in Hanover, London, 21–22 December 1871', in Marx and Engels 1989c.

—— 1871c, 'Jenny Marx (Tochter) an Ludwig und Gertrud Kugelmann 21.–22. December 1871', in Marx and Engels 1973s.

Marx, Jenny (senior) 1844, 'Jenny Marx to Karl Marx in Paris, Trier, between August 4 and 10, 1844', in Marx and Engels 1975c.

—— 1857a, 'Jenny Marx to Engels in Manchester, London, about 12 April 1857', in Marx and Engels 1983b.

—— 1857b, 'Jenny Marx an Engels um den 12. April 1857', in Marx and Engels 1973p.

—— 1863a, 'Jenny Marx to Engels in Manchester, London, beginning of November 1863', in Marx and Engels 1985c.

—— 1863b, 'Jenny Marx an Engels Anfang November 1863', in Marx and Engels 1972g.

—— 1866a, 'Jenny Marx to Johann Philipp Becker in Geneva, London, 29 January 1866', in Marx and Engels 1987c.

—— 1866b, 'Jenny Marx an Johann Philipp Becker 29. Januar 1866', in Marx and Engels 1973q.

—— 1867a, 'Jenny Marx to Ludwig Kugelmann in Hanover, London, 24 December 1867, 1 Modena Villas, Maitland Park', in Marx and Engels 1987c.

—— 1867b, 'Jenny Marx an Ludwig Kugelmann 24. December 1867', in Marx and Engels 1973q.

—— 1868a, 'Jenny Marx to Johann Philipp Becker in Geneva, London, after 10 January 1868, 1 Modena Villas, Maitland Park', in Marx and Engels 1987c.

—— 1868b, 'Jenny Marx an Johann Philipp Becker nach dem 10. Januar 1868', in Marx and Engels 1973r.

—— 1876a, 'Jenny Marx to Johann Philipp Becker in Geneva, London, between 16 and 20 August 1876', in Marx and Engels 1991c.

—— 1876b, 'Jenny Marx an Johann Philipp Becker zwichen dem 16. und 20. August 1876' in Marx and Engels 1973t.

Marx, Karl 1835a, 'Reflections of a Young Man on the Choice of a Profession', in Marx and Engels 1975a.

—— 1835b, 'Betrachtung eines Jünglings bei der Wahl eines Berufes', in Marx and Engels 1975e.

—— 1835c, 'The Union of Believers with Christ According to John 15:1–14, Showing Its Basis and Essence, Its Absolute Necessity, and Its Effects', in Marx and Engels 1975a.

—— 1835d, 'Die Vereinigung der Gläubigen mit Christo nach Johannes 15, 1–14, in ihrem Grund und Wesen, in ihrer unbedingten Notwendigkeit und in ihren Wirkungen dargestellt', in Marx and Engels 1975e.

—— 1836a, 'Feelings', in Marx and Engels 1975a.

—— 1836b, 'Empfindungen', in Marx and Engels 1975e.

—— 1836–7a, 'Transformation', in Marx and Engels 1975a.

—— 1836–7b, 'Umwandelung', in Marx and Engels 1975e.

—— 1837a, 'The Awakening', in Marx and Engels 1975a.

—— 1837b, 'Erwachen', in Marx and Engels 1975e.

—— 1837c, 'Creation', in Marx and Engels 1975a.

—— 1837d, 'Schöpfung', in Marx and Engels 1975e.

—— 1837e, 'Epigrams I–VIII', in Marx and Engels 1975a.

—— 1837f, 'Epigramme', in Marx and Engels 1975e.

—— 1837g, 'Human Pride', in Marx and Engels 1975a.

—— 1837h, 'Menschenstolz', in Marx and Engels 1975e.

—— 1837i, 'Invocation of One in Despair', in Marx and Engels 1975a.

—— 1837j, 'Des Verzweiflenden Gebet', in Marx and Engels 1975e.

—— 1837k, 'The Last Judgment: A Jest', in Marx and Engels 1975a.

—— 1837l, 'Weltgericht. Scherz', in Marx and Engels 1975e.

—— 1837m, 'Lucinda', in Marx and Engels 1975a.

—— 1837n, 'Lucinde', in Marx and Engels 1975e.

—— 1837o, 'The Pale Maiden: A Ballad', in Marx and Engels 1975a.

—— 1837p, 'Das bleiche Mädchen. Ballade', in Marx and Engels 1975e.

—— 1837q, 'Siren Song', in Marx and Engels 1975a.

—— 1837r, 'Sirengesang', in Marx and Engels 1975e.

—— 1837s, 'Three Little Lights', in Marx and Engels 1975a.

—— 1837t, 'Drei Lichtlein', in Marx and Engels 1975e.

—— 1839a, *Notebooks on Epicurean Philosophy*, in Marx and Engels 1975a.

—— 1839b, *Hefte zur epikureischen, stoischen und skeptischen Philosophie*, in Marx and Engels 1990c.

—— 1840–1a, *Difference Between the Democritean and Epicurean Philosophy of Nature with an Appendix*, in Marx and Engels 1975a.

—— 1840–1b, *Differenz der demokritischen und epikureischen Naturphilosophie im allgemenein nebst einem Anhange*, in Marx and Engels 1975e.

—— 1842a, 'The Attitude of Herwegh and Ruge to "The Free"', in Marx and Engels 1975a.

—— 1842b, 'Herweghs und Ruges Verhältnis zu den Freien. Brief von Georg Herweghs. Redigiert von Karl Marx', in Marx and Engels 1975e.

—— 1842c, 'The Divorce Bill', in Marx and Engels 1975a.

—— 1842d, 'Der Ehescheidungsgesetzentwurf', in Marx and Engels 1975e.

—— 1842e, 'The Divorce Bill: Editorial Note', in Marx and Engels 1975a.

—— 1842f, 'Der Ehescheidungsgesetzentwurf. Kritik der Kritik', in Marx and Engels 1975e.

—— 1842g, 'Exzerpte aus Charles de Brosses: Ueber den Dienst der Fetischengötter', in Marx and Engels 1976d.

—— 1842h, 'The Leading Article in No. 179 of the *Kölnische Zeitung*', in Marx and Engels 1975a.

—— 1842i, 'Der leitende Artikel in Nr. 179 der „Kölnische Zeitung"', in Marx and Engels 1975e.

—— 1842j, 'The Philosophical Manifesto of the Historical School of Law', in Marx and Engels 1975a.

—— 1842k, 'Der philosophische Manifest der historischen Rechtschule', in Marx and Engels 1975e.

—— 1842l, 'Proceedings of the Sixth Rhine Province Assembly. First Article: Debates on Freedom of the Press and Publication of the Proceedings of the Assembly of the Estates', in Marx and Engels 1975a.

—— 1842m, 'Die Verhandlungen des 6. Rheinischen Lantags. Erster Artikel: Debatten über Preßfreiheit und Publikation der Landständischen Verhandlungen', in Marx and Engels 1975e.

—— 1842n, 'Proceedings of the Sixth Rhine Province Assembly. Third Article: Debates on the Law on Thefts of Wood', in Marx and Engels 1975a.

—— 1842o, 'Verhandlungen des 6. Rheinischen Lantags. Dritter Artikel: Debatten über das Holzdiebstahlsgesetz', in Marx and Engels 1975e.

—— 1842p, 'Renard's Letter to Oberpräsident von Schaper', in Marx and Engels 1975a.

—— 1842q, 'An den Oberpräsident der Rheinprovinz von Schaper', in Marx and Engels 1990c.

—— 1842r, 'The Supplement to Nos. 335 and 336 of the Augsburg *Allgemeine Zeitung* on the Commissions of the Estates in Prussia', in Marx and Engels 1975a.

—— 1842s, 'Der Artikel in Nr. 335 und 336 der Augsburger „Allgemeinen Zeitung" über die ständischen Ausschüsse in Preußen', in Marx and Engels 1975e.

—— 1842t, 'Yet Another Word on *Bruno Bauer und die Akademische Lehrfreiheit* by Dr. O.F. Gruppe, Berlin, 1842', in Marx and Engels 1975a.

—— 1842u, 'Noch ein Wort über „Bruno Bauer und die akademische Lehrfreiheit" von Dr. O.F. Gruppe. Berlin 1842', in Marx and Engels 1975e.

—— 1842v, 'To Arnold Ruge in Dresden, February 10, 1842', in Marx and Engels 1975a.

—— 1842w, 'Marx an Arnold Ruge in Dresden, den 10ten Februar 1842', in Marx and Engels 1973n.

—— 1842x, 'To Arnold Ruge in Dresden, March 5, 1842', in Marx and Engels 1975a.

—— 1842y, 'Marx an Arnold Ruge in Dresden, den 5ten März 1842', in Marx and Engels 1973n.

—— 1842z, 'To Arnold Ruge in Dresden, March 20, 1842', in Marx and Engels 1975a.

—— 1842aa, 'Marx an Arnold Ruge in Dresden, den 20ten März 1842', in Marx and Engels 1973n.

—— 1842bb, 'To Arnold Ruge in Dresden, April 27, 1842', in Marx and Engels 1975a.

—— 1842cc, 'Marx an Arnold Ruge in Dresden, den 27. April 1842', in Marx and Engels 1973n.

—— 1842dd, 'To Arnold Ruge in Dresden, July 9, 1842', in Marx and Engels 1975a.

—— 1842ee, 'Marx an Arnold Ruge in Dresden, den 9ten Juli 1842', in Marx and Engels 1973n.

—— 1842ff, 'To Arnold Ruge in Dresden, November 30, 1842', in Marx and Engels 1975a.

—— 1842gg, 'Marx an Arnold Ruge in Dresden, den 30. Nov. 1842', in Marx and Engels 1973n.

—— 1843a, 'Comments on the Latest Prussian Censorship Instruction', in Marx and Engels 1975a.

—— 1843b, 'Bemerkungen über die neueste preußische Zensurinstruktion', in Marx and Engels 1975e.

—— 1843c, *Contribution to the Critique of Hegel's Philosophy of Law*, in Marx and Engels 1975c.

—— 1843d, *Zur Kritik der Hegelschen Rechtsphilosophie. Kritik des Hegelschen Staatsrechts*, in Marx and Engels 1974a.

—— 1843e, 'The Denunciation of the *Kölnische Zeitung* and the Polemic of the *Rhein- und Mosel-Zeitung*', in Marx and Engels 1975a.

—— 1843f, 'Die Denunziation der „Kölnischen" und die Polemik der „Rhein- und Mosel-Zeitung"', in Marx and Engels 1975e.

—— 1843g, 'Justification of the Correspondent from the Mosel', in Marx and Engels 1975a.

—— 1843h, 'Rechtfertigung des ††-Korrespondenten von der Mosel', in Marx and Engels 1975e.

—— 1843i, 'The Local Election of Deputies to the Provincial Assembly', in Marx and Engels 1975a.

—— 1843j, 'Die hiesige Landtagsabgeordnetenwahl', in Marx and Engels 1975e.

—— 1843k, 'Luther als Schiedsrichter zwischen Strauß und Feuerbach', in Marx and Engels 1974a.

—— 1843l, 'Marginal Notes to the Accusations of the Ministerial Rescript', in Marx and Engels 1975a.

—— 1843m, 'Randglossen zu den Anklagen des Ministerialreskripts', in Marx and Engels 1975e.

—— 1843n, 'A Passage from the Kreuznach Notebooks of 1843', in Marx and Engels 1975c.

—— 1843o, 'The *Rhein- und Mosel-Zeitung* as Grand Inquisitor', in Marx and Engels 1975a.

—— 1843p, 'Die „Rhein- und Mosel-Zeitung" als Großinquisitor', in Marx and Engels 1975e.

—— 1843q, 'To Arnold Ruge in Dresden, March 13, 1843', in Marx and Engels 1975a.

—— 1843r, 'Marx an Arnold Ruge in Dresden, 13. März 1843', in Marx and Engels 1973n.

—— 1843s, 'To Ludwig Feuerbach in Bruckberg, Kreuznach, October 3, 1843', in Marx and Engels 1975c.

—— 1843t, Marx an Ludwig Feuerbach in Bruckberg, 3. October 1843', in Marx and Engels 1973n.

—— 1844a, 'Comments on James Mill, Éléments d'économie politique', in Marx and Engels 1975c.

—— 1844b, 'Auszüge aus James Mills Buch „Éléments d'économie politique". Trad. par J.T. Parisot, Paris 1823', in Marx and Engels 1990c.

—— 1844c, 'Contribution to the Critique of Hegel's Philosophy of Law: Introduction', in Marx and Engels 1975c.

—— 1844d, 'Zur Kritik der Hegelschen Rechtsphilosophie. Einleitung', in Marx and Engels 1974a.

—— 1844e, 'Critical Marginal Notes on the Article "The King of Prussia and Social Reform. By A Prussian"', in Marx and Engels 1975c.

—— 1844f, 'Kritische Randglossen zu dem Artikel „Der König von Preußen und die Sozialreform. Von einem Preußen"', in Marx and Engels 1974a.

—— 1844g, *Economic and Philosophic Manuscripts of 1844*, in Marx and Engels 1975c.

—— 1844h, *Ökonomisch-philosophische Manuskripte aus dem Jahre 1844*, in Marx and Engels 1990c.

—— 1844i, 'Illustrations of the Latest Exercise in Cabinet Style of Frederick William IV', in Marx and Engels 1975c.

—— 1844j, 'Illustrationen zu der neuesten Kabinettsstilübung Friedrich Wilhelm IV', in Marx and Engels 1990c.

—— 1844k, 'Letters from the *Deutsch-Französische Jahrbücher*', in Marx and Engels 1975c.

—— 1844l, 'Briefe aus den „Deutsch-Französischen Jahrbüchern"', in Marx and Engels 1974a.

—— 1844m, *On the Jewish Question*, in Marx and Engels 1975c.

—— 1844n, *Zur Judenfrage*, in Marx and Engels 1974a.

—— 1844o, 'Marx to Heinrich Börnstein in Paris, Paris, Autumn 1844', in Marx and Engels 1982b.

—— 1844p, 'Marx an Heinrich Börnstein Herbst 1844', in Marx and Engels 1973n.

—— 1844q, 'To Ludwig Feuerbach in Bruckberg, Paris, August 11, 1844', in Marx and Engels 1975c.

—— 1844r, 'Marx an Ludwig Feuerbach in Bruckberg, 11. August 1844', in Marx and Engels 1973n.

—— 1845a, 'Draft of an Article on Friedrich List's Book *Das Nationale System der Politischen Oekonomie*', in Marx and Engels 1975d.

—— 1845b, 'Theses on Feuerbach (Original version)', in Marx and Engels 1976b.

—— 1845c, 'Thesen über Feuerbach', in Marx and Engels 1973a.

—— 1845d, 'Theses on Feuerbach (Edited by Engels)', in Marx and Engels 1976b.

—— 1845e, 'Thesen über Feuerbach', in Marx and Engels 1973a.

—— 1846a, 'Marx to Pavel Vasilyevich Annenkov in Paris, Brussels, 28 December, 1846', in Marx and Engels 1982b.

—— 1846b, 'Marx an Pawel Wassiljewittsch Annenkow 28. Dezember 1846', in Marx and Engels 1973n.

—— 1847a, 'The Communism of the *Rheinische Beobachter*', in Marx and Engels 1976c.

—— 1847b, 'Der Kommunismus des „Rheinischen Beobachters"', in Marx and Engels 1972a.

—— 1847c, 'Lamartine and Communism', in Marx and Engels 1976c.

—— 1847d, 'Lamartine und der Kommunismus', in Marx and Engels 1972a.

—— 1847e, 'Minutes of Marx's report to the London German Workers' Educational Society on November 30, 1847', in Marx and Engels 1976c.

—— 1847f, 'Moralising Criticism and Critical Morality: A Contribution to German Cultural History Contra Karl Heinzen', in Marx and Engels 1976c.

—— 1847g, 'Die moralisierende Kritik und die kritisierende Moral. Beitrag zur Deutschen Kulturgeschichte. Gegen Karl Heinzen von Karl Marx', in Marx and Engels 1972a.

—— 1847h, *The Poverty of Philosophy: Answer to the 'Philosophy of Poverty' by M. Proudhon*, in Marx and Engels 1976c.

—— 1847i, *Das Elend der Philosophie. Antwort auf Proudhons „Philosophie des Elends"*, in Marx and Engels 1972a.

—— 1847j, 'Remarks on the Article by M. Adolphe Bartels', in Marx and Engels 1976c.

—— 1847k, 'Bemerkungen zum Artikel von Herrn Adolph Bartels', in Marx and Engels 1972a.

—— 1848a, 'The Bourgeoisie and the Counter-Revolution', in Marx and Engels 1977b.

—— 1848b, 'Die Bourgeoisie und die Kontrerevolution', in Marx and Engels 1973c.

—— 1848c, 'The Chief Public Prosecutor and the *Neue Rheinische Zeitung*', in Marx and Engels 1977b.

—— 1848d, 'Die Oberprokuratur und die „Neue Rheinsche Zeitung"', in Marx and Engels 1973c.

—— 1848e, 'Confessions of a Noble Soul', in Marx and Engels 1977b.

—— 1848f, 'Bekenntnisse einer schönen Seele', in Marx and Engels 1973c.

—— 1848g, 'Counter-Revolution in Berlin', in Marx and Engels 1977b.

—— 1848h, 'Die Kontrerevolution in Berlin', in Marx and Engels 1973c.

—— 1848i, 'The Crisis in Berlin', in Marx and Engels 1977b.

—— 1848j, 'Die Berliner Krisis', in Marx and Engels 1973c.

—— 1848k, 'The *Débat Social* of February 6 on the Democrat Association', in Marx and Engels 1976c.

—— 1848l, 'Der „Débat social" vom 6. Februar über die Association démocratique', in Marx and Engels 1972a.

—— 1848m, 'A Decree of Eichmann's', in Marx and Engels 1977b.

—— 1848n, 'Ein Erlaß Eichmanns', in Marx and Engels 1973c.

—— 1848o, 'Drigalski – Legislator, Citizen and Communist', in Marx and Engels 1977b.

—— 1848p, 'Drigalski der Gesetzgeber, Bürger und Kommunist', in Marx and Engels 1973c.

—— 1848q, 'The Prussian Counter-Revolution and the Prussian Judiciary', in Marx and Engels 1977b.

—— 1848r, 'Die preußische Kontrerevolution und der preußische Richterstand Abfertigung', in Marx and Engels 1973c.

—— 1848s, 'Public Prosecutor "Hecker" and the *Neue Rheinische Zeitung*', in Marx and Engels 1977a.

—— 1848t, Der Staatsprokurator „Hekker" und die „Neue Rheinische Zeitung"', in Marx and Engels 1973b.

—— 1848u, 'Reply of Frederick William IV to the Delegation of the Civic Militia', in Marx and Engels 1977a.

—— 1848v, 'Antwort Friedrich Wilhelm IV. An die Deputation der Bürgerwehr', in Marx and Engels 1973b.

—— 1848w, 'Reply of the King of Prussia to the Delegation of the National Assembly', in Marx and Engels 1977a.

—— 1848x, 'Antwort des Königs von Preußen an die Deputation der Nationalversammlung', in Marx and Engels 1973b.

——1848y, 'The "Revolution of Cologne"', in Marx and Engels 1977a.

—— 1848z, 'Die „Kölnische Revolution"', in Marx and Engels 1973b.

—— 1848aa, 'Second Stage of the Counter-Revolution', in Marx and Engels 1977b.

—— 1848bb, 'Speech on the Question of Free Trade: Delivered to the Democratic Association of Brussels at Its Public Meeting of January 9, 1848', in Marx and Engels 1976c.

—— 1848cc, 'Rede über Frage des Freihandels, gehalten am 9.Januar 1848 in der Demokratischen Gesellschaft zu Brüssel', in Marx and Engels 1972a.

—— 1848dd, 'Three State Trials against the Neue Rheinische Zeitung', in Marx and Engels 1977b.

—— 1848ee, 'Drei Staatsprozesse gegen die „Neue Rheinische Zeitung"', in Marx and Engels 1973c.

—— 1848ff, 'Marx to Engels in Lausanne, Cologne, first half of November 1848', in Marx and Engels 1982b.

—— 1848gg, 'Marx an Engels Mitte November 1848', in Marx and Engels 1973n.

—— 1849a, 'The 18th of March', in Marx and Engels 1977c.

—— 1849b, 'Der 18. März', in Marx and Engels 1973c.

—— 1849c, 'The Berlin National-Zeitung to the Primary Electors', in Marx and Engels 1977b.

—— 1849d, 'Die Berliner „National-Zeitung" an die Urwähler', in Marx and Engels 1973c.

—— 1849e, 'The Hohenzollern General Plan of Reform', in Marx and Engels 1977c.

—— 1849f, 'Der Hohenzollernsche Gesamtreformplan', in Marx and Engels 1973c.

—— 1849g, 'Montesquieu LVI', in Marx and Engels 1977b.

—— 1849h, 'Montesquieu LVI', in Marx and Engels 1973c.

—— 1849i, 'The New Prussian Constitution', in Marx and Engels 1977c.

—— 1849j, 'Die neue preußische Verfassung', in Marx and Engels 1973c.

—— 1849k, 'Prussian Financial Administration under Bodelschwingh and Co.', in Marx and Engels 1977b.

—— 1849l, 'Preußische Finanzwirtschaft unter Bodelschwingh und Konsorten Stein', in Marx and Engels 1973c.

—— 1849m, 'The Summary Suppression of the Neue Rheinische Zeitung', in Marx and Engels 1977c.

—— 1849n, 'Die standrechtliche Beseitigung der „Neuen Rheinischen Zeitung"', in Marx and Engels 1973c.

—— 1849o, 'Three New Bills', in Marx and Engels 1977c.

—— 1849p, 'Drei neue Gesetzentwürfe', in Marx and Engels 1973c.

—— 1849q, 'The Trial of the Rhenish District Committee of Democrats', in Marx and Engels 1977b.

—— 1849r, 'Der Prozeß gegen den Rheinischen Kreisausschuß der Demokraten', in Marx and Engels 1973c.

—— 1850a, The Class Struggles in France, in Marx and Engels 1978.

—— 1850b, Die Klassenkämpfe in Frankreich 1848 bis 1850, in Marx and Engels 1973d.

—— 1851a, 'The Constitution of the French Republic Adopted November 4, 1848', in Marx and Engels 1978.

—— 1851b, 'Marx to Hermann Becker in Cologne, London, about 1 February 1851', in Marx and Engels 1982b.

—— 1851c, 'Marx an Hermann Becker um den 1. Februar 1851', in Marx and Engels 1973n.

—— 1851d, 'Marx to Engels in Manchester, London, 31 March 1851', in Marx and Engels 1982b.

—— 1851e, 'Marx an Engels 31. März 1851', in Marx and Engels 1973n.

—— 1851f, 'Marx to Engels in Manchester, London, 21 May 1851', in Marx and Engels 1982b.

—— 1851g, 'Marx an Engels 21. Mai 1851', in Marx and Engels 1973n.

—— 1851h, 'Marx to Joseph Weydemeyer in Frankfurt am Main, London, 27 June 1851', in Marx and Engels 1982b.

—— 1851i, 'Marx an Joseph Weydemeyer 27. Juni 1851', in Marx and Engels 1973n.

—— 1851j, 'Marx to Engels in Manchester, London, 14 August 1851', in Marx and Engels 1982b.

—— 1851k, 'Marx an Engels 14. August 1851', in Marx and Engels 1973n.

—— 1851l, 'Marx to Hermann Ebner in Frankfurt am Main, London, 15–22 August 1851', in Marx and Engels 1982b.

—— 1851m, 'Marx an Hermann Ebner 2. Hälfte August 1851', in Marx and Engels 1973n.

—— 1851n, 'Marx to Engels in Manchester, London, 23 September 1851', in Marx and Engels 1982b.

—— 1851o, 'Marx an Engels 23. September 1851', in Marx and Engels 1973n.

—— 1851p, 'Marx to Engels in Manchester, London, 19 October 1851', in Marx and Engels 1982b.

—— 1851q, 'Marx an Engels 19. Oktober 1851', in Marx and Engels 1973n.

—— 1851r, 'Marx to Hermann Ebner in Frankfurt am Main, London, 2 December 1851', in Marx and Engels 1982b.

—— 1851s, 'Marx an Hermann Ebner 2. Dezember 1851', in Marx and Engels 1973n.

—— 1852a, 'The Chartists', in Marx and Engels 1979a.

—— 1852b, 'Corruption at Elections', in Marx and Engels 1979a.

—— 1852c, *The Eighteenth Brumaire of Louis Bonaparte*, in Marx and Engels 1979a.

—— 1852d, *Der achtzehnte Brumaire des Louis Bonaparte*, in Marx and Engels 1973e.

—— 1852e, 'The Elections in England. – Tories and Whigs', in Marx and Engels 1979a.

—— 1852f, 'Result of the Elections', in Marx and Engels 1979a.

—— 1852g, 'Marx to Joseph Weydemeyer in New York, London, 20 February 1852', in Marx and Engels 1983a.

—— 1852h, 'Marx an Joseph Weydemeyer 20. Februar 1852', in Marx and Engels 1973o.

—— 1852i, 'Marx to Engels in Manchester, London, 30 March 1852', in Marx and Engels 1983a.

—— 1852j, 'Marx an Engels 30. März 1852', in Marx and Engels 1973o.

—— 1852k, 'Marx to Gustav Zerffi in Paris, London, 28 December 1852', in Marx and Engels 1983a.

—— 1852l, 'Marx an Gustav Zerffi 28. Dezember 1852', in Marx and Engels 1973o.

—— 1853a, 'Achievements of the Ministry', in Marx and Engels 1979b.

—— 1853b, 'The Attack on Francis Joseph. – The Milan Riot. – British Politics. – Disraeli's Speech. – Napoleon's Will', in Marx and Engels 1979a.

—— 1853c, 'The British Rule in India', in Marx and Engels 1979b.

—— 1853d, 'Defense. – Finances. – Decrease of the Aristocracy. – Politics', in Marx and Engels 1979a.

—— 1853e, 'Elections. – Financial Clouds. – The Duchess of Sutherland and Slavery', in Marx and Engels 1979a.

—— 1853f, 'The Future Results of British Rule in India', in Marx and Engels 1979b.

—— 1853g, 'Kossuth and Mazzini. – Intrigues of the Prussian Government. – Austro-Prussian Commercial Treaty. – *The Times* and the Refugees', in Marx and Engels 1979a.

—— 1853h, 'Layard's Motion. – Struggle over the Ten Hours' Bill', in Marx and Engels 1979b.

—— 1853i, 'The London Press. – Policy of Napoleon. – On the Turkish', in Marx and Engels 1979b.

—— 1853j, 'Lord Palmerston', in Marx and Engels 1979b.

—— 1853k, 'Manteuffel's Speech. – Religious Movement in Prussia. – Mazzini's Address. – London Corporation. – Russell's Reforms. – Labor Parliament', in Marx and Engels 1979b.

—— 1853l, 'Mazzini. – Switzerland and Austria. – The Turkish Question', in Marx and Engels 1979b.

—— 1853m, 'Parliamentary Debates. – The Clergy Against Socialism. – Starvation', in Marx and Engels 1979a.

—— 1853n, 'Prosperity. – The Labor Question', in Marx and Engels 1979b.

—— 1853o, *Revelations Concerning the Communist Trial in Cologne*, in Marx and Engels 1979a.

—— 1853p, *Enthüllungen über den Kommunisten-Prozeß zu Köln*, in Marx and Engels 1973e.

—— 1853q, 'Revolution in China and in Europe', in Marx and Engels 1979b.

—— 1853r, 'Riot at Constantinople. – German Table Moving. – The Budget', in Marx and Engels 1979b.

—— 1853s, 'The Russian Humbug. – Gladstone's Failure. – Sir Charles

Wood's East India Reforms', in Marx and Engels 1979b.

—— 1853t, The Russo-Turkish Difficulty. – Ducking and Dodging of the British Cabinet. – Nesselrode's Last Note. – The East India Question', in Marx and Engels 1979b.

—— 1853u, 'The Turkish Question in the Commons', in Marx and Engels 1979b.

—— 1853v, 'Urquhart. – Bem. – The Turkish Question in the House of Lords', in Marx and Engels 1979b.

—— 1853w, 'The War Question. – Doings of Parliament. – India', in Marx and Engels 1979b.

—— 1853x, 'The War Question. – Financial Matters. – Strikes', in Marx and Engels 1979b.

—— 1853y, 'The Western Powers and Turkey. – Imminent Economic Crisis. – Railway Construction in India', in Marx and Engels 1979b.

—— 1853z, 'Marx to Engels in Manchester, London, 22–23 March 1853', in Marx and Engels 1983a.

—— 1853aa, 'Marx an Engels 22./23. März 1853', in Marx and Engels 1973o.

—— 1853bb, 'Marx to Engels in Manchester, London, 2 June 1853', in Marx and Engels 1983a.

—— 1853cc, 'Marx an Engels 2. Juni 1853', in Marx and Engels 1973o.

—— 1853dd, 'Marx to Adolph Cluss in Washington, London, 5 October 1853', in Marx and Engels 1983a.

—— 1854a, 'Attack Upon Sevastopol. – Clearing of Estates in Scotland', in Marx and Engels 1980a.

—— 1854b, 'Debates in Parliament', in Marx and Engels 1980a.

—— 1854c, 'Declaration of War. – On the History of the Eastern Question', in Marx and Engels 1980a.

—— 1854d, 'The Documents of the Partition', in Marx and Engels 1980a.

—— 1854e, 'English and French War Plans. – Greek Insurrection. – Spain. – China', in Marx and Engels 1980a.

—— 1854f, 'The Greek Insurrection', in Marx and Engels 1980a.

—— 1854g, 'The Knight of the Noble Consciousness', in Marx and Engels 1979b.

—— 1854h, 'Der Ritter vom edelmütigen Bewußtsein', in Marx and Engels 1972b.

—— 1854i, 'Parliamentary Debates of February 22. – Pozzo di Borgo's Dispatch.

– The Policy of the Western Powers', in Marx and Engels 1980a.

—— 1854j, 'Reshid Pasha's Note. – An Italian Newspaper on the Eastern Question', in Marx and Engels 1980a.

—— 1854k, 'Revolutionary Spain', in Marx and Engels 1980a.

—— 1854l, 'Russian Diplomacy. – The Blue Book on the Eastern Question. – Montenegro', in Marx and Engels 1979b.

—— 1854m, 'The Secret Diplomatic Correspondence', in Marx and Engels 1980a.

—— 1854n, 'The War in the East', in Marx and Engels 1979b.

—— 1854o, 'Marx to Engels in Manchester, London, 29 April 1854', in Marx and Engels 1983a.

—— 1854p, 'Marx an Engels 29. April 1854', in Marx and Engels 1973o.

—— 1854q, 'Marx to Engels in Manchester, London, 3 May 1854', in Marx and Engels 1983a.

—— 1854r, 'Marx an Engels 3. Mai 1854', in Marx and Engels 1973o.

—— 1854s, 'Marx to Engels in Manchester, London, 26 October 1854', in Marx and Engels 1983a.

—— 1854t, 'Marx an Engels 26. Oktober 1854', in Marx and Engels 1973o.

—— 1855a, 'Agitation Against Prussia. – A Day of Fasting', in Marx and Engels 1980b.

—— 1855b, 'Agitation gegen Preußen – Ein Fasttag', in Marx and Engels 1974c.

—— 1855c, 'Agitation over the Tightening-Up of Sunday Observance', in Marx and Engels 1980b.

—— 1855d, 'Die Aufregung gegen die Verschärfung der Sonntagsfeier', in Marx and Engels 1974c.

—— 1855e, 'The Aims of the Negotiations. – Polemic Against Russia. – The Snowball Riot', in Marx and Engels 1980a.

—— 1855f, 'Anti-Church Movement. – Demonstration in Hyde Park', in Marx and Engels 1980b.

—— 1855g, 'Kirchliche Agitation – Eine Demonstration im Hyde Park', in Marx and Engels 1974c.

—— 1855h, 'The Association for Administrative Reform. – People's Charter', in Marx and Engels 1980b.

—— 1855i, 'Die Administrativreform-Assoziation – Die Charte', in Marx and Engels 1974c.

—— 1855j, 'The Bank of France. – Reinforcements to the Crimea. – The New Field Marshals', in Marx and Engels 1980b.

—— 1855k, 'Die französischen Bank – Verstärkungen nach der Krim – Die neuen Feldmarschalle', in Marx and Engels 1974c.

—— 1855l, 'The Buying of Commissions. – News from Australia', in Marx and Engels 1980b.

—— 1855m, 'Stellenkauf – Aus Australien', in Marx and Engels 1974c.

—— 1855n, 'Commentary on the Parliamentary Proceedings', in Marx and Engels 1980b.

—— 1855o, 'Kommentar zu den Parlamentsverhandlungen', in Marx and Engels 1974c.

—— 1855p, 'The Crisis in Trade and Industry', in Marx and Engels 1980a.

—— 1855q, 'Die Industrie- und Handelskrise', in Marx and Engels 1973f.

—— 1855r, 'A Critique of Palmerston's Latest Speech', in Marx and Engels 1980b.

—— 1855s, 'Zur Kritik der letzten Rede Palmerstons', in Marx and Engels 1974c.

—— 1855t, 'From Parliament', in Marx and Engels 1980b.

—— 1855u, 'Aus dem Parlamente', in Marx and Engels 1974c.

—— 1855v, 'From Parliament. – Gladstone at the Dispatch-Box', in Marx and Engels 1980b.

—— 1855w, 'Aus dem Parlamente – Gladstones Auftreten', in Marx and Engels 1974c.

—— 1855x, 'Ireland's Revenge', in Marx and Engels 1980b.

—— 1855y, 'Irlands Rache', in Marx and Engels 1974c.

—— 1855z, 'Layard', in Marx and Engels 1980b.

—— 1855aa, 'Layard', in Marx and Engels 1974c.

—— 1855bb, 'Lord John Russell', in Marx and Engels 1980b.

—— 1855cc, 'Lord John Russell', in Marx and Engels 1974c.

—— 1855dd, 'Miscellaneous Reports', in Marx and Engels 1980b.

—— 1855ee, 'Mitteilungen verscheidenen Inhalts', in Marx and Engels 1974c.

—— 1855ff, 'Palmerston', in Marx and Engels 1980b.

—— 1855gg, 'Palmerston und die Englische Oligarchie', in Marx and Engels 1974c.

—— 1855hh, 'Palmerston. – The Physiology of the Ruling Class of Great Britain', in Marx and Engels 1980b.

—— 1855ii, 'Palmerston – Physiologie der herrschenden Klassen Großbritanniens', in Marx and Engels 1974c.

—— 1855jj, 'Sunday Observance and the Publicans. – Clanricide', in Marx and Engels 1980a.

—— 1855kk, 'Die Bierwirte und die Sonntagsfeier – Clanricide', in Marx and Engels 1973f.

—— 1855ll, 'Marx to Engels in Manchester, London, 7 December 1855', in Marx and Engels 1983a.

—— 1855mm, 'Marx an Engels 7. Dezember 1855', in Marx and Engels 1973o.

—— 1855nn, 'Marx to Engels in Manchester, London, 14 December 1855', in Marx and Engels 1983a.

—— 1855oo, 'Marx an Engels 14. Dezember 1855', in Marx and Engels 1973o.

—— 1856a, 'The Monetary Crisis in Europe', in Marx and Engels 1986a.

—— 1856b, 'Revolution in Spain', in Marx and Engels 1986a.

—— 1856c, 'The Right Divine of the Hohenzollerns', in Marx and Engels 1986a.

—— 1856d, 'Marx to Engels in Manchester, London, 18 January 1856', in Marx and Engels 1983b.

—— 1856e, 'Marx an Engels 18. Januar 1856', in Marx and Engels 1973p.

—— 1856f, 'Marx to Engels in Manchester, London, 12 February 1856', in Marx and Engels 1983b.

—— 1856g, 'Marx an Engels 12. Februar 1856', in Marx and Engels 1973p.

—— 1856h, 'Marx to Engels in Manchester, London, 5 March 1856', in Marx and Engels 1983b.

—— 1856i, 'Marx an Engels 5. März 1856', in Marx and Engels 1973p.

—— 1856j, 'Marx to Jenny Marx in Trier, Manchester, 21 June 1856', in Marx and Engels 1983b.

—— 1856k, 'Marx an Jenny Marx 21. Juni 1856', in Marx and Engels 1973p.

—— 1856l, 'Marx to Engels in Manchester, London, 22 September 1856', in Marx and Engels 1983b.

—— 1856m, 'Marx an Engels 22. September 1856', in Marx and Engels 1973p.

—— 1856–7, 'Revelations of the Diplomatic History of the 18th Century', in Marx and Engels 1986a.

—— 1857a, 'B. Bauer's Pamphlets on the Collision with Russia', in Marx and Engels 1986a.

—— 1857b, 'The Coming Election in England', in Marx and Engels 1986a.

—— 1857c, 'Defeat of the Palmerston Ministry', in Marx and Engels 1986a.

—— 1857d, 'The Indian Revolt', in Marx and Engels 1986a.

—— 1857e, 'The Persian Treaty', in Marx and Engels 1986a.

—— 1857f, 'Sardinia', in Marx and Engels 1986a.

—— 1857g, 'The War Against Persia', in Marx and Engels 1986a.

—— 1857h, 'Marx to Engels in Manchester, London, 10 January 1857', in Marx and Engels 1983b.

—— 1857i, 'Marx an Engels 10. Januar 1857', in Marx and Engels 1973p.

—— 1857j, 'Marx to Engels in Manchester, London, 21 April 1857', in Marx and Engels 1983b.

—— 1857k, 'Marx an Engels 21. April 1857', in Marx and Engels 1973p.

—— 1857l, 'Marx to Engels in Manchester, London, 23 April 1857', in Marx and Engels 1983b.

—— 1857m, 'Marx an Engels 23. April 1857', in Marx and Engels 1973p.

—— 1857–8a, Economic Manuscripts of 1857–58 (First Version of Capital) [Grundrisse], in Marx and Engels 1986c.

—— 1857–8b, Outlines of the Critique of Political Economy (Rough Draft of 1857–58) [Second Instalment], in Marx and Engels 1987b.

—— 1857–8c, Ökonomische Manuskripte 1857/1858 [Grundrisse], in Marx and Engels 2005.

—— 1858a, 'Affairs in Prussia', in Marx and Engels 1980c.

—— 1858b, 'Affairs in Prussia (2)', in Marx and Engels 1980c.

—— 1858c, 'Blum', in Marx and Engels 1982a.

—— 1858d, 'The English Alliance', in Marx and Engels 1986a.

—— 1858e, 'The King of Prussia's Insanity', in Marx and Engels 1980c.

—— 1858f, 'The King of Prussia's Insanity (2)', in Marx and Engels 1980c.

—— 1858g, 'Mr Disraeli's Budget', in Marx and Engels 1986a.

—— 1858h, 'The New Ministry', in Marx and Engels 1980c.

—— 1858i, 'Pelissier's Mission to England', in Marx and Engels 1986a.

—— 1859a, A Contribution to the Critique of Political Economy, in Marx and Engels 1987b.

—— 1859b, 'A Historic Parallel', in Marx and Engels 1980c.

—— 1859c, 'Invasion!', in Marx and Engels 1980c.

—— 1859d, 'Invasion!', in Marx and Engels 1974d.

—— 1859e, 'Marx to Engels in Manchester, London, 16 March 1859', in Marx and Engels 1983b.

—— 1859f, 'Marx an Engels 16. März 1859', in Marx and Engels 1973p.

—— 1859g, 'Marx to Engels in Manchester, London, 28 May 1859', in Marx and Engels 1983b.

—— 1859h, 'Marx an Engels 28. Mai 1859', in Marx and Engels 1973p.

—— 1859i, 'Marx to Engels in Manchester, London, 13 August 1859', in Marx and Engels 1983b.

—— 1859j, 'Marx an Engels 13. August 1859', in Marx and Engels 1973p.

—— 1859k, 'Marx to Engels in Manchester, London, 19 November 1859', in Marx and Engels 1983b.

—— 1859l, 'Marx an Engels 19. November 1859', in Marx and Engels 1973p.

—— 1860a, 'Affairs in France', in Marx and Engels 1981.

—— 1860b, 'Events in Syria. – Session of the British Parliament. – The State of British Commerce', in Marx and Engels 1981.

—— 1860c, Herr Vogt, in Marx and Engels 1981.

—— 1860d, Herr Vogt, in Marx and Engels 1972c.

—— 1860e, 'The New Treaty Between France and England', in Marx and Engels 1981.

—— 1860f, 'Marx to Engels in Manchester, London, 9 February 1860', in Marx and Engels 1985c.

—— 1860g, 'Marx an Engels 9. Februar 1860', in Marx and Engels 1972g.

—— 1860h, 'Marx to Ferdinand Freiligrath in London, Manchester, 29 February 1860, 6 Thorncliffe Grove, Oxford Road', in Marx and Engels 1985c.

—— 1860i, 'Marx an Ferdinand Freligrath 29. Februar 1860', in Marx and Engels 1972g.

—— 1861a, 'Marx's Application for Naturalisation and Right of Domicile in Berlin', in Marx and Engels 1984.

—— 1861b, 'Antrag von Marx auf Naturalisierung und Wohnrecht in Berlin', in Marx and Engels 1972d.

—— 1861c, 'Marx's Passport, 1861', in Marx and Engels 1985c.

—— 1861d, 'Marx' Reispaß (ausgefertigt 11. April 1861)', in Marx and Engels 1972g.

—— 1861e, 'The Opinion of the Newspapers and the Opinion of the People', in Marx and Engels 1984.

—— 1861f, 'Die Meinung der Journale und die Meinung des Volkes', in Marx and Engels 1972d.

—— 1861g, 'Marx to Engels in Manchester, London, 18 January 1861', in Marx and Engels 1985c.

—— 1861h, 'Marx an Engels 18. Januar 1861', in Marx and Engels 1972g.

—— 1861i, 'Marx to Engels in Manchester, London, 10 May 1861', in Marx and Engels 1985c.

—— 1861j, 'Marx an Engels 10. Mai 1861', in Marx and Engels 1972g.

—— 1861k, 'Marx to Engels in Manchester, London, 12 July 1861', in Marx and Engels 1985c.

—— 1861l, 'Marx an Engels 12. Juli 1861', in Marx and Engels 1972g.

—— 1861–3a, *Economic Manuscript of 1861–63: A Contribution to the Critique of Political Economy*, in Marx and Engels 1988b.

—— 1861–3b, *Economic Manuscript of 1861–63 (Continuation): A Contribution to the Critique of Political Economy*, in Marx and Engels 1989a.

—— 1861–3c, *Theorie über den Mehrwert (Vierter Band des „Kapitals")*. *Erster Teil*, in Marx and Engels 1974e.

—— 1861–3d, *Economic Manuscript of 1861–63 (Continuation): A Contribution to the Critique of Political Economy*, in Marx and Engels 1989b.

—— 1861–3e, *Theorie über den Mehrwert (Vierter Band des „Kapitals")*. *Dritter Teil*, in Marx and Engels 1974f.

—— 1861–3f, *Economic Manuscript of 1861–63 (Continuation): A Contribution to the Critique of Political Economy*, in Marx and Engels 1991b.

—— 1861–3g, *Economic Manuscripts of 1861–63(Conclusion):AContributiontothe Critique of Political Economy*, in Marx and Engels 1994.

—— 1861–3h, *Ökonomisches Manuskript 1861–1863*, in Marx and Engels 1990d.

—— 1862a, 'Bread Manufacture', in Marx and Engels 1984.

—— 1862b, 'Die Brotfabrikation', in Marx and Engels 1972d.

—— 1862c, 'Chinese Affairs', in Marx and Engels 1984.

—— 1862d, 'Chinesisches', in Marx and Engels 1972d.

—— 1862e, 'The English Press and the Fall of New Orleans', in Marx and Engels 1984.

—— 1862f, 'Die englische Presse und der Fall von New Orleans', in Marx and Engels 1972d.

—— 1862g, 'French News Humbug. – Economic Consequences of War', in Marx and Engels 1984.

—— 1862h, 'Französischer Nachrichtenhumbug – Ökonomische Kriegskonsequenzen', in Marx and Engels 1972d.

—— 1862i, 'Workers' Distress in England', in Marx and Engels 1984.

—— 1862j, 'Die Arbeiternot in England', in Marx and Engels 1972d.

—— 1862k, 'Marx to Ferdinand Lassalle in Berlin, London, 16 June 1862', in Marx and Engels 1985c.

—— 1862l, 'Marx an Ferdinand Lasalle 16. Juni 1862', in Marx and Engels 1972g.

—— 1863a, 'Marx to Engels in Manchester, London, 9 April 1863', in Marx and Engels 1985c.

—— 1863b, 'Marx an Engels 9. April 1863', in Marx and Engels 1972g.

—— 1863c, 'Marx to Engels in Manchester, London, 2 December 1863', in Marx and Engels 1985c.

—— 1863d, 'Marx an Engels 2. Dezember 1863', in Marx and Engels 1972g.

—— 1864a, 'Inaugural Address of the Working Men's International Association', in Marx and Engels 1985a.

—— 1864b, 'Marx to Engels in Manchester, Zalt-Bommel, 20 January 1864', in Marx and Engels 1985c.

—— 1864c, 'Marx an Engels 20. Januar 1864', in Marx and Engels 1972g.

—— 1864d, 'Marx to Engels in Manchester, London, 16 June 1864', in Marx and Engels 1985c.

—— 1864e, 'Marx an Engels 16. Juni 1864', in Marx and Engels 1972g.

—— 1864f, 'Marx to Lion Philips in Aachen, London, 25 June 1864', in Marx and Engels 1985c.

—— 1864g, 'Marx an Lion Philips 25. Juni 1864', in Marx and Engels 1972g.

—— 1865a, 'On Proudhon (Letter to J.B. Schweitzer)', in Marx and Engels 1985a.

—— 1865b, 'Über P.-J. Proudhon. Brief an J.B. v. Schweitzer', in Marx and Engels 1973g.

—— 1865c, *Value, Price and Profit*, in Marx and Engels 1985a.

—— 1865d, 'Marx to Hermann Jung in London, London, 20 November 1865', in Marx and Engels 1987c.

—— 1865e, 'Marx an Hermann Jung 20. November 1865', in Marx and Engels 1973q.

—— 1865f, 'Marx to César de Paepe in Brussels, London, about 25 November 1865', in Marx and Engels 1987c.

—— 1865g, 'Marx an César de Paepe um den 25. November 1865', in Marx and Engels 1973q.

—— 1866a, 'Instructions for the Delegates of the Provisional General Council. The Different Questions', in Marx and Engels 1985a.

—— 1866b, 'Instruktionen für die Delegierten des Provisorischen Zentralrats zu den einzelnen Fragen', in Marx and Engels 1973g.

—— 1866c, 'Marx to Laura Marx in London, Margate, 20 March 1866, 5 Lansell's Place', in Marx and Engels 1987c.

—— 1866d, 'Marx an seine Tochter Laura 20. März 1866', in Marx and Engels 1973q.

—— 1866e, 'Marx to Engels in Manchester, London, 10 May 1866', in Marx and Engels 1987c.

—— 1866f, 'Marx an Engels 10. Mai 1866', in Marx and Engels 1973q.

—— 1866g, 'Marx to François Lafargue in Bordeaux, London, 12 November 1866', in Marx and Engels 1987c.

—— 1866h, 'Marx an François Lafargue 12. November 1866', in Marx and Engels 1973q.

—— 1866i, 'Marx to Engels in Manchester, London, 17 December 1866', in Marx and Engels 1987c.

—— 1866j, 'Marx an Engels 17. Dezember 1866', in Marx and Engels 1973q.

—— 1867a, *Capital: A Critique of Political Economy, Volume I*, in Marx and Engels 1996.

—— 1867b, *Das Kapital. Kritik der politischen Ökonomie. Erster Band Buch I: Der Produktionsprozeß des Kapitals*, in Marx and Engels 1972f.

—— 1867c, 'Outline of a Report on the Irish Question Delivered to the German Workers' Educational Society in London on December 16, 1867', in Marx and Engels 1985b.

—— 1867d, 'Aufzeichnung eines Vortrages von Karl Marx zur irischen Frage, gehalten im Deutschen Bildungsverein für Arbeiter in London am 16. Dezember 1867', in Marx and Engels 1973g.

—— 1867e, 'Speech at the Polish Meeting in London', in Marx and Engels 1985a.

—— 1867f, 'Rede auf dem Polenmeeting in London am 22. Januar 1867', in Marx and Engels 1973g.

—— 1867g, 'Marx to Engels in Manchester, Hanover, 24 April 1867', in Marx and Engels 1987c.

—— 1867h, 'Marx an Engels 24. April 1867', in Marx and Engels 1973q.

—— 1868a, 'Remarks on the Programme and Rules of the International Alliance of Socialist Democracy', in Marx and Engels 1985b.

—— 1868b, 'Marx to Engels in Manchester, London, 14 March 1868', in Marx and Engels 1987c.

—— 1868c, 'Marx an Engels 14. März 1868', in Marx and Engels 1973r.

—— 1868d, 'Marx to Ludwig Kugelman in Hanover, London, 6 April 1868', in Marx and Engels 1988c.

—— 1868e, 'Marx an Ludwig Kugelmann 6. April 1868', in Marx and Engels 1973r.

—— 1868f, 'Marx to Engels in Manchester, London, 7 July 1868', in Marx and Engels 1988c.

—— 1868g, 'Marx an Engels 7. Juli 1868', in Marx and Engels 1973r.

—— 1868h, 'Marx to Johann Baptist von Schweitzer in Berlin, London, 13 October 1868', in Marx and Engels 1988c.

—— 1868i, 'Marx an Johann Baptist von Schweitzer 13. Oktober 1868', in Marx and Engels 1973r.

—— 1868j, 'Marx to Sigfrid Meyer and August Vogt in New York, London, 28 October 1868', in Marx and Engels 1988c.

—— 1868k, 'Marx an Sigfrid Meyer und August Vogt 28. Oktober 1868', in Marx and Engels 1973r.

—— 1869a, 'Address to the National Labour Union of the United States', in Marx and Engels 1985b.

—— 1869b, 'Ireland from the American Revolution to the Union of 1801: Extracts and Notes', in Marx and Engels 1985b.

—— 1869c, 'Preface to the Second Edition of *The Eighteenth Brumaire of Louis Bonaparte*', in Marx and Engels 1985b.

—— 1869d, 'Vorwort zur Zweiten Ausgabe (1869) „Der achtzehnte Brumaire des Loius Bonaparte"', in Marx and Engels 1973g.

—— 1869e, 'Report of the General Council to the Fourth Annual Congress of the International Working Men's Association', in Marx and Engels 1985b.

—— 1869f, 'Marx to Eleanor Marx in Paris, London, 26 April 1869', in Marx and Engels 1988c.

—— 1869g, 'Marx an seine Tochter Eleanor, 26. April 1869', in Marx and Engels 1973r.

—— 1869h, 'Marx to Engels in Manchester, London, 29 March 1869', in Marx and Engels 1988c.

—— 1869i, 'Marx an Engels 29. März 1869', in Marx and Engels 1973r.

—— 1869j, 'Marx to Paul Lafargue in Paris, Manchester 2 June 1869', in Marx and Engels 1988c.

—— 1869k, 'Marx an Paul Lafargue 2. Juni 1869', in Marx and Engels 1973r.

—— 1869l, 'Marx to Engels in Manchester, London, 3 July 1869', in Marx and Engels 1988c.

—— 1869m, 'Marx an Engels 3. Juli 1869', in Marx and Engels 1973r.

—— 1869n, 'Marx to Engels in Manchester, London, 22 July 1869', in Marx and Engels 1988c.

—— 1869o, 'Marx an Engels 22. Juli 1869', in Marx and Engels 1973r.

—— 1869p, 'Marx to Engels in Manchester, London, 10 August 1869', in Marx and Engels 1988c.

—— 1869q, 'Marx an Engels 10. August 1869', in Marx and Engels 1973r.

—— 1869r, 'Marx to Engels in Manchester, Hanover, 25 September 1869', in Marx and Engels 1988c.

—— 1869s, 'Marx an Engels 25. September 1869', in Marx and Engels 1973r.

—— 1870a, 'Marx to Paul and Laura Lafargue in Paris, London, 28 July 1870', in Marx and Engels 1989c.

—— 1870b, 'Marx an Paul und Laura Lafargue 28. Juli 1870', in Marx and Engels 1973s.

—— 1871a, *The Civil War in France*, in Marx and Engels 1986b.

—— 1871b, *Der Bürgerkrieg in Frankreich: Adresse des Generalrats der Internationalen Arbeiterassoziation*, in Marx and Engels 1973h.

—— 1871c, 'To the Editor of *De Werker*', in Marx and Engels 1986b.

—— 1871d, 'An die Redaktion des „De Werker"', in Marx and Engels 1973h.

—— 1871e, First Draft of *The Civil War in France*, in Marx and Engels 1986b.

—— 1871f, *Erster Entwurf zum „Bürgerkrieg in Frankreich"*, in Marx and Engels 1973h.

—— 1871g, 'Record of Marx's Speech on the Position of the International Working Men's Association in Germany and England', in Marx and Engels 1986b.

—— 1871h, 'Aufzeichnung der Rede von Karl Marx über die Lage der Internationalen Arbeiterassoziation in Deutschland und England', in Marx and Engels 1973h.

—— 1872a, 'Declaration of the General Council of the International Working Men's Association Concerning Cochrane's Speech in the House of Commons', in Marx and Engels 1988a.

—— 1872b, 'On the Hague Congress: A Correspondent's Report of a Speech Made at a Meeting in Amsterdam on September 8, 1872', in Marx and Engels 1988a.

—— 1872c, 'Rede über den Haage Kongreß', in Marx and Engels 1973i.

—— 1872d, 'Report of the General Council to the Fifth Annual Congress of the International Working Men's Association, Held at The Hague, from the 2nd to the 7th September 1872', in Marx and Engels 1988a.

—— 1872e, 'Offizieller Bericht des Londoner Generalrats, verlesen in öffentlicher Sitzung des Internationalen Kongresses zu Haag', in Marx and Engels 1973i.

—— 1873a, 'Political Indifferentism', in Marx and Engels 1988a.

—— 1873b, 'Der politische Indifferentismus', in Marx and Engels 1973i.

—— 1874a, 'Marx to Engels in Ramsgate, Ryde, 15 July 1874, 11 Nelson Street', in Marx and Engels 1991c.

—— 1874b, 'Marx an Engels 15. Juli 1874', in Marx and Engels 1973s.

—— 1875a, *Critique of the Gotha Programme*, in Marx and Engels 1991a.

—— 1875b, *Kritik des Gothaer Programms*, in Marx and Engels 1973j.

—— 1875c, 'Epilogue to *Revelations Concerning the Communist Trial in Cologne*', in Marx and Engels 1991a.

—— 1875d, 'Nachwort zu „Enthüllungen über den Kommunisten-Prozeß zu Köln‴', in Marx and Engels 1973i.

—— 1875e, 'Marx to Engels in Ramsgate, Karlsbad, 21 August 1875, Germania, Schlossplatz', in Marx and Engels 1991c.

—— 1875f, 'Marx an Engels 21. August 1875', in Marx and Engels 1973t.

—— 1876a, 'Marx to Engels in Ramsgate, London, 25 May 1876', in Marx and Engels 1991c.

—— 1876b, 'Marx an Engels 25. Mai 1876', in Marx and Engels 1973t.

—— 1877a, 'Marx to Ferdinand Fleckes in Karlsbad, London, 21 January 1877', in Marx and Engels 1991c.

—— 1877b, 'Marx an Ferdinand Fleckes 21. Januar 1877', in Marx and Engels 1973t.

—— 1877c, 'Marx to Engels in Ramsgate, London, 23 July 1877', in Marx and Engels 1991c.

—— 1877d, 'Marx an Engels 23. Juli 1877', in Marx and Engels 1973t.

—— 1877e, 'Marx to Friedrich Adolph Sorge in Hoboken, London, 27 September 1877, 41 Maitland Park Road, N.W.', in Marx and Engels 1991c.

—— 1877f, 'Marx an Friedrich Adolphe Sorge, 27. September 1877', in Marx and Engels 1973t.

—— 1877g, 'Marx to Friedrich Adolph Sorge in Hoboken, London, 19 October 1877', in Marx and Engels 1991c.

—— 1877h, 'Marx an Friedrich Adolphe Sorge, 19. Oktober 1877', in Marx and Engels 1973t.

—— 1878a, 'Mr. George Howell's History of the International Working-Men's Association', in Marx and Engels 1991a.

—— 1878b, 'The Parliamentary Debate on the Anti-Socialist Law', in Marx and Engels 1991a.

—— 1879, 'Account of Karl Marx's Interview with the *Chicago Tribune* Correspondent', in Marx and Engels 1991a.

—— 1881a, 'Marginal Notes on Adolph Wagner's *Lehrbuch der politischen Oekonomie*', in Marx and Engels 1991a.

—— 1881b, 'Randglossen zu Adolph Wagner's „Lehrbuch der politischen Ökonomie‴', in Marx and Engels 1973j.

—— 1881c, 'Marx to Ferdinand Domela Nieuwenhuis in The Hague, London, 22 February 1881, 41 Maitland Park Road, N.W.', in Marx and Engels 1992.

—— 1881d, 'Marx an Ferdinand Domela Nieuwenhuis 22. Februar 1881', in Marx and Engels 1973u.

—— 1882a, 'Marx to Engels in London, Algiers, 8 April (Saturday) 1882', in Marx and Engels 1992.

—— 1882b, 'Marx an Engels 8. April 1882', in Marx and Engels 1973u.

—— 1882c, 'Marx to Laura Lafargue in London, Algiers, Thursday, 13 and 14 April 1882', in Marx and Engels 1992.

—— 1882d, 'Marx an Laura Lafargue 13./14. April 1882', in Marx and Engels 1973u.

—— 1882e, 'Marx to Engels in London, Paris, 30 September 1882', in Marx and Engels 1992.

—— 1882f, 'Marx an Engels 30. September 1882', in Marx and Engels 1973u.

—— 1885a, *Capital: A Critique of Political Economy, Volume II*, in Marx and Engels 1997a.

—— 1885b, *Das Kapital. Kritik der politischen Ökonomie. Zweiter Band. Buch II: Der Zirkulationsprozeß des Kapitals*, in Marx and Engels 1973m.

—— 1894a, *Capital: A Critique of Political Economy, Volume III*, in Marx and Engels 1997b.

—— 1894b, *Das Kapital. Kritik der politischen Ökonomie. Dritter Band. Buch III: Der Gesamtprozeß der kapitalistischen Produktion*, in Marx and Engels 1973x.

—— 1974 [1880–2], *The Ethnological Notebooks of Karl Marx*, edited by Lawrence Krader, Assen: Van Gorcum.

—— 2002, *Marx on Religion*, edited by John Raines, Philadelphia: Temple University Press.

—— 2006 [1844], *Sur la Question juive*, translated by Jean-François Poirier, edited by Daniel Bensaïd, Paris: La Fabrique Éditions.

Marx, Karl and Friedrich Engels 1845a, *The Holy Family, or Critique of Critical Criticism*, in Marx and Engels 1975d.

—— 1845b, *Die heilige Familie oder Kritik der kritischen Kritik*, in Marx and Engels 1974b.

—— 1845–6a, *The German Ideology: Critique of Modern German Philosophy According to Its Representatives Feuerbach, B. Bauer and Stirner, and of German Socialism According to Its Various Prophets*, in Marx and Engels 1976b.

—— 1845–6b, *Die deutsche Ideologie. Kritik der neuesten deutschen Philosophie in ihren Repräsentanten Feuerbach, B. Bauer und Stirner und des deutschen Sozialismus in seinen verschiedenen Propheten*, in Marx and Engels 1973a.

—— 1846a, 'Circular Against Kriege', in Marx and Engels 1976c.

—— 1846b, 'Zirkular gegen Kriege', in Marx and Engels 1972a.

—— 1848a, 'Arrests', in Marx and Engels 1977a.

—— 1848b, 'The Berlin Debate on the Revolution', in Marx and Engels 1977a.

—— 1848c, 'Die Berliner Debatte über die Revolution', in Marx and Engels 1973b.

—— 1848d, 'The Bill on the Compulsory Loan and Its Motivation', in Marx and Engels 1977a.

—— 1848e, 'Der Gesetzentwurf über die Zwangsanleihe und seine Motivierung', in Marx and Engels 1973b.

—— 1848f, 'The Civic Militia Bill', in Marx and Engels 1977a.

—— 1848g, 'Der Bürgerwehrgesetzentwurf', in Marx and Engels 1973b.

—— 1848h, 'Cologne in Danger', in Marx and Engels 1977a.

—— 1848i, 'Köln in Gefahr', in Marx and Engels 1973b.

—— 1848j, 'Demands of the Communist Party in Germany', in Marx and Engels 1977a.

—— 1848k, 'Forderungen der Kommunistischen Partei in Deutschland', in Marx and Engels 1973b.

—— 1848l, 'The Downfall of the Camphausen Government', in Marx and Engels 1977a.

—— 1848m, 'Sturz des Ministeriums Camphausen', in Marx and Engels 1973b.

—— 1848n, 'The Frankfurt Assembly Debates the Polish Question', in Marx and Engels 1977a.

—— 1848o, 'Die Polendebatte in Frankfurt', in Marx and Engels 1973b.

—— 1848p, 'German Professorial Baseness', in Marx and Engels 1977b.

—— 1848q, 'Deutsche Professorengemeinheit', in Marx and Engels 1973c.

—— 1848r, 'The Hansemann Government', in Marx and Engels 1977a.

—— 1848s, 'Das Kabinett Hansemann', in Marx and Engels 1973b.

—— 1848t, 'The Italian Liberation Struggle and the Cause of its Present Failure', in Marx and Engels 1977a.

—— 1848u, 'Der italienische Befreiungskampf und die Ursache seines jetzigen Mißlingens', in Marx and Engels 1973b.

—— 1848v, *The Manifesto of the Communist Party*, in Marx and Engels 1976c.

—— 1848w, *Manifest der Kommunistischen Partei*, in Marx and Engels 1972a.

—— 1848x, 'The New "Holy Alliance"', in Marx and Engels 1977b.

—— 1848y, 'Die neue „Heilige Allianz"', in Marx and Engels 1973c.

—— 1848z, 'News', in Marx and Engels 1977b.

—— 1848aa, 'Neuigkeiten', in Marx and Engels 1973c.

—— 1848bb, 'On the Polish Question: Speeches in Brussels, on February 22, 1848, on the Occasion of the Second Anniversary of the Cracow Insurrection', in Marx and Engels 1976c.

—— 1848cc, 'Reden auf der Gedenkfeier in Brüssel am 22. Februar 1848 zum 2. Jahrestag des Krakauer Aufstandes von 1846', in Marx and Engels 1972a.

—— 1848dd, 'The Position of the Parties in Cologne', in Marx and Engels 1977a.

—— 1848ee, 'Stellung der Parteien in Köln', in Marx and Engels 1973b.

—— 1848ff, 'Proudhon's Speech Against Thiers', in Marx and Engels 1977a.

—— 1848gg, 'Proudhons Rede gegen Thiers', in Marx and Engels 1973b.

—— 1848hh, 'Public Prosecutor Hecker Questions People Who Had Attended the Worringen Meeting', in Marx and Engels 1977a.

—— 1848ii, 'Report of the Frankfurt Committee on Austrian Affairs', in Marx and Engels 1977b.

—— 1848jj, 'Die Bericht des Frankfurter Ausschusses über die östreichischen Angelegenheiten', in Marx and Engels 1973c.

—— 1848kk, 'The Russian Note', in Marx and Engels 1977a.

—— 1848ll, 'Die russische Note', in Marx and Engels 1973b.

—— 1848mm, 'The Shield of the Dynasty', in Marx and Engels 1977a.

—— 1848nn, 'Das Schild der Dynastie', in Marx and Engels 1973b.

—— 1848oo, 'The Stupp Amendment', in Marx and Engels 1977a.

—— 1848pp, 'Das Amendement Stupp', in Marx and Engels 1973b.

—— 1849a, 'The English Soldier's Oath of Allegiance', in Marx and Engels 1977c.

—— 1849b, 'Der Eid der englischen Soldatten', in Marx and Engels 1973c.

—— 1849c, 'The First Trial of the *Neue Rheinische Zeitung*', in Marx and Engels 1977b.

—— 1849d, 'Der erste Preßprozeß der „Neuen Rheinischen Zeitung"', in Marx and Engels 1973c.

—— 1849e, 'Vienna and Frankfurt', in Marx and Engels 1977c.

—— 1849f, 'Wien und Frankfurt', in Marx and Engels 1973c.

—— 1850a, 'Review (January–February 1850)', in Marx and Engels 1978.

—— 1850b, 'Revue, Januar–Februar 1850', in Marx and Engels 1973d.

—— 1850c, 'Review (May to October 1850)', in Marx and Engels 1978.

—— 1850d, 'Revue, Mai bis Oktober 1850', in Marx and Engels 1973d.

—— 1850e, 'Reviews from the *Neue Rheinische Zeitung. Politisch-Ökonomische Revue* No. 2', in Marx and Engels 1978.

—— 1850f, 'Rezensionen aus der „Neuen Rheinische Zeitung. Politisch-ökonomische Revue". Zweites Heft', in Marx and Engels 1973d.

—— 1850g, 'Reviews from the *Neue Rheinische Zeitung. Politisch-Ökonomische Revue* No. 4', in Marx and Engels 1978.

—— 1850h, 'Rezensionen aus der „Neuen Rheinische Zeitung. Politisch-ökonomische Revue". Viertes Heft', in Marx and Engels 1973d.

—— 1852a, *The Great Men of the Exile*, in Marx and Engels 1979a.

—— 1852b, *Die großen Männer des Exils*, in Marx and Engels 1973e.

—— 1853, 'British Politics. – Disraeli. – The Refugees. – Mazzini in London. – Turkey', in Marx and Engels 1979b.

—— 1854, 'The European War', in Marx and Engels 1980a.

—— 1855a, 'From Parliament. – From the Theatre of War', in Marx and Engels 1980a.

—— 1855b, 'Aus dem Parliament – Vom Kriegsschauplatz', in Marx and Engels 1974c.

—— 1873a, 'The Alliance of Socialist Democracy and the International Working Men's Association. Report and Documents Published by Decision of The Hague Congress of the International', in Marx and Engels 1988a.

—— 1873b, 'Ein Komplot gegen die Internationale Arbeiterassoziation. Im Auftrage des Haager Kongresses verfaßter Bericht über das Trieben Bakunins und der Allianz der sozialistichen Demokratie', in Marx and Engels 1973i.

—— 1968, *Marx Engels Werke*, Volume 38, Berlin: Dietz.

—— 1969, *Marx and Engels Collected Works*, Volume 6, Moscow: Progress Publishers.

—— 1972a, *Marx Engels Werke*, Volume 4, Berlin: Dietz.

—— 1972b, *Marx Engels Werke*, Volume 9, Berlin: Dietz.

—— 1972c, *Marx Engels Werke*, Volume 14, Berlin: Dietz.

—— 1972d, *Marx Engels Werke*, Volume 15, Berlin: Dietz.

—— 1972e, *Marx Engels Werke*, Volume 22, Berlin: Dietz.

—— 1972f, *Marx Engels Werke*, Volume 23, Berlin: Dietz.

—— 1972g, *Marx Engels Werke*, Volume 30, Berlin: Dietz.

—— 1973a, *Marx Engels Werke*, Volume 3, Berlin: Dietz.

—— 1973b, *Marx Engels Werke*, Volume 5, Berlin: Dietz.

—— 1973c, *Marx Engels Werke*, Volume 6, Berlin: Dietz.

—— 1973d, *Marx Engels Werke*, Volume 7, Berlin: Dietz.

—— 1973e, *Marx Engels Werke*, Volume 8, Berlin: Dietz.

—— 1973f, *Marx Engels Werke*, Volume 10, Berlin: Dietz.

—— 1973g, *Marx Engels Werke*, Volume 16, Berlin: Dietz.

—— 1973h, *Marx Engels Werke*, Volume 17, Berlin: Dietz.

—— 1973i, *Marx Engels Werke*, Volume 18, Berlin: Dietz.

—— 1973j, *Marx Engels Werke*, Volume 19, Berlin: Dietz.

—— 1973k, *Marx Engels Werke*, Volume 20, Berlin: Dietz.

—— 1973l, *Marx Engels Werke*, Volume 21, Berlin: Dietz.

—— 1973m, *Marx Engels Werke*, Volume 24, Berlin: Dietz.

—— 1973n, *Marx Engels Werke*, Volume 27, Berlin: Dietz.

—— 1973o, *Marx Engels Werke*, Volume 28, Berlin: Dietz.

—— 1973p, *Marx Engels Werke*, Volume 29, Berlin: Dietz.

—— 1973q, *Marx Engels Werke*, Volume 31, Berlin: Dietz.

—— 1973r, *Marx Engels Werke*, Volume 32, Berlin: Dietz.

—— 1973s, *Marx Engels Werke*, Volume 33, Berlin: Dietz.

—— 1973t, *Marx Engels Werke*, Volume 34, Berlin: Dietz.

—— 1973u, *Marx Engels Werke*, Volume 35, Berlin: Dietz.

—— 1973v, *Marx Engels Werke*, Volume 36, Berlin: Dietz.

—— 1973w, *Marx Engels Werke*, Volume 39, Berlin: Dietz.

—— 1973x, *Marx Engels Werke*, Volume 25, Berlin: Dietz.

—— 1974a, *Marx Engels Werke*, Volume 1, Berlin: Dietz.

—— 1974b, *Marx Engels Werke*, Volume 2, Berlin: Dietz.

—— 1974c, *Marx Engels Werke*, Volume 11, Berlin: Dietz.

—— 1974d, *Marx Engels Werke*, Volume 13, Berlin: Dietz.

—— 1974e, *Marx Engels Werke*, Volume 26, Part 1, Berlin: Dietz.

—— 1974f, *Marx Engels Werke*, Volume 26, Part 3, Berlin: Dietz.

—— 1974g, *Marx Engels Werke*, Volume 37, Berlin: Dietz.

—— 1975a, *Marx and Engels Collected Works*, Volume 1, Moscow: Progress Publishers.

—— 1975b, *Marx and Engels Collected Works*, Volume 2, Moscow: Progress Publishers.

—— 1975c, *Marx and Engels Collected Works*, Volume 3, Moscow: Progress Publishers.

—— 1975d, *Marx and Engels Collected Works*, Volume 4, Moscow: Progress Publishers.

—— 1975e, *Marx Engels Gesamtausgabe*, Division 1, Volume 1, Berlin: Dietz.

—— 1976a, *On Religion*, Moscow: Progress.

—— 1976b, *Marx and Engels Collected Works*, Volume 5, Moscow: Progress Publishers.

—— 1976c, *Marx and Engels Collected Works*, Volume 6, Moscow: Progress Publishers.

—— 1976d, *Marx Engels Gesamtausgabe*, Division 4, Volume 1, Berlin: Dietz.

—— 1977a, *Marx and Engels Collected Works*, Volume 7, Moscow: Progress Publishers.

—— 1977b, *Marx and Engels Collected Works*, Volume 8, Moscow: Progress Publishers.

—— 1977c, *Marx and Engels Collected Works*, Volume 9, Moscow: Progress Publishers.

—— 1978, *Marx and Engels Collected Works*, Volume 10, Moscow: Progress Publishers.

—— 1979a, *Marx and Engels Collected Works*, Volume 11, Moscow: Progress Publishers.

—— 1979b, *Marx and Engels Collected Works*, Volume 12, Moscow: Progress Publishers.

—— 1980a, *Marx and Engels Collected Works*, Volume 13, Moscow: Progress Publishers.

—— 1980b, *Marx and Engels Collected Works*, Volume 14, Moscow: Progress Publishers.

—— 1980c, *Marx and Engels Collected Works*, Volume 16, Moscow: Progress Publishers.

—— 1981, *Marx and Engels Collected Works*, Volume 17, Moscow: Progress Publishers.

—— 1982a, *Marx and Engels Collected Works*, Volume 18, Moscow: Progress Publishers.

—— 1982b, *Marx and Engels Collected Works*, Volume 38, Moscow: Progress Publishers.

—— 1983a, *Marx and Engels Collected Works*, Volume 39, Moscow: Progress Publishers.

—— 1983b, *Marx and Engels Collected Works*, Volume 40, Moscow: Progress Publishers.

—— 1984, *Marx and Engels Collected Works*, Volume 19, Moscow: Progress Publishers.

—— 1985a, *Marx and Engels Collected Works*, Volume 20, Moscow: Progress Publishers.

—— 1985b, *Marx and Engels Collected Works*, Volume 21, Moscow: Progress Publishers.

—— 1985c, *Marx and Engels Collected Works*, Volume 41, Moscow: Progress Publishers.

—— 1985d, *Marx Engels Gesamtausgabe*, Division 1, Volume 3, Berlin: Dietz.

—— 1986a, *Marx and Engels Collected Works*, Volume 15, Moscow: Progress Publishers.

—— 1986b, *Marx and Engels Collected Works*, Volume 22, Moscow: Progress Publishers.

—— 1986c, *Marx and Engels Collected Works*, Volume 28, Moscow: Progress Publishers.

—— 1987a, *Marx and Engels Collected Works*, Volume 25, Moscow: Progress Publishers.

—— 1987b, *Marx and Engels Collected Works*, Volume 29, Moscow: Progress Publishers.

—— 1987c, *Marx and Engels Collected Works*, Volume 42, Moscow: Progress Publishers.

—— 1988a, *Marx and Engels Collected Works*, Volume 23, Moscow: Progress Publishers.

—— 1988b, *Marx and Engels Collected Works*, Volume 30, Moscow: Progress Publishers.

—— 1988c, *Marx and Engels Collected Works*, Volume 43, Moscow: Progress Publishers.

—— 1989a, *Marx and Engels Collected Works*, Volume 31, Moscow: Progress Publishers.

—— 1989b, *Marx and Engels Collected Works*, Volume 32, Moscow: Progress Publishers.

—— 1989c, *Marx and Engels Collected Works*, Volume 44, Moscow: Progress Publishers.

—— 1990a, *Marx and Engels Collected Works*, Volume 26, Moscow: Progress Publishers.

—— 1990b, *Marx and Engels Collected Works*, Volume 27, Moscow: Progress Publishers.

—— 1990c, *Marx Engels Werke*, Volume 40, Berlin: Dietz.

—— 1990d, *Marx Engels Werke*, Volume 43, Berlin: Dietz.

—— 1991a, *Marx and Engels Collected Works*, Volume 24, Moscow: Progress Publishers.

—— 1991b, *Marx and Engels Collected Works*, Volume 33, Moscow: Progress Publishers.

—— 1991c, *Marx and Engels Collected Works*, Volume 45, Moscow: Progress Publishers.

—— 1992, *Marx and Engels Collected Works*, Volume 46, Moscow: Progress Publishers.

—— 1994, *Marx and Engels Collected Works*, Volume 34, Moscow: Progress Publishers.

—— 1995, *Marx and Engels Collected Works*, Volume 47, Moscow: Progress Publishers.

—— 1996, *Marx and Engels Collected Works*, Volume 35, Moscow: Progress Publishers.

—— 1997a, *Marx and Engels Collected Works*, Volume 36, Moscow: Progress Publishers.

—— 1997b, *Marx and Engels Collected Works*, Volume 37, Moscow: Progress Publishers.

—— 2001a, *Marx and Engels Collected Works*, Volume 48, Moscow: Progress Publishers.

—— 2001b, *Marx and Engels Collected Works*, Volume 49, Moscow: Progress Publishers.

—— 2004, *Marx and Engels Collected Works*, Volume 50, Moscow: Progress Publishers.

—— 2005, *Marx Engels Werke*, Volume 42, Berlin: Dietz.

—— 2008, *Marx Engels Werke*, Volume 41, Berlin: Dietz.

Marx-Longuet, Jenny 1863, 'Jenny Marx-Longuet to Ludwig and Gertrud Kugelmann in Hanover, London, 12 May 1873', in Marx and Engels 1989c.

Massey, Marilyn Chapin 1983, *Christ Unmasked: The Meaning of The Life of Jesus in German Politics*, Chapel Hill: University of North Carolina Press.

Mayer, Gustav 1920, 'Die Junghegelianer unde der preussische Staat', *Historische Zeitschrift*, 121: 413–40.

McDonald, Lee and James A. Sanders (eds.) 2002, *The Canon Debate*, Peabody: Hendrickson.

McKinnon, Andrew M. 2006, 'Opium as Dialectics of Religion: Metaphor, Expression and Protest', in *Marx, Critical Theory, and Religion: A Critique of Rational Choice*, edited by Warren S. Goldstein, Leiden: Brill.

McLellan, David 1969, *The Young Hegelians and Karl Marx*, Basingstoke: Macmillan.

—— 1980, *Marx Before Marxism*, Second Edition, Basingstoke: Macmillan.

—— 1987, *Marxism and Religion: A Description and Assessment of the Marxist Critique of Religion*, New York: Harper and Row.

—— 1995, *Ideology*, Minneapolis: University of Minnesota Press.

Meeks, M. Douglas 1989, *God the Economist: The Doctrine of God and Political Economy*, Minneapolis: Fortress.

Milbank, John 1990, *Theology and Social Theory: Beyond Secular Reason*, Oxford: Blackwell.

Misrahi, Robert 1972, *Marx et la Question juive*, Paris: Éditions Gallimard.

—— 2004, *Un juif läic en France*, Paris: Médicis-Entrelacs.

Moggach, Douglas 2003, *The Philosophy and Politics of Bruno Bauer*, Cambridge: Cambridge University Press.

—— 2006, *The New Hegelians: Politics and Philosophy in the Hegelian School*, Cambridge: Cambridge University Press.

Molyneux, John 2008, 'More Than Opium: Marxism and Religion', *International Socialism*, 119, available at: <http://www.isj.org.uk/index.php4?id=456&issue=119>.

Müntzer, Thomas 1988, *The Collected Works of Thomas Müntzer*, translated by Peter Matheson, Edinburgh: T. and T. Clark.

Muravchik, Joshua 2003, *Heaven on Earth: The Rise and Fall of Socialism*, San Francisco: Encounter Books.

Ollman, Bertell 1971, *Alienation: Marx's Conception of Man in Capitalist Society*, Cambridge: Cambridge University Press.

Padover, Saul K. (ed.) 1974, *Karl Marx on Religion*, New York: McGraw Hill.

Peled, Yoav 1992, 'From Theology to Sociology: Bruno Bauer and Karl Marx on the Question of Jewish Emancipation', *History of Political Thought*, 13, 3: 463–85.

Perry, Marvin and Frederick M. Schweitzer 2005, *Antisemitism: Myth and Hate from Antiquity to the Present*, Basingstoke: Palgrave Macmillan.

Pietz, William 1985, 'The Problem of the Fetish I', *Res: Anthropology and Aesthetics*, 9: 5–17.

—— 1987, 'The Problem of the Fetish II: The Origin of the Fetish', *Res: Anthopology and Aesthetics*, 13: 23–45.

—— 1988, 'The Problem of the Fetish, III', *Res: Anthopology and Aesthetics*, 16: 105–23.

Pietz, William and Emily Apter (eds.) 1993, *Fetishism as Cultural Discourse*, Ithaca: Cornell University Press.

Price, Robert M. 2000, *Deconstructing Jesus*, Amherst: Prometheus Books.

Raines, John 2002, 'Introduction', in *Marx on Religion*, edited by John Raines, Philadelphia: Temple University Press.

Raines, John and Thomas Dean (eds.) 1970, *Marxism and Radical Religion: Essays Toward a Revolutionary Humanism*, Philadelphia: Temple University Press.

Ray, Larry 2006, 'Marx and the Radical Critique of Difference', *Engage Journal*, 3, avail-able at: <http://www.engageonline.org.uk/journal/index.php?journal_id=12&article_id=49>.

'Record of Marx's Interview with *The World* Correspondent' 1871, in Marx and Engels 1986b.

Roberts, John 2008a, 'The "Returns to Religion": Messianism, Christianity and the Revolutionary Tradition. Part I: "Wakefulness to the Future"', *Historical Materialism*, 16, 2: 59–84.

—— 2008b, 'The "Returns to Religion": Messianism, Christianity and the Revolutionary Tradition. Part II: The Pauline Tradition', *Historical Materialism*, 16, 3: 77–103.

Rose, Margaret A. 1984, *Marx's Lost Aesthetic: Karl Marx and the Visual Arts*, Cambridge: Cambridge University Press.

Rose, Paul Lawrence 1990, *Revolutionary Antisemitism in Germany from Kant to Wagner*, Princeton: Princeton University Press.

Rosen, Zvi 1977, *Karl Marx and Bruno Bauer: The Influence of Bruno Bauer on Marx's Thought*, The Hague: Nijhoff.

Rules of the Communist League 1850, in Marx and Engels 1978.

Schaper, Karl, Henry Bauer and Jospeh Moll 1847, 'The Central Authority to the League', in Marx and Engels 1976c.

Schleiermacher, Friedrich 1960 [1830], *The Christian Faith*, Edinburgh: T. and T. Clark.

Schmitt, Carl 2005 [1922], *Political Theology: Four Chapters on the Concept of Sovereignty*, translated by George Schwab, Chicago: University of Chicago Press.

Scott, Peter 1994, *Theology, Ideology and Liberation*, Cambridge: Cambridge University Press.

Sobrino, Jon 2004a [1982], *Jesus in Latin America*, Eugene: Wipf and Stock.

—— 2004b [1985], *The True Church and the Poor*, Eugene: Wipf and Stock.

Sorel, Georges 1961 [1908], *Reflections on Violence*, translated by T. Hulme and J. Roth, New York: Collier.

Stark, Rodney 1996, *The Rise of Christianity: How the Obscure, Marginal Jesus Movement Became the Dominant Religious Force in the Western World*, Princeton: Princeton University Press.

Stepelevich, Lawrence S. (ed.) 1997, *The Young Hegelians: An Anthology*, Amherst: Prometheus Books.

Stirner, Max 1845, *Der Einzige und Sein Eigentum*, Leipzig: Philipp Reclam.

—— 2005 [1845], *The Ego and His Own: The Case of the Individual Against Authority*, translated by Steven T. Byington, New York: Dover Publications.

Strauss, David Friedrich 1835, *Das Leben Jesu, kritisch bearbeitet*, Tübingen: C.F. Osiander.

—— 1836, *Das Leben Jesu, kritisch bearbeitet*, Second Edition, Tübingen: C.F. Osiander.

—— 1839, *Das Leben Jesu, kritisch bearbeitet*, Third Edition, Tübingen: C.F. Osiander.

—— 1840a, *Das Leben Jesu, kritisch bearbeitet*, Fourth Edition, Tübingen: C.F. Osiander.

—— 1840b, *Die christliche Glaubenslehre in ihrer geschichtlichen Entwicklung und im Kampfe mit der modernen Wissenschaft*, Tübingen: C.F. Osiander.

—— 1851, *Christian Märklin: Ein Lebens- und Charakterbild aus der Gegenwart*, Mannheim: Bassermann.

—— 1858–60, *Ulrich von Hutten*, Leipzig: Brockhaus.

—— 1864, *Das Leben Jesu für das deutsche Volk*, Leipzig: Brockhaus.

—— 1865, *Die Halben und die Ganzen*, Berlin: F. Duncker.

—— 1873, *Der alte und der neue Glaube: Ein Bekenntnis*, Bonn: Verlag von Emil Strauss.

—— 1902 [1835], *The Life of Jesus: Critically Examined*, translated by George Eliot, London: Swan Sonnenschein.

—— 1924 [1870], *Voltaire: 6 Vorträge*, Leipzig: A. Kröner.

—— 1978 [1849], *Christian Friedrich Daniel Schubarts Leben in seinen Briefen*, Königstein: Scriptor Verlag.

—— 1980 [1837], *Streitschriften zur Verteidigung meiner Schrift über das Leben Jesu und zur Charakteristik der gegenwärtigen Theologie*, Hildesheim: Olms.

—— 1983 [1837], *In Defence of My Life of Jesus Against the Hegelians*, translated by Marilyn Chapin Massey, Hamden: Archon Books.

—— 1991 [1862], *Hermann Samuel Reimarus und seine Schutzschrift für die vernünftigen Verehrer Gottes*, Hildesheim: Olms.

—— 1992 [1847], *Der Romantiker auf dem Throne der Cäsaren oder Julian der Abtrünnige*, Heidelberg: Manutius Verlag.

—— 1997 [1873], *The Old Faith and the New*, Amherst: Prometheus Books.

—— 2000 [1865], *Der Christus des Glaubens und der Jesus der Geschichte: eine Kritik des Schleiermacher'schen Lebens Jesu*, Waltrop: Spenner.

Suda, Max Josef 1978, 'The Critique of Religion in Karl Marx's *Capital*', *Journal of Ecumenical Studies*, 15, 1: 15–28.

Sundberg, Albert 1964, *The Old Testament of the Early Church*, Cambridge, MA.: Harvard University Press.

Sung, Jung Mo 2007, *Desire, Market, and Religion*, London: SCM.

Taylor, Charles 2007, *A Secular Age?*, Cambridge, MA.: Belknap.

Thiemann, Ronald F. 1985, 'Praxis: The Practical Atheism of Karl Marx', *Journal of Ecumenical Studies*, 22, 3: 544–9.

Thomas, Paul 1975, 'Karl Marx and Max Stirner', *Political Theory*, 3, 2: 159–79.

Thompson, Edward Palmer 1966, *The Making of the English Working Class*, New York: Vintage.

—— 1993, *Witness Against the Beast: William Blake and the Moral Law*, Cambridge: Cambridge University Press.

Thompson, Thomas L. 1992, *Early History of the Israelite People: From the Written and Archaeological Sources*, Leiden: Brill.

—— 1999, *The Mythic Past: Biblical Archaeology and the Myth of Israel*, New York: Basic Books.

—— 2005, *The Messiah Myth: The Near Eastern Roots of Jesus and David*, New York: Basic Books.

Troeltsch, Ernst 1992 [1911], *The Social Teaching of the Christian Churches*, two volumes, Louisville: Westminster John Knox Press.

Van Leeuwen, Arendt Theodoor 2002a [1972], *Critique of Earth*, Cambridge: James Clarke.

—— 2002b [1974], *Critique of Heaven*, Cambridge: James Clarke.

Weisman, Ze'ev 1998, *Political Satire in the Bible*, Atlanta: Scholar's Press.

Wellhausen, Julius 1994 [1885], *Prolegomena to the History of Israel: With a Reprint of the Article 'Israel' from the Encyclopaedia Britannica*, Atlanta: Scholar's Press.

Winter, Bruce (ed.) 1997, *Philo and Paul among the Sophists*, Cambridge: Cambridge University Press.

Wolfson, Murray 1982, *Marx: Economist, Philosopher, Jew: Steps in the Development of a Doctrine*, Basingstoke: Macmillan.

Zindler, Frank R. 2003, *The Jesus the Jews Never Knew: Sepher Toldoth Yeshu and the Quest for the Historical Jesus in Jewish Sources*, Austin: American Atheist Press.

Index

www.ingramcontent.com/pod-product-compliance
Lightning Source LLC
Chambersburg PA
CBHW060021030426
42334CB00019B/2126